Using Advanced MPI

Scientific and Engineering Computation
William Gropp and Ewing Lusk, editors; Janusz Kowalik, founding editor

A complete list of books published in the Scientific and Engineering Computation series appears at the back of this book.

Using Advanced MPI
Modern Features of the Message-Passing Interface

William Gropp
Torsten Hoefler
Rajeev Thakur
Ewing Lusk

The MIT Press
Cambridge, Massachusetts
London, England

This book was set in LATEX by the authors.

Library of Congress Cataloging-in-Publication Data

Gropp, William.
Using advanced MPI : modern features of the Message-Passing Interface / William Gropp, Torsten Hoefler, Rajeev Thakur, and Ewing Lusk.
    p. cm. — (Scientific and engineering computation)
Includes bibliographical references and index.
ISBN 978-0-262-52763-7 (pbk. : alk. paper)
1. Parallel programming (Computer science) 2. Parallel computers—Programming. 3. Computer interfaces. I. Hoefler, Torsten. II. Thakur, Rajeev. III. Lusk, Ewing. IV. Title.
QA76.642.G758   2014
005.7'11—dc23

2014033725

To Clare Gropp, Natalia (Tasche), Pratibha and Sharad Thakur, and Brigid Lusk

Contents

Series Foreword

The Scientific and Engineering Series from MIT Press presents accessible accounts of computing research areas normally presented in research papers and specialized conferences. Elements of modern computing that have appeared thus far in the series include parallelism, language design and implementation, system software, and numerical libraries. The scope of the series continues to expand with the spread of ideas from computing into new aspects of science.

This book describes how to use advanced features of the Message-Passing Interface (MPI), a communication library specification for both parallel computers and workstation networks. MPI has been developed as a community standard for message passing and related operations. Its adoption by both users and implementors has provided the parallel-programming community with the portability and features needed to develop application programs and parallel libraries that will tap the power of today's (and tomorrow's) high-performance computers.

William Gropp and Ewing Lusk, Editors

Foreword

Since its release in May 1994, the Message-Passing Interface (MPI) has become a de facto standard for parallel computations on distributed-memory clusters and supercomputers. All large-scale scientific computing applications and libraries use MPI; it is used on modest clusters, as well as on the most powerful supercomputers that have millions of cores; it is not expected to be replaced in the coming decade.

MPI has continued to evolve in order to provide new functionality and take advantage of evolving hardware. The MPI-2 version of the standard was released in July 1997, and MPI-3 was released in September 2013. In addition to these major releases, minor releases provided clarifications and corrections.

This book discusses MPI-3.0, the most recent version of the MPI standard. MPI-3 added important extensions to MPI-2, including the following:

- Support for nonblocking and sparse collective operations that can achieve greater scalability on large systems
- Significant changes in MPI one-sided communications that simplify semantics and enable better performance on modern hardware
- Support for shared-memory communication among MPI processes to better support hybrid shared-memory/message-passing programming
- New bindings for current Fortran (Fortran 2008)

These extensions are discussed and their use is illustrated in this book. In addition, the book covers other aspects of MPI that were poorly covered in previous publications. These include parallel I/O, data-intensive computations, and programming patterns that help in designing scalable codes.

The four authors of this book have been heavily involved in the activities of the MPI Forum that led to the release of MPI-3; two of them have been involved in the MPI Forum since its inception and coauthored highly successful books on MPI-1 and MPI-2; each of them contributed to the implementation of MPI. Therefore, I expect this new book to become a necessary tool for programmers who want to understand and use the latest features of MPI and to write efficient programs for modern clusters and supercomputers.

Marc Snir
Director, Mathematics and Computer Science Division
Argonne National Laboratory
Michael Faiman and Saburo Muroga Professor
Department of Computer Science, University of Illinois at Urbana Champaign
July 2014

Preface

MPI (Message-Passing Interface) is a standard library interface for writing parallel programs. MPI was developed in two phases by an open forum of parallel computer vendors, library writers, and application developers. The first phase took place in 1993–1994 and culminated in the first release of the MPI standard, which we call MPI-1. A number of important topics in parallel computing had been deliberately left out of MPI-1 in order to speed its release, and the MPI Forum began meeting again in 1995 to address these topics, as well as to make minor corrections and clarifications to MPI-1 that had been discovered to be necessary. The MPI-2 standard was released in the summer of 1997. After a long delay, the MPI-3 standard was released in September of 2012. The official standard documents for MPI, including the official versions of MPI-1, MPI-2, and MPI-3, are available on the web at http://www.mpi-forum.org. More polished versions of the standard documents for MPI-1 and MPI-2 are published by MIT Press in the two volumes of *MPI—The Complete Reference* [22, 61].

These official documents and the books that describe them are organized so that they will be useful as reference works. The structure of the presentation is according to the chapters of the standard, which in turn reflects the subcommittee structure of the MPI Forum.

In 1994, two of the present authors, together with Anthony Skjellum, wrote *Using MPI: Portable Programming with the Message-Passing Interface* [24], a quite differently structured book on MPI-1, taking a more tutorial approach to the material. A second edition [25] of that book brought the material up to date with MPI-2. A third edition [26] has now appeared as a companion to this book, covering the most recent additions and clarifications to the material of MPI, and bringing it up to date with MPI-3 and in various other ways as well.

This book takes the same tutorial, example-driven approach to its material that *Using MPI* does, applying it to the topics of MPI-2 and MPI-3. These topics include parallel I/O, dynamic process management, remote memory operations, and external interfaces.

About This Book

Following the pattern set in *Using MPI*, we do not follow the order of chapters in the MPI standard, nor do we follow the order of material within a chapter as in the standard. Instead, we have organized the material in each chapter according to the complexity of the programs we use as examples, starting with simple examples and moving to more complex ones. We do assume that the reader is familiar with at least the simpler aspects of MPI-1. It is not necessary to have read *Using MPI*, but it wouldn't hurt.

This book is a major update to *Using MPI-2* [27], which described the features added to MPI by the MPI-2 standard in 1997. MPI-3 made major changes to some parts of MPI, particularly the remote memory access or one-sided communication; added some new features such as nonblocking and neighborhood collectives; and added new language bindings for Fortran 2008. Other parts of MPI were left essentially unchanged, such as the parallel I/O and dynamic process features. Some chapters in this book, such as those for parallel I/O and dynamic processes, are relatively minor updates from *Using MPI-2*. Others, such as the remote memory access chapters, have been significantly rewritten to make use of the new features and changes in MPI-3. Still others are entirely new and describe features introduced in MPI-3.

We begin in Chapter 1 with an overview of the current situation in parallel computing, many aspects of which have changed in the past five years. We summarize the new topics covered in MPI-2 and MPI-3 and their relationship to the current and (what we see as) the near-future parallel computing environment.

Chapter 2 covers several new classes of collective communication routines that are especially valuable for writing scalable applications. It also covers a replacement for the graph topology routines from MPI-1; the design of the MPI-1 routines does not scale to today's systems that may have more than a million MPI processes.

Because remote memory access is a large and complex topic, the discussion is divided into two chapters. Chapter 3 covers the basics of remote memory access and a simple synchronization model. Chapter 4 covers more general types of remote memory access and more complex synchronization models.

Chapter 5 shows how MPI-3 has extended the remote memory interface to provide a portable way to use memory shared between MPI processes, using the C or Fortran expressions for assignment and reference to update and access the data rather than MPI communication calls. The subtle and tricky issue of memory consistency is covered here.

Chapter 6 discusses how MPI can be used with other programming models, particularly ones that use multiple threads within an MPI process. Such programming approaches are increasingly common in large parallel applications written with MPI, and this chapter touches on some of the benefits and challenges of using threads correctly. It also introduces the MPI_Message, a new feature in MPI-3 to aid in certain types of multithreaded programming.

Chapter 7 describes the parallel I/O features of MPI, how to use them in a graduated series of examples, and how they can be used to get high performance, particularly on today's parallel file systems.

Chapter 8 covers new features of MPI-3 that handle very large data, such as file operations that return more than 2 gigabytes of data (the largest that can be represented in a 4-byte signed integer).

Chapter 9 introduces a new feature of MPI-3, an interface to permit both the expert programmer and the tool developer to access performance data that the MPI implementation may be collecting, as well as accessing and modifying parameters that control the behavior of the implementation. These are powerful features that can give you insight and control over the performance of your MPI application.

Chapter 10 covers MPI's relatively straightforward approach to dynamic process management, including both spawning new processes and dynamically connecting to running MPI programs.

In Chapter 11 we describe a new binding of MPI to Fortran. This binding takes advantage of features added to the Fortran 2008 standard, including ones added specifically to provide a better interface to MPI from Fortran.

Chapter 12 covers some of the other features of MPI that are especially useful for writers of software libraries. We also summarize the parts of MPI that we did not cover in either this book or *Using MPI*.

In Chapter 13 we summarize our journey through the new types of parallel programs enabled by MPI, comment on the current status of MPI implementations, and speculate on future directions for MPI.

Appendix A describes how to obtain supplementary material for this book, including complete source code for the examples, and related MPI materials that are available on the web.

In addition to the normal subject index, there is an index for the definitions of the MPI functions, constants, and terms used in this book.

We try to be impartial in the use of C and Fortran in the book's examples. The MPI standard has tried to keep the syntax of its calls similar in C and Fortran; in fact, MPI-3 introduces a new language binding for Fortran 2008 that is close to the C binding. When we need to refer to an MPI function without regard to language, we use the C version just because it is a little easier to read in running text.

This book is not a reference manual, in which MPI functions would be grouped according to functionality and completely defined. Instead we present MPI functions informally, in the context of example programs. Precise definitions are given in the MPI-3 standard [46]. Nonetheless, to increase the usefulness of this book to someone working with MPI, we have provided the bindings in C and Fortran for each MPI function that we discuss. These listings can be found set off in boxes located near where the functions are introduced. Arguments that can be of several types (typically message buffers) are defined as `void*` in C. In the Fortran boxes, such arguments are marked as being of type `<type>`. This means that one of the appropriate Fortran data types should be used. To find the "binding box" for a given MPI routine, one should use the appropriate bold-face reference in the Function and Term Index: **C** for C and **f90** for Fortran. For the few routines from the Fortran 2008 binding for MPI for which binding boxes are provided, the label in the index is **f08**.

Acknowledgments

We thank all those who participated in the MPI Forum. Their dedication to creating a standard for parallel computing has transformed computational science, bringing the power of parallel computing to all branches of science and engineering.

Our interactions with the many users of MPICH have been the source of ideas, examples, and code fragments. Other members of the MPICH group at Argonne have made critical contributions to MPICH and other MPI-related tools that we have used in the preparation of this book.

Gail Pieper, technical writer in the Mathematics and Computer Science Division at Argonne, was our indispensable guide in matters of style and usage and vastly improved the readability of our prose.

Natalia Berezneva designed and created many figures for this edition of the book.

Using Advanced MPI

1 Introduction

MPI (Message-Passing Interface) is a portable, standard interface for writing parallel programs using a distributed-memory programming model. It is widely used for writing parallel applications, particularly in science and engineering domains, on systems of all sizes—from laptops to clusters to the largest and most powerful supercomputers in the world. MPI originated in 1994 as a standardization of message-passing practice, and it has since been significantly expanded twice—first with MPI-2 in 1997 and then to MPI-3 in 2012 [46].

This book is on the use of the more advanced features of MPI and assumes familiarity with the basics of programming with MPI, such as are covered in the companion volume in this series, *Using MPI* [26].

1.1 MPI-1 and MPI-2

The MPI standardization process began in late 1992 with a workshop at the Supercomputing '92 conference. A group, calling itself the MPI Forum, started meeting regularly every six weeks thereafter, with the goal of defining a standard interface for message passing. The MPI Forum included technical representatives from various computer (and supercomputer) system vendors, researchers from universities and national laboratories working on communication libraries, and application and library developers who were users of communication libraries. The United States, Europe, and Japan were represented. The Forum's efforts focused on standardizing existing practice since many different communication libraries already existed at the time—one from each supercomputer vendor and several research efforts. The first version of the MPI standard (MPI-1) was released in the summer of 1994. MPI-1 supported all the basic functionality needed in a message-passing library, such as point-to-point communication (blocking and nonblocking), collective communication, datatypes to describe data layout in memory, virtual process topologies, error codes and classes, and bindings for both C and Fortran 77. MPI constituted a major advance over all existing message-passing libraries in terms of features, precise semantics, standardized interface, and the potential for highly optimized implementations on all platforms, resulting in the ability for users to write truly portable and performant parallel programs. Implementations of MPI, led by the MPICH implementation [23], were available immediately on all platforms, which led to the widespread adoption of MPI in parallel applications.

About a year after MPI-1 was released, the MPI Forum again resumed meeting to explore additions to the MPI standard that went beyond the basic message-passing concepts of MPI-1. This effort resulted in the MPI-2 standard, released in 1997.

MPI-2 had three major new features: an extensive interface to efficiently support parallel file I/O from an MPI program; support for one-sided (put/get) communication, as opposed to the two-sided (send/receive) communication in MPI-1; and dynamic process management, namely, the ability to create additional processes in a running MPI program and the ability for separately started MPI applications to connect to each other and communicate. MPI-2 also had other features such as precisely defined semantics for multithreaded MPI communication, bindings for Fortran 90 and C++, and support for mixed-language programming.

1.2   MPI-3

MPI-2 was finished in 1997; implementations of most of the new standard appeared shortly thereafter. Over the next decade, MPI filled the needs of most computational science codes that demanded a high-performance, highly scalable programming system. However, ten years is a long time in computing; and were many changes both in the computing environment and in the practice of computing that necessitated an update to MPI. These included the following:

- The scale of massively parallel systems increased significantly, with machines with over a million cores delivered in 2013.

- Single-core processors vanished; virtually all "processors" were now symmetric multiprocessors with shared memory. Even the term processor became ill-defined: Is it a core in a chip? The chip itself? Interaction with shared-memory programming and with threads became important to applications.

- Remote direct memory access (RDMA) support in networks became mainstream, particularly through the widespread adoption of InfiniBand as a commodity network fabric. Networks, especially those designed for the highest-performance parallel computers, became increasingly capable, adding support for remote atomic memory operations and accelerated collective communication.

- C and Fortran both evolved, requiring updates to the MPI interfaces. Enhancements in Fortran offered the hope of an MPI binding that addressed many of the issues discussed at length in the MPI-2 standard (see especially Section 10.2.2 in [45]). C++ also evolved, becoming much richer and powerful; the MPI C++ binding was woefully outdated.

- Experience had been gained with nonblocking collective communication, combined with disappointing experience with threads on HPC platforms. The MPI-2 expectation had been that nonblocking collectives would be implemented by the user by simply running a blocking collective from within a separate thread. However, the overhead of using threads (already recognized as a potential problem in MPI-2) meant that this approach was too inefficient on some important platforms.

- A great deal of interest in fault tolerance and how MPI would work when faults were frequent had arisen.

- While MPI-2 RMA was used by some applications, it had failed to live up to the expectations of the MPI Forum. Limitations of the model had been documented [6], and a major overhaul of this part of MPI clearly was needed.

- A long list of generally minor errata had accumulated.

With all of these and more, the MPI Forum reconvened in 2008 to first release minor updates to MPI-2 (MPI 2.1 in 2008 and MPI 2.2 in 2009) and to begin developing MPI-3. After many meetings and several years of work, MPI-3 was finally released in September 2012. This book covers many of the more advanced features in MPI introduced in MPI-3. Because some of those are about one-sided communication, which was a major part of *Using MPI-2* [27], this book was written as a replacement for that book and includes other parts of MPI, such as the parallel I/O and dynamic process features, that were introduced in MPI-2.

1.3   Parallelism and MPI

This book, like *Using MPI*, uses examples to illustrate the use of MPI. These may be full example programs (which we present as much as possible) or code fragments where a full program would be too long. While we use a range of examples, one problem will be used in several places. This problem is a computation on a regular grid or mesh, distributed across all processes. Regular meshes arise in many applications, from the solution of elliptic, parabolic, and hyperbolic partial differential equations (PDEs), to linear algebra, where the "mesh" is a matrix, to graphics, where the mesh is a pixel array. More complex data structures often make use of MPI in a way similar to how MPI is used with regular meshes, and regular mesh code is simpler to describe and to provide complete example codes. Because this example will be used several times in this book, we describe it here. To provide a specific example, we will describe two simple simulations that are computed on a

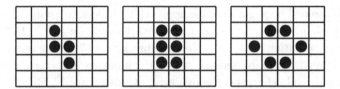

Figure 1.1: Three turns in Conway's Game of Life

regular mesh. The description is similar to that of the Poisson problem in *Using MPI*, Section 4.1, though there are some differences that set the stage for discussions later in this book. We begin by describing the approach without reference to any parallelism. This is often a good approach, because it lets you concentrate first on designing a correct implementation. We will then apply parallelism by decomposing the problem into smaller subproblems. An alternative approach that can be more effective in some cases is to express the maximum degree of parallelism as separate computations and then aggregate them together.

1.3.1 Conway's Game of Life

Our first simulation is Conway's Game of Life, popularized in Martin Gardner's column in *Scientific American* [18]. The rules for this game are simple. There is a board, like a chess board. On each square, there can be either life or no life (think of the square as being occupied or empty). For each turn of the game, the following rules are applied to determine whether each square at the end of the turn is occupied:

- If the square is occupied and if either two or three (not more and not less) of the surrounding eight squares are occupied, then that square is occupied at the end of the turn (continues to live).

- If the square is not occupied, and there are exactly three occupied surrounding squares, then that square is occupied at the end of the turn (birth).

Three consecutive turns in this game are shown in Figure 1.1.

This game is an example of a *cellular automaton* and has many interesting properties. For example, the population of this game (on an unbounded board) can be unbounded—there are initial configurations whose populations grow without bound.

1.3.2 Poisson Solver

Our second simulation is the solution of the Poisson problem

$$\nabla^2 u(x,y) \;=\; \frac{\partial^2 u}{\partial x^2}(x,y) + \frac{\partial^2 u}{\partial y^2}(x,y) = f(x,y) \qquad (1.1)$$

$$u(x,y) \;=\; g(x,y) \text{ on the boundary}$$

on the unit square $[0,1] \times [0,1]$, with the value of $u(x,y)$ specified on the boundary. A simple approach to approximate the solution to this problem is to approximate $u(x,y)$ on a regular mesh, defined by the points (x_i, y_j), with $0 \le i \le n$ and $0 \le j \le n$, where $x_i = i/n$ and $y_j = j/n$. To simplify the notation, we will use $u_{i,j}$ to denote the approximation to $u(x_i, y_j)$. Using the simplest second-order finite-difference approximation to the second derivatives in Equation 1.1, we have these equations:

$$u_{0,j} \;=\; g(0,y_j) \text{ for } 0 \le j \le n$$
$$u_{n,j} \;=\; g(1,y_j) \text{ for } 0 \le j \le n$$
$$u_{i,0} \;=\; g(x_i,0) \text{ for } 0 \le i \le n$$
$$u_{i,n} \;=\; g(x_i,1) \text{ for } 0 \le i \le n$$

$$\frac{u_{i+1,j} - 2u_{i,j} + u_{i-1,j}}{h^2}$$
$$+\frac{u_{i,j+1} - 2u_{i,j} + u_{i,j-1}}{h^2} \;=\; f(x_i,y_j) \qquad (1.2)$$
$$\text{for } 1 \le i,j \le n-1.$$

The last equation can be rewritten as

$$4u_{i,j} = (u_{i+1,j} + u_{i-1,j} + u_{i,j+1} + u_{i,j-1}) - h^2 f(x_i,y_j) \qquad \text{for } 1 \le i,j \le n-1 \quad (1.3)$$

This is a system of linear equations for the unknown values $u_{i,j}$. Such problems can be solved in many ways. For systems where the total number of equations is large, iterative methods are often employed. One of the simplest methods takes Equation 1.3 and computes a new iterate at each point by using the right hand side of the equation:

$$u_{i,j}^{k+1} = \frac{1}{4}\left((u_{i+1,j}^k + u_{i-1,j}^k + u_{i,j+1}^k + u_{i,j-1}^k) - h^2 f(x_i,y_j)\right) \qquad \text{for } 1 \le i,j \le n-1 \quad (1.4)$$

Here, $u_{i,j}^k$ is the approximation to $u(x_i,y_k)$ at the kth iteration. This is known as *Jacobi's method* and it converges to the solution of the system of equations as k

becomes large. Much better methods are known; but for the purposes of showing how to program such problems using MPI, this algorithm is sufficient.

For Jacobi's method, to compute the value of the new approximation $u_{i,h}^k$, we could use the following code:

```
for (i=1; i<n; i++)
  for (j=1; j<n; j++)
    unew[i][j] = 0.25 * ((u[i+1][j] + u[i-1][j] +
                          u[i][j+1] + u[i][j-1]) - h*h*f[i][j]);
```

In the case of Conway's Game of Life, the computation is

```
for (i=1; i<n; i++)
    for (j=1; j<n; j++) {
        nbrs = u[i+1][j+1] + u[i+1][j]   + u[i+1][j-1] +
               u[i][j+1]    +              u[i][j-1]    +
               u[i-1][j+1] + u[i-1][j+1] + u[i-1][j-1];
        if (nbrs == 3 || nbrs + u[i][j] == 3)
            unew[i][j] = 1;
        else
            unew[i][j] = 0;

    }
```

In this version of Life, we fix the values of u and *unew* along the boundaries. More sophisticated versions can apply periodic boundary conditions or grow the mesh as life expands.

Note that both Conway's Game of Life and the Jacobi method consist of loops over all of mesh points and that the values for unew could be computed in any order. Also note that the value of unew[i][j] depends only on a few values from u—the four values immediately left, right, above, and below for the Jacobi method and the eight surrounding values for Life. These two patterns of data dependency are illustrated in Figure 1.2 and are called *stencils*. In the case of the Jacobi method (Figure 1.2(a)), this is a five-point or plus stencil; for Life, it is a nine-point or star stencil.

To parallelize this computation, we need to divide the work across many processes. One common and simple way is by *regular domain decomposition*: divide the data into regular, equal-sized (or approximately equal-sized) pieces, and assign each piece to a different process. For a regular mesh data structure, the easiest decomposition is to divide the mesh into slices as shown in Figure 1.3.

Looking at the full mesh, one can set that the process with rank r has the part of the mesh defined by $s_r \leq i < s_{r+1}$ and $0 \leq j \leq n$, where s_r defines the

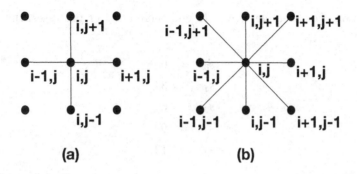

Figure 1.2: A 5-point stencil (a) and a 9-point stencil (b)

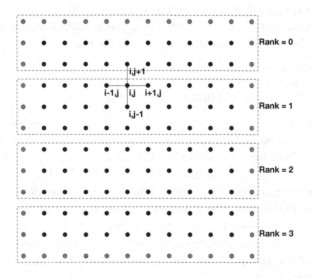

Figure 1.3: A 1-D decomposition of a 2-D mesh

decomposition. For example, if $n = 11$ and there are four processes, the values of s_r would be

$$s_0 = 0$$
$$s_1 = 3$$
$$s_2 = 6$$
$$s_3 = 9$$
$$s_4 = 12$$

Note that each process stores only the part of the mesh that it "owns." In the example here, each process might declare

```
double u[3][12];
```

since the mesh is 12×12 and there are four processes, so each process takes one fourth of the mesh. We'll see shortly that we need to expand this storage slightly, but the important point is that with domain decomposition the data is divided among the processes and, hence, for a fixed-size problem the amount of storage needed *per process* goes down as more processes are used.

With the decomposition described above, the code that is executed on each process is almost the same. For the Jacobi method, the code is now

```
for (i=0; i<localN; i++)
  for (j=1; j<n; j++)
    unew[i][j] = 0.25 * ((u[i+1][j] + u[i-1][j] +
                          u[i][j+1] + u[i][j-1]) - h*h*f[i][j]);
```

Here, `localN` is computed as $s_{r+1} - s_r$. But note that there are two problems with this code. First, for i=0, it requires the value of `u[0-1][j]` or `u[-1][j]`. Second, for i=LocalN-1, it requires `u[LocalN-1+1][j]` or `u[LocalN][j]`. In our simple decomposition, these values belong to the processes with ranks $r - 1$ and $r + 1$, respectively. To compute with these values, we must communicate them from their owning processes to this process. And, of course, we must have some place to put them. The most common approach is to add two rows to our local data structure, one above and one below, as shown in Figure 1.4. These extra locations are called *halo* or *ghost* cells.

Now, the declaration is

```
double u[5][12];
```

and the code is

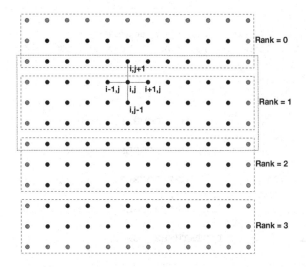

Figure 1.4: Ghost or halo region for the local mesh

```
// communication to fill in ghost cells
for (i=1; i<=localN; i++)
  for (j=1; j<n; j++)
    unew[i][j] = 0.25 * ((u[i+1][j] + u[i-1][j] +
                          u[i][j+1] + u[i][j-1]) - h*h*f[i][j]);
```

In Fortran, this can be made a little cleaner because the declaration can define the range of indices. For example, using sr and $srp1$ for s_r and s_{r+1}, respectively, the Fortran declaration would be

```
double precision u(sr-1:srp1,0:n)
```

In this book, we'll see a number of ways to perform this communication. In the companion book, *Using MPI* [26], the use of point-to-point communication is described, and we assume in this book that you are familiar with the use of point-to-point communication for problems of this type. For reference, Figure 1.5 shows one example for the simple 1-D decomposition. To use this code, it is necessary to compute the ranks of the neighbors. In most cases, the best approach is to use the virtual process topology functions of MPI, such as `MPI_Cart_create` and `MPI_Cart_shift`, in order to determine the ranks of the neighboring processes.

Several important points must be considered when looking at regular meshes.

```
#include "mpi.h"
void exchng1(int nx, int s, int e, double a[nx+2][e-s+1],
             MPI_Comm comm1d, int nbrbottom, int nbrtop)
{
  MPI_Request req[4];
  int         ny = e - s + 1;

  MPI_Irecv(&a[1][0],    nx, MPI_DOUBLE, nbrbottom,
            0, comm1d, &req[0]);
  MPI_Irecv(&a[1][ny-1], nx, MPI_DOUBLE, nbrtop,
            1, comm1d, &req[1]);
  MPI_Isend(&a[1][ny-2], nx, MPI_DOUBLE, nbrtop,
            0, comm1d, &req[2]);
  MPI_Isend(&a[1][1],    nx, MPI_DOUBLE, nbrbottom,
            1, comm1d, &req[3]);
  MPI_Waitall(4, req, MPI_STATUSES_IGNORE);
}
```

Figure 1.5: One possible halo-exchange implementation, using MPI nonblocking communication. See Figure 4.16 in *Using MPI* [26] for the Fortran version of this routine.

1. The decomposition. The one-dimensional decomposition that we showed is the simplest, but it limits to n the number of processes that can be used. In addition, the amount of data that must be communicated is the same independent of the number of processes used. Thus, parallelism, while reducing the amount of computation performed on each process, doesn't reduce the amount of communication. This limits the performance of a parallel code that uses such a simple decomposition. Higher-dimensional decompositions, while more complex to describe and to code, provide more parallelism and reduce the amount of communication needed.

2. The precise decomposition and the precise assignment of the parts of the mesh to the processes can have a significant impact on performance. In our example, the pieces of the decomposed mesh were assigned to processes in rank order. This approach is easy but not necessarily best for performance; other assignment orders can be used. In *Using MPI* [26], the use of the process topology routines is described. These routines can be used to create a new communicator in which the simple rank ordering of our examples should provide a good choice of assignment of mesh pieces to processes. Note, how-

ever, that these optimizations are only approximate, particularly for modern multicore processors. MPI also provides some routines to work directly with meshes distributed across the processes in an MPI program; we will discuss them in Section 7.4.

3. The decomposition here assumes that each process works equally fast. This is not always true on modern systems; for example, the operating system or even the user's runtime may steal time from one or more of the compute cores on a multiprocessing chip. When this assumption of equal compute time per process fails, we say that a *load imbalance* exists. Fortunately, as we'll see in Chapter 6, one can use MPI to take advantage of features on multicore chips to address some issues of load balance and imbalance.

4. In these examples, we've spent little time on the boundary conditions for the problem, other than to define them in the definition of the Poisson problem. Handling the boundary conditions is often straightforward, yet can require more code than is needed for the interior of the mesh or grid, which is why we skipped over that detail. In a real calculation, the boundary conditions will need to be handled, which may add significantly to the code.

5. Many problems have much more complex data structures. In fact, a number of parallel languages have provided easy-to-use features for the sort of regular mesh we've described here. Yet those languages have not been successful. One reason is that many (perhaps most) problems require some specialized data structure that is not quite the same as a regular mesh. A strength of MPI is that it is equally easy (or hard) to use with almost any choice of data structure. For example, most of the ideas used in this section also apply when solving problems on an irregular or unstructured mesh, including the notion of stencils and halo or ghost cells. And with proper care in choosing the data structures and methods, the code can be kept relatively easy to use; one example is the PETSc library [3] that provides a powerful framework for solving (among other things) linear systems of equations arising from the discretization of PDEs on unstructured meshes.

1.4   Passing Hints to the MPI Implementation with `MPI_Info`

MPI provides a mechanism by which the user can pass "hints" to the implementation. Hints are suggestions from the user about choices that may improve performance. An implementation may ignore the hints. We briefly introduce the hints mechanism here because hints are used in many parts of MPI, such as parallel I/O, remote memory access, and dynamic processes. Details on their specific use in various areas are given in the respective chapters.

1.4.1 Motivation, Description, and Rationale

MPI contains some complex functions with potentially long and unwieldy argument lists. In addition, some functions interact with external objects such as the operating system or file system in ways that are unlikely to be uniform across the wide range of platforms on which MPI programs are expected to run. In order to preserve at least some measure of portability for MPI programs, some arguments need to be optional.

The answer to all of these problems is the info object. The info object is an opaque object (of type `MPI_Info` in C and `integer` in Fortran) that provides a flexible mechanism for dealing with complex, optional, or nonportable options on certain MPI function calls. In some ways it is a general "mini-database" of (key, value) pairs. MPI provides functions to create and delete info objects, to access and update an info object by adding and deleting these pairs, and to access the pairs either by key or by number in sequence. Both keys and values are character strings.

This type of functionality (managing sets of strings) doesn't seem to have much to do with message passing; what is it doing as part of the MPI standard? The MPI Forum felt that no existing library provided the flexibility needed, was available on all platforms, and was language-neutral. Therefore it had to specify one of its own. We will see how it is used with an example related to parallel I/O; a more through description is given in other chapters where info is used.

1.4.2 An Example from Parallel I/O

Several parallel file systems can benefit from "hints" given to the file system about how the application program will interact with the file system. These hints contain information known to the programmer or user that may be difficult or impossible for the file system to figure out by itself and that may allow the file system to perform useful optimizations in handling the application's I/O requests. For example, optimizations may be possible if the file system knows that the file will be read only once and in a sequential fashion. This hint can be given to the file system via the info object as follows.

---

int **MPI_Info_create**(MPI_Info *info)

int **MPI_Info_set**(MPI_Info info, const char *key, const char *value)

int **MPI_Info_free**(MPI_Info *info)

Table 1.1: C bindings for the info functions used in this chapter

---

```
MPI_Info myinfo;
MPI_File myfile;
MPI_Comm mycomm;

MPI_Info_create(&myinfo);
MPI_Info_set(myinfo, "access_style", "read_once,sequential");
MPI_File_open(mycomm, "myfile", MPI_MODE_RDONLY, myinfo,
              &myfile);
MPI_Info_free(&myinfo);
```

Note that one can free the info object after it has been used in the call to `MPI_-File_open`; the info object belongs to the user, not the system, and its content is extracted by the system when it is used as an argument in an MPI call.

The key `access_style` is a reserved key in MPI, and the values for it are also reserved. An MPI implementation is free to ignore this hint, but if it recognizes `access_style`, it should also recognize the values specified in the MPI standard. It can also recognize additional values not defined in the standard. The standard contains all the reserved keys for the info object and describes their possible values. Implementations are allowed to recognize other keys and values as well, at some risk to the portability of programs that use them. C and Fortran bindings for the info functions used above are given in Tables 1.1 and 1.2.

1.5   Organization of This Book

This book is organized around accomplishing different tasks in MPI. Chapter 2 discusses features of MPI that are especially important for working with large numbers of processes. Since systems are already in use with over 1 million cores, and since the number of cores in even mid-sized clusters is over $10,000$, the techniques in this chapter can help ensure that an MPI program performs well on all sizes of systems. Chapters 3 and 4 introduce the one-sided communication model in MPI. This alternative to two-sided message passing offers both better performance and

---

MPI_INFO_CREATE(info, ierror)
        integer info, ierror

MPI_INFO_SET(info, key, value, ierror)
        integer info, ierror
        character*(*) key, value

MPI_INFO_FREE(info, ierror)
        integer info, ierror

Table 1.2: Fortran bindings for the info functions used in this chapter

simpler programming in many cases and is increasingly important because modern interconnects now provide hardware support for many one-sided operations. Chapter 5 covers the related issue of using shared memory with MPI. This new feature, added in MPI-3, provides MPI programs with a way to make better use of multicore processors without needing to use a separate programming approach such as threads or OpenMP. Chapter 6 covers hybrid programming for those cases where combining MPI with threads and programming systems with a thread-like model of parallelism is appropriate. Chapter 7 describes parallel I/O in MPI, including the critical role of collective I/O in achieving high performance. Chapter 8 covers routines that were added in MPI-3 to handle the case of very large data sizes, such as individual messages containing more than two gigabytes of data. Chapter 9 describes new features in MPI that allow the programmer (or even better, new tools) to provide more insight and control into the performance of MPI programs. We describe this as a chapter on debugging because we consider performance and correctness as requirements of parallel programs, and these features of MPI help the programmer to address problems with both types of requirements. Chapter 10 covers the features in MPI that permit the creation of new processes during the execution of an MPI program. While this capability has had limited use, and some supercomputers do not support it, it has found use especially in prototype systems and in supporting certain programming paradigms. Chapter 11 covers the new Fortran 2008 language bindings added to MPI. In this book, we use the older Fortran 9x binding because many existing MPI programs use that binding, and because the new Fortran binding is similar in style and appearance to the C binding, and hence one can easily see how to use the new Fortran binding when looking at examples in C. Nevertheless, we do explain how to use the new Fortran binding, and we discuss some issues that may slow its adoption. Chapter 13 looks at how MPI may change and offers a few final comments on programming parallel computers with MPI.

2 Working with Large-Scale Systems

From the beginning, MPI has always been defined with large-scale systems in mind. Collective operations and scalable communicator and group operations have been designed to support highly parallel abstract machines. However, system design and implementation has changed over the past several years, and the exponential growth in processing elements has led to numbers of MPI processes that were unthinkable fifteen years ago. One unexpected problem at large scale has been the interference between synchronization and small local delays, called system noise. Such local delays may introduce less than 1% overhead at each core, but each delay can propagate through synchronization to other processes. Overheads from propagating system noise have been identified as a major performance-limiting factor in parallel systems [54]. Research has also shown that noise events become deterministic with scale and thus form a *noise barrier*, a certain performance limit that cannot be crossed under noise, no matter how fast the network or machine is [36]. In addition, new and more dynamic application domains, such as graph analytics, have discovered MPI as an implementation system and require more flexible interfaces.

On the hardware level, we observe a mix of sparse constant-degree topologies, such as fat tree or torus networks, being scaled to very large node counts. In addition, the number of cores per node is still on an exponential trajectory. Thus it is becoming increasingly important to efficiently map user computations to the underlying sparse network topology connecting multicore nodes. Low-diameter networks, such as Dragonfly [41], mitigate negative effects of bad process placement. Nevertheless, adapting applications to the physical topology will improve efficiency of those systems as well.

MPI addresses these needs by introducing and improving several new concepts in the latest versions of the standard: nonblocking collective operations, distributed graph topologies, neighborhood collectives, and advanced communicator creation routines. In this chapter, we discuss concepts that are most relevant for large-scale systems (while they can be used on small systems, they are likely to have the biggest impact at large scales). Thus, the features discussed here often directly impact scalability of parallel MPI codes.

MPI-3 introduced nonblocking versions of all collective communication operations. Such *nonblocking collectives* can be used to relax synchronization to mitigate system noise as well as to implement efficient termination detection algorithms for large-scale graph analytics. MPI-2.2 defined a new scalable specification of application graphs [35] that enables efficient process-to-node mappings for parallel execution. A new class of collective operations, neighborhood collectives, were introduced in MPI-3 to perform communication in user-definable static neighborhoods. Moreover, two new communicator management functions were added in MPI-3. The first function allows programmers to create new communicators by invoking a call only on the subset of processes that form the new communicator, as opposed to the old interface, where all processes of the old communicator needed to call the creation function. The second function defines a nonblocking communicator duplication routine needed for the implementation of truly nonblocking libraries without threads.

2.1   Nonblocking Collectives

Nonblocking collective operations are conceptually simple but enable us to solve complex problems and apply essential optimizations. Let us begin our discussion with an example: parallel computation of a two-dimensional Fast Fourier Transformation (2-D FFT).

2.1.1   Example: 2-D FFT

We solve the 2-D problem by distributing it in one dimension across all processes and using local one-dimensional FFTs. Figure 2.1 shows an example transformation of a 16×16 points FFT on four processes. Let us assume that the data is distributed in the y direction, i.e., each process has four complete lines in the x direction. Each process can now independently transform its local four lines with four local 1-D FFTs (Step A in Figure 2.1). To complete the 2-D FFT, we need to perform the same 1-D transformation in the y direction (Step C in Figure 2.1). The necessary data ordering (complete y lines at each process) can be expressed with a parallel transpose using `MPI_Alltoall` of the input array (Step B in Figure 2.1).

On most architectures, FFT is dominated by the parallel transpose time; therefore, communication optimizations are crucial. Many teams have looked at optimizing the communication in FFT, and several have enabled computation/communication overlap of the communication of the ith line with the 1-D transformation of the $(i + 1)$th line. This overlap is most commonly performed by using nonblocking point-to-point communication, sending blocks of data to each process separately. This approach, however, leads to rather complex mechanical code transformations that reduce the readability and maintainability of the application code base. In addition, using separate point-to-point communication specifies a communication schedule and pattern statically instead of allowing the MPI implementation to select the best alltoall algorithm and message schedule for the particular architecture.

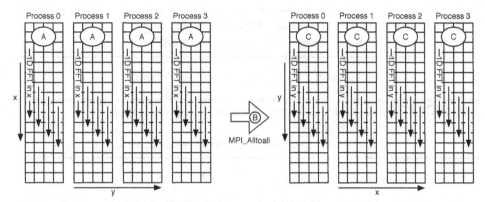

Figure 2.1: Schematic view of the parallel two-dimensional FFT

Thus, this kind of transformation lowers abstraction and eliminates performance portability.

Yet the general idea of overlapping computation and communication in parallel FFT is fundamentally useful. A nonblocking alltoall allows programmers to maintain the high level of abstraction, and thus programmer friendliness, as well as the performance portability. We present source code as well as a more detailed discussion of FFT and software pipelining in Section 2.1.5.

In general, nonblocking collectives combine nonblocking functionality, a well-known concept from point-to-point communication, with collective communication. Let us quickly recapitulate those two orthogonal concepts. The main intent of nonblocking point-to-point communication is to avoid deadlocks and enable overlap of communication and computation. We note that MPI guarantees only freedom from deadlock, in other words, a nonblocking function will return irrespective of the state of any remote process. Overlap of computation and communication *may* be possible and generally depends on the details and quality of the implementation used. Yet nonblocking semantics are powerful and can be used to construct complex distributed applications. An interesting side-effect is that nonblocking semantics allow the programmer to *defer synchronization* to the point where the operation completes (in a test or wait call).

Collective communication functions, such as `MPI_Bcast` or `MPI_Alltoall`, offer a convenient set of communication operations defined on groups of processes. Their semantics allow users to express a certain communication problem declaratively. This declarative concept, which defines what to do and not how to do it, allows the implementation to use optimized communication algorithms for each target architecture, leading to the well-known *performance portability* of collec-

---

int **MPI_Ibcast**(void* buffer, int count, MPI_Datatype datatype, int root,
                MPI_Comm comm, MPI_Request *request)

Table 2.1: C binding for nonblocking broadcast

MPI_IBCAST(buffer, count, datatype, root, comm, request, ierror)
                <type> buffer(*)
                integer count, datatype, root, comm, request, ierror

---

Table 2.2: Fortran binding for nonblocking broadcast

tive operations. (As always, the MPI standard guarantees only the semantics; the performance depends on the quality of the MPI implementation.) Because of the higher-level of abstraction, using collective communication often leads to more concise and more elegant formulations of a problem as compared with expressing it with point-to-point communication [20].

Nonblocking collectives combine the benefits of nonblocking and collective operations and thus offer mechanisms for preventing deadlocks, overlapping communication with computation, and deferring synchronization together with elegant high-level and performance-portable group communication. In fact, the combined semantics are much more than the sum of the two parts and enable the development of novel protocols to solve complex problems, such as the solution to the dynamic sparse data exchange described in Section 2.1.6.

MPI-3 defines a simple interface for nonblocking collectives: It allows programmers to call nonblocking collectives by adding an "I" (for immediate) to the name and a request output parameter to the blocking version. For example, the nonblocking version of `MPI_Bcast(buffer, count, datatype, root, comm)` is `MPI_Ibcast(buffer, count, datatype, root, comm, request)`. The full signatures for C and Fortran are shown in Tables 2.1 and 2.2, respectively.

The output request is the same as the request object from point-to-point communication and can be used in the usual test and wait functions to check for completion of the operation. It can also be mixed with requests from point-to-point communication in functions such as `MPI_Waitall`, `MPI_Waitany`, and `MPI_-Waitsome` and their nonblocking equivalents `MPI_Testall`, `MPI_Testany`, and `MPI_Testsome`. The nonblocking collective functions (e.g., `MPI_Ibcast`) must be called collectively in the same order on all processes in the communicator. They return *immediately* as the prefix suggests, irrespective of the state of remote pro-

cesses. However, the corresponding blocking completion routines (e.g., wait) will
not return before the operation is locally complete, which may depend on the state
of remote processes involved in the operation.

2.1.2 Example: Five-Point Stencil

Figure 2.2 shows how a simple five-point stencil code (e.g., representing a two-
dimensional Poisson solver, cf. Section 1.3.2) can be expressed with collective communication. Let us focus on processes 1 to 4. Each process is the center of a
communication pattern where it receives data from its four neighbors and sends
data to its four neighbors. This exchange can be expressed by a collective gather
(receive from neighbors) or scatter (send to neighbors) on a communicator that
includes only direct neighbors of each process. For simplicity, we omit the details
of message sizes and buffers. The right side of Figure 2.2 shows all four communicators. Each process is the root of its own communicator and member of four
neighbor communicators called east, west, north, and south. For example, process 1 in the figure is the root of communicator A, and communicators B and C
are its east and south communicators owned by processes 3 and 2, respectively
(north and west are omitted for simplicity). Any blocking collective operation on
all four communicators at the same time would lead to a deadlock because of the
cyclic matching ordering dependency (i.e., one cannot find a valid order in which
the collectives can be called without deadlocking).

For example, the following code would deadlock:

```
MPI_Comm comm[5]= {c_my, c_north, c_south, c_east, c_west};
for (i=0; i<5; ++i) {
  MPI_Scatter(sbf[i], ct, dt, rbf[i], ct, dt, 0, comm[i]);
}
```

MPI-3's nonblocking collectives support the start of nonblocking group communications in any order as long as they are completed without additional remote
dependencies. This feature allows us to transform the previously deadlocking code
into a correct version:

```
MPI_Comm comm[5] = {c_my, c_north, c_south, c_east, c_west};
MPI_Request rq[5];
for (i=0; i<5; ++i) {
 MPI_Iscatter(sbf[i], ct, dt, rbf[i], ct, dt, 0, comm[i], &rq[i]);
}
MPI_Waitall(5, rq, MPI_STATUSES_IGNORE);
```

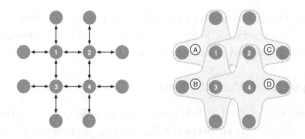

Figure 2.2: Example where blocking collectives always deadlock. The left side shows the messaging pattern and the right side shows a communicator layout that can be used with scatter/gather.

---

int **MPI_Iscatter**(const void* sendbuf, int sendcount, MPI_Datatype sendtype,
        void* recvbuf, int recvcount, MPI_Datatype recvtype, int root,
        MPI_Comm comm, MPI_Request *request)

int **MPI_Igather**(const void* sendbuf, int sendcount, MPI_Datatype sendtype,
        void* recvbuf, int recvcount, MPI_Datatype recvtype, int root,
        MPI_Comm comm, MPI_Request *request)

Table 2.3: C bindings for nonblocking scatter and gather

Similarly, one could use nonblocking `MPI_Igather` calls to implement the stencil example. Tables 2.3 and 2.4 show the C and Fortran interfaces, respectively, for nonblocking scatter and gather. However, this example is only intended to illustrate issues with overlapping communicators. We provide a better solution for collective communications for the Poisson stencil problem in Section 2.3.1.

2.1.3   Matching, Completion, and Progression

The matching of nonblocking collectives defines which collective invocation at one process is linked to which collective invocation at another process. Blocking collective operations are matched trivially since exactly one collective operation can be active on a communicator at any time. For example, the following program is incorrect:

MPI_ISCATTER(sendbuf, sendcount, sendtype, recvbuf, recvcount, recvtype, root,
          comm, request, ierror)
          <type> sendbuf(*), recvbuf(*)
          integer sendcount, sendtype, recvcount, recvtype, root, comm,
             request, ierror

MPI_IGATHER(sendbuf, sendcount, sendtype, recvbuf, recvcount, recvtype, root,
          comm, request, ierror)
          <type> sendbuf(*), recvbuf(*)
          integer sendcount, sendtype, recvcount, recvtype, root, comm,
             request, ierror

Table 2.4: Fortran bindings for nonblocking scatter and gather

---

```
if (rank==0)
  MPI_Gather(sbf, sct, tp, rbf, rct, tp, 0, comm);
else
  MPI_Scatter(sbf, sct, tp, rbf, rct, tp, 0, comm);
```

Nonblocking collectives behave similarly and match in their issuing order on each communicator. Thus the program above would still be incorrect even if the collective invocations were nonblocking. Note that the stencil example with nonblocking collectives is correct because each collective is started on a different communicator. Multiple nonblocking collective operations can be in progress at any time and complete independently. That means that the completion of a collective means nothing for the completion of another collective, and, in general, nonblocking collectives can complete in any order. Tags are offered in point-to-point communications because it is sometimes necessary to differentiate between different control flows and matches. This behavior can be emulated by using different communicators that form their own matching scope for the different collective communications. But this technique should be used cautiously because communicators may consume significant resources.

Nonblocking point-to-point communication is not always completed if the sender or receiver do not call MPI functions. In the worst case, the communication does not *progress* and is delayed until both processes call test or wait. Similarly, nonblocking collective communications do not guarantee progress, and all communication may happen during test or wait calls. Progress issues are much more important for collectives than for point-to-point because collective algorithms are often multistage communications. For example, consider the binomial tree in Figure 2.3, which

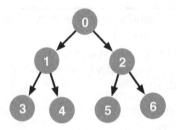

Figure 2.3: Binomial tree as used in some broadcast implementations

is a possible implementation of broadcast. The root process 0 will most likely send
the first two messages during the start of the MPI_Ibcast. However, it is unlikely
that the message has already arrived when process 1 calls MPI_Ibcast. Thus, if
the other processes are not progressed (e.g., by calling MPI), then the messages
cannot advance beyond those processes.

High-quality implementations may offer asynchronous progress facilities or even
allow the user to control related parameters (e.g., the invocation of a progress
thread). If such features are not available, the programmer can always advance
collective communications manually by calling nonblocking completion (test) or
other MPI routines. However, the correct timing of manual progress calls is tricky:
if they are called too infrequently, communications will not progress asynchronously
leading to reduced overlap; if they are called too frequently, the call overheads will
diminish performance gains resulting from the overlap.

2.1.4   Restrictions

Nonblocking collective operations cannot be canceled like nonblocking point-to-
point operations. Nonblocking collectives do *not* match with blocking collectives.
This restriction is intended to allow different algorithms for each type, because
implementors often minimize nonoverlappable overheads of nonblocking collectives
while they minimize absolute latency of blocking collectives. Send buffers as well
as the vector buffers needed for vector (v- and w-) collectives must not be modified
while the operation is in progress.

We now present three use cases that demonstrate how nonblocking collectives
can be used to address three separate concerns in large-scale computing: (1) communication overheads, (2) system noise, and (3) scalable coordination.

```
for (x=0; x<n/p; ++x) fft_1d(/* x-th stencil */);

// pack data for alltoall
MPI_Alltoall(&in, n/p*n/p, cplx_t, &out, n/p*n/p,
             cplx_t, comm);
// unpack data from alltoall and transpose

for (y=0; y<n/p; ++y) fft_1d(/* y-th stencil */);

// pack data for alltoall
MPI_Alltoall(&in, n/p*n/p, cplx_t, &out, n/p*n/p,
             cplx_t, comm);
// unpack data from alltoall and transpose
```

Figure 2.4: Example code for an FFT with blocking `MPI_Alltoall`

2.1.5   Collective Software Pipelining

One major concern at large scale is the overhead of communication. As fixed problems are scaled to larger numbers of processes, the relative share of communication time often increases drastically. Collective communications can become a significant serial bottleneck as their completion times grow at least logarithmically, often superlinearly, with the number of processes involved. Yet they are often the most elegant way to express global data dependencies, as we demonstrated with the FFT example.

Figure 2.4 shows how the FFT can be expressed with blocking `MPI_Alltoall` calls. Note that pack and unpack could be done on the fly by using MPI datatypes (see [32]). We use the packing scheme for clarity.

One way to decrease communication overheads is to overlap communication with computation so that the cores can continue computing while the network and memory subsystems move the data. This technique can lead to performance improvements of up to 2x. Let us reconsider the example from Figure 2.1. The 16×16 array is distributed between four processes. Each process computes its 1-D FFTs line by line. Instead of waiting for all lines to be processed, we can greedily start to communicate any set of transformed lines. Doing so allows us to construct a software pipeline that overlaps the communication of the ith line with the computation of the $(i + 1)$st. Obviously, the first and last line cannot be overlapped (this is also known as pipeline startup and teardown).

Figure 2.5 shows how the communication and 1-D FFT computation can be

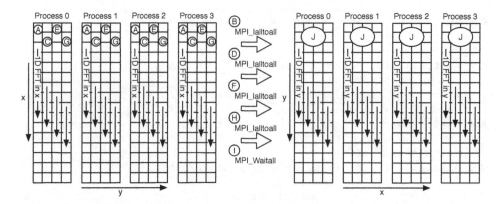

Figure 2.5: Schematic view of the pipelined parallel two-dimensional FFT

---

int **MPI_Ialltoall**(const void* sendbuf, int sendcount, MPI_Datatype sendtype,
                       void* recvbuf, int recvcount, MPI_Datatype recvtype,
                       MPI_Comm comm, MPI_Request *request)

Table 2.5: C binding for nonblocking alltoall

pipelined. Steps B and C, D and E, F and G overlap each other while steps A and H cannot be overlapped. The transformation in the y direction (Step J) can finish only after all communications are complete (Step I). The code shown in Figure 2.6 implements a slightly more generic version.

The C and Fortran interfaces for nonblocking alltoall are shown in Tables 2.5 and 2.6, respectively.   This basic structure of the source and software pipelining in general leaves several questions open: (1) How many lines should be collocated in a single `MPI_Ialltoall`? (2) When should each `MPI_Ialltoall` call be completed? and (3) How should progress be handled? We cannot provide absolute answers to those questions because they depend on the details of the system and MPI implementation. Nonetheless, we will discuss each question below.

How many lines should be collocated in a single `MPI_Ialltoall`?   In Figure 2.5 we start an `MPI_Ialltoall` after the processing of each line.   The source code provides a parameter, nb, that sets the number of blocks to be sent and hence allows programmers to define the size of each block.

```
MPI_Request req[nb];
for (b=0; b<nb; ++b) { // loop over blocks
  for (x=b*n/p/nb; x<(b+1)*n/p/nb; ++x)
      fft_1d(/* x-th stencil*/);

  // progress all previous operations (see text)
  for (i=max(0,b-nt); i<b; ++i)
    MPI_Test(&req[i], &flag, MPI_STATUS_IGNORE);

  // pack b-th block of data for alltoall
  MPI_Ialltoall(&in, n/p*n/p/bs, cplx_t, &out, n/p*n/p,
             cplx_t, comm, &req[b]);
}
MPI_Waitall(nb, req, MPI_STATUSES_IGNORE);

// modified unpack data from alltoall and transpose
for (y=0; y<n/p; ++y) fft_1d(/* y-th stencil */);
// pack data for alltoall
MPI_Alltoall(&in, n/p*n/p, cplx_t, &out, n/p*n/p, cplx_t,
             comm);
// unpack data from alltoall and transpose
```

Figure 2.6: Example code for an FFT with nonblocking MPI_Alltoall using software pipelining

MPI_IALLTOALL(sendbuf, sendcount, sendtype, recvbuf, recvcount, recvtype, comm, request, ierror)

                        `<type> sendbuf(*), recvbuf(*)`

                        `integer sendcount, sendtype, recvcount, recvtype, comm, request, ierror`

Table 2.6: Fortran binding for nonblocking alltoall

The ideal block size depends on the time to perform the 1-D FFT of n elements ($T_{FFT}(n)$), the latency to complete the `MPI_Ialltoall` of n elements on p processes ($T_{A2A}(n,p)$), and the nonoverlappable fraction ($\delta(n)$). Each of these time functions can be determined by using semi-analytic performance modeling where a model function is parametrized with observed runtime values [33]. The time to perform the software pipelined $n \times n$ 2-D FFT computation if each process holds $k = \frac{n}{p}$ lines is $T(n) = T_{FFT}(n) + (k-1)\max\{T_{FFT}(n) + \delta(n) \cdot T_{A2A}(n,p), T_{A2A}(n,p)\} + T_{A2A}(n) + kT_{FFT}(n)$. The minimal time is approximated when $T_{FFT}(n) + \delta(n) \cdot T_{A2A}(n,p) = T_{A2A}(n,p)$, which can be easily solved for n.

Simple performance models like this are often helpful in finding good parameters for various software pipelining codes.

When should each `MPI_Ialltoall` call be completed?   In our example figure and code, the nonblocking collectives are completed as late as possible right before the data is needed. However, when hundreds of thousands of lines are to be communicated, it may not advisable to have tens of thousands of collectives active at the same time because each running operation consumes resources and may slow the progress of other operations. In the extreme case, the program may exhaust internal implementation resources and new collective invocations may generate an MPI exception. We can simply complete some operations earlier (e.g., by using `MPI_Wait`) to limit the number of outstanding nonblocking collective operations.

How should progression be handled?   Message progression is an intricate topic. Our code example progresses the last `nt` outstanding operations during each iteration. If `nt` is set to `nb`, all outstanding operations are tested in each iteration, which may cause high overheads. If `nt` is set to zero, no tests are performed.

The ideal value for `nt` depends on the MPI implementation. If the implementation offers full asynchronous progress then `nt` should be zero. Otherwise, `nt` needs to be tuned to the implementation to achieve highest overlap. It is also safe to ignore manual progression initially as it is a pure performance property and difficult to tune.

Unfortunately, no perfect answer exists for the general topic of progression of point-to-point and collective communications on today's hardware. Manual progress causes additional code complexity and many unknowns, as explained above. Automatic asynchronous progression may cause significant overheads in the MPI implementation and may thus not always be beneficial to the application [34].

---

int **MPI_Ibarrier**(MPI_Comm comm, MPI_Request *request)

Table 2.7: C binding for nonblocking barrier

MPI_IBARRIER(comm, request, ierror)
        integer comm, request, ierror

Table 2.8: Fortran binding for nonblocking barrier

2.1.6 A Nonblocking Barrier?

One of the first questions reverberating through the MPI Forum when nonblocking collectives were first introduced was: "But what is a nonblocking barrier good for?" The synchronization semantics of the `MPI_Barrier` simply didn't seem to fit the nonblocking semantics that defer and thus relax synchronization.

In spite of this seeming semantic conflict, nonblocking barriers are tremendously useful. The `MPI_Ibarrier` call allows a process to announce that it has reached a certain point in its computation locally, without depending on any other process. The operation can complete, however, only after all processes have announced their local completion. In fact, the necessary synchronization may happen asynchronously. Tables 2.7 and 2.8 show the C and Fortran bindings for the nonblocking barrier, respectively.

To explain these semantics further, let us consider the following anecdote. A mine is operated by a group of mine workers who share a single elevator that goes up and down once per shift. Each worker has to complete a task that is independent of the other workers, and once the task is done, his shift ends. Yet he has to wait for the other workers before he can start the elevator. With blocking semantics, each worker would proceed to the elevator and wait there until all workers arrived; none of the waiting workers would be allowed to do anything else. With nonblocking semantics, a finished worker would leave a note at the elevator that he's done and would be free to continue other work or take a break. From time to time, all finished workers would check the elevator to see whether all other workers left a note.

The benefits are evident: workers that finish their essential task can continue with other nonessential tasks while still notifying all others about their status. Furthermore, the workers would be able to coordinate other workers or help them. To illustrate this, let us assume that, in addition to the main task, each worker oversees the safety of his neighbors by periodically checking whether they are doing well. In the blocking case, a finished worker could not indicate that he is finished *and* return to his workplace to monitor his colleagues. In the nonblocking case, one could easily do so.

Most readers will probably not work in a mine, so let us continue with an example from parallel computing. Many N-body codes distribute the physical domain across different processes such that each process is responsible for a fixed physical space and the particles therein. The computation is often divided into two phases: the computation of the forces at each particle and the movement of each particle along the forces. Particles may cross from one process's area to another during the movement phase. Since the force computations are local, only the originating process knows which particles are leaving its area and where they are going. This creates an interesting problem where each process has a set of data items to send to a small number of other processes. The destination processes typically do not know how much they will receive from which other process. In addition, the send-to relations are somewhat localized (particles have maximum velocity) and change rapidly (each iteration moves different particles to different processes). This problem, called Dynamic Sparse Data Exchange (DSDE), is central to many computations such as graph computations (e.g., breadth first search), sparse matrix computations with sparsity mutations, and particle codes. We will first describe possible solutions to this problem and then present a solution that illustrates the semantic power of nonblocking collectives and presents a use case for `MPI_Ibarrier`.

A trivial solution to this problem is to exchange the data sizes with an `MPI_Alltoall` that sets up an `MPI_Alltoallv` for the communication of the actual data. This simple solution sends p^2 data items for a communicator of size p. Thus, it is practical only if nearly all processes have data for nearly all other processes. This is often not the case, however, as most communications in scalable codes are confined in a local neighborhood around each sending process.

A second solution would be to reduce the problem to return only the number of messages that each process needs to receive. Each process would then receive all messages from `MPI_ANY_SOURCE` (after determining the size with `MPI_Probe()` and allocating a receive buffer). This can be accomplished with `MPI_Reduce_scatter` using addition as the operation. The input array of size p would be filled with a one at index i if the source process has a message to send to process i, and zero otherwise. However, this protocol still sends p^2 data items to communicate all the metadata. The counting could also be performed by using the one-sided `MPI_Accumulate` function (cf. Chapter 3). This would be asymptotically optimal but would require a fast implementation of `MPI_Accumulate`.

We will now describe a simple algorithm using a nonblocking barrier in combination with nonblocking synchronous sends. The algorithm comprises two phases:

```
MPI_Request reqs[m]; // we send m messages

for (i=0; i < m; ++i)
  MPI_Issend(sbuf[i], size[i], type, dst[i], tag, comm,
             &reqs[i]);

MPI_Request barrier_request;
int barrier_done=0, barrier_active=0;
while (!barrier_done) {
  MPI_Iprobe(MPI_ANY_SOURCE, tag, comm, &flag, &stat);
  if (flag) {
    // allocate buffer and receive msg
  }
  if (!barrier_active) {
    int flag;
    MPI_Testall(m, reqs, &flag, MPI_STATUSES_IGNORE);
    if (flag) {
      MPI_Ibarrier(comm, &barrier_request);
      barrier_active = 1;
    }
  } else {
    MPI_Test(&barrier_request, &barrier_done,
             MPI_STATUS_IGNORE);
  }
}
```

Figure 2.7: Example code for nonblocking MPI_Barrier in the dynamic sparse data exchange problem

In the first phase, each process sends all its messages by using nonblocking synchronous sends. Note that synchronous sends complete only after they have been matched to a receive. In the second phase, each process enters a loop in which it checks the completion of all its sends without blocking (checking with MPI_Iprobe and receiving any found messages). If all sends are complete, the process starts a nonblocking barrier and then continues to receive messages from other processes in the loop. The processes exit the loop collectively once the nonblocking barrier completes. The code in Figure 2.7 shows the complete algorithm.

This algorithm elegantly solves the metadata exchange problem by combining local synchronous send semantics with global collective synchronization semantics. More detailed information about the DSDE problem and performance results can be found in [37]. This example is intended to demonstrate the potential of combining nonblocking collective semantics with point-to-point messages and can act as a blueprint for designing other algorithms involving other collective operations.

2.1.7   Nonblocking Allreduce and Krylov Methods

Krylov methods are a class of algorithms for the iterative solution of linear systems. The most famous is the Conjugate Gradient (CG) algorithm; other, such as GMRES or BiCGStab, are also commonly used in applications. These methods are often the methods of choice for large systems of equations (with billions of unknowns) on extreme-scale systems. A key part of all of these algorithms is one or more dot or inner products, which require the use of `MPI_Allreduce`. These allreduce operations can limit the scalability of these algorithms, particularly on systems without hardware support for fast `MPI_Allreduce` operations. Fortunately, these algorithms can be adjusted to use nonblocking reduction operations, taking advantage of `MPI_Iallreduce`, the nonblocking version of `MPI_Allreduce`. A good reference for versions of Conjugate Gradient that can use nonblocking reduction operations is [19]. One of the algorithms in that paper, called "groppcg," is very close to the original CG algorithm. For example, where the original algorithm has a dot product (allreduce) before the application of the matrix M, the "groppcg" algorithm uses the following:

$$\cdots$$

$$\delta_{local} \;=\; p_{local}^{T} s_{local}$$
$$\texttt{Iallreduce}(\delta_{local}, \delta, \ldots, \&req)$$
$$q \;=\; Ms$$
$$\texttt{Wait}(\&req)$$
$$\alpha \;=\; \gamma/\delta$$
$$\cdots$$

Here, p_{local} and s_{local} are the vector elements local to the process, and δ_{local} is the result of the dot produce of those local elements. The reduction of the sums (δ_{local}) from each process is carried out by an `MPI_Iallreduce` that is issued before beginning the matrix-vector product, which will also involve communication (since the vectors are distributed across the processes). Once that matrix-vector product is complete, the algorithm must wait for the nonblocking allreduce to complete and can then use the result in δ to compute the next value of α used in the CG algorithm. C and Fortran bindings for `MPI_Iallreduce` are shown in Tables 2.9 and 2.10, respectively.

---

int **MPI_Iallreduce**(const void* sendbuf, void* recvbuf, int count,
         MPI_Datatype datatype, MPI_Op op, MPI_Comm comm,
         MPI_Request *request)

Table 2.9: C binding for nonblocking allreduce

MPI_IALLREDUCE(sendbuf, recvbuf, count, datatype, op, comm, request, ierror)
         <type> sendbuf(*), recvbuf(*)
         integer count, datatype, op, comm, request, ierror

Table 2.10: Fortran binding for nonblocking allreduce

2.2   Distributed Graph Topologies

MPI offers a facility, called *process topology*, to attach information about the communication relationships between processes to a communicator. Its initial purpose was to provide support for addressing communication partners. It enabled a programmer to specify the topology once during setup and then reuse it in different parts of the code and pass it transparently to communication libraries. As an example of a simple process topology consider our two-dimensional stencil-based Poisson solver (cf. Section 1.3.2). The user would simply create a 2-D Cartesian process topology that specifies all communication relationships between processes. Figure 2.8 illustrates the process topology for a 4×4 process grid.

The process-topology mechanism not only simplifies the management of communication relationships for the programmer but also provides information about the application's communication behavior to the MPI implementation. The MPI implementation can transparently use this knowledge to perform various optimizations, such as adapting communication buffer resources, improving communication setup, or optimizing process layouts. In addition, the interface offers the option to renumber processes according to the underlying communication network properties or memory system.

The original MPI-1 standard provided two interfaces to specify process communication topologies: the Cartesian and general graph topology constructors. Cartesian constructors specify the number of dimensions (d) and the size of each dimension ($s_1, \ldots, s_d$). The MPI implementation then constructs a d-dimensional Cartesian topology with $\prod_1^d s_d$ processes. Figure 2.8 can be described by $d = 2$ and $s_1 = 4$, $s_2 = 4$. More details about this interface and the special query functions are provided in *Using MPI* [26]. However, many regular and irregular communica-

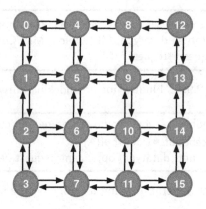

Figure 2.8: A 4 × 4 2-D Cartesian process topology

tion patterns cannot be represented by Cartesian graphs. For example, 2-D 9-point stencils as used in the Game of Life example (cf. Section 1.3.1) and 3-D 19-point or 27-point stencils require communication "over the edges" of the Cartesian communicator. For these and other applications, MPI offers the general graph topology constructor to specify arbitrary communication relations.

The MPI-1 general graph topology interface is not scalable to large communicators because each process has to specify all communication relationships between all processes in a communicator. This legacy interface requires amounts of memory that grow between linear and quadratically with respect to the number of processes in the communicator. In addition to being fundamentally nonscalable, the MPI-1 interface allows users to specify only unweighted and undirected communication relations between processes and thus does not provide sufficient information to the MPI implementation to guide the optimization efficiently. Since the benefits of the process-topology mechanism are expected to be highest at large scale, this interface needed to be improved.

Therefore, MPI-2.2 introduced a highly scalable *distributed* graph topology interface [35]. This interface does not require the complete graph to be specified at each process. Instead, it offers two interface variants. The "adjacent" interface requires each process to specify all its neighbors, and the "general" distributed interface allows each process to specify an arbitrary edge in the graph.

The distributed interface does not allow users to query the complete graph at any process, since doing so would introduce a new scalability problem. Instead, a process can query for just its direct incoming neighbors to post receive operations, and

---

int **MPI_Dist_graph_neighbors_count**(MPI_Comm comm, int *indegree,
        int *outdegree, int *weighted)

int **MPI_Dist_graph_neighbors**(MPI_Comm comm, int maxindegree, int sources[],
        int sourceweights[], int maxoutdegree, int destinations[],
        int destweights[])

Table 2.11: C bindings for distributed process topology query interfaces

---

MPI_DIST_GRAPH_NEIGHBORS_COUNT(comm, indegree, outdegree, weighted,
        ierror)
        integer comm, indegree, outdegree, ierror
        logical weighted

MPI_DIST_GRAPH_NEIGHBORS(comm, maxindegree, sources, sourceweights,
        maxoutdegree, destinations, destweights, ierror)
        integer comm, maxindegree, sources(*), sourceweights(*),
           maxoutdegree, destinations(*), destweights(*), ierror

---

Table 2.12: Fortran bindings for distributed process topology query interfaces

outgoing neighbors to post send operations. The function `MPI_Dist_graph_-`
`neighbors_count` returns the number of incoming and outgoing neighbors of
the calling process and the function `MPI_Dist_graph_neighbors` returns the
exact neighborhood structure. The C and Fortran interfaces for both functions are
shown in Tables 2.11 and 2.12. If `maxoutdegree` or `maxindegree` is smaller than
the actual number of neighbors, the implementation truncates the list. Both functions can be called only on communicators of type `MPI_DIST_GRAPH` as returned
by the function `MPI_Topo_test`.

The adjacent interface should be used if all neighboring nodes of all processes are
easily known to the programmer. This situation is often true for codes on regular
grids where the neighbors can be computed. The interface specifies each edge at
two processes, once at the source process as an outgoing edge and once at the target
process as an incoming edge. This requires twice as much memory during topology
creation but does not require any communication in the creation routine. Thus, we
recommend using this interface whenever possible. The C and Fortran interfaces
are shown in Tables 2.13 and 2.14. The function accepts `comm_old` and returns
`comm_dist_graph`, a copy of `comm_old` (including the same processes) with the

---

int **MPI_Dist_graph_create_adjacent**(MPI_Comm comm_old, int indegree,
        const int sources[], const int sourceweights[], int outdegree,
        const int destinations[], const int destweights[], MPI_Info info,
        int reorder, MPI_Comm *comm_dist_graph)

Table 2.13: C binding for distributed process topology adjacent creation interface

---

MPI_DIST_GRAPH_CREATE_ADJACENT(comm_old, indegree, sources,
        sourceweights, outdegree, destinations, destweights, info, reorder,
        comm_dist_graph, ierror)
        integer comm_old, indegree, sources(*), sourceweights(*), outdegree,
        destinations(*), destweights(*), info, comm_dist_graph, ierror
        logical reorder

Table 2.14: Fortran binding for distributed process topology adjacent creation interface

topology information attached. The function requires six parameters that specify the calling process's local adjacency list. The parameter `indegree` specifies the number of incoming edges, and the arrays `sources` and `sourceweights`, both of size `indegree`, specify the source processes and the edge weights, respectively. Similarly, the parameter `outdegree` specifies the number of outgoing edges and the parameters `destinations` and `destweights` include the destination processes and edge weights, respectively. The parameter `reorder` can be used to indicate whether the MPI implementation may renumber the processes in the new communicator and is explained in Section 2.2.4. The `info` argument is explained in Section 2.2.3.

To demonstrate the adjacent interface, let us extend the 5-point stencil of the two-dimensional Poisson example to a 9-point stencil including "over the edge" communications for the Game of Life example (cf. Section 1.3.1) as shown in Figure 2.9. This stencil shape cannot be easily represented as a Cartesian topology.[1] Here, process 5 would specify the processes 0, 1, 2, 4, 6, 8, 9, and 10 as outgoing and incoming communication neighbors. The neighborhood relations in this case can be easily computed at each process and passed to the topology constructor. The code in Figure 2.10 demonstrates how to create this graph topology.

---

[1]One can always arrange the communication to include the diagonal messages in messages along Cartesian dimensions, but instead it would be more efficient to send them directly to the diagonal neighbors by defining a graph topology and specifying the diagonal neighbors.

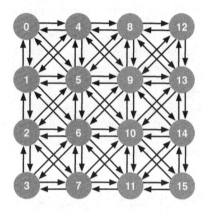

Figure 2.9: A 4×4 2-D process topology with "over the edge" communications as used in the Game of Life

---

int **MPI_Dist_graph_create**(MPI_Comm comm_old, int n, const int sources[],
        const int degrees[], const int destinations[], const int weights[],
        MPI_Info info, int reorder, MPI_Comm *comm_dist_graph)

Table 2.15: C binding for scalable process topology general interface

The general distributed graph interface allows the programmer to specify any edge at any process. Tabled 2.15 and 2.16 shows the C and Fortran interfaces. Similar to the adjacent constructor, `comm_old` is the input communicator, `comm_dist_graph` is the new output communicator, and `reorder` constrains process reordering as described in Section 2.2.4. The `info` argument is explained in Section 2.2.3. The remaining four parameters specify parts of the distributed graph in an adjacency list format similar to the compressed sparse row (CSR) format. The parameter n specifies the number of source nodes for which the calling process specifies edges. The array `sources` of size n specifies each of those source processes. The array `degrees` of size n specifies the outdegree for each of the vertices in the array `sources`. The array `destinations` of size $\sum_i$ sources$_i$ lists a destination for each edge.

This interface is significantly more complex than the adjacent interface and should be used only if the specification of the neighborhood relationships is not easy to compute or requires communication to distribute the information about all adjacent processes to each process. The MPI implementation needs to perform

```
int pdims[2]={0,0};
// compute good (rectangular) domain decomposition
MPI_Dims_create(np, 2, pdims);
int px = pdims[0], py = pdims[1];

// create Cartesian topology as helper
int periods[2] = {0,0};
MPI_Cart_create(comm, 2, pdims, periods, 0, &topocomm);

// get my local x,y coordinates
int coords[2];
MPI_Cart_coords(topocomm, rank, 2, coords);
int rx = coords[0], ry = coords[1];

// distributed graph structures
int pos=0, neighbors[8];

// compute Cartesian neighbors
int north, south, east, west;
MPI_Cart_shift(topocomm, 0, 1, &west, &east);
MPI_Cart_shift(topocomm, 1, 1, &north, &south);
neighbors[pos++] = north; neighbors[pos++] = south;
neighbors[pos++] = east; neighbors[pos++] = west;

// compute "over the edge" neighbors
int northwest = (ry-1)*px+(rx-1);
if (ry-1 >= 0 && rx-1 >= 0) neighbors[pos++] = northwest;
int northeast = (ry-1)*px+(rx+1);
if (ry-1 >= 0 && rx+1 < px) neighbors[pos++] = northeast;
int southwest = (ry+1)*px+(rx-1);
if (ry+1 < py && rx-1 >= 0) neighbors[pos++] = southwest;
int southeast = (ry+1)*px+(rx+1);
if (ry+1 < py && rx+1 < px) neighbors[pos++] = southeast;

MPI_Dist_graph_create_adjacent(comm, pos, &neighbors[0],
    MPI_UNWEIGHTED, pos, &neighbors[0], MPI_UNWEIGHTED,
    MPI_INFO_NULL, 1, &comm_dist_graph);

/* read data in the new rank order of comm_dist_graph */
```

Figure 2.10: Example code for adjacent graph creation

MPI_DIST_GRAPH_CREATE(comm_old, n, sources, degrees, destinations, weights,
        info, reorder, comm_dist_graph, ierror)
        integer comm_old, n, sources(*), degrees(*), destinations(*),
            weights(*), info, comm_dist_graph, ierror
        logical reorder

Table 2.16: Fortran binding for scalable process topology general interface

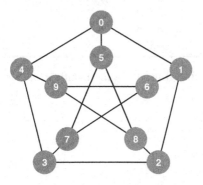

Figure 2.11: The Peterson graph connecting 10 processes

communication operations to build local adjacency information at each process.

2.2.1 Example: The Peterson Graph

Let us assume we want to arrange our process topology according to the neighborhood relations in the well-known unweighted Peterson graph as shown in Figure 2.11. We replace each undirected edge (u, v) with a pair of directed edges (u, v) and (v, u). In the adjacent specification, as shown in Table 2.17, each process specifies all incoming and outgoing edges. The same topology can be specified through the general distributed graph topology interface. An example specification is shown in Table 2.18.

2.2.2 Edge Weights

The distributed graph topology interface accepts edge weights for each communication edge. If the graph is unweighted, the user can specify MPI_UNWEIGHTED instead of the array argument. The meaning of the edge weights is not defined by

process	indegree	sources	outdegree	destinations
0	3	1,4,5	3	1,4,5
1	3	0,2,6	3	0,2,6
2	3	1,3,7	3	1,3,7
3	3	2,4,8	3	2,4,8
4	3	0,3,9	3	0,3,9
5	3	0,7,8	3	0,7,8
6	3	1,8,9	3	1,8,9
7	3	2,5,9	3	2,5,9
8	3	3,5,6	3	3,5,6
9	3	4,6,7	3	4,6,7

Table 2.17: Adjacent distributed graph specification for the Peterson Graph

process	n	sources	degrees	destinations
0	3	0,4,6	1,2,1	1,3,0,8
1	2	2,8	1,1	0,5
2	0	-	-	-
3	4	1,2,6,9	1,1,2,1	0,3,1,6
4	4	0,3,5,8	1,1,1,1	5,0,7,6
5	2	3,5	1,1	4,0
6	5	1,3,5,7,9	1,1,1,3,1	2,8,8,2,5,9,7
7	0	-	-	-
8	2	1,4	1,1	6,9
9	4	0,2,8,9	1,1,1,1	4,7,3,4

Table 2.18: An example general distributed graph specification for the Peterson Graph

the MPI standard and one can easily envision different semantics such as message
counts, data volume, maximum message size, or even message latency hints. A
high-quality MPI implementation will most likely use the weights to improve lo-
cality and place processes connected by heavy edges closer together. Additional
details are implementation specific.

MPI implementations can also use the info argument to allow the programmer
to select semantics from a set of supported hints. Some examples are discussed in
[35].

2.2.3   Graph Topology Info Argument

The info argument can be used to provide additional information to the MPI implementation. Info arguments never change the semantics of the program, and libraries
may choose to ignore the information. However, high-quality implementations will
provide a set of possible hints to guide internal optimizations.

For example, a user could ensure that the process topology includes all possible communications, and the implementation can then establish connections only
between processes that are connected in the topology. As mentioned above, the
info argument could also be used to communicate the exact semantics of the edge
weights to the implementation. Many additional uses are possible, and users are
advised to consult the MPI implementation's documentation.

2.2.4   Process Reordering

One of the major features of MPI's topology interface is that it can easily be used to
adapt the MPI process layout to the underlying network and system topology. This
process is also called topology mapping. The user can specify a weighted application
communication topology, and the implementation can use its internal knowledge
about the system topology to provide a new process-to-location mapping to the
user. The MPI implementation can either perform this optimization transparently
and simply relocate the processes without the programmer's involvement, or it
can provide a new mapping to the programmer. Most process-mapping problems
are NP-hard, but a high-quality MPI implementation will provide some heuristic
solutions [70, 38].

As an example, let us consider an application whose communication pattern is
represented by the weighted Bull graph shown in the left side of Figure 2.12. Let
us assume that the weights represent the message sizes in gigabytes and that the
application is to be run on a set of dual-core machines. The first, unoptimized
mapping simply maps the processes linearly to the cores as shown in the middle

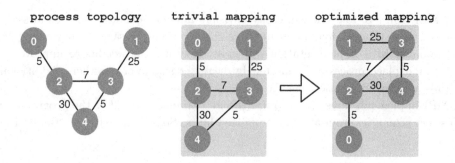

Figure 2.12: The weighted Bull graph, a trivial mapping, and an optimized mapping to three dual-core nodes

part of the figure. This causes a total network communication volume of 65 GB. The optimized mapping, a simple renumbering of the ranks from $[0, 1, 2, 3, 4]$ to $[1, 3, 2, 4, 0]$, shown in the right part, reduces the network load to 17 GB, which can lead to significant energy and time savings during the program execution.

The programmer needs to explicitly allow the MPI implementation to return a new mapping by setting the `reorder` argument to true; otherwise, a process in `comm_dist_graph` will have the same rank as in `comm_old`. If the ranks are permuted, the programmer may need to redistribute the data from a process with rank i in `comm_old` to the new process with rank i in `comm_dist_graph`. This redistribution leads to additional overheads and complications. We therefore suggest that, whenever possible, the topology graph be built and the reordering done *before* the input data is read, so that it can be read in the final order. If this is not possible, programmers can use a redistribution protocol.

2.3 Collective Operations on Process Topologies

The main benefits of MPI's process topology interface are the ability to remap processes and determine the communicating partners. The topology interface, however, contains only helper functions and cannot perform any communication tasks itself. In order to achieve the highest performance, communication must be scheduled carefully to avoid endpoint congestion.

Let us assume the code shown in Figure 2.13 for the stencil example with the topology shown in Figure 2.8. The distributed graph query interface provides no guarantees on the order of the processes returned in the `sources` and destinations arrays returned by `MPI_Dist_graph_neighbors`. Let us assume that the order of destinations is (4,1), (4,9,6,1), and (4,9,12) at processes 0, 5, and 8, respectively. Figure 2.14 depicts this scenario. If we execute the code above, process 4 would receive four messages "at the same time"[2] from its neighbors. This creates congestion at process 4 and delays the whole execution. To prevent this congestion, the user could generate a communication schedule where each process receives only from one other process "at the same time" (per logical communication round). This can be expressed as a graph-coloring problem where the number of colors is the number of required communication rounds. For the "over the edges" 2-D Cartesian example we can compute analytically that the minimum number of rounds is eight. A good schedule would be where all processes send "simultaneously" in each direction.

The graph coloring problem is NP-hard in the general case, and determining and implementing a good communication schedule can thus be difficult. In addition, users often perform a second optimization for the "over the edge" communication. Messages along the diagonals are sent in two steps along the Cartesian dimensions; for example, the message for north-west is first sent to the north process and then passed on to the west process. In this way, users trade off injection overheads (reducing the number of messages to 1/2) with bandwidth (diagonal messages are sent twice through the network). One can easily envision a generalization of this principle where more complex communications are performed within neighborhoods (e.g., broadcast trees in local densely connected neighborhoods). The selection of the best schedule is highly machine dependent, and a manual point-to-point specification is thus not portable across machines.

2.3.1 Neighborhood Collectives

MPI-3 provides communication functions specified on graph topologies, which are called *neighborhood collective operations*. The two main calls are `MPI_-Neighbor_allgather` and `MPI_Neighbor_alltoall`. Their respective vector versions `MPI_Neighbor_allgatherv`, `MPI_Neighbor_alltoallv`, and `MPI_Neighbor_alltoallw` are also provided. The neighborhood allgather gathers a message from each incoming neighbor in the process topology and stores them into a contiguous buffer. Each process specifies a single send buffer; thus, allgather can also be seen as a neighborhood broadcast from a sender's perspective. In a neighborhood alltoall, each process specifies a different message buffer

---

[2]The notion of time in an MPI program is weak. We use the term informally to provide some intuition and thus mark it with quotes.

```
int ideg, odeg, wgt;
MPI_Dist_graph_neighbors_count(comm_dist_graph, &ideg,
                               &odeg, &wgt);

int *in  = (int*)malloc(ideg * sizeof(int));
int *out = (int*)malloc(odeg * sizeof(int));

MPI_Dist_graph_neighbors(comm_dist_graph, ideg, in,
         MPI_UNWEIGHTED, odeg, out, MPI_UNWEIGHTED);

MPI_Request rreqs[ideg], sreqs[odeg];

for (step = 0; step < nsteps; step++) {
  for (int i=0; i<ideg; ++i) MPI_Irecv(rbuf[i], rcnt[i],
                             MPI_DOUBLE, in[i*size], 99,
                             comm_dist_graph, &rreqs[i]);
  for (int i=0; i<odeg; ++i) MPI_Isend(sbuf[i], scnt[i],
                             MPI_DOUBLE, out[i*size], 99,
                             comm_dist_graph, &sreqs[i]);

  /* perform computation of independent stencils */

  MPI_Waitall(ideg, rreqs, MPI_STATUSES_IGNORE);
  MPI_Waitall(odeg, sreqs, MPI_STATUSES_IGNORE);

  /* perform computation of dependent stencils */
}
```

Figure 2.13: Example code for communication on a distributed graph topology

for each outgoing process and receives into a different buffer from each incoming process, similar to regular alltoall. The function interfaces for C and Fortran are shown in Tables 2.19 and 2.20, and Figure 2.15 shows a schematic overview of the communication buffers.

We note that all communication-only traditional collectives, such as broadcast, gather, and scatter, and excluding all reductions, can be expressed as neighborhood collectives with specially crafted topologies. Programmers should never do so, however, because the traditional collective interfaces specify the structure declaratively, whereas extracting the structure from arbitrary communication patterns is hard. Using a similar argument, we strongly recommend users to use the Cartesian topology interface instead of the distributed graph topology interface whenever possible.

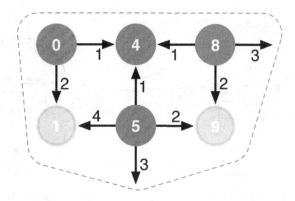

Figure 2.14: Congestion scenario in neighborhood communication. The numbers at the arrows denote the logical communication order (time) relative to the source process.

---

int **MPI_Neighbor_allgather**(const void* sendbuf, int sendcount,
        MPI_Datatype sendtype, void* recvbuf, int recvcount,
        MPI_Datatype recvtype, MPI_Comm comm)

int **MPI_Neighbor_alltoall**(const void* sendbuf, int sendcount,
        MPI_Datatype sendtype, void* recvbuf, int recvcount,
        MPI_Datatype recvtype, MPI_Comm comm)

Table 2.19: C bindings for neighborhood allgather and alltoall functions

---

MPI_NEIGHBOR_ALLGATHER(sendbuf, sendcount, sendtype, recvbuf, recvcount,
        recvtype, comm, ierror)
        <type> sendbuf(*), recvbuf(*)
        integer sendcount, sendtype, recvcount, recvtype, comm, ierror

MPI_NEIGHBOR_ALLTOALL(sendbuf, sendcount, sendtype, recvbuf, recvcount,
        recvtype, comm, ierror)
        <type> sendbuf(*), recvbuf(*)
        integer sendcount, sendtype, recvcount, recvtype, comm, ierror

---

Table 2.20: Fortran bindings for neighborhood allgather and alltoall functions

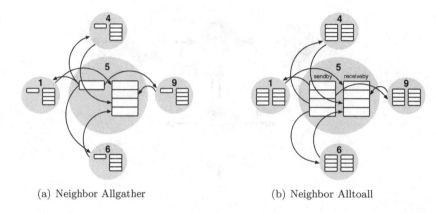

(a) Neighbor Allgather   (b) Neighbor Alltoall

Figure 2.15: Communication schemes for neighborhood collectives

The order of the send and receive buffers for (distributed) graph process topologies is the order of processes returned by the neighbor query functions `MPI_-Graph_neighbors` (which is deprecated and should never be used) or `MPI_-Dist_graph_neighbors`. For Cartesian topologies, the order is defined by the order of dimensions, first negative and then positive. If Cartesian topologies are not periodic, the buffers at the boundary processes that point to nonexisting processes must still exist but are neither read nor written during the communication.

The following listing shows how the communication part of the Poisson problem (as shown in Figure 1.5) can be expressed as a portable neighborhood collective. This call replaces the 13 lines, assuming that the topology and the communication buffers are set up correctly.

```
MPI_Neighbor_alltoall(sbuf, size, MPI_DOUBLE, rbuf, size,
                      MPI_DOUBLE, comm_dist_graph);
```

2.3.2 Vector Neighborhood Collectives

Neighborhood collectives also support the specification of different buffer sizes for each outgoing and incoming process. The standard `MPI_Neighbor_allgatherv` and `MPI_Neighbor_alltoallv` variants allow users to specify different numbers of elements of the same type. As in traditional vector collectives, the size lists are specified as an integer array. Tables 2.21 and 2.22 show the C and Fortran bindings.

---

int **MPI_Neighbor_allgatherv**(const void* sendbuf, int sendcount,
        MPI_Datatype sendtype, void* recvbuf, const int recvcounts[],
        const int displs[], MPI_Datatype recvtype, MPI_Comm comm)

int **MPI_Neighbor_alltoallv**(const void* sendbuf, const int sendcounts[],
        const int sdispls[], MPI_Datatype sendtype, void* recvbuf,
        const int recvcounts[], const int rdispls[], MPI_Datatype recvtype,
        MPI_Comm comm)

Table 2.21: C bindings for neighborhood allgather and alltoall vector functions

---

MPI_NEIGHBOR_ALLGATHERV(sendbuf, sendcount, sendtype, recvbuf,
        recvcounts, displs, recvtype, comm, ierror)
        <type> sendbuf(*), recvbuf(*)
        integer sendcount, sendtype, recvcounts(*), displs(*), recvtype,
          comm, ierror

MPI_NEIGHBOR_ALLTOALLV(sendbuf, sendcounts, sdispls, sendtype, recvbuf,
        recvcounts, rdispls, recvtype, comm, ierror)
        <type> sendbuf(*), recvbuf(*)
        integer sendcounts(*), sdispls(*), sendtype, recvcounts(*),
          rdispls(*), recvtype, comm, ierror

Table 2.22: Fortran bindings for neighborhood allgather and alltoall vector functions

The function `MPI_Neighbor_alltoallw`, shown in Table 2.23 (C binding) and Table 2.24 (Fortran binding), enables users to specify different datatypes for each incoming or outgoing neighbor. This function can be used to enable efficient zero-copy communication in process neighborhoods [32]. Figure 2.16 shows the code for a zero-copy version of the normal 2-D Cartesian stencil. Figure 2.17 illustrates the scheme.

2.3.3 Nonblocking Neighborhood Collectives

All neighborhood collectives also have nonblocking variants that enable overlap of communication and computation. These nonblocking collectives are conceptually identical to those discussed in Section 2.1 and are thus not further discussed here. The following listing shows an example.

```
int pdims[2]={0,0};
// compute good (rectangular) domain decomposition
MPI_Dims_create(np, 2, pdims);
int px = pdims[0];
int py = pdims[1];

// create Cartesian topology
int periods[2] = {0,0};
MPI_Cart_create(comm, 2, pdims, periods, 0, &topocomm);

// row-major order - bx and by are the x and y dimensions
#define ind(i,j) (j)*(bx+2)+(i)

// create north-south datatype
MPI_Datatype north_south_type;
MPI_Type_contiguous(bx, MPI_DOUBLE, &north_south_type);
MPI_Type_commit(&north_south_type);
// create east-west type
MPI_Datatype east_west_type;
MPI_Type_vector(by, 1, bx+2, MPI_DOUBLE, &east_west_type);
MPI_Type_commit(&east_west_type);

int sizes[4] = {size, size, size, size};
MPI_Aint sdispls[4] = {ind(1,1), ind(1,by), ind(bx,1),
                       ind(1,1)},
         rdispls[4] = {ind(1,0), ind(1,by+1), ind(bx+1,1),
                       ind(0,1)};
MPI_Datatype stypes[4] = {north_south_type,north_south_type,
                          east_west_type,east_west_type},
             rtypes[4] = {north_south_type,north_south_type,
                          east_west_type,east_west_type};

MPI_Neighbor_alltoallw(sbuf, sizes, sdispls, stypes, rbuf,
                       sizes, rdispls, rtypes, topocomm);
```

Figure 2.16: Example code for using MPI_Neighbor_alltoallw for 2-D stencil communication

---

int **MPI_Neighbor_alltoallw**(const void* sendbuf, const int sendcounts[],
        const MPI_Aint sdispls[], const MPI_Datatype sendtypes[],
        void* recvbuf, const int recvcounts[], const MPI_Aint rdispls[],
        const MPI_Datatype recvtypes[], MPI_Comm comm)

Table 2.23: C binding for neighborhood alltoallw, allowing different datatypes

---

MPI_NEIGHBOR_ALLTOALLW(sendbuf, sendcounts, sdispls, sendtypes, recvbuf,
        recvcounts, rdispls, recvtypes, comm, ierror)
        <type> sendbuf(*), recvbuf(*)
        integer(kind=mpi_address_kind) sdispls(*), rdispls(*)
        integer sendcounts(*), sendtypes(*), recvcounts(*), recvtypes(*),
        comm, ierror

Table 2.24: Fortran binding for neighborhood alltoallw, allowing different datatypes

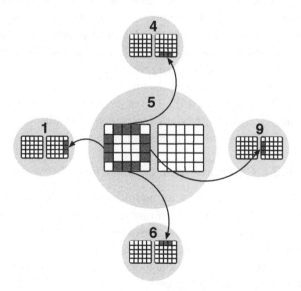

Figure 2.17: Zero-copy implementation of the 2-D stencil. The send data is gathered from the source array directly, and the received data is deposited into the target array.

---

int **MPI_Comm_idup**(MPI_Comm comm, MPI_Comm *newcomm,
            MPI_Request *request)

Table 2.25: C binding for nonblocking communicator duplication

---

```
MPI_Request req;
MPI_Ineighbor_alltoall(sbuf, size, MPI_DOUBLE, rbuf, size,
    MPI_DOUBLE, comm_dist_graph, &req);

/* perform computation of independent stencils */

MPI_Wait(&req, MPI_STATUS_IGNORE);
```

2.4   Advanced Communicator Creation

Communicators provide isolated communication contexts for point-to-point and collective communications. These contexts can be used for communication isolation in modular libraries or to create smaller process subgroups to cooperate on separate tasks. MPI-2 offered three interfaces to create new communicators: `MPI_Comm_dup` to duplicate a communicator, `MPI_Comm_split` to split a communicator using colors, and `MPI_Comm_create` to create arbitrary communicators. MPI-3 added two new functions: `MPI_Comm_idup` for nonblocking communicator duplication and `MPI_Comm_create_group` to noncollectively create a new communicator. We now describe both mechanisms.

2.4.1   Nonblocking Communicator Duplication

We construct a library that performs an unoptimized alternating prefix operation. The operation is defined as $a \cdot b$ if a is on an even rank and b/a if a is on an odd rank. For example, if three processes have the values (2, 4, 2), then the result (distributed to the three processes) is (2, 2, 4).

We now describe how to write a nonblocking communication library with automatic initialization by using `MPI_Comm_idup` (see Tables 2.25 and 2.26 for C and Fortran bindings). For our library, we use two kinds of structures: a request structure `MY_Request` that identifies one particular operation and a communicator structure `_opcomm` that is not visible to the user; both structures are shown in Figure 2.18.

MPI_COMM_IDUP(comm, newcomm, request, ierror)
            integer comm, newcomm, request, ierror

Table 2.26: Fortran binding for nonblocking communicator duplication

---

```
typedef struct {
  MPI_Request sreq, rreq;
  MPI_Comm comm;
  double *sbuf, *rbuf;
  int count, r, s, recvstarted;
  enum {MUL, DIV} op;
} MY_Request;

typedef struct {
  MPI_Comm comm;
  MPI_Request dupreq;
  int duped;
} _opcomm;
```

Figure 2.18: Data structures for nonblocking communication library

Our library offers a nonblocking initialization routine `MY_Ioperation`. Our implementation of this routine only initializes the request and adds all relevant arguments to it, as shown in Figure 2.19.

All actual operations are performed in the nonblocking progression function, which is shown in Figure 2.20. Good library design requires us to separate the library communication from the user communication such that messages cannot cross-match [39]. This can easily achieved by duplicating the user-passed communicator; however, our nonblocking library has to perform this duplication in nonblocking manner. Thus, at each invocation, the library reads an attribute from the communicator that specifies the status of the nonblocking comm-dup operation. If the attribute does not exist, the `MPI_Comm_idup` needs to be started and attached to the communicator. If the attribute exists, the library queries the status and, if needed, progresses the nonblocking communicator duplication. If the communicator is already duplicated, the library can execute the communication logic.

Similar to `MPI_Comm_dup`, `MPI_Comm_idup` also copies all associated key values, topology information, and info hints to the new communicator. However, there is no nonblocking equivalent of `MPI_Comm_dup_with_info`, which duplicates a

```
void MY_Ioperation(double *sbuf, double *rbuf, int count,
                   MPI_Comm comm, MY_Request *req) {

  req->comm = comm;
  req->sbuf = sbuf;
  req->rbuf = rbuf;
  req->count = count;

  MPI_Comm_rank(comm, &req->r);
  MPI_Comm_size(comm, &req->s);

  if (req->r % 2 == 0) req->op = DIV; else req->op = MUL;
}
```

Figure 2.19: Example code for initializing the nonblocking communication operation

communicator and associates a user-provided info object with the new communicator (see Section 9.2). Therefore, in MPI 3.0, communicators created using nonblocking communicator duplication will always inherit all info objects from the old communicator.

2.4.2 Noncollective Communicator Creation

Prior to MPI-3, communicators could only be created *collectively* by using functions such as MPI_Comm_dup, MPI_Comm_split, or MPI_Comm_create. These functions are defined to be collective over the input communicator; in other words, they must be called by all processes in that communicator. This requirement is obvious for MPI_Comm_dup, where the new communicator contains all processes of the old communicator, and also for MPI_Comm_split, where the split is performed by comparing color values from all processes. However, it is not obvious why MPI_Comm_create, which creates an arbitrary new communicator (e.g., a proper subset of the processes in the old communicator), must be called collectively on the old communicator.

Indeed, the collective nature of this call creates problems in certain scenarios. For example, a failed process cannot participate in collective communications.[3]

---

[3] Some believe that the MPI standard requires programs to abort on any failure. This is false. The standard simply does not mandate any particular behavior after a fault, and in fact provides a comprehensive error-reporting mechanism (see Section 12.1.3). As is true for most other standards, the MPI standard leaves it up to the implementation to decide what happens after an error. See

```
int MY_Progress(MY_Request *req) {

  _opcomm *oc = ... /* query opcomm attribute from req->comm */

  /* start duplicating communicator */
  if (oc == NULL) {
    MPI_Comm_idup(req->comm, &req->comm, &oc->dupreq);
    oc = (_opcomm*)malloc(sizeof(_opcomm));
    oc->duped = 0;
    ... = oc; /* attach op as opcomm attribute to comm */
  } else if (oc->duped == 0) {
    int flag = 0;
    MPI_Test(&oc->dupreq, &flag, MPI_STATUS_IGNORE);
    if (flag) oc->duped = 1;
    else return 0;
  }

  if (!req->recvstarted && req->r > 0) {
    MPI_Irecv(req->rbuf, req->count, MPI_DOUBLE, req->r-1, 99,
              req->comm, &req->rreq);
    req->recvstarted = 1;
  }

  int flag, i;
  MPI_Test(&req->rreq, &flag, MPI_STATUS_IGNORE);
  if (flag == 1) {
    if (req->op == MUL)
      for (i=0; i<req->count; ++i)
        req->rbuf[i] = req->sbuf[i] * req->rbuf[i];
    else
      for (i=0; i<req->count; ++i)
        req->rbuf[i] = req->sbuf[i] / req->rbuf[i];
    if (req->r < req->s)
      MPI_Isend(req->rbuf, req->count, MPI_DOUBLE, req->r+1,
                99, req->comm, &req->sreq);
  }

  flag = 0;
  MPI_Test(&req->sreq, &flag, MPI_STATUS_IGNORE);
  if (flag == 1) return 1;
  else return 0;
}
```

Figure 2.20: Example code for nonblocking communication progression function

---

int **MPI_Comm_create_group**(MPI_Comm comm, MPI_Group group, int tag,
            MPI_Comm *newcomm)

Table 2.27: C binding for noncollective communicator creation

---

MPI_COMM_CREATE_GROUP(comm, group, tag, newcomm, ierror)
            integer comm, group, tag, newcomm, ierror

Table 2.28: Fortran binding for noncollective communicator creation

Thus, a communicator with a single failed process cannot be used for any collective communication. It can thus also not be used to create a new communicator with MPI_Comm_create. This restriction essentially disables all collectives on this communicator until program termination. One workaround would be to hierarchically merge intercommunicators to create a new communicator excluding the failed process. However, this mechanism is clumsy and slow.

To avoid this limitation, MPI-3 added a new *noncollective* communicator creation routine, MPI_Comm_create_group, where only members of the created communicator need to call the routine. The C and Fortran bindings are shown in Tables 2.27 and 2.28. The function creates a new communicator among all processes in the group group. It needs to be called only by all processes in this group, and it returns the new communicator object newcomm.

As an example use case, let us assume that we have a failure detector that eventually and collectively (among all alive processes) declares a set of processes as failed. In this case, MPI_Comm_create_group can be used to recreate a working communicator with all alive processes. The code in Figure 2.21 demonstrates such a check and creation.

A second use case could arise in a communication where a set of process groups solves a problem jointly. We assume that each group performs collective communications to work on its isolated task. If the load within the process groups varies, for example, if groups create more work dynamically in an unpredictable way, then intergroup load balancing is required [14]. For example, some groups would be able to free processes because of a lighter load, and some groups would require more processes to tackle their work. If two groups discover that they could exchange some processes, the collective nature of MPI-2 communicator creation routines would

---

[29] for a discussion of what fault tolerance means in MPI. Some of the more general issues in fault tolerance and resilience for extreme-scale systems are discussed in [7, 8].

```
int k;
int *failed;
fdetect(&k, failed, comm); /* failure detector declared k
                              processes in array failed as dead */

/* check if this process is destined to die */
int dead = 0;
for (int i=0; i<k; ++i) if (my_rank == failed[i]) dead = 1;

if (!dead) {
  MPI_Group group, egroup;
  MPI_Comm_group(comm, &group);
  MPI_Group_excl(group, k, failed, &egroup);

  /* create new communicator */
  MPI_Comm newcomm;
  MPI_Comm_create_group(comm, egroup, 99, &newcomm);
  /* restart from fdetect if MPI_Comm_create_group fails */
} else {
  /* abort the process */
}
```

Figure 2.21: Example code for creating a new communicator that excludes failed processes

require a coordination of all groups, whereas MPI_Comm_create_group would allow the two groups to exchange processes in isolation from the other groups. One could also easily implement mechanisms where idle processes are added to a pool of processes that then itself steals work from other process groups. Such advanced group load balancing requires noncollective communicator creation routines to work efficiently.

3 Introduction to Remote Memory Operations

Two principal approaches exist for communicating data between cooperating processes: message passing and direct access to the memory in the remote process. MPI-1 provides a powerful and complete interface for the message-passing approach. MPI-2 added, and MPI-3 greatly extended, remote memory operations that provide a way to directly access memory in another process, through operations that *put* data to, *get* data from, or *update* data at a remote process. Unlike message passing, the program running on the remote process does not need to call any routines to match the put or get operations. Thus, remote memory operations can offer both greater performance (when there is sufficient support in hardware for the operations) and greater functionality, simplifying some kinds of parallel programming.

The MPI remote memory operations grew out of several approaches for parallel programming based on remote memory operations,[1] just as MPI-1 standardized message passing by drawing on experiences with research systems and commercial message-passing systems. Perhaps the most important of the early research systems was *bulk synchronous parallel*, often abbreviated as BSP [30, 59, 71]. In the BSP style of parallel programming, programs are divided into sections, one where there is no communication between the processes and one where there is only communication; the sections are separated by barriers. Communication of data between processes is handled by remote memory operations that put or get data, and these operations are all nonblocking (in the MPI sense). Completion of these operations is handled by a single communication barrier, hence the term "bulk synchronous."[2]

Several proprietary implementations of remote memory operations have been developed. IBM introduced LAPI [58] and provided it on its distributed-memory systems starting with the IBM SP. Perhaps the most significant and successful is SHMEM, introduced by Cray for the T3D. This interface has been used on a wide variety of systems; there is now an OpenSHMEM [53] effort that has created a standard description of this interface.

Another programming model that takes advantage of one-sided operations is the Partitioned Global Address Space (PGAS) programming model. In this model, programs in a distributed memory system have a global address space or a similar mechanism that allows any process to access data in another process through load

---

[1] These are also called one-sided operations because only one of the two processes is directly involved, from the programmer's standpoint, in the operation.

[2] The term "bulk synchronous" is sometimes used to describe programming with separate computation and communication phases, even when the communication is accomplished by two-sided message passing.

and store operations. The most important languages for this model are Unified Parallel C or UPC [15] and Fortran 2008 [47], which includes Co-Arrays. These are arrays distributed across all processes in a parallel Fortran program. Co-Arrays have a long history, first proposed in "F--" [51] and having a number of implementations often known as Co-Array Fortran or CAF. A related system is Global Arrays [49], which we will discuss in Section 4.6.

Equally important with the development of programming models and good implementations of the remote memory operations has been the development of hardware support for remote memory operations. Early research systems, such as U-Net [73], have led to network systems that support remote memory operations in hardware, both commodity networks such as InfiniBand and proprietary networks for supercomputers [1, 10]. These make it possible to deliver high performance for programs and programming systems that make careful use of the one-sided or remote memory operations. We'll explain later in this chapter why we emphasized the "careful use" of one-sided operations.

All of the above contributed to the design of the MPI remote memory programming model. In addition, the MPI design makes the remote memory operations have the same "look and feel" as other MPI routines, including permitting the use of MPI datatypes and allowing collective operations on any communicator, not just MPI_COMM_WORLD (which is a restriction of many of the prior systems). Moreover, the MPI model is designed to be implementable on a wide range of systems, from workstation networks with no special hardware for remote memory operations to tightly coupled parallel computers with fast, fully coherent shared-memory hardware. For readers who are familiar with the MPI-2 one-sided model but not the MPI-3 one-sided model, MPI-3 greatly extended the MPI-2 model, addressing many of the limitations that had limited the applicability of the MPI-2 one-sided model for many applications.

The MPI remote memory operations must be distinguished from the shared-memory programming model. In the usual shared-memory model, there is a single address space, shared by multiple threads of execution. References to memory, regardless of location, are accomplished simply by referencing variables. A major advantage of this model is that programs can be written by using familiar variable reference and assignment (load and store) statements; new syntax or routines are not required. However, the model has several disadvantages. The most obvious is that supporting this model efficiently requires special hardware. A less obvious problem is that simultaneous access by several different threads to the same memory location can lead to hard-to-find errors; correcting this problem requires providing a way to control or synchronize access to shared data. The approach used in shared-memory models uses some combination of sophisticated compilers and special routines to provide, for example, locks to synchronize access to shared variables. While shared-memory appears to many to be an easier to use programming model than message-passing, it is surprisingly difficult to write correct shared-memory programs [4, 5].

This chapter introduces the MPI remote memory model. Rather than covering all the functions in each category, as the MPI standard [46] does, this chapter introduces functions as they are needed to illustrate their use. Specifically, we cover here the routines used to initiate remote memory operations and the simplest of the three methods provided by MPI for completing remote memory operations.

The following chapter continues the discussion of more general models of memory access, including ones that do not require the target process to make any MPI calls. Chapter 5 covers the use of MPI's remote memory access routines for using shared memory between processes.

3.1   Introduction

The message-passing model provides a *cooperative* way of moving data from one process to another: one process performs a send, and the destination process performs a receive. Only when the receive completes does the destination process have the data. This approach has a number of important properties. One is that changes in the memory of the receiver can happen only when the receiver allows them (by calling one of the MPI receive routines) and only in the memory locations that are specified as the receive buffer in those routines. Thus, it is clear from the program both what memory locations can be modified by another process (often called a *remote* process) and at what points in the program this can happen. These properties can aid in ensuring that the program is correct and in debugging it if it isn't.

The requirement of message passing that data transfers be cooperative has its disadvantages as well. Two main areas of limitation are expressiveness (the ease with which programs may be written) and performance.

While in principle any parallel program can be written by using message passing, in practice some programs are much harder to write than others. The requirement that every send be matched with a receive demands careful planning and can add complexity to a code. It is difficult to provide with message passing a way for one process to access or modify data held by another process, since both processes must cooperate to perform the operation. An example is a single counter (for example, a counter of the number of errors seen) that is shared by many processes. How can a

process add a value to this counter? With message passing, it must send a message
to the process that "owns" the counter, asking that process to update the value.
That process in turn must check for these messages. Doing so greatly complicates
the program, particularly if the MPI implementation is single threaded or does not
want to use a thread solely to update this value (as in Section 6.4).

In addition, the cooperative nature of message passing introduces an order into
the delivery of data; in some cases, the order isn't important to the application.
Enforcing the order has performance costs, in terms both of specifying which data
must be delivered first and of extra overhead in implementing message matching.

MPI-2 introduced, and MPI-3 extended, a new approach for moving data from
one process to another that eliminates the drawbacks of message passing while
retaining many of the advantages. This approach, called *remote memory access*
(RMA), provides a way to move data from one process to another with a single
routine that specifies both where the data is coming from and where it is going
to. An RMA operation is a kind of combined send and receive; the calling process
specifies both the send buffer and the receive buffer. Because a single call is used,
these routines are also called *one-sided communication* routines.

Using the RMA approach involves three main steps:

1. Define the memory of the process that can be used for RMA operations, pre-
   serving the advantage of limiting what memory can be modified by a remote
   process. This is accomplished by defining a *memory window* and creating
   a new MPI object, the MPI window object `MPI_Win`. MPI provides four
   routines to create a new `MPI_Win`, depending on exactly how the memory
   will be used. We cover these with examples in Sections 3.3, 4.8.4, and 5.2.

2. Specify the data to be moved and where to move it. MPI-2 defined just
   three routines: `MPI_Put`, `MPI_Get`, and `MPI_Accumulate`. MPI-3 added
   seven more that are variations on these three. See Section 3.4 for details on
   the original three; some of the others are covered in Sections 4.4.2. When we
   describe the behavior of one of the original three routines, it applies to all
   similar routines unless specifically noted. The routines are:

   Put. `MPI_Put` and `MPI_Rput`

   Get. `MPI_Get` and `MPI_Rget`

   Accumulate. `MPI_Accumulate` and `MPI_Raccumulate`. In addition,
   these new read-modify-write routines are considered to be variations on
   accumulate: `MPI_Get_accumulate`, `MPI_Rget_accumulate`,
   `MPI_Fetch_and_op`, and `MPI_Compare_and_swap`.

3. Specify how we know that the data is available. In other words, what is the RMA equivalent to the completion of a receive? MPI provides three ways (with several variations in one of those) to accomplish this. The simplest, which corresponds to the simplest BSP and SHMEM models, is described in Section 3.5 and is the only method described in this chapter. The others are described in the next chapter.

Section 3.2 contrasts message passing with remote memory access. The MPI functions introduced are described in more detail in the following three sections (Sections 3.3 through 3.5). Section 3.6 contains two examples: an alternative to the Poisson problem described in Section 1.3.2, and a dense matrix-vector multiply. The chapter closes with some discussion of memory coherence and RMA performance issues.

3.2 Contrast with Message Passing

Before going into the details of remote memory operations, we begin with a simple RMA example and compare it with point-to-point message passing. In this example we will concentrate on the RMA routines most closely related to `MPI_-Send` and `MPI_Recv`. This example emphasizes the similarities between RMA and message-passing operations. Later we will see how to use RMA in situations where a message-passing solution is much more difficult.

To see the similarities between RMA and message passing, let us consider sending data from one process to another. Specifically, process 0 is sending `n ints` in `outbuf` to the variable `inbuf` in process 1.

Figures 3.1 and 3.2 show the correspondence between the message-passing operations and remote memory operations, respectively. For example, the memory window object serves a role similar to that of a communicator in message passing. `MPI_Put`, like `MPI_Isend`, initiates a data transfer. `MPI_Win_fence` completes the data transfer initiated by `MPI_Put`, much as `MPI_Wait` completes the transfer initiated by `MPI_Isend`.

These figures also show some of the differences. Note that this example uses no remote memory operation corresponding to `MPI_Irecv`; instead, the destination of the data is specified as arguments to the window creation on process 1. There is also an `MPI_Win_fence` call *before* the `MPI_Put` call. These differences will be covered below. The call to `MPI_Win_create` passes `MPI_BOTTOM` as the buffer address and 0 for the size of the local window for rank 0; this is simply a way to indicate that this process is making no memory available (C users could also pass

```
/* Create communicator for separate context for processes
   0 and 1 */
MPI_Comm_rank(MPI_COMM_WORLD, &rank);
MPI_Comm_split(MPI_COMM_WORLD, rank <= 1, rank, &comm);

/* Only processes 0 and 1 execute the rest of this */
if (rank > 1) return;

/* Process 0 sends and Process 1 receives */
if (rank == 0) {
    MPI_Isend(outbuf, n, MPI_INT, 1, 0, comm, &request);
}
else if (rank == 1) {
    MPI_Irecv(inbuf, n, MPI_INT, 0, 0, comm, &request);
}
/* Allow other operations to proceed (communication or
   computation) */
...
/* Complete the operation */
MPI_Wait(&request, MPI_STATUS_IGNORE);

/* Free communicator */
MPI_Comm_free(&comm);
```

Figure 3.1: Example code for sending data from one process to another with non-blocking message passing

NULL as the buffer address). An alternative version of Figure 3.2 is possible that uses MPI_Get on process 1 instead of MPI_Put on process 0. In this case, there is an RMA routine corresponding to MPI_Irecv, but not to MPI_Isend.

Figure 3.3 shows the relationship between the local memory windows on two processes and both put and get operations, emphasizing that the origin of a put or a get operation can be anywhere in memory, but the target must be in a memory window.

A more subtle issue that has been passed over here has to do with when a program may access variables that are also used in RMA operations. With message passing, the rules are (relatively) natural and easy to follow: between the beginning of the message-passing operation and the end of the operation, whether it is a send or a receive, the buffer for the data should not be accessed. With shared memory and RMA, the rules are more complex because of the one-sided nature of the operation:

```
/* Create memory window for separate context for processes
   0 and 1 */
MPI_Comm_rank(MPI_COMM_WORLD, &rank);
MPI_Comm_split(MPI_COMM_WORLD, rank <= 1, rank, &comm);

/* Only processes 0 and 1 execute the rest of this */
if (rank > 1) return;

if (rank == 0) {
    MPI_Win_create(MPI_BOTTOM, 0, sizeof(int),
                   MPI_INFO_NULL, comm, &win);
}
else if (rank == 1) {
    MPI_Win_create(inbuf, n * sizeof(int), sizeof(int),
                   MPI_INFO_NULL, comm, &win);
}

/* Process 0 puts into process 1 */
MPI_Win_fence(0, win);
if (rank == 0)
    MPI_Put(outbuf, n, MPI_INT, 1, 0, n, MPI_INT, win);

/* Allow other operations to proceed (communication or
   computation) */
...
/* Complete the operation */
MPI_Win_fence(0, win);

/* Free the window */
MPI_Win_free(&win);
```

Figure 3.2: Example code for sending data from one process to another with remote memory operations

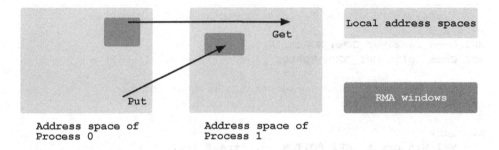

Figure 3.3: Remote memory access window on two processes. The shaded area covers a single window object made up of two windows.

When can data in the process that is not directly involved (via an MPI_Put or MPI_Get call) in the data transfer be used? While the general rules are somewhat complex, there are simple rules that will ensure a correct program; some of these are presented in Section 3.7.

This example makes remote memory operations look more complex than message passing. The reason is that the operation is "sending data from one process to another." Message passing is very natural for this operation, whereas RMA is not the most natural approach, although the operation can be implemented with RMA. We will see later other operations that are more natural with RMA.

In addition, this example has used a collective routine, MPI_Win_fence, to complete the remote memory operations. This provides a simple RMA model, but it is not the most general. A method that does not involve collective completion operations is described in Section 4.1.

3.3 Memory Windows

The first step in using RMA is to define the memory that will be available for remote memory operations. The memory in a process that can be accessed by another process through the use of the RMA routines is called a *memory window* into the process. It is called a window because MPI limits what part of a process's memory is accessible to other processes. That is, just as MPI_Recv limits where a message can be received (in the buffer specified by arguments to MPI_Recv), a memory window limits where data may be written with one-sided routines such as MPI_Put or MPI_Accumulate) or read from with one-sided routines such as MPI_Get. (We'll see additional one-sided communication routines in Section 4.4.2.)

A memory window is local memory (memory in the calling MPI process) that is made available to RMA operations. It is a contiguous section of memory, described as base address plus size in bytes.

MPI provides several routines for creating memory windows. The first that we will describe, `MPI_Win_create`, is used to tell MPI what memory windows are available, and is the only one that creates a window with memory specified by the user when the window is created (others allocate memory for the user or allow the user to attach memory after the `MPI_Win` is created). Following the analogy with the message-passing operations, in addition to specifying where data may be stored or read, we need to specify which MPI processes have access to that data. Since one of the reasons for using the RMA interface is to allow several different processes to access (read, write, or update) a memory location, the most natural way to describe the processes that can access a memory window is with an MPI group.

Since an MPI group is involved, it is not surprising that the MPI group used is the group of an MPI (intra)communicator. Since a communicator is involved, it isn't surprising that the operation to create the memory windows is collective over the communicator.

This is enough to define the memory that forms the local memory window and the processes that can access that memory window (also called window or local window). Two additional arguments must be provided. The first is the displacement unit. This is used to simplify accesses with a single datatype. Typical values are either 1 (all accesses are in terms of byte *offsets*) or the size of a data item (e.g., `sizeof(double)`). Sections 3.4.1 through 3.4.3 cover this argument in more detail.

The second required argument is an info argument that can be used to improve performance. This is covered in more detail in Section 3.8. It is always correct to use `MPI_INFO_NULL` for this argument.

The value returned is called an MPI *window object*, which represents the collection of windows defined by the collective `MPI_Win_create` call. A window object must be passed to all RMA routines that perform RMA operations. The window object serves the same role for RMA operations that the MPI communicator does for message-passing operations. The C and Fortran bindings for `MPI_Win_create` and `MPI_Win_free` are shown in Tables 3.1 and 3.2.

A note on terminology. A *window* refers to a region of memory within a single process. The output `MPI_Win` object from `MPI_Win_create` (or any of the other window creation routines) is called a "window object" and describes the collection of windows that are the input to the `MPI_Win_create` call. It might have been

---

int **MPI_Win_create**(void *base, MPI_Aint size, int disp_unit, MPI_Info info,
            MPI_Comm comm, MPI_Win *win)

int **MPI_Win_free**(MPI_Win *win)

Table 3.1: C bindings to create and free an RMA window object

---

MPI_WIN_CREATE(base, size, disp_unit, info, comm, win, ierror)
            <type> base(*)
            integer(kind=MPI_ADDRESS_KIND) size
            integer disp_unit, info, comm, win, ierror

MPI_WIN_FREE(win, ierror)
            integer win, ierror

Table 3.2: Fortran bindings to create and free an RMA window object

easier if the individual regions of memory were called something like facets or panes (as in window panes), but that is not what was chosen in the MPI standard. Instead, the term "window object" is always used for the object returned by a call to `MPI_-Win_create` or the other three routines that create an `MPI_Win`, and the term "window" is used for the local memory region.

When a window object is no longer needed, it should be freed with a call to `MPI_-Win_free`. This is a collective call; all of the processes that formed the original window must call `MPI_Win_free` collectively. `MPI_Win_free` should be called only when all RMA operations are complete; the completion of RMA operations is described in Section 3.5, 4.1 and 4.11. As with the other routines that free an MPI opaque object, the address of the object is passed; on return, it will be set to `MPI_WIN_NULL`.

3.3.1 Hints on Choosing Window Parameters

This section covers some suggestions for picking the parameters for `MPI_Win_-create`. Choices related to performance are covered separately in Section 3.8. The use of the displacement unit for heterogeneous RMA communication is covered in Section 3.4.1.

Local window and displacement unit. Often, the local window should be chosen as a single array, declared or allocated in the calling program. The size of the window should be the size of the array. If the local window is a simple type, such as `double` in C or `DOUBLE PRECISION` in Fortran, then the displacement unit should be the size of that type. Otherwise, a displacement unit of one should be used.

Info. The info argument is used only to provide performance-tuning options. A value of `MPI_INFO_NULL` is always valid. See Section 3.8.1 for an info value that can be used when only `MPI_Win_fence` is used to complete RMA operations.

3.3.2 Relationship to Other Approaches

In SHMEM, the single program model is exploited; variables that are statically declared (e.g., most variables in Fortran) are guaranteed (by the compiler and the loader) to have the same local address. Thus, a program can use the address of a local variable as the address of that same variable (in the single program model) in another process. In this case, no special routines are needed to indicate what local memory is available for RMA operations; all memory is "preregistered." Accessing dynamically allocated memory requires communicating the addresses between the processes; in this case, the programmer is responsible for keeping track of the location of a remote memory area (remote memory window in MPI terms). MPI handled this for the programmer through `MPI_Win_create`. The routine `MPI_-Win_allocate`, which is described in Section 4.3 and provides the memory to the user, may be able to allocate memory in such a way that the base address is the same in all processes (this is sometimes called *symmetric allocation*, which may reduce the storage and communication overheads), but there is no guarantee in MPI that this will happen.

In IBM's LAPI [58], memory is allocated specifically for RMA operations. This is similar to `MPI_Win_allocate`, described in Section 4.3.

3.4 Moving Data

Now that we've identified the memory that can participate in remote memory operations, we need to specify how to move data between two processes. MPI provides several sets of routines to specify what data to move. The three simplest routines are `MPI_Put` to put data into a remote memory window, `MPI_Get` to get data from a remote memory window, and `MPI_Accumulate` to update data in a remote window. `MPI_Put` is like "store to remote memory" or "write to remote memory."

The specification of the data to put is identical to that in an `MPI_Send`: buffer address, count, and datatype. The data to be moved can be anywhere in memory; it does not need to be in a window. This is called the *origin address*; origin here refers to the process making the call, not the source of the data.

The specification of where to put the data on the remote node is slightly different from that of where the data comes from. The destination of the data is always relative to the memory window on the destination process. Thus, instead of a buffer address, the location to put the data is given by the offset, which is relative to the window's base address. The offset argument is combined with the displacement unit that was specified when the window was created (the `disp_unit` parameter to `MPI_Win_create`) to determine exactly where the data will be placed (see Section 3.4.1). Then, just as in message passing, this location is combined with the count and datatype to determine which locations in memory receive data. The remote process is specified with a relative rank in the window object, just as the destination of an `MPI_Send` is specified with a relative rank in a communicator. The relationship between window objects, local windows, and RMA operations is shown in Figure 3.4. A more detailed diagram of an `MPI_Put` operation is shown in Figure 3.5.

We've said that `MPI_Put` is like a combined send and receive. This isn't quite correct. It is more like a combined nonblocking send and nonblocking receive. That is, `MPI_Put` is a nonblocking communication routine. There is no blocking version of `MPI_Put`. This is a deliberate choice in MPI, and it is worth spending some time to explain why the RMA communication routines are nonblocking.

One of the benefits of nonblocking RMA operations is that they allow many data motion operations to be completed with a single operation (the `MPI_Win_-fence` that we've seen in the examples in Section 3.2). One of the contributions to the latency of point-to-point message passing is the need to complete each message-passing operation separately (even when using multiple completion operations, such as `MPI_Waitall`, the MPI implementation must be prepared to complete each individually with `MPI_Wait`). Separating the initiation of data motion from the completion of that data motion is important in achieving high performance. With the MPI RMA operations, any number of `MPI_Put` operations can be completed efficiently by a single `MPI_Win_fence` call.

Section 4.2 shows how to implement a kind of blocking put operation. There could also be a buffered put (the analogue of `MPI_Bsend`); again, this is easy for an application programmer to do and isn't needed as part of the MPI standard.

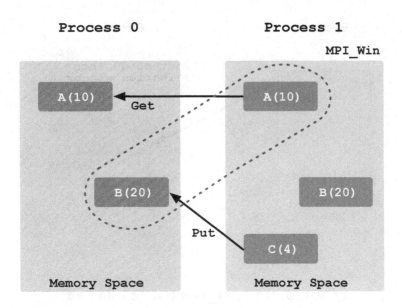

Figure 3.4: Windows, put, and get. Process 0 gets data from A on process 1. Process 1 puts data into B on process 0. The window object is made up of the array B on process 0 and the array A on process 1.

---

int **MPI_Put**(const void *origin_addr, int origin_count,
         MPI_Datatype origin_datatype, int target_rank, MPI_Aint target_disp,
         int target_count, MPI_Datatype target_datatype, MPI_Win win)

int **MPI_Get**(void *origin_addr, int origin_count, MPI_Datatype origin_datatype,
         int target_rank, MPI_Aint target_disp, int target_count,
         MPI_Datatype target_datatype, MPI_Win win)

Table 3.3: C bindings for RMA put and get routines

The BSP routine `bsp_put` is in fact a buffered put; the BSP counterpart to `MPI_-Put` is `bsp_hpput` (hp for "high performance"). In OpenSHMEM, `shmemput` is nonblocking in the same way as `MPI_Put`.

A counterpart to `MPI_Put` is the routine `MPI_Get`, which gets data *from* the remote process and returns that data to the calling process. This takes the same

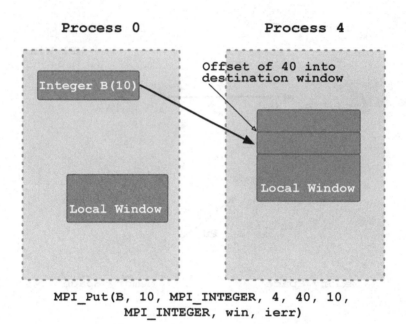

```
MPI_Put(B, 10, MPI_INTEGER, 4, 40, 10,
        MPI_INTEGER, win, ierr)
```

Figure 3.5: Illustration of an MPI put operation. Note that the data sent is *not* in the local window.

MPI_PUT(origin_addr, origin_count, origin_datatype, target_rank, target_disp, target_count, target_datatype, win, ierror)

    \<type> origin_addr(*)

    integer(kind=MPI_ADDRESS_KIND) target_disp

    integer origin_count, origin_datatype, target_rank, target_count, target_datatype, win, ierror

MPI_GET(origin_addr, origin_count, origin_datatype, target_rank, target_disp, target_count, target_datatype, win, ierror)

    \<type> origin_addr(*)

    integer(kind=MPI_ADDRESS_KIND) target_disp

    integer origin_count, origin_datatype, target_rank, target_count, target_datatype, win, ierror

Table 3.4: Fortran bindings for RMA put and get routines

arguments as `MPI_Put`, but the data moves in the opposite direction. The C and Fortran bindings for `MPI_Put` and `MPI_Get` are shown in Tables 3.3 and 3.4.

3.4.1 Reasons for Using Displacement Units

Why do MPI memory windows have a displacement unit, rather than defining everything in terms of byte displacements? One reason is clarity in programming (byte offsets can be confusing), and the second reason is correctness for heterogeneous systems. To understand both of these, consider the following task: Put four `int`s into a remote window, starting at the 11th `int` (10th numbering from zero). Let the remote window be created on process 3 with this code:

```
int A[20];
disp_unit = 1;  /* displacements in bytes */
MPI_Win_create(A, 20*sizeof(int), disp_unit, ..., &win);
```

Then, to store into `A[10]` through `A[13]`, process 1 would call

```
target_offset = 10 * sizeof(int);
MPI_Put(B, 4, MPI_INT, 3, target_offset, 4, MPI_INT, win);
```

Because process 3 specified a displacement unit in bytes (`disp_unit = 1`), the `target_offset` used by process 1 must be computed in bytes.

If, instead, process 3 creates the window explicitly as an array of integers with

```
int A[20];
disp_unit = sizeof(int); /* displacements in ints */
MPI_Win_create(A, 20*sizeof(int), disp_unit, ..., &win);
```

then process 1 can put data into `A[10]` through `A[13]` with

```
target_offset = 10;
MPI_Put(B, 4, MPI_INT, 3, target_offset, 4, MPI_INT, win);
```

Certainly the second approach is more *convenient* for RMA communication operations. However, it is *essential* when the MPI processes use different data representations, such as in a heterogeneous cluster of workstations. For example, in the above case, let us assume that process 1 uses 4-byte integers and process 3 uses 8-byte integers. In the first case, the use of a byte offset displacement unit leads to the wrong action: process 1 is specifying a byte offset of `10*sizeof(int)`, but the size of an `int` on process 1 is 4 bytes, leading to an offset of 40 bytes. But on process 3, with its 8-byte integers, this refers to `A[5]` (`5*sizeof(int)`). Using displacement units in terms of the local type at the time the window object

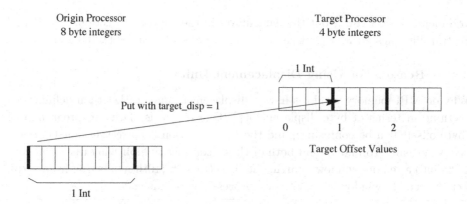

Figure 3.6: Data size offset computation

is created ensures that programs will be portable to heterogeneous environments. Figure 3.6 shows how an `MPI_Put` operation can move data to the correct location, even when the two processes have different data lengths, when the displacement unit is set to the size of the data item (an integer in this case) rather than a single byte.

Why, then, ever use a displacement unit of 1 (byte displacement)? One case is with a window that contains several different data types. For example, a sparse matrix is often represented as three separate arrays: two of type integer and one of type double precision. If these arrays were in a single window (for example, they were allocated in a single Fortran common block), it would be easiest to use byte displacements to access the individual elements.[3] If byte displacements are used, however, the application is not portable to heterogeneous systems where the basic datatypes have different lengths.

3.4.2   Cautions in Using Displacement Units

Note that the location in a remote memory window that is accessed by an RMA operation depends on combining the offset specified on the *origin* process with the displacement unit that was specified on the *target* process. This is a potential source of error: the displacement unit used is *not* the one specified in the `MPI_-Win_create` call on the process that is originating the RMA (e.g., `MPI_Put`) call.

---

[3] We say easiest because Fortran defines the ratio of sizes of numeric types; thus a displacement size of type integer could also be used, even with the double-precision entries.

MPI_SIZEOF(x, size, ierror)
>   <type> x
>   integer size, ierror

Table 3.5: Fortran binding for finding the size of a variable

In order to avoid potential problems in understanding RMA code, the displacement units should be either one for all processes in the window or the size of the same basic type.

3.4.3 Displacement Sizes in Fortran

Until recently, Fortran had no counterpart to the C `sizeof` operator. MPI provides Fortran users with the routine `MPI_SIZEOF`. This routine takes as input a variable of any numeric intrinsic type and returns the size in bytes of that type. The variable may be a scalar or an array; the size returned is the size of a single element of that type. This routine may be used only when using the `mpi` or `mpi_f08` module. The binding for `MPI_SIZEOF` is shown in Table 3.5. Note that some implementations of MPI may only allow scalars for the variable; our examples are careful not to use an array as an argument to `MPI_SIZEOF`.

If your application is using the `mpif.h` include file, you may not be able to use `MPI_SIZEOF`. In that case, in order to get the size of a datatype to be used in computing a displacement, the function `MPI_Type_size` may be used with MPI predefined datatypes such as `MPI_REAL` and `MPI_INTEGER`.

3.5 Completing RMA Data Transfers

MPI provides many different ways to complete data transfers. This section discusses a simple barrier like method. Other methods are described in Chapter 4.

In many computations, data exchange happens in phases; computation occurs between communication phases. In the MPI RMA model described in this chapter, these phases are separated with `MPI_Win_fence`. `MPI_Win_fence` is collective over all processes in the group associated with the window object passed to `MPI_-Win_fence`. `MPI_Win_fence` completes any RMA operations that started since the last call to `MPI_Win_fence` and ensures that any local stores to the memory window will be visible to RMA operations (e.g., code like `a(10) = 3` where `a` is part of the local window) before any RMA operations that follow the `MPI_Win_-fence` call. A good rule for using `MPI_Win_fence` is to ensure that between

---

int **MPI_Win_fence**(int assert, MPI_Win win)

Table 3.6: C binding for window fence

MPI_WIN_FENCE(assert, win, ierror)
              integer assert, win, ierror

Table 3.7: Fortran binding for window fence

any pair of successive `MPI_Win_fence` calls, there may be either local stores (assignments to variables in the process) to the (local) memory window or RMA put or accumulate operations (or neither), but not both local stores and RMA put or accumulate operations. If there are no RMA put operations between a pair of `MPI_Win_fence` calls, there may be both load and RMA get operations on the memory window.

Programming remote memory operations using `MPI_Win_fence` is much like the BSP model or the OpenSHMEM programming model. It is the *least* like shared memory. It is most suitable for "data parallel" applications, where each process is performing operations on a shared, distributed data structure.

`MPI_Win_fence` has an additional argument named `assert`, that provides information about the fence that can be used by some MPI implementations to provide better performance. A value of zero for the `assert` argument is always valid. Other values are described in Section 3.8.2. The C and Fortran bindings for `MPI_Win_fence` are shown in Tables 3.6 and 3.7.

One common use of `MPI_Win_fence` is to alternate between RMA accesses to a memory window and accesses by local loads and stores from the local process. When used this way, `MPI_Win_fence` can be thought of a "toggling" between the two kinds of accesses. However, `MPI_Win_fence` is more general. `MPI_Win_fence` separates RMA accesses (particularly `MPI_Put` and `MPI_Accumulate`) from non-RMA accesses that store data into any local window. The `assert` argument can be used to indicate exactly what kind of operations `MPI_Win_fence` is separating; this is covered in detail in Section 3.8.2.

The code fragment in Figure 3.7 shows an example of using `MPI_Win_fence` to complete RMA operations and to separate RMA operations from local loads and stores. Note that in this example, `MPI_Win_fence` is not a toggle between RMA and local accesses. To be more specific, when using `MPI_Win_fence` for RMA synchronization, all RMA operations must be bracketed by `MPI_Win_fence` calls;

```
MPI_Win_create(A, ..., &win);
MPI_Win_fence(0, win);
if (rank == 0) {
    /* Process 0 puts data into many local windows */
    MPI_Put(... , win);
    MPI_Put(... , win);
}
/* This fence completes the MPI_Put operations initiated
   by process 0 */
MPI_Win_fence(0, win);

/* All processes initiate access to some window to extract data */
MPI_Get(... , win);
/* The following fence completes the MPI_Get operations */
MPI_Win_fence(0, win);

/* After the fence, processes can load and store
   into A, the local window */
A[rank] = 4;
printf("A[%d] = %d\n", 0, A[0]);

/* We need a fence between stores and RMA operations */
MPI_Win_fence(0, win);

MPI_Put(... , win);
/* The following fence completes the preceding Put */
MPI_Win_fence(0, win);
```

Figure 3.7: Example using `MPI_Win_fence` to separate RMA operations from local load/stores and to complete RMA operations

an `MPI_Win_fence` is needed both to start and to complete any RMA operation.

3.6 Examples of RMA Operations

In this section we present two examples that use RMA operations. The first is a ghost-cell update, similar to those used for finite difference, finite volume, and finite element computations. The second computes a matrix-vector product using a distributed dense matrix and vector.

3.6.1   Mesh Ghost Cell Communication

This section provides an alternative approach to the Poisson problem, a simple partial differential equation, described in Section 1.3. In solving partial differential equations, the solution often is approximated on a mesh of points that is distributed among the processes. In the simplest case, shown in Figure 1.3, the mesh is regular, and it is partitioned among the processes with a simple, one-dimensional decomposition. In more complex cases, the decomposition among processes can be multidimensional, and the grid itself can be irregular. We will start with the simple decomposition. To compute the discretization at every point on the part of the mesh that is local to the process, we need the value of the neighboring points; these are called the *ghost cells* or *ghost points*. An example is illustrated in Figure 1.4.

We will declare the local part of the distributed mesh with

---
double precision a(0:nx+1,s-1:e+1)

We let a(i,j) stand for $a(x_i, y_j)$, where the coordinates of a mesh point are given by (x_i, y_j). As discussed in *Using MPI* [26], this approach follows the natural representation of a mesh but is different from the "matrix" interpretation of a two-dimensional array. See Appendix C in *Using MPI* [26] for more details. The declaration of a represents a slice of the mesh, where each process has rows (that is, ranges of the mesh in the y-coordinate) s to e (for *start* to *end*), and there are nx columns (ranges of the mesh in the x-coordinate), plus a column for the boundary conditions on the left and right.

The algorithm for communicating the neighbor information to the ghost cells can be summarized as follows:

1. Initiate send a(*,e) in the local process to a(*,s-1) in the top neighbor.

2. Initiate send a(*,s) in the local process to a(*,e+1) in the bottom neighbor.

3. Complete all data transfers.

We saw implementation of this algorithm that uses point-to-point message passing in Section 1.3.2, Figure 1.5. To convert this to use remote memory operations, one can combine the pairs of MPI_Irecv and MPI_Isend into either MPI_-Put or MPI_Get operations. The third step of the algorithm requires a simple MPI_Win_fence call, replacing the MPI_Waitall in Figure 1.5.

To use the RMA routines, we must first define an MPI window object in which the data will be moved (with either MPI_Put or MPI_Get). The following code creates a window where each local window is the (local part of the) mesh, including the ghost cells:

```
integer sizedouble, ierr, win
double precision A(0:nx+1,s-1:e+1)

call MPI_SIZEOF(A(0,s), sizedouble, ierr)
call MPI_WIN_CREATE(A, (nx+2)*(e-s+3)*sizedouble, sizedouble, &
                    MPI_INFO_NULL, MPI_COMM_WORLD, win, ierr)
```

The code to use RMA to exchange ghost-cell values is shown in Figure 3.8. The displacements at the targets are offset by one; this offset is necessary to skip the first ghost cell on the left. It corresponds to a(0,s-1) and a(0,e+1) which is used to store the boundary conditions and does not need to be transferred (note that the point-to-point version in Figure 1.5 sent and received with a(1,*)). Note that we can store into A both with MPI_Put and read values from A; we don't need separate windows for the different parts of A. However, if we wanted to both store into A with statements such as A(i,j) = ... and with MPI_Put, we must either separate the stores into the local window and the MPI_Put operations with a MPI_Win_fence or put the parts of A that we access with MPI_Put into separate MPI window objects.

The RMA code in Figure 3.8 is similar to the point-to-point version in Figure 1.5. We have replaced two send-receive pairs with two MPI_Put operations, and we have replaced the MPI_Waitall on four requests with a simple MPI_Win_fence. The major difference is that there is an MPI_Win_fence at the *beginning* of the code to indicate that local stores to A must complete and that RMA operations can now take place.

Determining the target displacement.   In the example above, the first MPI_-Put call appears to take the bottommost edge of the mesh on the calling process and put it into the topmost ghost edge of the destination (or target) process. But does it? In the example, the displacement for the target window (top_ghost_-disp) is computed by using the *local process*'s window. In other words, the code computes the location of the top ghost cells on process bottom_nbr using the calling process's parameters. As Figure 3.9 shows, this strategy can lead to errors if each process does not have an identically sized mesh. In our example, if the values of s and e are not the same on all processes, the wrong value of top_ghost_disp will be computed.

To obtain the correct target displacement for the ghost cells on the top edge of the neighbor's mesh, we may need to communicate this information to the process

```
subroutine exchng1(a, nx, s, e, win, &
                   bottom_nbr, top_nbr)
use mpi
integer nx, s, e, win, bottom_nbr, top_nbr
double precision a(0:nx+1,s-1:e+1)
integer ierr
integer(kind=MPI_ADDRESS_KIND) bottom_ghost_disp, top_ghost_disp

call MPI_WIN_FENCE(0, win, ierr)
! Put bottom edge into bottom neighbor's top ghost cells
! See text about top_ghost_disp
top_ghost_disp = 1 + (nx+2)*(e-s+2)
call MPI_PUT(a(1,s), nx, MPI_DOUBLE_PRECISION, &
             bottom_nbr, top_ghost_disp, nx, &
             MPI_DOUBLE_PRECISION, win, ierr)
! Put top edge into top neighbor's bottom ghost cells
bottom_ghost_disp = 1
call MPI_PUT(a(1,e), nx, MPI_DOUBLE_PRECISION, &
             top_nbr, bottom_ghost_disp, nx, &
             MPI_DOUBLE_PRECISION, win, ierr)
call MPI_WIN_FENCE(0, win, ierr)
return
end
```

Figure 3.8: Code using RMA to exchange ghost cell values

that is performing the MPI_Put operation. The easiest way to do so is with point-to-point message passing: as part of the process of setting up the windows and preparing to communicate, every process sends to its top neighbor the value to use for the target displacement in the MPI_Put. This code is shown in Figure 3.10. The one in the expression for my_top_ghost_disp puts the displacement at the first ghost point in the mesh (skipping the mesh point representing the boundary). This code also introduces a new predefined MPI datatype: MPI_AINT. This is the MPI datatype that corresponds to the address-sized integers defined by MPI: MPI_Aint in C and integer (kind=MPI_ADDRESS_KIND) in Fortran. This datatype and MPI_OFFSET for offset-sized integers were added in MPI 2.2. It also uses MPI_Sendrecv instead of a pair of separate MPI_Send and MPI_Recv calls since the latter depends on sends of short (one integer) messages happening even without a receive being posted at the target (an *unsafe* communication).

An alternative approach is to communicate the mesh parameters s and e; then

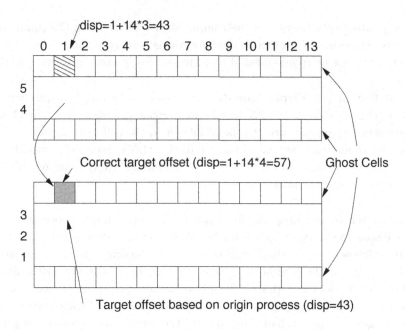

Figure 3.9: Illustration of the different target displacements needed when each local mesh is of a different size

```
integer sizedouble, ierr, win
integer (kind=MPI_ADDRESS_KIND) top_ghost_disp, my_top_ghost_disp
double precision A(0:nx+1,s-1:e+1)

call MPI_SIZEOF(A(0,s), sizedouble, ierr)
call MPI_WIN_CREATE(A, (nx+2)*(e-s+3)*sizedouble, sizedouble, &
                 MPI_INFO_NULL, MPI_COMM_WORLD, win, ierr)
! Compute the displacement into my top ghost cells
my_top_ghost_disp = 1 + (nx+2)*(e-s+2)
call MPI_SENDRECV(my_top_ghost_disp, 1, MPI_AINT, top_nbr, 0, &
                 top_ghost_disp, 1, MPI_AINT, bottom_nbr, 0, &
                 MPI_COMM_WORLD, MPI_STATUS_IGNORE, ierr)
```

Figure 3.10: Code to send to neighboring processes the displacement values to be used in MPI_Put operations

the appropriate displacements can be computed. We have shown the communication of the displacements in order to illustrate the general case and to note that the displacements must be communicated as address-sized integers with `MPI_AINT`.

More on the target displacement. The type of the target displacement is `INTEGER (kind=MPI_ADDRESS_KIND)` in Fortran and `MPI_Aint` in C. Care must be taken to pass the correct type of integer in the call to `MPI_Put` and any place where an address-sized integer is required. This is especially important in Fortran when not using the `mpi` or `mpi_f08` modules, since type mismatches will not be caught by the compiler.

An alternative to sending displacements. In the example above, we had to send the displacement value needed for the `MPI_Put` operation for the ghost cells on the top edge because the displacement needed at the origin process (the process calling `MPI_Put`), in the general case, might not be easy to calculate. Alternatively, instead of putting data into ghost cells only on remote processes, we can put data into the ghost cells of the process on the top, starting at a displacement of one; and we can get the ghost cells for our part of the grid on the top edge by getting grid data from the first column of the process on the top. That is, for the ghost values, we can put into the bottommost row (displacement of one), and for the top ghost cells, we get from the first row (displacement of `(nx+2)+1` double-precision values). The routine that we use to get the data is `MPI_Get`, and the code for this is shown in Figure 3.11.

Note that we can use both `MPI_Put` and `MPI_Get` operations on the window. We can do so because the memory locations being accessed as targets of the `MPI_-Put` and `MPI_Get` operations do not overlap (see Section 3.7.3 and Section 11.7 of [46]). Also note that this code has no explicit reference to the `bottom_nbr`: the "get from top neighbor" replaces the "put to bottom neighbor."

Playing with the displacement unit. In our example, we used a displacement unit of `sizedouble`, the number of bytes in a `DOUBLE PRECISION` data item. This is the most obvious choice, but other choices exist. One choice is to make the displacement unit the size of an entire row[4] of A, rather than a single element of A.

---

[4]Recall that we have defined a row of the array a as a row of the mesh, that is, the elements corresponding to constant y value. Readers who are used to the matrix interpretation of two-dimensional arrays are reminded that the jth row of the mesh, corresponding to y_j, is a`(:,j)`, which in the *matrix* interpretation of a, is a column. We use the mesh interpretation because no matrices are involved in our example.

```
subroutine exchng1(a, nx, s, e, win, &
                   bottom_nbr, top_nbr)
use mpi
integer nx, s, e, win, bottom_nbr, top_nbr
integer (kind=MPI_ADDRESS_KIND) offset
double precision a(0:nx+1,s-1:e+1)
integer ierr

call MPI_WIN_FENCE(0, win, ierr)
! Get top edge from top neighbor's cells after the ghost cells
offset = nx + 3
call MPI_GET(a(1,e+1), nx, MPI_DOUBLE_PRECISION, top_nbr, &
             offset, nx, MPI_DOUBLE_PRECISION, win, ierr)
! Put top edge into top neighbor's ghost cell row
offset = 1
call MPI_PUT(a(1,e), nx, MPI_DOUBLE_PRECISION, top_nbr, &
             offset, nx, MPI_DOUBLE_PRECISION, win, ierr)
call MPI_WIN_FENCE(0, win, ierr)

return
end
```

Figure 3.11: Alternative code for exchanging ghost cells that mixes puts and gets

If the window is defined with a displacement unit of (nx+2)*sizedouble, then the offset that is used in MPI_Put is just the row number. In other words, instead of (nx+2)*(m+1), we can use simply m+1. If we do so, however, we must send an extra element, not just the interior part (e.g., we must send nx+1 values starting from a(0,m) rather than nx values starting from a(1,m)). Even the need to send nx+1 elements instead of nx elements can be avoided by carefully defining the local window; we leave that as an exercise for the reader.

Using datatypes.   The simple one-dimensional decomposition is not scalable to a large number of processes. In that case, one should use a higher-dimensional decomposition. In the case of our two-dimensional mesh, we might declare the local mesh as

```
double precision a(sx-1:ex+1,sy-1:ey+1)
```

This includes ghost cells on all four sides. When sending the top and bottom rows of ghost cells, we can use essentially the same code as before. For the left and right edges, however, the data is not contiguous in memory. This is a perfect place to use MPI datatypes, specifically the `MPI_Type_vector` routine to construct a datatype for columns of the local mesh. The code to construct the window object and the datatypes for the columns is shown in Figures 3.12 and 3.13. As in the previous cases, we also need to send the offsets to be used as the target displacements and the strides needed for the target datatypes (if every local mesh has exactly the same size, we can dispense with this step; we include it to show what is needed in the general case).

With the window object and datatype for a row defined, we can now write the code to fill the ghost cells on all four sides (this is assuming a five-point stencil). The code is shown in Figure 3.14. In a Fortran 90 environment, the variables describing the displacements and datatypes to use for the neighbors could be placed in a derived type, much as a C programmer would put them into a structure.

Performance issues.   Using MPI datatypes is certainly the clearest and simplest approach and offers the possibility of good performance. In practice, unfortunately, not all MPI implementations provide high performance when using derived data-types for communication [56]. If the highest performance is required, one may need to avoid the use of derived datatypes. In this case, two approaches are possible.

The first is to move the data into a buffer, collecting the data from a row in A into contiguous memory locations. For example, to move the top row of A into a buffer on the neighboring process, one could use the code in Figure 3.15. This approach replaces the single `MPI_Put` call that uses the `coltype` datatype. Note that it uses a different window object, `winbuf`, from that used to move columns of A. This requires a separate set of `MPI_Win_fence` calls.

The second approach is to put all of the ghost cells into contiguous memory locations, even those that were moved into columns of A. That is, rather than put the ghost cells in A, we put them into a different array, `aghost`. This array has `2*nx+2*ny` elements. We can create the window with the following code:

```fortran
integer win, sizedouble, ierr
integer (kind=MPI_ADDRESS_KIND) right_ghost_disp, &
        left_ghost_disp, top_ghost_disp
integer (kind=MPI_ADDRESS_KIND) my_right_Ghost_disp, &
        my_left_Ghost_disp, myTopghost_disp
double precision a(sx-1:ex+1,sy-1:ey+1)

! nx is the number of (non-ghost) values in x, ny in y
nx = ex - sx + 1
ny = ey - sy + 1
call MPI_SIZEOF(A(sx-1,sy-1), sizedouble, ierr)
call MPI_WIN_CREATE(a, (ex-sx+3)*(ey-sy+3)*sizedouble, &
                    sizedouble, MPI_INFO_NULL, MPI_COMM_WORLD, &
                    win, ierr)
! Exchange information on the offsets
! Compute the displacement into my right ghost cells
my_right_Ghost_disp = 2*(nx+2)-1
call MPI_SENDRECV(my_right_Ghost_disp, 1, MPI_AINT, right_nbr, &
                  0, right_ghost_disp, 1, MPI_AINT, left_nbr, &
                  0, MPI_COMM_WORLD, MPI_STATUS_IGNORE, ierr)
! Compute the displacement into my top ghost cells
myTopghost_disp = (nx + 2)*(ny + 1) + 1
call MPI_SENDRECV(myTopghost_disp, 1, MPI_AINT, top_nbr, 0, &
                  top_ghost_disp, 1, MPI_AINT, bottom_nbr, 0, &
                  MPI_COMM_WORLD, MPI_STATUS_IGNORE, ierr)
! Compute the displacement into my left ghost cells
my_left_Ghost_disp = nx + 2
call MPI_SENDRECV(my_left_Ghost_disp, 1, MPI_AINT, left_nbr, 0,&
                  left_ghost_disp, 1, MPI_AINT, right_nbr, 0, &
                  MPI_COMM_WORLD, MPI_STATUS_IGNORE, ierr)
```

Figure 3.12: Code to exchange displacement values in preparation for using MPI_Put in the example in Figure 3.14

```fortran
integer coltype, left_coltype, right_coltype

! Vector type used on origin
call MPI_TYPE_VECTOR(1, ny, nx+2, MPI_DOUBLE_PRECISION, &
                     coltype, ierr)
call MPI_TYPE_COMMIT(coltype, ierr)

! Exchange stride information needed to build the left and right
! coltypes
call MPI_SENDRECV(nx, 1, MPI_INTEGER, left_nbr, 2, &
                  right_nx, 1, MPI_INTEGER, right_nbr, 2, &
                  MPI_COMM_WORLD, MPI_STATUS_IGNORE, ierr)
call MPI_SENDRECV(nx, 1, MPI_INTEGER, right_nbr, 3, &
                  left_nx, 1, MPI_INTEGER, left_nbr, 3, &
                  MPI_COMM_WORLD, MPI_STATUS_IGNORE, ierr)
call MPI_TYPE_VECTOR(1, ny, left_nx + 2, MPI_DOUBLE_PRECISION, &
                     left_coltype, ierr)
call MPI_TYPE_COMMIT(left_coltype, ierr)
call MPI_TYPE_VECTOR(1, ny, right_nx + 2, MPI_DOUBLE_PRECISION, &
                     right_coltype, ierr)
call MPI_TYPE_COMMIT(right_coltype, ierr)
```

Figure 3.13: Code to create vector datatypes to be used at the origin and at the targets in the example in Figure 3.14

```fortran
integer winbuf, ierr
double precision aghost(MAX_GHOST)

nx = ex - sx + 1
ny = ey - sy + 1
! MAX GHOST must be at least 2*nx + 2*ny
call MPI_SIZEOF(aghost(1), sizedouble, ierr)
call MPI_WIN_CREATE(aghost, (2*nx+2*ny)*sizedouble, &
                    sizedouble, MPI_INFO_NULL, &
                    MPI_COMM_WORLD, winbuf, ierr)
```

Figure 3.16 shows the corresponding code to collect data into buffer arrays and then move it with MPI_Put. Note that two separate local buffer arrays, buf1 and buf2, are used. Recall that RMA data movement operations (MPI_Put here) are all nonblocking in the MPI sense. That is, the data buffer must not be modified until the operation completes. Thus, just as separate buffers are needed for MPI_Isend, they are needed for the MPI_Put calls here.

```
subroutine exchng2(a, sx, ex, sy, ey, win, &
     left_nbr, right_nbr, top_nbr, bot_nbr, &
     right_ghost_disp, left_ghost_disp, &
     top_ghost_disp, coltype, right_coltype, left_coltype)
use mpi
integer sx, ex, sy, ey, win, ierr
integer left_nbr, right_nbr, top_nbr, bot_nbr
integer coltype, right_coltype, left_coltype
double precision a(sx-1:ex+1,sy-1:ey+1)
integer (kind=MPI_ADDRESS_KIND) right_ghost_disp, &
        left_ghost_disp, top_ghost_disp, bot_ghost_disp
integer nx

nx = ex - sx + 1

call MPI_WIN_FENCE(0, win, ierr)
! Put bottom edge into bottom neighbor's top ghost cells
call MPI_PUT(a(sx,sy), nx, MPI_DOUBLE_PRECISION, bot_nbr, &
             top_ghost_disp, nx, MPI_DOUBLE_PRECISION, &
             win, ierr)
! Put top edge into top neighbor's bottom ghost cells
bot_ghost_disp = 1
call MPI_PUT(a(sx,ey), nx, MPI_DOUBLE_PRECISION, top_nbr, &
             bot_ghost_disp, nx, MPI_DOUBLE_PRECISION, &
             win, ierr)
! Put right edge into right neighbor's left ghost cells
call MPI_PUT(a(ex,sy), 1, coltype, &
             right_nbr, left_ghost_disp, 1, right_coltype, &
             win, ierr)
! Put left edge into the left neighbor's right ghost cells
call MPI_PUT(a(sx,sy), 1, coltype, &
             left_nbr, right_ghost_disp, 1, left_coltype, &
             win, ierr)
call MPI_WIN_FENCE(0, win, ierr)
return
end
```

Figure 3.14: Code to exchange ghost values for a two-dimensional decomposition of the mesh

```
! Create a special window for the ghost cells
call MPI_WIN_CREATE(abuf, ..., winbuf, ierr)
...
ny = ey - sy + 1
nx = ex - sx + 1
do i=1,ny
    bufleft(i)  = a(1,sy+i-1)
    bufright(i) = a(nx,sy+i-1)
enddo
call MPI_WIN_FENCE(0, winbuf, ierr)
call MPI_PUT(bufleft, ny, MPI_DOUBLE_PRECISION, left_nbr, &
             0, ny, MPI_DOUBLE_PRECISION, winbuf, ierr)
... similar code for the right edge with bufright
call MPI_WIN_FENCE(0, winbuf, ierr)
... code to unpack the data in the local memory to the ghost
... cells
```

Figure 3.15: Code to move ghost cell data without using derived datatypes but using a second window object

For unstructured grid problems, a slight variation of the separate ghost array is to put all of the "ghost" points at the end of the local array.

3.6.2   Combining Communication and Computation

In many applications, a common step is to receive data and then combine that data with other local data with a simple operation, such as addition. In this section, we consider a slightly more elaborate example: forming a matrix-vector product with the matrix and the vector distributed across two processes.

We can write this as follows, with the lines indicating the division of data among the two processes.

$$\begin{pmatrix} w_0 \\ w_1 \end{pmatrix} = \begin{pmatrix} A_{00} & | & A_{01} \\ A_{10} & | & A_{11} \end{pmatrix} \begin{pmatrix} v_0 \\ v_1 \end{pmatrix}$$

We can expand this to show the four separate matrix-vector multiplications.

$$w_0 = A_{00}v_0 + A_{01}v_1$$
$$w_1 = A_{10}v_0 + A_{11}v_1.$$

Assume that process 0 has w_0, v_0, and the first block column of A: A_{00} and A_{10} and that process 1 has w_1, v_1, and the second block column of A: A_{01} and A_{11}.

```
call MPI_WIN_FENCE(0, winbuf, ierr)
! Put bottom edge into bottom neighbor's ghost cells
nx = ex - sx + 1
call MPI_PUT(a(sx,sy), nx, MPI_DOUBLE_PRECISION, &
          bottom_nbr, 0, nx, MPI_DOUBLE_PRECISION, winbuf, ierr)
! Put top edge into top neighbor's ghost cells
call MPI_PUT(a(sx,ey), nx, MPI_DOUBLE_PRECISION, &
          top_nbr, nx, nx, MPI_DOUBLE_PRECISION, winbuf, ierr)
! Put left edge into left neighbor's ghost cells
ny = ey - sy + 1
do i=sy,ey
    buf1(i-sy+1) = a(sx,i)
enddo
call MPI_PUT(buf1, ny, MPI_DOUBLE_PRECISION, &
            left_nbr, 2*nx, ny, MPI_DOUBLE_PRECISION, &
            winbuf, ierr)
! Put right edge into right neighbor's ghost cells
do i=sy,ey
    buf2(i-sy+1) = a(ex,i)
enddo
call MPI_PUT(buf2, ny, MPI_DOUBLE_PRECISION, &
            right_nbr, 2*nx+ny, ny, MPI_DOUBLE_PRECISION, &
            winbuf, ierr)
call MPI_WIN_FENCE(0, winbuf, ierr)
! ... use data in aghost ...
```

Figure 3.16: Code to exchange ghost cell information in a 2-D decomposition without using derived datatypes. For simplicity, this code assumes that all processes have the same values for nx and ny.

Process 0 can thus compute $t_0^0 = A_{00}v_0$ and $t_1^0 = A_{10}v_0$; process 1 can compute $t_0^1 = A_{01}v_1$ and $t_1^1 = A_{11}v_1$. The temporary t_i^j stands for the result on the jth process of multiplying the ith block of the matrix times the ith block of the vector. The computation of w is then

$$w_0 = t_0^0 + t_0^1$$
$$w_1 = t_1^0 + t_1^1,$$

where the superscript on t indicates which process computed the value.

If this was implemented with message passing, the natural approach would look something like the following for process 0, and where there are only two processes. Here, t(rank)(i) is used for t_i^{rank}.

```
int MPI_Accumulate(const void *origin_addr, int origin_count,
                   MPI_Datatype origin_datatype, int target_rank, MPI_Aint target_disp,
                   int target_count, MPI_Datatype target_datatype, MPI_Op op,
                   MPI_Win win)
```

Table 3.8: C bindings for RMA accumulate routine

```
double t[2][VEC_SIZE], buf[VEC_SIZE], w[VEC_SIZE];
... each process computing t(rank)(i) for i=0,1
if (rank == 0) {
   /* Send t(0)(1) = t[1] to process 1 */
   MPI_Isend(t[1], n, MPI_DOUBLE, 1, 0, MPI_COMM_WORLD, &req[0]);
   /* Receive t(1)(0) from process 1 into buf */
   MPI_Irecv(buf, n, MPI_DOUBLE, 1, 0, MPI_COMM_WORLD, &req[1]);
   /* Complete the communication */
   MPI_Waitall(2, req, MPI_STATUSES_IGNORE);
   for (i=0; i<n; i++) w[i] = t[0][i] + buf[i];
}
```

We have discussed how to replace the message-passing in code such as this with RMA operations. Doing so involves moving the data in t[] twice: once from process 1 to process 0, ending up in the temporary vector buf, and then once more as it is loaded and added to t[0] in the for loop. This can be inefficient. Each time data is moved, the opportunity is lost to do some computing. A better approach would be to move the data in t and immediately add it to the t for rank zero to form w on rank zero.

MPI provides a way to accomplish a move and combine as a single operation. The routine MPI_Accumulate allows data to be moved and combined, at the destination, using any of the predefined MPI reduction operations, such as MPI_SUM. The arguments to MPI_Accumulate have the same form as for MPI_Put, with the addition of an MPI_Op argument. The C and Fortran bindings for MPI_Accumulate are shown in Tables 3.8 and 3.9.

Using MPI_Accumulate, we can replace the message passing *and* remove the for loop, as shown in the following code (again, this is for process 0):

```
MPI_Win win;
/* Create a window with w */
MPI_Win_create(w, n*sizeof(double), sizeof(double),
               MPI_INFO_NULL, MPI_COMM_WORLD, &win);
if (rank == 0) {
```

MPI_ACCUMULATE(origin_addr, origin_count, origin_datatype, target_rank,
　　　　　target_disp, target_count, target_datatype, op, win, ierror)
　　　　　<type> origin_addr(*)
　　　　　integer(kind=MPI_ADDRESS_KIND) target_disp
　　　　　integer origin_count, origin_datatype, target_rank, target_count,
　　　　　　　target_datatype, op, win, ierror

Table 3.9: Fortran bindings for RMA accumulate routine

```
/* compute t[0][0] in w and t[0][1] in buf */
...
/* Add this value to w on the remote process */
MPI_Win_fence(0, win);
MPI_Accumulate(buf, n, MPI_DOUBLE, 1, 0, n, MPI_DOUBLE,
               MPI_SUM, win);
MPI_Win_fence(0, win);
}
```

MPI_Accumulate is not quite as general as the MPI collective computation routines (e.g., MPI_Reduce, MPI_Allreduce, MPI_Reduce_scatter, or MPI_-Scan) because only the predefined reduction operations, such as MPI_SUM or MPI_LAND, are allowed. User-defined operations may not be used with RMA accumulate operations such as MPI_Accumulate. This restriction was made by the MPI Forum to allow and encourage more efficient implementations of MPI_-Accumulate. In addition, there are restrictions on the datatype arguments. It is always correct to use the basic MPI datatypes, as long as they are valid for the operation. In addition, unlike in MPI_Reduce and other collective reduction functions, one may use a derived datatype where every component is the same basic datatype. For example, the vector types constructed in Figure 3.13 may be used with RMA accumulate functions.

Concurrent updates using accumulate. Now consider the case with more than two processes. If there are p processes, then the result w_i on the ith process is computed from the local contribution $A_{ii}v_i$ and $p-1$ contributions from the other $p-1$ processes. With message passing[5] (e.g., MPI_Isend and MPI_Irecv), or the RMA routines MPI_Put, and MPI_Get, one buffer is needed to receive data from

---

[5]See Section 7.2.2 in *Using MPI* [26] for how this can be implemented with MPI_Reduce_scatter.

each process that is contributing data. With `MPI_Accumulate`, each process can contribute directly to the result vector `w`, as shown below:

```
double t[MAX_RANK][MAX_VEC];
MPI_Win win;
/* Create a window with w */
MPI_Win_create(w, n*sizeof(double), sizeof(double),
               MPI_INFO_NULL, MPI_COMM_WORLD, &win);
/* compute t[rank][i] in t[i] and t[rank][rank] in w */
...
/* Add this value to w on the remote process */
MPI_Win_fence(0, win);
for (i=0; i<p; i++) {
    if (i != myrank)
        MPI_Accumulate(t[i], n, MPI_DOUBLE, i,
                       0, n, MPI_DOUBLE, MPI_SUM, win);
}
MPI_Win_fence(0, win);
```

A special operation allowed for `MPI_Accumulate` is `MPI_REPLACE`. The effect of this operation is to replace the value at the target process with the value provided on the origin process. We do not need this operation for this example, but it can come in handy. In addition, it emphasizes that `MPI_Accumulate`, unlike `MPI_-Put` or `MPI_Get`, may be used to update the same locations in a memory window with multiple calls without separating the calls with an `MPI_Win_fence` (or other window synchronization routine). The next section helps us understand the reason for this, as well as the rules for when a memory location may be accessed with RMA operations and when with local loads and stores.

3.7   Pitfalls in Accessing Memory

To understand the rules for access to data in memory windows, that is, when can one use an RMA operation and when a local load or store, one must consider in more detail what might happen when data in memory is referenced. The issues here are quite subtle; one must remember that the MPI standard is designed to be implementable on a wide range of hardware platforms, even those that do not have any hardware support for shared-memory or remote memory operations. Understanding the reasons for the rules in this section often requires thinking of things that can go wrong.

```
/* This code has undefined behavior */
double b[10];

for (i=0; i<10; i++) b[i] = rank * 10.0 + i;

MPI_Win_create(b, 10*sizeof(double), sizeof(double),
               MPI_INFO_NULL, MPI_COMM_WORLD, &win);
MPI_Win_fence(0, win);
if (rank == 0) {
  b[2] = 1./3.;
}
else if (rank == 1) {
  /* Store my value of b into process 0's window, which is
     process 0's array b */
  MPI_Put(b, 10, MPI_DOUBLE, 0, 0, 10, MPI_DOUBLE, win);
}
MPI_Win_fence(0, win);
```

Figure 3.17: Example of conflicting put and store operations. This code has undefined behavior.

3.7.1   Atomicity of Memory Operations

When can a program access a variable with local load or store? That is, when can the operations for using a value in a variable (load) or assigning a value in a variable (store) be used without interfering with RMA operations? Consider the code in Figure 3.17. What is the value of b[2] at the end of the code?

A number of possibilities arise. The most obvious is that b[2] is either the value 1./3. or 12.0. But that assumes that either b[2] = 1./3. or that the MPI_Put for b[2] succeeds completely, that is, that either one of the operations to store a value into b[2] succeeds, and the other does not. Unfortunately, that may not be what happens within the computer (this also applies to shared-memory programming, by the way). For example, assume that the hardware moves only four bytes at a time and that a double is eight bytes long. Then putting a value into b[2] will require two separate operations by the computer hardware. In the code in Figure 3.17, there are four possibilities for the result, not two, depending on the order in which each of the two parts of b[2] are stored. These four possibilities are shown in Figure 3.18. Because of this behavior, a programmer cannot depend on any particular result; MPI-2, therefore, defined such conflicting accesses as erroneous—that is, the program is incorrect. This is a strong statement, and indeed it proved

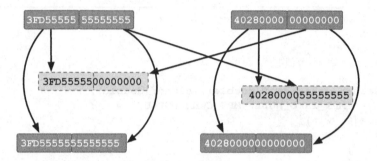

Figure 3.18: The four possible results for b[2] in Figure 3.17. The dashed boxes show possible, but incorrect, results. The box on the top left contains 1/3 (as a floating-point value) and is the value stored by process 0 in the example in Figure 3.17. The box on the top right contains 12 (also in floating point) and is the value passed to MPI_Put by process 1.

too strong a statement for some valid uses of RMA [6]. In MPI-3, conflicting or overlapping accesses are undefined rather than erroneous. The difference between erroneous and undefined is that in the former case, an MPI implementation could return an error (and abort). In the latter case, the program is still correct but the results are undefined. By making the result undefined, programs that can accept an undefined result can continue.

This example may seem a little contrived, since many computers will guarantee to store even an eight-byte double or DOUBLE PRECISION in a single operation. But even for double-precision complex values, two operations may be required. And for a structure, of course, a number of operations will be required.

This illustrates an important point: Operations in a programming language that appear to be a single operation, such as a store to a variable, an increment (e.g., i++ in C), or an array operation (e.g., A = 0 for an array A in Fortran), may not be a single operation in the hardware. Operations that are performed as a single operation, without any possibility of another operation modifying the result of the operation, are called *atomic*, because they are the smallest, indivisible operations.

3.7.2   Memory Coherency

Some computer systems do not even provide memory systems that are fully coherent. For example, data in cache (representing a copy of data in memory) that is updated may not cause data in memory or in another cache (representing the same memory address) to be updated before some other process references the same memory locations. Such systems are said to *not* have coherent memory caches. Most computers today do provide coherent caches, but performance implications arise, and some special high-performance systems may trade memory coherency for greater performance. MPI RMA is designed to work with both memory coherent and incoherent systems; this approach promotes maximum portability, but it does introduce some restrictions to allow relatively efficient implementation even when no hardware support is provided for coherent memory. We'll say more about this in Section 4.10.

3.7.3   Some Simple Rules for RMA

We have seen that maintaining the consistency of memory when two different agents may modify a word can be difficult. On some systems, sophisticated hardware is used to ensure that updates are atomic and memory is coherent and to give the expected results. However, MPI is designed so that RMA can be used even when such hardware support is not available, although MPI-3 adds support for systems with such hardware support (see Section 4.10). In order to accomplish this, certain rules must be followed when using the RMA operations. A complete description is given in the MPI-3 standard, Section 11.7. In this section, we provide rules that are sufficient for writing correct code but that are slightly stricter than required.

Also, as is clear from above, reading from memory with either local loads or RMA get (e.g., `MPI_Get`) is less restrictive than writing to memory with either local stores or puts and accumulates (e.g., `MPI_Put` and `MPI_Accumulate`). For that reason, we divide the cases to consider into whether the memory window is merely accessed (that is, an RMA get such as `MPI_Get` and load) or is modified (that is, put or accumulate, e.g., `MPI_Put` or `MPI_Accumulate`, or store). These rules also apply to the other RMA communication routines that we'll cover in the next chapter.

Overlapping put and accumulate operations.   The targets of two RMA put operations in the same destination window must not overlap. This rule prevents problems such as the one illustrated in Figure 3.17 (but involving two put operations rather than a put and a local store).

Note that the RMA accumulate operations such as `MPI_Accumulate` allow (and even encourages) overlapping operations. A few restrictions exist here as well. When the targets overlap, both the basic MPI datatype (for example, `MPI_INT`) and the operation (for example, `MPI_SUM`) must be the same.

To make remote memory stores to overlapping locations, one can use the operation `MPI_REPLACE` in an RMA accumulate operation. Note, however, that if two accumulate operations are accessing the same locations in the target window from different origin processes, MPI does not specify in which order they make their replacements. For example, if two processes are making calls like this

---

MPI_Accumulate(a, 2, **MPI_DOUBLE**, ..., **MPI_REPLACE**, win);

---

then at the target, the location at displacement 0 may get the value from one process and the location at displacement 1 may get its value from the other process. MPI guarantees only that the updates don't break a basic datatype.[6] Put and accumulate operations between two `MPI_Win_fence` calls must not overlap under any circumstances (otherwise the result is undefined). Similarly, overlapping accesses (gets) may be accomplished with a variant of `MPI_Accumulate`, which is `MPI_Get_accumulate`.

Local stores and RMA updates. Stores into the local window and `MPI_-Put` or `MPI_Accumulate` operations into that window must be separated by an `MPI_Win_fence` (or other RMA synchronization) call.

Local loads and RMA get. Local loads and RMA get operations may access any part of the window that has not been updated by an RMA update (RMA put or accumulate) or local store operation.

The easy rule. The simplest rule is as follows:

1. Do not overlap accesses on windows (except for accumulate operations such as `MPI_Accumulate`).

2. Separate non-RMA accesses from RMA accesses with `MPI_Win_fence`.

This is stricter than required by MPI, but it is often easy to accomplish.

So far, we have referred only to `MPI_Win_fence` as the routine to use in separating RMA updates, accesses, local loads, and local stores. In the next chapter, we will introduce some additional MPI routines that may be used to separate the accesses. In those cases, these same rules apply.

---

[6]The MPI standard, in Section 11.7.1, refers to "locations" and says that the results may vary only as much as computer arithmetics are not commutative or associative. This suggests the interpretation that we have used here, but the actual text is unclear.

3.7.4 Overlapping Windows

One can have several MPI window objects whose local windows overlap. The rules in MPI for using these windows are very restrictive; see item 3, page 455, in [46], Section 11.7 (Semantics and Correctness). The restrictions were made by the MPI Forum to allow for relatively efficient implementations on systems without hardware support for shared-memory coherency. Because of the performance issues and the complexities of the rules for correct use, we recommend avoiding the use of overlapping windows.[7]

3.7.5 Compiler Optimizations

When one process modifies data in another process, there is a risk that because the compiler has placed the variable into a register, the modified result won't be seen by the target process. The simplest fix for this in C or Fortran (2003 or later) is to declare the variable that is given to `MPI_Win_create` as the local memory window as `volatile`.[8] For example, in the grid example, we might use

```
integer sizedouble, ierr, win
double precision, volatile :: a(0:nx+1,s-1:e+1)

call MPI_SIZEOF(a(0,s), sizedouble, ierr)
call MPI_WIN_CREATE(a, (nx+2)*(e-s+3)*sizedouble, sizedouble, &
                    MPI_INFO_NULL, MPI_COMM_WORLD, win, ierr)
```

In addition, if the array A is then passed to other routines, it may have to be declared as `volatile` in those routines as well.

Using `volatile` has its drawbacks, however. Most important, it forces the compiler to reload any element of the variable from memory rather than using a previously loaded value that is already in a register. The result can be a significant loss in performance. Fortunately, there is a work-around. The key is that the MPI RMA operations (that are completed by `MPI_Win_fence`) can update the local window any time between the two `MPI_Win_fence` calls that separate them from other operations. Thus, a correct MPI program cannot rely on the updates happening before the `MPI_Win_fence` that completes the RMA operations. For C, this is enough: since the local window is an argument to the `MPI_Win_create` routine that returned the window object, and the window object is an

---

[7]These rules are the reason there is no `MPI_Win_dup`, since a duplicated window object would involve overlapping memory windows.

[8]We will see shortly that for C and `MPI_Win_fence` synchronization, `volatile` is not necessary.

input to `MPI_Win_fence`, the C compiler must take into account the possibility that `MPI_Win_fence` will access the local window through a pointer stored in the window object. Thus, we do not need `volatile` in C when using `MPI_-Win_fence` synchronization. Note that we are *not* saying that `MPI_Win_fence` actually performs the updates, only that it *could* do so. The C compilers must assume the same and therefore reload the value of any part of the local memory window that is in the register after the call to `MPI_Win_fence`.

The situation is different in Fortran. Fortran pointers are much more restrictive (which allows the compiler more flexibility in generating fast code), and in this case the Fortran compiler will not conclude that `MPI_Win_fence` might update the variable provided to `MPI_Win_create` as the local memory window. A simple fix exists. Consider the routine

```
subroutine MPE_WIN_FENCE(base, assert, win, ierr)
use mpi
double precision base(*)
integer assert, win, ierr
call MPI_WIN_FENCE(assert, win, ierr)
end
```

If we call this routine from our Fortran program instead of just `MPI_Win_fence`, passing it the same array (as `base`) that we used with `MPI_Win_create`, then the Fortran compiler will assume that we might have changed the variable `base` (the local window), particularly if we define `MPE_Win_fence` with the following interface definition:

```
INTERFACE MPE_WIN_FENCE
    subroutine MPE_WIN_FENCE(base, assert, win, ierr)
    double precision, intent(inout) :: base(*)
    integer, intent(in) :: assert, win
    integer, intent(out) :: ierr
    end subroutine MPE_WIN_FENCE
END INTERFACE
```

The MPI standard provides an alternative approach. The routine `MPI_F_-SYNC_REG`, available only in Fortran, takes a single argument, the variable that needs to be protected from the compiler. For example, if `base` is the variable, we would insert

```
call MPI_F_SYNC_REG(base)
```

after the call to `MPI_Win_fence`.

3.8   Performance Tuning for RMA Operations

MPI provides a number of ways to aid an MPI implementation in performing RMA operations efficiently. This section discusses how to specify special cases to `MPI_-Win_create` and `MPI_Win_fence` to allow the MPI implementation to optimize the RMA operations.

3.8.1   Options for `MPI_Win_create`

The `MPI_Win_create` call has an info argument that can be used to provide hints to the MPI implementation. Three predefined hints exist. Their info keys are:

accumulate_ordering. The value of this key controls how much the order in which a sequence of accumulate operations from the same origin process to the same target process respects the order in which they were called (program order). The default is to preserve the program order. See Section 4.6.1.

accumulate_ops. If the value is `same_op`, the user promises that concurrent accumulate operations to the same target location (displacement) will use the same MPI operation, such as `MPI_SUM`. If the value is `same_op_no_-op`, then concurrent accumulate operations to the same target location use either the same operation or `MPI_NO_OP`. The default value for this key is `same_op_no_op`.

no_locks. If the value is set to `true`, this key states that this local window is never used with locks (see Section 4.1 for a discussion of locks). None of the examples in this chapter use locks. This hint may be used with any RMA code that uses only `MPI_Win_fence` for synchronization.

The following example shows how to use `no_locks` with the info argument to `MPI_Win_create`.

```
MPI_Info info;
MPI_Info_create(&info);
MPI_Info_set(info, "no_locks", "true");
MPI_Win_create(..., info, ...);
MPI_Info_free(&info);
```

MPI implementations may ignore the `no_locks` key; however, it never hurts to provide this info value when creating a window object when locks are not used.

The MPI-3 standard, in an "advice to implementors" in Section 11.2.5, mentions that `MPI_Win_free` internally requires a barrier to ensure that all operations, from

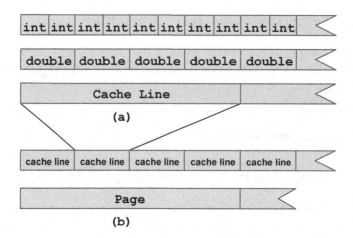

Figure 3.19: Alignments of data items. Part (a) shows how basic datatypes such as int and double fit into a cache line. Part (b) shows how cache lines fit into a memory page.

any source, have completed, unless every process involved in creating a window sets no_locks to true. Thus, while MPI_Win_free is collective over all the processes in the group that formed the window object, it need not be a barrier.

Choice of local window. The memory in a computer is organized into a hierarchy of elements, each with its own size. At the very top of the hierarchy are registers that hold a single word (often 32 or 64 bits) of data. The next level of hierarchy is usually one or more levels of cache. Each level of cache is made up of *cache lines*, 4 to 128 (or more) bytes in length. Below the cache memory are *memory pages*, typically 4K to 16K bytes (but may be larger) in size. Data motion in a computer usually happens in units of these natural sizes. For example, data is moved between memory and cache in units of the cache line size.

In addition, each larger item is typically *aligned* to begin at the start of the next smallest item. That is, a page always starts at the beginning of a cache line, and a cache line always starts at the beginning of a memory word. Another way to say this is that a smaller item never crosses a boundary between two larger items. This is shown in Figure 3.19. Note that the sizes and alignments are all nested.

Some MPI implementations will be more efficient if the base address is aligned on one of these boundaries; aligning on a page boundary will guarantee that the base address is also aligned on word and cache boundaries. It may also help if the size of the local window is an exact multiple of the page size, particularly for systems without hardware support for shared memory.

On some Unix systems, C users may use `posix_memalign` or `memalign` instead of `malloc` to get good data alignments for dynamically allocated data. The page size can be determined with the Unix function `getpagesize`.[9] Some Unix systems provide the function `valloc`, which returns memory aligned with the system page size.

Another option is to allocate the memory used for the local memory window with `MPI_Alloc_mem` or with `MPI_Win_allocate` and to free that memory with `MPI_Free_mem`. Because these routines are required for memory used with RMA lock and unlock routines, we discuss `MPI_Alloc_mem`, `MPI_Win_allocate`, and `MPI_Free_mem` routines with lock and unlock in the next chapter.

3.8.2   Options for `MPI_Win_fence`

`MPI_Win_fence` provides a general collective RMA synchronization, which makes it relatively simple to use. In the general case, each call to `MPI_Win_fence` will complete any RMA operations that were started since the last call to `MPI_Win_fence`. In addition, `MPI_Win_fence` must ensure that any local load and store operations are also complete before any RMA operations that follow the `MPI_Win_fence` call access the memory window. Ensuring that everything is in order is potentially expensive; for example, it may require flushing caches or making a copy of the memory window. To allow an implementation to optimize for cases where such operations are unnecessary because of the structure of the user's code, the `MPI_Win_fence` call has an argument, `assert`, that allows the user to provide information to MPI about how much work `MPI_Win_fence` may need to perform. The `assert` argument can contain any combination of the following four values; they can be combined by using bitwise or (|) in C and integer addition in Fortran.

MPI_MODE_NOSTORE. The local window was not updated by local stores (or local get or receive calls) since the last call to `MPI_Win_fence`. This refers to operations that occurred *before* the fence call.

   `MPI_MODE_NOSTORE` may be used, for example, for the ghost cells in a mesh computation, where the local window that contains the ghost cells is read only with local loads. This works only if the ghost cells are all that is exposed or if the entire array is used as read only and writes are done to another array.

---

[9]The function `getpagesize` returns the system page size, which may be different from the page size used by the hardware. However, the system page size is likely to be a good size to use because the system will want to size and align pages for efficient operation.

Consider the case where the data is read from the array b, the corresponding
window is called win_b, and the data is computed in the array a; a is not
in a memory window (or not in an overlapping memory window, as discussed
in Section 3.7.4). Since there are no stores to b between the two calls to
MPI_Win_fence, the MPI_MODE_NOSTORE assertion may be used on the
second call to MPI_Win_fence. This is shown below:

```
MPI_Win_create(b, n*sizeof(double), sizeof(double),
               MPI_INFO_NULL, MPI_COMM_WORLD, &win_b);
...
MPI_Win_fence(0, win_b);
MPI_Put(buf, m, MPI_DOUBLE, nbr, 0, m, MPI_DOUBLE, win_b);
...   update array a using information in array b
...   EXCEPT for any ghost cells
MPI_Win_fence(MPI_MODE_NOSTORE, win_b);
...   update the parts of a that depend on the ghost cells
...   in b
```

MPI_MODE_NOPUT. The local window will not be updated by put or accumulate
calls between this fence call and the next fence call.

This basically says that no changes will be made by remote processes to the
local window before the *next* fence call. The local process can modify the
data in the local memory window using stores. Another name for this mode
could have been "no RMA update."

This flag can help implementations that do not have hardware support for
memory coherency, by informing them that the memory window will not be
changed by any RMA operations (this includes hardware where a cache-flush
might otherwise be required to maintain correct operations).

MPI_MODE_NOPRECEDE. The fence will not complete any sequence of RMA calls
made by the process calling MPI_Win_fence. If this assertion is given by
any process in the window group, then it must be given by all processes in
the group. Thus, no RMA calls can be made by *any* process in the group
of the window, on this window object, since the last MPI_Win_fence call.
This refers to the operations that occurred *before* the fence call. It used to
state that no process in the window object's group made any RMA calls on
this window. In other words, there isn't anything to complete. Another name
for this mode could have been "no RMA completion."

MPI_MODE_NOSUCCEED. No RMA calls will be made on this window between this fence call and the next fence call. If the assertion is given by any process in the window group, then it must be given by all processes in the group. This is used to indicate that following this fence, no RMA calls will be made by any process in this window object's group before the next fence call. Another name for this mode could have been "no RMA start."

These assert flags may be combined. As an example, the code in Figure 3.8 can be augmented with all four of the assertion values:

```
call MPI_WIN_FENCE(MPI_MODE_NOPRECEDE, win, ierr)
! Put bottom edge into bottom neighbor's top ghost cells
top_ghost_disp = 1 + (nx+2)*(e-s+2)
call MPI_PUT(a(1,s), nx, MPI_DOUBLE_PRECISION, &
             bottom_nbr, top_ghost_disp, nx, &
             MPI_DOUBLE_PRECISION, win, ierr)
! Put top edge into top neighbor's bottom ghost cells
bottom_ghost_disp = 1
call MPI_PUT(a(1,e), nx, MPI_DOUBLE_PRECISION, &
             top_nbr, bottom_ghost_disp, nx, &
             MPI_DOUBLE_PRECISION, win, ierr)
call MPI_WIN_FENCE(MPI_MODE_NOSTORE + MPI_MODE_NOPUT + &
                   MPI_MODE_NOSUCCEED, win, ierr)
```

The first MPI_Win_fence call does not complete any RMA operations, and so MPI_MODE_NOPRECEDE may be used. Note that the window may have been updated by local stores; in fact, it almost certainly was, so MPI_MODE_NOSTORE must not be used in the first fence call.

The second fence call completes only RMA operations. Thus, MPI_MODE_NOSTORE can be used. Since no RMA calls follow the fence, we can use MPI_MODE_NOSUCCEED. MPI_MODE_NOPUT is redundant here because MPI_MODE_NOSUCCEED states that there are no RMA calls of any kind between this fence call and the next one. MPI_MODE_NOPUT could be used where MPI_Get operations were being made between two fence calls but no RMA put or accumulate operations.

Almost every use of MPI_Win_fence can specify some assert values. A good practice is to specify assert values because doing so allows the MPI implementation to optimize the performance of MPI_Win_fence and forces the programmer to examine closely how the MPI RMA operations are being used. Such examination will help detect any erroneous use of RMA that violates the rules set forth in Section 3.7.

4 Advanced Remote Memory Access

The previous chapter introduced remote memory access programming and showed how to use RMA for updating the ghost cells in a distributed mesh. This chapter explores some of the more advanced capabilities of RMA, including other ways to synchronize RMA communication and additional ways to specify communication, including read-modify-write operations.

4.1 Passive Target Synchronization

One requirement of the RMA routines in the previous chapter was the need for all processes that created a window object to call `MPI_Win_fence` to separate RMA operations from local loads and stores and to complete RMA operations. In other words, while the individual put, get, and accumulate operations are one sided and are called by a single process (instead of the two processes required to use send-receive-style message passing), we required a collective operation (`MPI_-Win_fence`) to complete the RMA operations. In this section, we will relax this requirement in two ways.

In Chapter 3, both the origin and target processes of an RMA operation must call `MPI_Win_fence` to complete the RMA call (along with all other processes that are in the window object's group). This is called *active target* synchronization, because the target is actively involved in the process. In many cases, however, a process may want to access data in a remote (target) process without that process being required to call any MPI routines. This is called *passive target* synchronization. In MPI, passive target synchronization is accomplished by using MPI *locks* at the origin process. When communication is targeted at a single process, this is accomplished with the routines `MPI_Win_lock` and `MPI_Win_unlock` at the origin process.

To perform a passive target RMA operation, one uses one-sided communication routines such as `MPI_Put`, `MPI_Get`, and/or `MPI_Accumulate`, just as when using active target synchronization. Instead of surrounding the RMA calls with calls to `MPI_Win_fence`, however, one begins the sequence of RMA calls with `MPI_Win_lock` and end the sequence of RMA calls with `MPI_Win_unlock`. The lock and unlock operations apply only to a specific remote window (specified by a rank), not the entire window object (that is, not all ranks); the specific window is indicated by a `rank` in the group of the window object. These two calls define an *access epoch*: between `MPI_Win_lock` and `MPI_Win_unlock`, a process may access the memory window of a remote process. The bindings for C and Fortran, respectively, for `MPI_Win_lock` and `MPI_Win_unlock` are shown in Tables 4.1

---

int **MPI_Win_lock**(int lock_type, int rank, int assert, MPI_Win win)

int **MPI_Win_unlock**(int rank, MPI_Win win)

Table 4.1: C bindings for locks

MPI_WIN_LOCK(lock_type, rank, assert, win, ierror)
      integer lock_type, rank, assert, win, ierror

MPI_WIN_UNLOCK(rank, win, ierror)
      integer rank, win, ierror

Table 4.2: Fortran bindings for locks

and 4.2. Another version permits access to *all* processes in a window; we'll see this later in this chapter.

The name `lock` is an unfortunate one because these MPI operations do not behave the way shared-memory locks or mutexes do. Instead, they are really "begin passive target access" and "end passive target access." Specifically, when referring to a remote window, all that the `MPI_Win_lock` and `MPI_Win_unlock` pair says is that the RMA operations between them will be complete when `MPI_Win_-unlock` returns; and, depending on the lock type (see below), they may occur atomically with respect to other RMA accesses to the same remote memory window. We will discuss this in more detail in Section 4.4. Only when referring to the local window (that is, when the `rank` in the lock call is the rank of the calling process in the window object's group) do these routines behave like conventional locks. The reason is that with passive target synchronization, one must use `MPI_Win_lock` and `MPI_Win_unlock` around accesses to ones own local window to ensure that RMA operations from other processes do not modify the data unexpectedly.

4.2   Implementing Blocking, Independent RMA Operations

The most elementary use of lock and unlock is to create a blocking version of the RMA data-movement commands that do not require the target to make any MPI calls. To do so, we simply surround the RMA call with lock and unlock. Figure 4.1 shows an implementation of a blocking put operation.

The use of `MPI_LOCK_SHARED` allows several RMA operations to act on the same window (not just window object) at the same time. If you want to ensure that only one process at a time can perform RMA operations on the target win-

```
int MPE_Blocking_put(const void *buf, int count,
                     MPI_Datatype dtype, int target_rank,
                     MPI_Aint target_offset, int target_count,
                     MPI_Datatype target_dtype, MPI_Win win)
{
    int err;

    MPI_Win_lock(MPI_LOCK_SHARED, target_rank, 0, win);
    err = MPI_Put(buf, count, dtype, target_rank, target_offset,
                  target_count, target_dtype, win);
    MPI_Win_unlock(target_rank, win);
    return err;
}
```

Figure 4.1: Blocking, independent (passive target) put operation

dow, MPI_LOCK_EXCLUSIVE must be used. This guarantees that no other RMA operation has any access, whether put, get, or accumulate, to the window at the target process.

In other words, MPI_LOCK_SHARED is used when the purpose of the lock is simply to allow one or more RMA operations to complete, independently of any action by the target or other process. When you want to guarantee atomic (undivided) access to a window on a particular process, MPI_LOCK_EXCLUSIVE must be used. We will see in Section 4.4 an example where MPI_LOCK_EXCLUSIVE is required.

Note that when MPI_LOCK_SHARED is used, the user must ensure that no concurrent operations access or modify the same or overlapping parts of the window, with the exception of multiple accumulate calls that all use the same type signatures and same operation (these are the same restrictions on MPI_Accumulate as in the previous chapter). MPI_LOCK_SHARED should be used primarily with MPI_Get when no chance exists that an RMA put or accumulate operation will be changing the contents of the window.

Using MPI_Win_lock in MPI protects only the window at a specific rank within a window object. This feature improves scalability: a distributed data structure is thus protected by separate locks on each process. We'll see how to gain access to all processes for passive target RMA in Section 4.8.2.

What if we want to permit overlapping puts? That is, what if we wish to relax the restriction that only non-overlapping sections of memory in the target window can be updated? Two approaches are possible. The first requires an exclusive lock rather than a shared lock. That is, you must change the lock type from MPI_-

LOCK_SHARED to MPI_LOCK_EXCLUSIVE. This ensures that only one blocking
put operation at a time can be performed on the window at the selected rank. While
correct, however, this approach prevents any concurrency in access to the window,
even for non-overlapping accesses. The second approach, as long as only predefined
datatypes or derived datatypes made up of the same predefined datatypes are used,
is to replace the call to MPI_Put with MPI_Accumulate, using the MPI_REPLACE
operation as described in Section 3.6.2.

4.3   Allocating Memory for MPI Windows

In Chapter 3, any variable or memory location could be used as the local window
for RMA operations. Passive target operations, however, can be more difficult to
implement. The MPI standard therefore allows implementations to restrict the use
of passive target RMA (that is, using MPI_Win_lock and MPI_Win_unlock)
to memory windows that have been allocated in specific ways. For most uses,
the best way in MPI-3 is to allocate the memory when the window is created,
using MPI_Win_allocate. One can allocate the memory separately by using
MPI_Alloc_mem and then provide it to MPI_Win_create. Both MPI_Win_-
allocate and MPI_Alloc_mem allocate size bytes of memory and return a
pointer to the allocated memory in baseptr. The following sections show how to
use MPI_Alloc_mem so that it is clear how the allocated memory is returned to
the user. The code to use MPI_Win_allocate is similar, with the only difference
being the additional arguments needed to create the window object. In most cases,
it is better to use MPI_Win_allocate because this allows the MPI implementation to coordinate the allocation of the memory across the processes in the group
that is forming the MPI window object.

4.3.1   Using **MPI_Alloc_mem** and **MPI_Win_allocate** from C

The C version of MPI_Alloc_mem uses the type void * for the returned type,
even though the actual parameter that must be passed is the address of a pointer
(e.g., void **). This choice of binding makes it easier to pass the address of
a pointer to a particular datatype. For example, the following code allocates 10
doubles:

```
double *d_ptr;
MPI_Alloc_mem(10*sizeof(double), MPI_INFO_NULL, &d_ptr);
```

If the last formal argument was typed as void **, the third actual argument
would need to be cast to that type:

---

int **MPI_Win_allocate**(MPI_Aint size, int disp_unit, MPI_Info info,
                MPI_Comm comm, void *baseptr, MPI_Win *win)

int **MPI_Alloc_mem**(MPI_Aint size, MPI_Info info, void *baseptr)

int **MPI_Free_mem**(void *base)

Table 4.3: C bindings for memory allocation and deallocation routines. The pointer is returned in `baseptr`.

```
MPI_Alloc_mem(10*sizeof(double), MPI_INFO_NULL, (void **)&d_ptr)
```

The MPI Forum felt that the convenience of avoiding the extra cast outweighed the potential confusion in the binding, since returning a pointer to an `int`, for example, requires an argument of type `int **`. The same approach is used by `MPI_Buffer_detach`, which also returns a pointer, and in the copy callback function used in attribute caching.

The `info` argument is provided to allow the user to specify, for example, different locations or properties for the allocated memory. For example, on a multichip node, specifying how the memory is allocated to the different chips might offer performance advantages. The null value, `MPI_INFO_NULL`, is always valid and will be the only value that we will use in our examples. No predefined info keys exist for use with `MPI_Alloc_mem`; implementations define the keys that they support.

The use of `MPI_Win_allocate` to allocate memory is similar. The parameters are similar to those of `MPI_Win_create` but return the memory that was allocated in `baseptr`. Using `MPI_Win_allocate` rather than separate `MPI_Alloc_-mem` and `MPI_Win_create` may allow the MPI implementation to optimize the allocation of memory and the communication of the information that is needed to create the `MPI_Win`.

To free memory allocated with `MPI_Alloc_mem` or `MPI_Win_allocate`, one must use the routine `MPI_Free_mem`. The C and Fortran bindings, respectively, for the memory allocation routines are shown in Tables 4.3 and 4.4.

4.3.2 Using **MPI_Alloc_mem** and **MPI_Win_allocate** from Fortran 2008

Fortran 2008 made major strides in providing a standard way to interoperate with routines written in C. In particular, one can now take a pointer returned from a

---

MPI_WIN_ALLOCATE(size, disp_unit, info, comm, baseptr, win, ierror)
        integer disp_unit, info, comm, win, ierror
        integer (kind=MPI_ADDRESS_KIND) size, baseptr

MPI_ALLOC_MEM(size, info, baseptr, ierror)
        integer info, ierror
        integer(kind=MPI_ADDRESS_KIND) size, baseptr

MPI_FREE_MEM(base, ierror)
        <type> base(*)
        integer ierror

Table 4.4: Fortran bindings for memory allocation and deallocation routines

C routine and associate it with a Fortran pointer. Using this interface, one can now use a Fortran standard interface to access memory allocated by MPI. While we have not used the Fortran 2008 binding for MPI in this book, other than in Chapter 11, this is one place where the Fortran 2008 binding can't follow the C binding.

Using MPI_Alloc_mem or MPI_Win_allocate from Fortran 2008 to allocate memory is a two-step process. First, obtain a C-style pointer from the MPI routine. In Fortran 2008, such a pointer is declared with type (C_PTR), using the ISO_-C_BINDING. Second, that C pointer is associated with a Fortran pointer by calling the Fortran routine C_F_POINTER. The following example allocates a 10 × 10 array of double-precision values, using MPI_Alloc_mem, whose Fortran 2008 binding is shown in Table 4.5:

```
use mpi_f08
use, intrinsic :: ISO_C_BINDING
type(C_PTR) :: p
double precision, dimension(:,:), pointer :: a
integer, dimension(2) :: arrayshape
...
! Determine the size of storage to allocate
arrayshape = (/10,10/)
call MPI_Sizeof(1.0d0, sizeofdouble, ierr)
size = sizeofdouble * arrayshape(1) * arrayshape(2)
! Get the C pointer from MPI
call MPI_Alloc_mem(size, MPI_INFO_NULL, p, ierr)
! Associate the C pointer with the Fortran pointer
! for the array a with the dimensions given by arrayshape
call C_F_POINTER(p, a, arrayshape)
```

MPI_Alloc_mem(size, info, baseptr, ierror)
    use, intrinsic :: ISO_C_BINDING, only : C_PTR
    integer(kind=MPI_ADDRESS_KIND), intent(in) :: size
    type(MPI_Info), intent(in) :: info
    type(C_PTR), intent(out) :: baseptr
    integer, optional, intent(out) :: ierror

MPI_Win_allocate(size, disp_unit, info, comm, baseptr, win, ierror)
    use, intrinsic :: ISO_C_BINDING, only : C_PTR
    integer(kind=MPI_ADDRESS_KIND), intent(in) :: size
    integer, intent(in) :: disp_unit
    type(MPI_Info), intent(in) :: info
    type(MPI_Comm), intent(in) :: comm
    type(C_PTR), intent(out) :: baseptr
    type(MPI_Win), intent(out) :: win
    integer, optional, intent(out) :: ierror

MPI_Free_mem(base, ierror)
    type(*), dimension(..), intent(in), asynchronous :: base
    integer, optional, intent(out) :: ierror

Table 4.5: Fortran definition of `MPI_Alloc_mem`, `MPI_Win_allocate`, and `MPI_Free_mem` in the `mpi_f08` module.

```
...
! Free the memory
call MPI_Free_mem(a, ierr)
```

This code works for compilers that support the C_PTR type from the ISO_C_-BINDING. If your compiler does not support this or if you do not have the mpi_f08 module, you may need to use a nonstandard, though common, extension to Fortran, described next.

4.3.3 Using MPI_ALLOC_MEM and MPI_WIN_ALLOCATE from Older Fortran

Older versions of Fortran do not have pointers of the same kind that C does. One cannot use the MPI memory allocation routines from standard-conforming versions of Fortran before Fortran 2008. However, some Fortran implementations provide an extension, often referred to as "Cray pointers" or "integer pointers," that may be used. A "Cray pointer" is much like a C pointer rather than a Fortran 90

pointer. In the declaration, a "Cray pointer" is named, and the Fortran variable
that the pointer will point at is also named. The space for this second variable is
not allocated. In the following example, the pointer is p, and the variable it points
to is u(0:50,0:20).

```
double precision u
pointer (p, u(0:50,0:20))
integer (kind=MPI_ADDRESS_KIND) size
integer sizeofdouble, ierror
! careful with size (must be MPI_ADDRESS_KIND)
call MPI_SIZEOF(1.0d0, sizeofdouble, ierror)
size = 51 * 21 * sizeofdouble
call MPI_ALLOC_MEM(size, MPI_INFO_NULL, p, ierror)
...
... program may now refer to u, including passing it
... to MPI_WIN_CREATE
...
call MPI_FREE_MEM(u, ierror)   ! not p!
```

Note that in MPI_Free_mem, the variable that the pointer points at, not the
pointer itself, is passed.

If "Cray pointers" are not available, the best approach is often to use a C program
to allocate the array with MPI_Win_allocate or MPI_Alloc_mem and then pass
this array as an argument to a Fortran routine.

4.4   Another Version of NXTVAL

In *Using MPI* [26], Section 7.1.2, we introduced the NXTVAL routine. This routine provided a shared counter; any process could request a value from this counter,
which was then incremented. This is a "fetch-and-add" operation, a common building block for certain types of distributed algorithms. The versions presented in
Using MPI used point-to-point message passing and required either a separate
process or thread or periodic polling by one process. In this section, we will see
how to implement a fetch-and-add operation using RMA. Because this is such a
powerful building block, we generalize our NXTVAL routine to support any number
of counters, and for scalability, we will distribute the counters among the processes.

Our first attempt might look something like the following, where the counter is
on process rank and at displacement idx in the window:

```
/* This code is erroneous */
int one = 1;
MPI_Win_allocate(..., &win);
```

```
...
MPI_Win_lock(MPI_LOCK_EXCLUSIVE, rank, 0, win);
MPI_Get(&value, 1, MPI_INT, rank, idx, 1, MPI_INT, win);
MPI_Accumulate(&one, 1, MPI_INT,
               rank, idx, 1, MPI_INT, MPI_SUM, win);
MPI_Win_unlock(rank, win);
```

However, this is not correct: two problems exist. First, the MPI standard explicitly says that accessing (with an RMA get such as MPI_Get or a local load) and updating (with an RMA put or accumulate) the same location in the same access epoch (the time between two MPI_Win_fence calls or MPI_Win_lock and MPI_Win_unlock) has undefined behavior (in MPI-2, it was erroneous). Even if the MPI standard permitted overlapping accesses by MPI_Accumulate and MPI_Get, these functions are nonblocking and can complete in any order as long as they complete by the time MPI_Win_unlock returns (with one exception—sequences of accumulate calls are ordered by default; see Section 4.6.1). The MPI standard does not specify an order in which RMA operations must complete, other than for sequences consisting only of RMA accumulate operations, as discussed in Section 4.6.1.

In some implementations, these operations may complete in the order that they appear, particularly on loosely coupled systems with no shared-memory hardware support. On other systems, enforcing an ordering may be expensive, and hence the MPI Forum decided not to require it in general. For example, in applications such as the ghost-point exchange in Section 3.6.1, ordering is not required, and enforcing an ordering can reduce performance. For operations such as fetch and add, however, the lack of ordered operations is inconvenient. Specifically, the lack of ordering means that loosening the access restrictions to allow overlapping access from the same origin process isn't sufficient to allow using the above code to implement fetch and add.

Because of the weak synchronization provided by MPI_Win_lock and MPI_Win_unlock and the restrictions on overlapping access to memory windows by RMA operations, it turns out to be surprisingly hard to implement a fetch-and-add operation using only the three operations MPI_Put, MPI_Get, and MPI_Accumulate (See [27], Section 6.5.4). Recognizing this situation and the general value of the routines that combine a read, modify, and write of the new value into a single atomic (unbreakable) operation, MPI-3 expanded the one-sided communication routines with several routines for such operations. Before showing these routines, however, we will start with another approach that doesn't work. Understanding why it doesn't work will provide a better understanding of `MPI_Win_-lock` and `MPI_Win_unlock`.

4.4.1   The Nonblocking Lock

An obvious approach for implementing fetch and add is to use two locks: one to complete the `MPI_Get` and, in a separate step, the `MPI_Accumulate` operations, and the other to establish a *critical section*. Only one process is allowed to be "in" the critical section at any time; in shared-memory code locks are commonly used to implement critical sections. Thus, at first glance, it looks like we could use a window object where the counters are distributed among the processes with ranks 0 to `size-1` (`size` being the size of the communicator used to create `counterWin`) and where an exclusive lock on rank `size-1` is used solely to provide the critical section. The code for NXTVAL might look like that in Figure 4.2.

But this code will not work because `MPI_Win_lock`, except when called with the target rank the same as the rank of the calling process, may be *nonblocking*. That is, just as the RMA put, get, and accumulate operations are nonblocking, so may `MPI_Win_lock` be nonblocking. All the `MPI_Win_lock` call does is to establish an access epoch, indicating that RMA calls on the specified window object and rank may be made, until the matching `MPI_Win_unlock`. If the lock type is `MPI_LOCK_EXCLUSIVE`, it also ensures that the RMA operations are performed atomically with respect to other processes at the target.

Note that when `MPI_Win_lock` is called with the rank of the calling process (so the lock is being acquired for the local memory window), the MPI standard specifies that `MPI_Win_lock` must block until the lock is acquired. The reason is that when using passive target RMA operations, one must call `MPI_Win_lock` and `MPI_Win_unlock` around any local loads and stores (See Section 4.10). Since the local loads and stores may happen at any time, the `MPI_Win_lock` call in this particular case must block until the lock is acquired. But in all other cases, `MPI_Win_lock` may be nonblocking. And it turns out that this is important for performance in the case where the amount of data moved in the RMA operation is small [68].

4.4.2   NXTVAL with `MPI_Fetch_and_op`

What we need is a way to both read and update a value in a single, unbreakable step. In general, such operations are called read-modify-write operations. MPI-3 added several of these operations, and one of them is just what we need for NXTVAL. This operation is the "fetch-and-perform operation" and is accomplished

```
/* Erroneous code */
int MPE_Counter_nxtval(MPI_Win counterWin, int num, int *value)
{
    int one = 1;
    int rank, size;
    MPI_Aint idx;
    /* Computed rank and idx for counter "num" */
    /* Counters are distributed across the first size-1 processes;
       the last process is used for the exclusive lock */
    ... size = ...;  rank = num % (size-1); idx = num / (size-1);

    /* Acquire access to the counter (on rank size-1) */
    MPI_Win_lock(MPI_LOCK_EXCLUSIVE, size-1, 0, counterWin);

    /* Once we get the lock, we can fetch the counter value */
    MPI_Win_lock(MPI_LOCK_SHARED, rank, MPI_MODE_NOCHECK,
                 counterWin);
    MPI_Get(value, 1, MPI_INT, rank, idx, 1, MPI_INT, counterWin);
    MPI_Win_unlock(0, counterWin);

    /* And update the value */
    MPI_Win_lock(MPI_LOCK_SHARED, rank, MPI_MODE_NOCHECK,
        counterWin);
    MPI_Accumulate(&one, 1, MPI_INT, rank, idx, 1, MPI_INT,
        MPI_SUM, counterWin);
    MPI_Win_unlock(rank, counterWin);

    /* Release the counter */
    MPI_Win_unlock(size-1, counterWin);
    return 0;
}
```

Figure 4.2: Erroneous attempt to implement NXTVAL using two locks

with the routines MPI_Get_accumulate or MPI_Fetch_and_op. MPI_Get_-
accumulate is a generalization of MPI_Accumulate and follows similar rules.
Because a "fetch and perform operation" is often used with a single word, MPI
provides MPI_Fetch_and_op, a simplified version of MPI_Get_accumulate for
operating on a single data item. This simplified version is just what we need.
The parameters for MPI_Fetch_and_op are these: a single value to accumulate
(origin_addr) of type datatype with operation op at location target_disp

---

int **MPI_Fetch_and_op**(const void *origin_addr, void *result_addr,
             MPI_Datatype datatype, int target_rank, MPI_Aint target_disp,
             MPI_Op op, MPI_Win win)

Table 4.6: C binding for RMA fetch and accumulate

MPI_FETCH_AND_OP(origin_addr, result_addr, datatype, target_rank, target_disp,
             op, win, ierror)
             <type> origin_addr(*), result_addr(*)
             integer(kind=MPI_ADDRESS_KIND) target_disp
             integer datatype, target_rank, op, win, ierror

Table 4.7: Fortran binding for RMA fetch and accumulate

in window object `win`. These are almost identical to `MPI_Accumulate`, except that only one element is accumulated. The major difference is the second argument, `result_addr`. The value of the target location before the accumulate operation is returned here. The C and Fortran bindings, respectively, are shown in Tables 4.6 and 4.7.

With this function, the implementation of NXTVAL is simple and is shown in Figure 4.3. Note that this code relies on computing the rank and displacement for the selected counter; that computation in turn requires knowing the number of processes in the MPI memory window (`counterWin`). The next section shows how we make this value available to this code.

4.4.3   Window Attributes

To implement NXTVAL for any number of counters, we need to know how many processes are in the group of the memory window. The classic solution is to define a new structure that contains this size and the other data needed by the implementation, which in this case is just the memory window `counterWin`. Another need also exists. The routine works by creating an MPI window object that the user passes to the counter routine when a new value is needed. When the user is done with the routine, the user frees the window by using `MPI_Win_free`. However, this does not free the allocated memory. Even though this is a small amount of memory, it is a storage leak and in a long-running application could eventually exhaust the available memory. The classic solution is to require the user to call a

```
int MPE_Counter_nxtval(MPI_Win counterWin, int counterNum,
    int *value)
{
    const int one = 1;
    int        lrank, flag, size, *attrval;
    MPI_Aint  lidx;
    /* Compute the location of the counter */
    MPI_Win_get_attr(counterWin, MPE_COUNTER_KEYVAL, &attrval,
        &flag);
    if (!flag) return -1;   /* Error: counterWin not correctly
                                setup */
    size = (MPI_Aint)attrval;   /* We stored the integer as a
                                    pointer */
    lrank = counterNum % size;
    lidx  = counterNum / size;
    /* Update and return the counter */
    MPI_Win_lock(MPI_LOCK_SHARED, 0, lrank, counterWin);
    MPI_Fetch_and_op(&one, value, MPI_INT,
                    lrank, lidx, MPI_SUM, counterWin);
    MPI_Win_unlock(lrank, counterWin);
    return 0;
}
```

Figure 4.3: Implementing a shared counter

free routine, perhaps called MPE_Counter_free. However, this depends on the user's remembering to call this routine and not simply calling MPI_Win_free.

We'll see how to accomplish both these needs by using *attributes*. Attributes on MPI communicators were introduced in *Using MPI* [26], Section 6.2. The MPI-2 standard added attributes to both MPI datatypes and RMA window objects. Attributes allow information to be cached on a window object according to a keyval. In addition, attributes allow the user to associate routines that are called when the object is duplicated or freed. The C and Fortran bindings, respectively, for window attributes are shown in Tables 4.8 and 4.9.

With these functions, we can create a keyval (MPE_COUNTER_KEYVAL in our example) that is known only to the NXTVAL routines. We will use this attribute value to remember the size of the communicator that was used to form the memory window. In addition, we use the attribute to provide a function that is called automatically by the MPI implementation when the window object is freed. This function is the delete routine associated with the keyval and is specified as the

---

int **MPI_Win_create_keyval**(MPI_Win_copy_attr_function *win_copy_attr_fn,
      MPI_Win_delete_attr_function *win_delete_attr_fn, int *win_keyval,
      void *extra_state)

int **MPI_Win_free_keyval**(int *win_keyval)

int **MPI_Win_set_attr**(MPI_Win win, int win_keyval, void *attribute_val)

int **MPI_Win_get_attr**(MPI_Win win, int win_keyval, void *attribute_val, int *flag)

int **MPI_Win_delete_attr**(MPI_Win win, int win_keyval)

Table 4.8: C bindings for window object attribute routines

MPI_WIN_CREATE_KEYVAL(win_copy_attr_fn, win_delete_attr_fn, win_keyval,
      extra_state, ierror)
      external win_copy_attr_fn, win_delete_attr_fn
      integer win_keyval, ierror
      integer(kind=MPI_ADDRESS_KIND) extra_state

MPI_WIN_FREE_KEYVAL(win_keyval, ierror)
      integer win_keyval, ierror

MPI_WIN_SET_ATTR(win, win_keyval, attribute_val, ierror)
      integer win, win_keyval, ierror
      integer(kind=MPI_ADDRESS_KIND) attribute_val

MPI_WIN_GET_ATTR(win, win_keyval, attribute_val, flag, ierror)
      integer win, win_keyval, ierror
      integer(kind=MPI_ADDRESS_KIND) attribute_val
      logical flag

MPI_WIN_DELETE_ATTR(win, win_keyval, ierror)
      integer win, win_keyval, ierror

Table 4.9: Fortran bindings for window object attribute routines

MPI_Win_delete_fn argument of the keyval when the attribute key is created.

The code to create the MPI_Win for NXTVAL, including the creation and use of the attribute to ensure that the allocated data is freed, is shown in Figure 4.4. Note that we have used MPI_Alloc_mem to create the counter memory.

The code to free the counters is shown in Figure 4.5. With this code, a separate MPE_Counter_free routine is unnecessary; the user may simply use MPI_-Win_free on the counter window. This code introduces one of five predefined attributes on memory windows: MPI_WIN_BASE provides the base address of the local window, and this allows us to determine the address of memory that we need to free.

The four other attributes are MPI_WIN_SIZE for the size (in bytes) of the local memory window, MPI_WIN_DISP_UNIT for the displacement unit chosen when the window object was created, MPI_WIN_CREATE_FLAVOR for which routine was used to create the window (e.g., MPI_WIN_FLAVOR_CREATE is the value that the attribute points to if MPI_Win_create was used to create the window object), and MPI_WIN_MODEL for the memory model for the window (see Section 4.10).

A curious feature.   The MPI_Win_create_keyval routine contains a MPI_-Win_copy_attr_function. Under no circumstance, however, would this routine be called. For communicators and datatypes, the respective duplicate functions (MPI_Comm_dup and MPI_Type_dup) are the only functions that cause a keyval's copy function to be invoked. But as we have mentioned before, the rules for overlapping accesses make any kind of "duplicate window" operation nearly useless. Thus, as the MPI standard is currently written, the copy function provided when creating a keyval for a window object has no purpose.

If the MPI standard were to be extended, an MPI_Win_dup function could be defined, perhaps by loosening the restrictions on overlapping access to memory windows or by having MPI_Win_dup allocate new memory windows. In that case, a copy function would become important. By providing the copy function argument now, the MPI Forum has ensured that future extensions are not constrained.

4.5   An RMA Mutex

For many operations, one wants to be able to establish a critical section or mutual exclusion among the processes. A simple way to do so is to use a counter. The value is initially zero, indicating that no process holds the mutex. To attempt to obtain the mutex, a process uses a fetch-and-increment operation to add one to the counter. If the value was zero, the process now holds the mutex. If the

```
extern int MPE_COUNTER_KEYVAL;
extern int MPEi_CounterFree(MPI_Win counter_win, int keyval,
                            void *attr_val, void *extra_state);

void MPE_Counter_create(MPI_Comm comm, int num,
                        MPI_Win *counter_win)
{
  int size, rank, lnum, lleft, i, *counterMem=0;
  MPI_Aint counterSize;

  MPI_Comm_rank(comm, &rank);
  MPI_Comm_size(comm, &size);

  lnum  = num / size;
  lleft = num % size;
  if (rank < lleft) lnum++;
  counterSize = lnum * sizeof(int);
  if (counterSize > 0) {
    MPI_Alloc_mem(counterSize, MPI_INFO_NULL, &counterMem);
    for (i=0; i<lnum; i++) counterMem[i] = 0;
  }
  /* By using MPI_Alloc_mem first, we ensure that the initial
     value of the counters are zero.  See text */
  MPI_Win_create(counterMem, counterSize, sizeof(int),
                 MPI_INFO_NULL, comm, counter_win);

  /* Create key if necessary and store the number of counters */
  if (MPE_COUNTER_KEYVAL == MPI_KEYVAL_INVALID) {
    MPI_Win_create_keyval(MPI_WIN_NULL_COPY_FN,
                          MPEi_CounterFree,
                          &MPE_COUNTER_KEYVAL, NULL);
  }
  MPI_Win_set_attr(*counter_win, MPE_COUNTER_KEYVAL,
                   (void*)(MPI_Aint)num);
}
```

Figure 4.4: Code to create the window object and counter memory used for NXTVAL

original value was not zero (because some other process acquired the mutex first), then the process must decrement the counter by one and try again. We can use MPI_Fetch_and_op to implement this feature, as shown in Figure 4.6. Similar to NXTVAL, our routine supports an arbitrary number of mutexes and uses the same

```
int MPEi_CounterFree(MPI_Win counter_win, int keyval,
                     void *attr_val, void *extra_state)
{
  int counter_flag, *counterMem;

  MPI_Win_get_attr(counter_win, MPI_WIN_BASE,
                   &counterMem, &counter_flag);

  /* Free the memory used by the counter */
  if (counter_flag && counterMem)
    MPI_Free_mem(counterMem);

  return MPI_SUCCESS;
}
```

Figure 4.5: Routine to free memory allocated in NXTVAL, using the delete function on the keyval MPE_COUNTER_KEYVAL

distribution of the counters among the processes of the memory window.

This example introduces a new routine (also new to MPI, added in MPI-3), MPI_Win_flush. This routine can be used within a passive target access epoch to force the completion of all RMA routines called to that point that target the process rank specified in the call to the flush routine. In this case, the call to MPI_Win_flush causes the MPI_Fetch_and_op to complete, allowing the code to examine the result in oldval. Without the call to MPI_Win_flush, it would be necessary to end the access epoch by calling MPI_Win_unlock, then calling MPI_Win_lock again if oldval was not zero so that MPI_Accumulate could be called. MPI_Win_flush completes all pending operations from the calling process to the indicated target process at both the origin and the target process. The routine MPI_Win_flush_local completes RMA operations locally, that is, just at the origin process. After MPI_Win_flush_local returns, all buffers passed to the pending RMA routines may be reused. In this code, we could have used MPI_Win_flush_local because the MPI_Fetch_and_op is atomic; and once the result value is returned in oldval, the code can continue. The C and Fortran bindings, respectively, for these routines are shown in Tables 4.10 and 4.11.

The routine to release the mutex is even simpler; we need only decrement the counter, using MPI_Accumulate, as shown in Figure 4.7.

This implementation has its drawbacks; however, it is correct and reliable. The implementation of fast, fair, and scalable mutexes and other shared data structures

```
#include "mpi.h"
extern int MPE_MUTEX_KEYVAL;
int MPE_Mutex_acquire(MPI_Win mutex_win, int num) {
  int      mone = -1, one=1, oldval;
  int      lrank, flag, size, *attrval;
  MPI_Aint lidx;

  /* Compute the location of the counter */
  MPI_Win_get_attr(mutex_win, MPE_MUTEX_KEYVAL, &attrval, &flag);
  if (!flag) return -1;   /* Error: counterWin not setup */
  size = (int)(MPI_Aint)attrval;   /* We stored the integer as a
                                      pointer */
  lrank = num % size; lidx  = num / size;

  MPI_Win_lock(MPI_LOCK_SHARED, lrank, 0, mutex_win);
  do {
    MPI_Fetch_and_op(&one, &oldval, MPI_INT,
                     lrank, lidx, MPI_SUM, mutex_win);
    MPI_Win_flush(lrank, mutex_win);
    if (oldval == 0) break;
    MPI_Accumulate(&mone, 1, MPI_INT, lrank, lidx, 1, MPI_INT,
                   MPI_SUM, mutex_win);
    MPI_Win_flush(lrank, mutex_win);
    /* We could wait a little bit, depending on oldval */
  } while (1);
  MPI_Win_unlock(lrank, mutex_win);
  return 0;
}
```

Figure 4.6: Simple mutex implemented with fetch and op: acquire

int **MPI_Win_flush**(int rank, MPI_Win win)

int **MPI_Win_flush_local**(int rank, MPI_Win win)

Table 4.10: C bindings for routines to complete pending RMA operations

```
#include "mpi.h"
extern int MPE_MUTEX_KEYVAL;
int MPE_Mutex_release(MPI_Win mutex_win, int num)
{
  int mone = -1;
  int      lrank, flag, size, *attrval;
  MPI_Aint lidx;

  /* Compute the location of the counter */
  MPI_Win_get_attr(mutex_win, MPE_MUTEX_KEYVAL, &attrval, &flag);
  if (!flag) return -1;          /* Error: counterWin setup */
  size = (int)(MPI_Aint)attrval; /* We stored the integer as a
                                         pointer */
  lrank = num % size; lidx  = num / size;

  MPI_Win_lock(MPI_LOCK_SHARED, lrank, 0, mutex_win);
  MPI_Accumulate(&mone, 1, MPI_INT, lrank, lidx, 1, MPI_INT,
              MPI_SUM, mutex_win);
  MPI_Win_unlock(lrank, mutex_win);
  return 0;
}
```

Figure 4.7: Simple mutex implemented with fetch and op: release

MPI_WIN_FLUSH(rank, win, ierror)
          integer rank, win, ierror

MPI_WIN_FLUSH_LOCAL(rank, win, ierror)
          integer rank, win, ierror

Table 4.11: Fortran bindings for routines to complete pending RMA operations

is a major area of study; see [2, 48, 72] for some classic examples of the issues that arise in different environments.

4.6   Global Arrays

As an example of how an existing high-level library for one-sided operations can be implemented using the standard MPI one-sided operations, we consider the Global Arrays library [43, 50].

The Global Arrays library is a collection of routines that allows the user to define and manipulate a multidimensional array that is distributed across all processes of a parallel program. A number of different datatypes are supported, including `integer`, `real`, `double precision`, and `complex`. The Global Arrays library is large and powerful; in addition to operations for writing to and reading from any part of a global array, it provides a range of operations from linear algebra, including `ga_diag` for solving the generalized eigenvalue problem, `ga_lu_solve` for solving a system of linear equations by LU factorization, and `ga_dgemm` for performing matrix-matrix multiplies.

In this section we describe an implementation of a small subset of a library similar to the Global Arrays library. Our simple subset has the following routines:

ga_create. Creates a new global array.

ga_free. Frees a global array.

ga_put. Puts data into an arbitrary 2-D subsection of a global array.

ga_get. Gets data from an arbitrary 2-D subsection of a global array.

ga_acc. Accumulates data into an arbitrary 2-D subsection of a global array. Unlike `MPI_Accumulate`, the entire accumulation is atomic.

The major differences between our library and the Global Arrays library, beyond offering far fewer capabilities, are the simpler distribution of the global array among processes (to simplify the code that we present) and the more general datatypes and process groups. The latter come essentially "for free" by exploiting the datatypes and groups in MPI.

Most of these operations are fairly obvious. The `ga_create` and `ga_free` are needed to manage the global array itself. The routines `ga_put`, `ga_get`, and `ga_acc` are similar to `MPI_Put`, `MPI_Get`, and `MPI_Accumulate`, though with one important difference for `MPI_Accumulate` as mentioned above: the accumulate operation is atomic for the entire operation, not on an element-by-element basis.

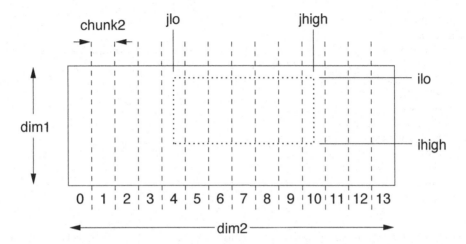

Figure 4.8: Decomposition of a global 2-D array. The rectangle given by coordinates (ilo, jlo) to (ihigh, jhigh) shows a typical region that can be accessed or modified with the global array routines. Vertical dashed lines show the decomposition of the global array across 14 processes. The global array has dimensions dim1 by dim2.

Let's begin with an overview of the design. We use a pointer to a structure,[1] called GA, which contains information about the global array. For simplicity in the examples, we require that the array have two dimensions and be decomposed into groups of columns as shown in Figure 4.8. We also assume Fortran ordering and indexes that start from one. Thus, the local rectangles on each process are stored in contiguous memory locations.

This design immediately gives us most of the members of the data pointed at by GA: we need an MPI window object to contain the global array and some ints to hold the sizes of the array and how it is decomposed among the processes. It is also useful to know the MPI datatype that corresponds to the data type for the array and the size of an element of this data type. For cases where the datatype is MPI_-INTEGER, MPI_DOUBLE_PRECISION, or MPI_DOUBLE_COMPLEX, this matches the original Global Arrays library. In our version, we can allow any contiguous datatype (we will use the size, not the extent, of the datatype in our example code, again for simplicity). The ga->lock_win element is explained in Section 4.6.3.

---

[1] We use a pointer to the structure instead of the structure itself so that users always see the pointer. This approach improves modularity and makes it easier to modify the implementation without forcing users to rebuild all their code.

```
#include "mpi.h"
#include <stdlib.h>
/* We make GA a pointer to this structure so that users always
   have a pointer, never the actual structure */
typedef struct _GA {
    MPI_Win        ga_win;
    MPI_Win        lock_win;
    /* Datatype and size */
    MPI_Datatype dtype;
    int            dtype_size;
    /* sizes of the global array */
    int            dim1, dim2, chunk2;
} *GA;
```

Figure 4.9: Header file for global arrays. Additional information, such as the address and size of the local memory window, could be stored here as well.

The contents of a GA are shown in the header file in Figure 4.9. The implementation of our GA library is in C; a Fortran interface may be provided by using tools such as bfort [28].

4.6.1 Create and Free

Now that we have all the members of GA, we can describe the code to create and free a new global array.

The code for ga_create is shown in Figure 4.10. The routine MPE_Mutex_-create is used to create one mutex for every process in the window object. This will be used to enforce the semantics of accesses in our global array library, which requires that accumulate updates be atomic for the entire accumulate, not just each element as in MPI.

This code shows the use of the info argument in the call to create the window. For example, consider this code:

```
MPI_Win_lock(MPI_LOCK_SHARED, trank, 0, win);
MPI_Accumulate(buf1, n, MPI_INT,
               trank, 0, n, MPI_INT, MPI_SUM, win);
MPI_Accumulate(buf2, n, MPI_INT,
               trank, 0, n, MPI_INT, MPI_SUM, win);
MPI_Win_unlock(trank, win);
```

```
#include "ga.h"
int ga_create(MPI_Comm comm, int dim1, int dim2,
              MPI_Datatype dtype, GA *ga)
{
    GA        new_ga;
    int       size, chunk2, sizeoftype;
    MPI_Aint  local_size;
    MPI_Info  info;
    void      *ga_win_ptr;

    /* Get a new structure */
    new_ga = (GA)malloc(sizeof(struct _GA));
    if (!new_ga) return 0;
    /* Determine size of GA memory */
    MPI_Comm_size(comm, &size);
    chunk2 = dim2 / size;
    /* Require size to exactly divide dim2 */
    if ((dim2 % size) != 0) MPI_Abort(comm, 1);
    MPI_Type_size(dtype, &sizeoftype);
    local_size = dim1 * chunk2 * sizeoftype;

    /* Specify ordering of accumulate operations (this is the
       default behavior in MPI-3) */
    MPI_Info_create(&info);
    MPI_Info_set(info,"accumulate_ordering", "rar,raw,war,waw");

    /* Allocate memory and create window */
    MPI_Win_allocate(local_size, sizeoftype, info, comm,
                     &ga_win_ptr, &new_ga->ga_win);
    MPI_Info_free(&info);

    /* Create critical section window */
    MPE_Mutex_create(comm, size, &new_ga->lock_win);

    /* Save other data and return */
    new_ga->dtype      = dtype;   new_ga->dtype_size = sizeoftype;
    new_ga->dim1       = dim1;    new_ga->dim2       = dim2;
    new_ga->chunk2     = chunk2;
    *ga                = new_ga;
    return 1;
}
```

Figure 4.10: Code to create a global array

MPI guarantees that the first `MPI_Accumulate` will complete before the second. This is often what the programmer expects (even though these routines are non-blocking), but it can reduce performance, because the MPI implementation must ensure that order of completion. The info key `accumulate_ordering` allows the user to specify the ordering that is required for accumulate operations on a window. Ordering applies only to accumulate operations; regular put and get operations are unordered (but we can use `MPI_Win_flush` to force them to complete, which provides a partial ordering). The values of this key are any combination of the following, separated by commas:

rar. Read after read. Reads complete at the target in the order in which they are issued. (There are several accumulate routines, such as `MPI_Get_-accumulate` and `MPI_Fetch_and_op`, that read and return data.)

raw. Read after write. Reads complete at the target *after* any writes that were issued before the reads.

war. Write after read. Writes complete at the target *after* any reads that were issued before the writes.

waw. Write after write. Writes complete at the target in the order in which they are issued.

none. No ordering.

The default value for `accumulate_ordering` is `rar,raw,war,waw`. To allow the MPI implementation maximum flexibility in processing accumulate operations, you should specify the value as `none`. MPI-2 provided no control of this ordering; that behavior is the same as specifying `none` for `accumulate_ordering`.

The code to free a global array is shown in Figure 4.11. Similar to the code for the NXTVAL routine, we use the window attribute `MPI_WIN_BASE` to find the memory that must be freed after the window object for the global array is freed.

An alternative to using a GA structure is to use the MPI window object, specifically `ga_win`, and use window attributes to store the rest of the data, as we did for the NXTVAL routine.

4.6.2   Put and Get

The routines for `ga_put` and `ga_get` are relatively simple. The code for `ga_put` is shown in Figure 4.12; `ga_get` is similar. The basic algorithm is as follows:

```
#include "ga.h"
int ga_free(GA ga)
{
    int flag;
    void *ga_win_ptr;

    MPI_Win_get_attr(ga->ga_win, MPI_WIN_BASE, &ga_win_ptr,
                     &flag);
    MPI_Win_free(&ga->ga_win);
    if (flag && ga_win_ptr)
        MPI_Free_mem(ga_win_ptr);
    MPE_Mutex_free(&ga->lock_win);

    free(ga);
    return 0;
}
```

Figure 4.11: Code to free a global array

1. Determine the rank of the process holding the leftmost column to update (ga_put) or get (ga_get).

2. Acquire a mutex to ensure that no other process is updating this process. We'll see in the description of ga_acc why MPI_LOCK_EXCLUSIVE cannot be used in this case.

3. Begin an access epoch for that rank.

4. For each column of data to be updated or fetched from that target process, perform the RMA (put or get) operation.

5. Complete the RMA.

6. Release the mutex.

7. Continue to the next rank until the last specified column (jhigh) has been reached.

For simplicity, these routines put or get one column of data at a time; a more sophisticated implementation would check for special cases, such as entire columns, or use an MPI datatype created with MPI_Type_vector to access all the required columns on a remote process with a single RMA call. Using an MPI datatype

```
#include "ga.h"
int ga_put(GA ga, int ilo, int ihigh, int jlo, int jhigh,
           void *buf)
{
    int       jcur, jfirst, jlast, j, rank;
    MPI_Aint disp;

    jcur = jlo;
    while (jcur <= jhigh) {
        rank   = (jcur - 1) /ga->chunk2;
        jfirst = rank * ga->chunk2 + 1;
        jlast  = (rank + 1) * ga->chunk2;
        if (jlast > jhigh) jlast = jhigh;

        MPE_Mutex_acquire(ga->lock_win,rank);

        /* Using lock_shared allows get accesses to proceed */
        MPI_Win_lock(MPI_LOCK_SHARED, rank, MPI_MODE_NOCHECK,
                     ga->ga_win);
        for (j=jcur; j<=jlast; j++) {
            disp = (j - jfirst) * ga->dim1 + (ilo - 1);
            MPI_Put(buf, ihigh - ilo + 1, ga->dtype,
                    rank, disp, ihigh - ilo + 1, ga->dtype,
                    ga->ga_win);
            buf = (void *)( ((char *)buf) +
                            (ihigh - ilo + 1) *  ga->dtype_size );
        }
        MPI_Win_unlock(rank, ga->ga_win);

        MPE_Mutex_release(ga->lock_win,rank);
        jcur = jlast + 1;
    }
    return 0;
}
```

Figure 4.12: Code for ga_put

eliminates the for loop and replaces a set of MPI_Put or MPI_Get operations
with a single MPI_Put or MPI_Get. The code to use a datatype instead of the
for loop is shown in Figure 4.13. One can use MPI_Type_create_resized to
avoid creating the vectype in each iteration of the while loop; that is left as an
exercise for the reader.

```
MPI_Type_vector(jlast-jcur+1, ihigh-ilow+1, ga->dim1, ga->dtype,
                &vectype);
MPI_Type_commit(&vectype);
MPI_Put(buf, (jlast-jcur+1)*(ihigh-ilow+1), ga->dtype, rank,
        (jcur-jfirst)*ga->dim1 + (ilow-1), 1, vectype, ga->ga_win);
MPI_Type_free(&vectype);
buf = (void *)( ((char *)buf) +
                (jlast-jcur+1)*(ihigh-ilow+1) *  ga->dtype_size );
```

Figure 4.13: Code to replace the `for` loop in `ga_put` using MPI datatypes

These routines have two tricky parts. The first is the computation of the address of the buffer to pass to the RMA routines. The code presented here assumes that a `char *` pointer is in bytes (this is common but not universal and is not required by the C standard). The other tricky part is the calls to `MPE_Mutex_acquire` and `MPE_Mutex_release`. We need these because the semantics for `ga_acc` is that the entire accumulate takes place atomically. Thus, we can't let any other process put or accumulate into *any* of the processes that this accumulate will access. By using the mutexes for each of the processes that will be accessed, we ensure that the `ga_acc` is atomic.

In these examples, an assert argument of `MPI_MODE_NOCHECK` is provided to `MPI_Win_lock`. This value may be used when it is known that no other process will attempt to call `MPI_Win_lock` on the same window object and process. In our case, because of the call to `MPE_Mutex_lock`, we know that no other process can call `MPI_Win_lock` for this process and window. The `MPI_Win_lock` and `MPI_Win_unlock` calls in this case are used only to complete the RMA operations between them.

4.6.3 Accumulate

The global array version of accumulate, `ga_acc`, is a bit more interesting. In the Global Arrays library, `ga_acc` is both one sided and atomic. By atomic, we mean that the action is indivisible; if there are multiple accumulate operations to the same part of a global array, all elements contributed by a single `ga_acc` operation are accumulated before another `ga_acc` operation is allowed to modify any of the same elements of the global array. To implement this, we first acquire *all* of the mutual exclusion locks that we are going to need and then perform the accumulate operations. We can release the mutual exclusion locks as we complete the accumulate operations in each window. The code for `ga_acc` is shown in Figure 4.14. Just as for the cast of `ga_put`, a more efficient version of this routine could use `MPI_Type_vector` to replace the inner loop with a single `MPI_Accumulate` call.

It is often dangerous for a routine to depend on acquiring several mutexes, as `ga_acc` does here. In the general case, if there are several processes each of which needs several mutexes, each process may acquire one of the mutexes needed by the others and then wait forever for one of the other mutexes. This is the *dining philosophers* problem, where processes are replaced by philosophers and mutexes by forks, with each philosopher needing two forks to eat; if each philosopher seizes a fork, the philosophers starve, each waiting for another the relinquish a fork.

The current code does not suffer from this problem because the mutexes are acquired in strict rank-increasing order: if a process requires several mutexes, it acquires all that it needs, or it blocks because a process has gotten the mutex ahead of it. If it has blocked, it cannot interfere with the success of the process that already holds the mutex. However, if we made major changes to our library, such as providing more general decompositions of the global array among the processes, this algorithm would have to be reevaluated.

4.6.4   The Rest of Global Arrays

Now that we have a fetch and increment and a mutex routine, we can complete our implementation of our simplified Global Arrays library. As we noted in the beginning of this section, there are many features of Global Arrays that our simple implementation doesn't provide. Some are relatively straightforward. For example, Global Arrays provides a way to create and use mutexes; these can be provided by using our `MPI_Mutex_create` routine. Other features require more work; for example, Global Arrays provides versions of put, get, and accumulate that are nonblocking and that are completed by waiting on a special handle. These can be implemented in MPI by using a group of RMA communication routines that return an `MPI_Request`. These are `MPI_Rput`, `MPI_Rget`, `MPI_Raccumulate`, and `MPI_Rget_accumulate`. These RMA operations are completed with any of the routines, such as `MPI_Wait` or `MPI_Testany`, that complete an `MPI_Request`. A full implementation of the nonblocking versions in global arrays requires the use of another advanced MPI feature, *generalized requests*, described in Section 12.1.2.

```
#include "ga.h"
int ga_acc(GA ga, int ilo, int ihigh, int jlo, int jhigh,
           void *buf)
{
  int      jcur, jfirst, jlast, j, rank, rank_first, rank_last;
  MPI_Aint disp;

  /* In order to ensure that the entire update is atomic, we must
     first mutex-lock all of the windows that we will access */
  rank_first = (jlo - 1) / ga->chunk2;
  rank_last  = (jhigh - 1) / ga->chunk2;
  for (rank = rank_first; rank <= rank_last; rank++) {
      MPE_Mutex_acquire(ga->lock_win, rank);
  }

  jcur = jlo;
  while (jcur <= jhigh) {
    rank   = (jcur - 1) /ga->chunk2;
    jfirst = rank * ga->chunk2 + 1;
    jlast  = (rank + 1) * ga->chunk2;
    if (jlast > jhigh) jlast = jhigh;

    MPI_Win_lock(MPI_LOCK_SHARED, rank, MPI_MODE_NOCHECK,
                 ga->ga_win);
    for (j=jcur; j<=jlast; j++) {
        disp = (j - jfirst) * ga->dim1 + (ilo - 1);
        MPI_Accumulate(buf, ihigh - ilo + 1, ga->dtype,
                       rank, disp, ihigh - ilo + 1, ga->dtype,
                       MPI_SUM, ga->ga_win);
        buf = (void *)( ((char *)buf) +
                    (ihigh - ilo + 1) *  ga->dtype_size);
    }
    MPI_Win_unlock(rank, ga->ga_win);

    MPE_Mutex_release(ga->lock_win, rank);
    jcur = jlast + 1;
  }
  return 0;
}
```

Figure 4.14: Code for global array accumulate. Note that all target processes are locked with MPE_Mutex_lock before any is updated.

4.7   A Better Mutex

The mutex that we implemented for the Global Arrays library is a simple *spinlock*. This is fast and simple as long as there is no contention for the lock. However, if several processes attempt to acquire the same mutex at the same time, the spinlock has several problems. It is inefficient because the processes attempt to access and update the same data location. It is *unfair* because no guarantee exists that the process that has been waiting the longest to acquire the mutex will be the next to succeed. A much better mutex, called an *MCS lock* for the initials of its creators, is described in [44].

We will sketch the approach and the solution using MPI RMA here; we refer the reader to [44] for a clear and detailed description of the approach. The main idea is to maintain a list of the processes that wish to acquire the mutex. This list is very simple; it has at most one element for each process. In our implementation, shown in Figure 4.16, process 0 stores the rank of the process that *most recently* requested the mutex—in other words, the tail of the list of processes waiting for the mutex and the process holding the mutex. The code to initialize the MCS lock is shown in Figure 4.15. As we've done before, we store the rank of the calling process in an attribute, since this information is needed later.

The code to acquire the lock is shown in Figure 4.16. A process acquires the mutex by adding itself to the tail of the list; we use MPI_Fetch_and_op with an operation of MPI_REPLACE, targeting the location of the tail pointer on process 0 (this is the "fetch-and-store" operation in the original paper). If the previous value for the tail pointer was a rank of −1, then the process has the mutex. Otherwise, it has the rank of the previous tail of the list. It uses that information to inform that process that it is next; this is done by using MPI_Accumulate with an operation of MPI_REPLACE (this is an atomic put). It waits for the lock by spinning on a location in its own window; we'll see that this location is updated by a process executing the mutex release. This spin loop calls MPI_Win_sync, which ensures that any updates to the window from another process are visible to the calling process. This is discussed in more detail in Section 4.10.

The code to release this mutex is shown in Figure 4.17. The process that holds the mutex notifies the next process that it now holds the mutex by clearing the "blocked" flag in that process, using the MPI_Put call just before the MPI_Win_-unlock_all at the end of the routine. This requires a little care, because a process could be adding itself to the tail of the list but may not have completed yet the step where it notifies the previous tail process of its rank. This problem is solved by using a powerful accumulate operation known as *compare and swap*, which is provided

---

int **MPI_Compare_and_swap**(const void *origin_addr, const void *compare_addr,
        void *result_addr, MPI_Datatype datatype, int target_rank,
        MPI_Aint target_disp, MPI_Win win)

Table 4.12: C binding for compare and swap

MPI_COMPARE_AND_SWAP(origin_addr, compare_addr, result_addr, datatype,
        target_rank, target_disp, win, ierror)
        <type> origin_addr(*), compare_addr(*), result_addr(*)
        integer(kind=MPI_ADDRESS_KIND) target_disp
        integer datatype, target_rank, win, ierror

Table 4.13: Fortran binding for compare and swap

in MPI by the function `MPI_Compare_and_swap`. The C and Fortran bindings
for this function are shown in Tables 4.12 and 4.13, respectively. This function
compares the value at `compare_addr` with the value at `target_disp`; if they
are the same, the value at `target_disp` is replaced with the value at `origin_-`
`addr`. The original value at `target_disp` is returned in `result_addr` whether
or not the comparison succeeded. The MCS lock release code uses this function
to test whether the tail of the list is the calling process. In that case, the calling
process is the only member of the list, and it can set the list to empty (a rank of -1
is used here). If another process was in the list, the calling process has to wait, if
necessary, until that process has stored its rank in `lmem[nextRank]` (this is the
`do ... while` step). The calling process then informs that process that it now
holds the mutex. This notification is performed with `MPI_Accumulate`, with the
operation `MPI_REPLACE`. This is an atomic put operation, which is needed since
the target process is accessing the same location in the memory window.

4.8   Managing a Distributed Data Structure

To understand more clearly the differences between the MPI RMA model and
shared memory, particularly the use of pointers in shared memory, let us look at
the implementation of a list containing character keys and values that is distributed
among all the processes in an MPI communicator. We first describe a shared-
memory implementation of a routine that searches for a given key and returns the
corresponding value. We next show what must be changed in order to implement the

```
static int MCS_LOCKRANK = MPI_KEYVAL_INVALID;
enum { nextRank=0, blocked=1, lockTail=2 };

void MCSLockInit(MPI_Comm comm, MPI_Win *win)
{
  int       *lmem, rank;
  MPI_Aint winsize;
  MPI_Comm_rank(comm,&rank);

  if (MCS_LOCKRANK == MPI_KEYVAL_INVALID)
    MPI_Win_create_keyval(MPI_WIN_NULL_COPY_FN,
                          MPI_WIN_NULL_DELETE_FN,
                          &MCS_LOCKRANK, (void*)0);

  winsize = 2 * sizeof(int);
  if (rank == 0) winsize += sizeof(int);
  MPI_Win_allocate(winsize, sizeof(int), MPI_INFO_NULL, comm,
                   &lmem, win);
  lmem[nextRank] = -1;
  lmem[blocked]  = 0;
  if (rank == 0) {
    lmem[lockTail] = -1;
  }
  MPI_Win_set_attr(*win, MCS_LOCKRANK, (void*)(MPI_Aint)rank);
  MPI_Barrier(comm);
}
```

Figure 4.15: Implementation of an MCS lock with MPI: initialization

same operations using MPI RMA. We then add the ability to allow some processes to insert elements in the list while others may be searching the list, again showing both shared-memory and RMA implementations.

4.8.1 A Shared-Memory Distributed List Implementation

In this section, we consider a list distributed among processes as shown in Figure 4.18. We describe here the routine FindElm that searches through the list. In Section 4.8.4, we'll describe how the list might be created.

A shared-memory implementation is relatively simple. We start with a simple list element defined by the structure ListElm, shown in Figure 4.19. We also include a pointer to the head of the list and code to initialize the head to point to an empty

```
void MCSLockAcquire(MPI_Win win)
{
  int  flag, myrank, predecessor, *lmem;
  void *attrval;

  MPI_Win_get_attr(win, MCS_LOCKRANK, &attrval, &flag);
  myrank = (int)(MPI_Aint)attrval;
  MPI_Win_get_attr(win, MPI_WIN_BASE, &lmem, &flag);
  lmem[blocked] = 1; /* In case we are blocked */
  MPI_Win_lock_all(0, win);
  MPI_Fetch_and_op(&myrank, &predecessor, MPI_INT,
                   0, lockTail, MPI_REPLACE, win);
  MPI_Win_flush(0, win);
  if (predecessor != -1) {
    /* We didn't get the lock.  Add us to the tail of the list */
    MPI_Accumulate(&myrank, 1, MPI_INT, predecessor,
                   nextRank, 1, MPI_INT, MPI_REPLACE, win);
    /* Now spin on our local value "blocked" until we are
       given the lock */
    do {
      MPI_Win_sync(win);   /* Ensure memory updated */
    } while (lmem[blocked] == 1);
  }
  // else we have the lock
  MPI_Win_unlock_all(win);
}
```

Figure 4.16: Implementation of an MCS lock with MPI: acquire

element (this will simplify some code when we add the ability to modify the list). We assume that all processes can access the head pointer, as well as the character strings pointed at by the key and value fields in each list element (because they are all stored in shared memory).

The code to find an element in the list that matches a particular key is then simple, as shown in Figure 4.20. C programmers might reduce the code to five lines by replacing the while loop with a for loop that handles the initialization, test, and advancement to the next list element, but the form here is easier for Fortran programmers to follow and, more importantly, will be easier to compare with the MPI RMA version that we consider next. Note also that we enclose the loop within a critical section, implemented with a mutex. We assume that the routines lock_mutex and unlock_mutex are provided by the shared-memory

```
void MCSLockRelease(MPI_Win win)
{
  int nullrank = -1, zero=0, myrank, curtail, flag, *lmem;
  void *attrval;

  MPI_Win_get_attr(win, MCS_LOCKRANK, &attrval, &flag);
  myrank = (int)(MPI_Aint)attrval;
  MPI_Win_get_attr(win, MPI_WIN_BASE, &lmem, &flag);
  MPI_Win_lock_all(0, win);
  if (lmem[nextRank] == -1) {
    /* See if we're waiting for the next to notify us */
    MPI_Compare_and_swap(&nullrank, &myrank, &curtail, MPI_INT,
                         0, lockTail, win);
    if (curtail == myrank) {
      /* We are the only process in the list */
      MPI_Win_unlock_all(win);
      return;
    }
    /* Otherwise, someone else has added themselves to the list.*/
    do {
      MPI_Win_sync(win);
    } while (lmem[nextRank] == -1);
  }
  /* Now we can notify them.  Use accumulate with replace instead
     of put since we want an atomic update of the location */
  MPI_Accumulate(&zero, 1, MPI_INT, lmem[nextRank], blocked,
                 1, MPI_INT, MPI_REPLACE, win);
  MPI_Win_unlock_all(win);
}
```

Figure 4.17: Implementation of an MCS lock with MPI: release

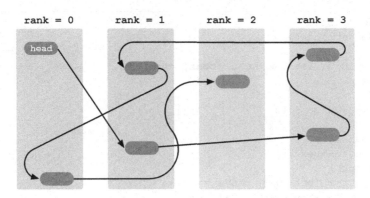

Figure 4.18: An example of a list distributed among four processes

```
typedef struct _listelm {
    struct _listelm *next;
    char *key, *value; } ListElm;

/* Initial head element:
ListElm headval = { 0, 0, 0 };
static ListElm *head = &headval;
*/
```

Figure 4.19: Definition of a list element and list pointer for the shared-memory implementation of a distributed list. The comment shows how the head of the list might be declared. These definitions are stored in the include file list.h.

programming environment. This critical section ensures that the list is not modified by another routine, such as an insert or delete, while the findElm routine is executing. The routine returns a copy of the result value; this ensures that if the list element is deleted by a later routine, the value returned remains valid.

4.8.2 An MPI Implementation of a Distributed List

In MPI, we cannot directly access the list elements on other processes (see Chapter 5 for an exception for processes on the same node). Instead, we must use RMA operations to access them. In addition, we cannot use a simple pointer to identify a list element. In the distributed case, we need to know the rank of the process that holds the element and the displacement within the window of the

```
#include "list.h"
#include <string.h>

char *FindElm(ListElm *head, const char *key)
{
  ListElm *ptr;
  char     *value = 0;

  lock_mutex();
  ptr = head->next;
  while (ptr) {
    if (strcmp(ptr->key, key) == 0) {
      value = strdup(ptr->value);
      break;
    }
    ptr = ptr->next;
  }
  unlock_mutex();
  return value;
}
```

Figure 4.20: Shared-memory version of `FindElm`

element. Thus, instead of using a pointer (`ListElm *`) to access elements, we define a structure `RemotePointer`, shown in Figure 4.21, which shows the header file `Dlist.h`. The `RemotePointer` structure also includes a `local_pointer` field. If the list element is on the local process, this field is the address of the list element and is used only on that process. The `local_pointer` is not required, since the address of an element on a local process can be computed from the displacement; but having this data precomputed can improve the performance of the RMA implementation of `FindElm`. The header file that contains the definition of `RemotePointer` also contains a definition of a list element that replaces the pointer to the next list element (`struct _listelm *next` in the shared-memory case) with a `RemotePointer`. In addition, the list elements themselves contain character arrays for the `key` and `value` rather than pointers to `key` and `value` strings. These could also have been implemented by using `RemotePointer` to point to the storage locations in a memory window, but for many applications, it is both simpler and more efficient (in time if not in memory) to store these directly

```
#define MAX_KEY_SIZE 64
#define MAX_VALUE_SIZE 256

typedef struct {
    MPI_Aint disp;              /* Displacement in window */
    int      rank;             /* Rank (process) */
    void     *local_pointer;   /* Local address of data pointed
                                  at (if data local) */
    } RemotePointer;
typedef struct {
    RemotePointer next;
    /* For simplicity, we make the key and value stay within the
       structure.  In a more general case, they too could use
       RemotePointer */
    char         key[MAX_KEY_SIZE],
                 value[MAX_VALUE_SIZE];
    } ListElm;

/* The head starts on process 0 at an unknown displacement */
extern MPI_Win      listmutex;
extern MPI_Datatype listelmType, dptrType;
extern RemotePointer nullDptr;
extern int MPE_LISTWIN_KEY_RANK;

#define DispInListElm( _dptr, _field ) \
    (MPI_Aint)&(((ListElm *)((_dptr).disp))->_field)
```

Figure 4.21: Header file Dlist.h for distributed list code. The local_pointer field is declared as void * to provide a general "remote pointer"; however, in the code in these examples, we could have used ListElm *local_pointer.

within the list element.[2]

The last part of Dlist.h contains a few global variables that will simplify the implementation. One is the MPI datatype, listelmType, that will be used to access a list element (ListElm). Since a ListElm contains a remote pointer as well as character arrays, we use an MPI datatype to access a ListElm on a remote process. Not shown here is the list element that head points to; this is a ListElm on process 0 with displacement 0, and with key = "\0".

---

[2]The same efficiency argument often holds in the shared-memory case as well, but for simplicity we have used the simplest and most general form in this case.

```
/* Create a type for the RemotePointer */
blens[0]  = 1;  blens[1]  = 1;
displs[0] = 0;  dtypes[0] = MPI_AINT;
MPI_Get_address(&head.disp, &disp_base);
MPI_Get_address(&head.rank, &displs[1]);
displs[1] = displs[1] - disp_base;
dtypes[1] = MPI_INT;
MPI_Type_create_struct(2, blens, displs, dtypes, &dptrType);

/* Create the datatype for ListElm */
dtypes[0] = dptrType;    blens[0] = 1;
dtypes[1] = MPI_CHAR;    blens[1] = MAX_KEY_SIZE;
dtypes[2] = MPI_CHAR;    blens[2] = MAX_VALUE_SIZE;
MPI_Type_create_struct(3, blens, displs, dtypes,
                          &listelmType);
MPI_Type_commit(&dptrType);
MPI_Type_commit(&listelmType);
```

Figure 4.22: Code to create the `listelmType` datatype used to access an entire list element with MPI RMA and `dptrType` used to access a `RemotePointer`

The code to construct the datatype `listelmType` is fairly simple and is shown in Figure 4.22. We use the MPI datatype `MPI_AINT` that corresponds to an `MPI_-Aint`. Note that we do not need to transfer the `void *local_pointer` field. At the same time, we construct a datatype for a `RemotePointer`; we'll need this later for the insert routine.

The rest of the header file `Dlist.h` includes:

nullDptr. A special `RemotePointer` that serves as a null pointer (similar to `NULL` for regular pointers). The name `Dptr` is short for "distributed memory pointer."

MPE_LISTWIN_KEY_RANK. An attribute keyval that allows us to cache the rank of the calling process in the group of the window, on the window object. Without this, we would need to either pass the rank as a separate argument to all the routines or extract the rank using `MPI_Win_get_group`.

DispInListElm. This is used to compute displacements. We'll see its use later in Section 4.8.4.

Along with creating the `MPI_Win` for the list, we attach to the window object an attribute that contains the rank of the process in the communicator that was used to create the window object. It is possible to compute this rank just given the window object, but using an attribute is much more efficient.

With these preliminaries, we are ready to describe the RMA version of `FindElm`. The code in Figure 4.23 parallels the shared-memory code, but with some important differences.

- We use our mutex routine, `MPE_Mutex_acquire`, from Section 4.5 to provide the critical section.

- We use `MPI_Win_lock_all` and `MPI_Win_unlock_all` to establish an access epoch to *all* processes in the window. `MPI_Win_lock_all` acts like an `MPI_Win_lock` to every process in the window object, with the lock type of `MPI_LOCK_SHARED`. Using these routines makes it much easier to follow the links from process to process, rather than using `MPI_Win_lock` and `MPI_Win_unlock` around each access to a remote element. C and Fortran bindings, respectively, for these routines are in Tables 4.14 and 4.15.

- To complete the RMA operations with the access epoch, we use the `MPI_-Win_flush` routine. We could use `MPI_Win_flush_local` here instead; this routine only completes the RMA operations locally. But in this case (a get), it means that the RMA operation must have completed at the target process as well.

- Because we must use an `MPI_Win_flush` to complete any `MPI_Get` operation, we get an entire list element, including the `key` and `value`, in a single operation, rather than first checking the `key` and then obtaining either the `value` (if the `key` matched) or the `next` pointer (if the `key` did not match). We also make a copy of the list element that we will look at. This approach is almost always more efficient that using multiple get/flush or lock/get/unlock operations.

- We get the remote list element into a `local_copy`.

- For better performance, where the data is local, we use the `local_pointer` field in `RemotePointer` rather than either using `MPI_Get` on the local process or computing the local pointer from the window base and displacement.

- The end of the list is indicated by a `rank` of `-1`. We use this rather than using a window displacement of zero (`disp` in `RemotePointer`) because a displacement of zero is a valid location. The `nullDptr` is a null

---

int **MPI_Win_lock_all**(int assert, MPI_Win win)

int **MPI_Win_unlock_all**(MPI_Win win)

Table 4.14: C bindings to allow passive target access to all processes

---

MPI_WIN_LOCK_ALL(assert, win, ierror)
          integer assert, win, ierror

MPI_WIN_UNLOCK_ALL(win, ierror)
          integer win, ierror

Table 4.15: Fortran bindings to allow passive target access to all processes

RemotePointer and is defined this way with a rank of -1 and a displacement of zero.

4.8.3 Inserting into a Distributed List

To see how to insert into a distributed list, we'll first look at a shared-memory version of InsertElm, just as we did for FindElm. This code is shown in Figure 4.24. We assume that the list is sorted by key; the insert routine inserts the element into the correct location in the list. The code is straightforward; the while loop finds the pointer to the list elements before (last_ptr) and after (ptr) the element to be inserted (here is where having head point to a first element helps; there is no special code for handling the head). No element is inserted if key is found. Note that a mutex lock is used around access to the list to prevent concurrent inserts from corrupting the list data structures. Finally, we assume that malloc and strdup may be used to allocate sharable memory.

These two shared-memory codes are fairly simple, but they illustrate one of the more subtle issues in writing parallel programs. In both InsertElm and FindElm, a single mutex lock is used to protect the list. As a result, only one process at a time can use the list. This restriction makes this code *nonscalable*: as more processes are added, the program may not run faster. Note that if there is no DeleteElm, only an InsertElm, and if we have write ordering,[3] we may be able to avoid locks in the FindElm routine by carefully ordering the updates to the list elements in

---

[3]Write ordering means that stores to memory appear to all processes in the order they are written and are not reordered by the compiler or the memory system hardware.

```
#include "Dlist.h"

char *FindElm(RemotePointer head, MPI_Win win, const char *key)
{
 static ListElm local_copy;
 ListElm        *local_copy_ptr;
 RemotePointer  ptr;
 int            myrank, *attrval, flag;
 MPI_Group      win_group;

 MPI_Win_get_attr(win, MPE_LISTWIN_KEY_RANK, &attrval, &flag);
 if (!flag) {
   /* win not properly initialized */
   return 0;
 }
 myrank = (int)(MPI_Aint)attrval;  /* We store the rank in
                the attrval, which is an address-sized value */

 ptr = head;
 MPI_Win_lock_all(0, win);
 while (ptr.rank >= 0) {
   /* Make sure we have the data */
   if (ptr.rank != myrank) {
      MPI_Get(&local_copy, 1, listelmType,
            ptr.rank, ptr.disp, 1, listelmType, win);
      MPI_Win_flush(ptr.rank, win);
      local_copy_ptr = &local_copy;
   } else
      local_copy_ptr = (ListElm *)(ptr.local_pointer);

   if (strcmp(local_copy_ptr->key, key) == 0) {
      MPI_Win_unlock_all(win);
      return local_copy_ptr->value;
   }
   ptr = local_copy_ptr->next;
 }
 MPI_Win_unlock_all(win);
 return 0;  /* Did not find key */
}
```

Figure 4.23: Code to find an element in an unchanging distributed list using RMA. Note that this code is not thread safe because it uses a static variable (local_copy).

```c
#include "list.h"
#include <stdlib.h>
#include <string.h>

void InsertElm(ListElm *head, const char *key, const char *value)
{
    ListElm *ptr, *last_ptr, *new_ptr;
    int     compare;

    /* Lock list, find insertion point */
    lock_mutex();

    last_ptr = head;
    ptr      = head->next;
    while (ptr) {
        compare = strcmp(ptr->key, key);
        if (compare == 0) {
            /* Duplicate key. Ignore */
            unlock_mutex(); return; }
        if (compare > 0) {
            /* Insert before this element */
            break;
        }
        last_ptr = ptr;
        ptr      = ptr->next;
    }

    /* Create and insert new element */
    if ( !(new_ptr = (ListElm *)malloc(sizeof(ListElm))) )
        abort();
    new_ptr->key   = strdup(key);
    new_ptr->value = strdup(value);
    if (! new_ptr->key || ! new_ptr->value) abort();
    new_ptr->next  = ptr;
    last_ptr->next = new_ptr;

    unlock_mutex();
}
```

Figure 4.24: Shared-memory code to insert an element into a list

`InsertElm`. Such code is fragile because write ordering is not a requirement of C or Fortran, and code that runs on one system may fail on another. However, with those assumptions, we do not need to use a mutex around the `FindElm` routine because we can ensure that the list is always valid (this is why the last pointer operation is the assignment to `last_ptr->next` in `InsertElm`).

4.8.4   An MPI Implementation of a Dynamic Distributed List

To implement a list that is dynamically updated by different processes, we need to be able to perform the following operations:

1. Allocate (and free) memory that is part of the list, making that memory accessible through an MPI window object.

2. Ensure that concurrent updates to the list are race free and correct.

The routines that we've used so far to create a memory window require that all the memory that will be used for MPI RMA communication be provided at the moment the window object is created. For a dynamically changing data structure, this isn't possible. In fact, in MPI-2, the user had to provide a block of memory, implement their own version of `malloc`, and hope that they allocated enough space. MPI-3 provides a new type of RMA window creation that allows one to add and remove memory from the memory window at any time. This routine is `MPI_-Win_create_dynamic`. Memory is added and removed from a memory window with `MPI_Win_attach` and `MPI_Win_detach`. We'll see how this is used to insert elements into a distributed list later, but to see how these are used, the following code is similar to using `MPI_Win_create` to initialize a window object.

```
MPI_Win_create_dynamic(MPI_INFO_NULL, MPI_COMM_WORLD, &win);
b = (char *)malloc(size);
MPI_Win_attach(win, b, size);
MPI_Barrier(MPI_COMM_WORLD);
... it is now safe to perform RMA communication on win
... origin processes will need to know the location of b
... on the target process
...
... Before detaching, ensure that no process will access the
... memory b.  An MPI_Barrier could be used here.
MPI_Win_detach(win, b);
free(b);
MPI_Win_free(&win);
```

---

int **MPI_Win_create_dynamic**(MPI_Info info, MPI_Comm comm, MPI_Win *win)

int **MPI_Win_attach**(MPI_Win win, void *base, MPI_Aint size)

int **MPI_Win_detach**(MPI_Win win, const void *base)

Table 4.16: C bindings for routines to use dynamically allocated memory with RMA memory windows

---

MPI_WIN_CREATE_DYNAMIC(info, comm, win, ierror)
        integer info, comm, win, ierror

MPI_WIN_ATTACH(win, base, size, ierror)
        integer win, ierror
        <type> base(*)
        integer(kind=MPI_ADDRESS_KIND) size

MPI_WIN_DETACH(win, base, ierror)
        integer win, ierror
        <type> base(*)

Table 4.17: Fortran bindings for routines to use dynamically allocated memory with RMA memory windows

The code for inserting an element, shown in Figures 4.25, 4.26, and 4.27, has more differences with its shared-memory counterpart than FindElm does. Like the shared-memory version, we get the next field from the head pointer. In this case, we use MPI_Get to read that field from the head element. To do that, we need the datatype to read (the dptrType we created), the rank of the process with the data (headDptr.rank), and the displacement in the target window of the data.

Computing this displacement is not hard but requires care, which is why we have defined the macro DispInListElm. We make the assumption that all processes have the same sized address space (e.g., the size of MPI_Aint or void* is the same on all processes). This macro takes a RemotePointer to a ListElm and the name of a field within a ListElm and returns the displacement to that field within that ListElm. The definition for DispInListElm from Figure 4.21 is repeated below for ease of reference.

```
#define DispInListElm( _dptr, _field ) \
        (MPI_Aint)&(((ListElm *)((_dptr).disp))->_field)
```

This macro computes the displacement on the target using the following steps:

1. Cast the displacement to a pointer to a `ListElm`. This *cast* is valid, even if it points to memory that isn't valid on the calling process (remember, the displacement is to a `ListElm` on some other process).

2. Select the address of the desired field of `ListElm` from this pointer; e.g., `ptr->field_name`. This is still valid on the calling process, since all we've done is compute an address.

3. Cast this address to an `MPI_Aint`. This is the displacement of the field *on the target process*.

With this macro, we use `MPI_Get` to find the pointer to the first list element after the head. For each element after that, we need to access at least the `key` field of the list element, so we read the entire list element into a local copy, `elmOfptr`. This is perhaps the biggest difference with the share memory code, as we explicitly make a copy of the element before examining the `key` and `next` fields. The update to the `next` field of the previous element is set with an `MPI_Put` operation. Again, we use the `DispInListElm` macro to compute the displacement of that element of the `ListElm` at the *target* process so that we only update the `next` field.

Finally, Figure 4.28 shows how the dynamic memory window is created, the use of a keyval for the attribute used to pass the rank of the calling process to the other routines, and how the head element is created. The final step is to broadcast the location of the head element on the process at rank zero to all the other processes. This dummy head element stays fixed on process zero; both the `FindElm` and `InsertElm` routines start by accessing the head element to find the first "real" element of the list.

4.8.5   Comments on More Concurrent List Implementations

The implementations that we've shown restrict one process at a time to examining or modifying the list. For some applications, this is adequate, but for others, greater parallelism is required. Unfortunately, it is significantly harder to correctly implement such list operations, even in shared memory. One of the easiest approaches is to use more mutexes, for example, one per list element, providing finer-grain control. Another option is to use "lock-free" algorithms, which can atomically update the list pointers. In shared memory, this algorithm uses a "compare and swap"

```
#include "mpi.h"
#include "Dlist.h"
#include <string.h>

int InsertElm(RemotePointer headDptr,
              const char *key, const char *value,
              MPI_Win listwin)
{
  RemotePointer dptr, last_dptr, new_dptr;
  int           compare;
  ListElm       elmOfptr, *new_lptr;
  int           *attrval, myrank, flag;


  MPI_Win_get_attr(listwin, MPE_LISTWIN_KEY_RANK, &attrval,
                     &flag);
  if (!flag) {
    /* Listwin not properly initialized */
    return 1;
  }
  myrank = (int)(MPI_Aint)attrval;   /* We store the rank in the
                                        attrval, which is an
                                        address-sized value */

  MPE_Mutex_acquire(listmutex,0);
```

Figure 4.25: An RMA routine to insert an element in a list that may be modified
by other processes: routine initialization code

operation. This is an atomic operation that compares two values and performs a
swap between two other values if the comparison is true. MPI provides this with the
routine MPI_Compare_and_swap, and the MPI standard provides an illustration
of its use in Example 11.22 [46]. While the code in that example works only with
list elements that contain a single integer as the value, it is fairly straightforward
to extend it to our distributed list.

However, there is one additional problem to providing greater parallelism in the
list operations. The MPI standard says that data accessed by put and get routines
must not overlap accesses with accumulate routines; puts and gets must also be
disjoint. Since MPI_Win_lock_all does not provide exclusive access (the lock-
type is always MPI_LOCK_SHARED), another MPI process, executing, for example,
an InsertElm routine, may use MPI_Put on the same element. The behavior of

```
last_dptr = headDptr;
MPI_Win_lock_all(0, listwin);
MPI_Get(&dptr, 1, dptrType, last_dptr.rank,
   DispInListElm(last_dptr,next), 1, dptrType, listwin );
MPI_Win_flush(last_dptr.rank, listwin);

while (dptr.rank != nullDptr.rank) {
  MPI_Get(&elmOfptr, 1, listelmType, dptr.rank, dptr.disp,
          1, listelmType, listwin);
  MPI_Win_flush(dptr.rank, listwin);
  /* elm is what ptr points to (i.e., *ptr) */
  compare = strcmp(elmOfptr.key, key);
  if (compare == 0) {
    /* Duplicate key.  Ignore */
    MPI_Win_unlock_all(listwin);
    return 0;
  }
  if (compare > 0) break; /* Insert in front of this */
  last_dptr = dptr;
  dptr      = elmOfptr.next; /* i.e., ptr->next */
}
```

Figure 4.26: An RMA routine to insert an element in a list that may be modified by other processes: code to find the insert location

MPI in this case is undefined.

Fixing this is a bit tricky. We could use the MPI RMA routine that permits overlapping access in a get operation: `MPI_Get_accumulate`. However, this routine can be used only with predefined datatypes or derived datatypes consisting of the same predefined type, not a derived datatype containing different predefined types (i.e., `listelmType`). We could instead use `MPI_BYTE` as the datatype, with a count that is the size of the structure. For a homogeneous system, this is likely to work as long as the data in the list is not updated (which is the assumption in this routine).

Now is a good time to explain this restriction. The danger in concurrent accesses to a data word is that while one process is updating the data, another is reading it and gets a data word that contains both some of the old and some of the new bits. For example, an update to an 8-byte word might happen 4 bytes at a time. Thus it would be possible for a read of those 8 bytes to get 4 old and 4 new bytes. The restriction in MPI that the datatypes need to be predefined (and the same) in

```
/* Create new element */
MPI_Alloc_mem(sizeof(ListElm), MPI_INFO_NULL, &new_lptr);
strncpy(new_lptr->key, key, MAX_KEY_SIZE);
strncpy(new_lptr->value, value, MAX_VALUE_SIZE);
new_lptr->next = dptr;
MPI_Win_attach(listwin, new_lptr, sizeof(ListElm));

new_dptr.rank = myrank;
MPI_Get_address(new_lptr,&new_dptr.disp);
MPI_Put(&new_dptr, 1, dptrType, last_dptr.rank,
    DispInListElm(last_dptr,next), 1, dptrType,
        listwin);
MPI_Win_unlock_all(listwin);
MPE_Mutex_release(listmutex,0);
return 0;
}
```

Figure 4.27: An RMA routine to insert an element in a list that may be modified by other processes: code to insert the element into the proper location

overlapping accesses is intended to let the MPI implementation use hardware where possible to ensure that the accessed return either the old or the new data, and not a mixture of the two. In this case, using MPI_BYTE provides no guarantee that the data read was not partially updated by another operation. This is a similar problem to that illustrated in Figure 3.18, where there are two conflicting updates to a memory word.

4.9   Compiler Optimization and Passive Targets

In Section 3.7.5 we discussed the danger that a value updated in memory may be ignored because the compiler is using a copy placed in a register. The same issues apply to passive target synchronization. Fortran programmers should consider using a volatile or asynchronous attribute (where available), using MPI_-F_SYNC_REG, or passing the local memory window to a dummy or near-dummy routine (e.g., an MPE_Win_lock that takes the local window, as well as the window object, as an argument). However, C programmers don't need to use volatile, at least when the lock type is MPI_LOCK_EXCLUSIVE, since accesses to the local window still require using MPI_Win_lock and MPI_Win_unlock.

```
...
MPI_Win_create_dynamic(MPI_INFO_NULL, MPI_COMM_WORLD, &listwin);

MPI_Win_create_keyval(MPI_WIN_NULL_COPY_FN,
                      MPI_WIN_NULL_DELETE_FN,
                      &MPE_LISTWIN_KEY_RANK, (void*)0);
MPI_Win_set_attr(listwin, MPE_LISTWIN_KEY_RANK,
                 (void*)(MPI_Aint)wrank);

headDptr.rank = 0;
if (wrank == 0) {
  ListElm *headLptr;
  MPI_Alloc_mem(sizeof(ListElm), MPI_INFO_NULL, &headLptr);
  MPI_Get_address(headLptr, &headDptr.disp);
  headLptr->next.rank = -1;
  headLptr->next.disp = (MPI_Aint)MPI_BOTTOM;
  MPI_Win_attach(listwin, headLptr, sizeof(ListElm));
}
MPI_Bcast(&headDptr.disp, 1, MPI_AINT, 0, MPI_COMM_WORLD);
```

Figure 4.28: Code to create the memory window for the distributed list and distribute information about the head pointer

4.10 MPI RMA Memory Models

An important part of any discussion of shared memory or remotely accessed and updated memory is the *memory model*. Roughly, the memory model describes what happens when different processes or threads access the same memory locations, and what "same" means for memory locations.

Programmers often believe that loads and stores happen in the order in which they have been written in the program and that all the stores to data complete before the next statement is executed in the program. However, this is not promised by either the programming language or by most (particularly the fastest) computer hardware. A system that guarantees that, in each thread or process, each statement is executed in the order that it appears, is said to be *sequentially consistent*.[4]

In MPI, the memory model for RMA is built around an abstraction of *public* and *private* memory. The private memory is the memory that belongs to the process

---

[4]This is an approximate definition. The entire topic of memory models is very difficult, filled with subtle yet important issues. This section is meant as a high-level introduction; the reader is encouraged to read more definitive works on memory models.

and within which operations described by statements in the programming language normally happen. Another way to think about this is that an MPI program that does not use any RMA has only private memory. Load and store operations, that is, variable assignment and references, use the private memory. The public memory is memory that is exposed for MPI RMA operations. The public memory is not necessarily distinct from the private memory, but updates to the public memory by other processes with MPI RMA operations may not be immediately visible to the process. Rather, the MPI standard describes (in excruciating detail) how the MPI RMA synchronization routines, such as `MPI_Win_fence` or `MPI_Win_-unlock`, make contents of the public memory and the private memory match. For example, a call to `MPI_Win_fence` ensures that the public memory is a copy of the private memory, and that any changes made to the public memory are copied into the private memory. The different assertions for `MPI_Win_fence` provide information that an implementation can use to avoid making one of these copies. It is also the reason why RMA routines must be used to update the local memory window when that window is exposed to RMA updates from other processes—if both the public memory and the corresponding private memory were updated, it would be prohibitively complex to ensure a correct result at the end of an RMA synchronization such as `MPI_Win_fence`. This memory model is illustrated in Figure 4.29(A) and is called the "separate" memory model.

When MPI-2 RMA was defined, some implementations were expected to have specialized memory used for RMA operations; hence, special steps would be needed to make this public memory consistent with the private memory of the process. For example, passive target operations could have been implemented entirely within memory managed by the network-interface hardware on the node.

However, in most implementations of MPI, the public and private memory are not different memory locations. Changes that are made to the "public" memory (an MPI memory window) will eventually become visible to the program because they are the same memory locations. This is illustrated in Figure 4.29(B), and is called the "unified" memory model. This might seem to simplify most of the problems with RMA accesses, but the key word in the above is *eventually*. Even though Figure 4.29 shows the process memory as a simple box, and store and load operations as simple arrows, the situation is much more complex in a real system [5]. One reason for this is that memory operations take a long time, relative to a processor clock cycle or an integer addition, and thus, for performance reasons, processors implement most memory operations as nonblocking operations and may not even enforce any ordering. For similar reasons, a compiler may reorder the execution of statements in a program in a way that preserves the serial computation but may not be what

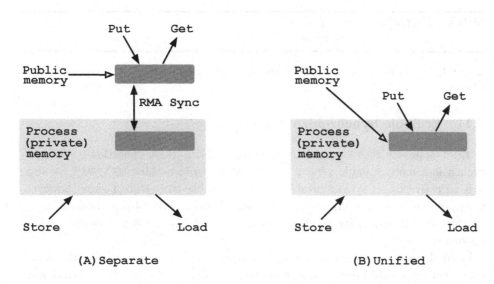

Figure 4.29: Illustration of the MPI separate (A) and unified (B) memory models

---

int **MPI_Win_sync**(MPI_Win win)

Table 4.18: C routine to synchronize the public and private memory for a window

is expected for a parallel execution [4].

Thus, even with the "unified" memory model, the programmer must ensure that all RMA operations have completed and that the data has arrived at its destination. All the MPI RMA synchronization routines ensure this. In addition, the public and private memories can be synchronized when using passive target RMA by calling MPI_Win_sync. The C and Fortran bindings for MPI_Win_sync are shown in Tables 4.18 and 4.19, respectively. Note that even in the unified case, MPI_Win_-sync is useful because of that pesky "eventually."

To determine whether the MPI environment provides the unified or separate memory model, one can check the the MPI_WIN_MODEL attribute on the window. The value of this attribute is a pointer to an integer that can have one of two values: MPI_WIN_UNIFIED or MPI_WIN_SEPARATE for the unified and separate memory models, respectively. In principle, different windows in the same window object could have different memory models, though this is unlikely with current MPI implementations.

MPI_WIN_SYNC(win, ierror)
           integer win, ierror

Table 4.19: Fortran routine to synchronize the public and private memory for a window

4.11 Scalable Synchronization

A third approach may be used to synchronize MPI RMA operations. This approach is a more scalable version of `MPI_Win_fence`. Like `MPI_Win_fence`, it is an active target synchronization method. Unlike `MPI_Win_fence`, however, the approach is not collective over the group of the window object. Instead, these routines are called only for the processes that are origins, targets, or both for RMA operations.

From the grid ghost-point exchange used in Chapter 3 to introduce the RMA operations, it should be clear that collective synchronization is stronger than necessary. A process can continue past the ghost-point exchange once the RMA operations to the neighbors (that is, with the neighbors as targets) have completed and any RMA operations targeting this process have also completed. The third MPI synchronization approach allows us to express this degree of synchronization.

4.11.1 Exposure and Access Epochs

To understand this approach, we first introduce the concept of an *exposure epoch*. This is the period of time when a local window may be the target of RMA operations. In other words, it is the time when the local window is exposed to changes made by other processes. This is the counterpart to the access epoch first mentioned in Section 4.1. The routine `MPI_Win_post` begins an exposure epoch and `MPI_Win_wait` ends an exposure epoch for the local window. These calls take as an argument the window object whose local window is being exposed. In addition, `MPI_Win_post` takes an MPI group as an argument. This is the group of processes that will be making RMA operations with this local window as the target. We emphasize this in the argument list by using the name `from_group` for this group: it is the group from which RMA calls will be coming.

An access epoch is simply the period of time when a process is making RMA calls on a window object. Most of this chapter has discussed the use of `MPI_-Win_lock` and `MPI_Win_unlock` to establish an access epoch for passive target synchronization. For general active target synchronization, an access epoch is

---

int **MPI_Win_start**(MPI_Group to_group, int assert, MPI_Win win)

int **MPI_Win_complete**(MPI_Win win)

int **MPI_Win_post**(MPI_Group from_group, int assert, MPI_Win win)

int **MPI_Win_wait**(MPI_Win win)

Table 4.20: C routines for scalable active target synchronization

---

MPI_WIN_START(to_group, assert, win, ierror)
        integer to_group, assert, win, ierror

MPI_WIN_COMPLETE(win, ierror)
        integer win, ierror

MPI_WIN_POST(from_group, assert, win, ierror)
        integer from_group, assert, win, ierror

MPI_WIN_WAIT(win, ierror)
        integer win, ierror

Table 4.21: Fortran routines for scalable active target synchronization

started with `MPI_Win_start` and completed with `MPI_Win_complete`. Just like `MPI_Win_post`, `MPI_Win_start` takes an MPI group as an argument; this group indicates the processes that will be targets of RMA calls made by this process. We emphasize this by using the name `to_group` in the argument list: it is the group to which RMA calls are being made. The C and Fortran bindings, respectively, for all four routines are shown in Tables 4.20 and 4.21. As you might expect from the name `MPI_Win_wait`, there is an `MPI_Win_test` that is the nonblocking version of `MPI_Win_wait`.

4.11.2 The Ghost-Point Exchange Revisited

We can rewrite the ghost-point exchange code from Section 3.6.1 by replacing the `MPI_Win_fence` calls that surround the RMA operations with combinations of `MPI_Win_start`, `MPI_Win_post`, `MPI_Win_wait`, and `MPI_Win_complete`. Doing so comprises two parts.

First, we must construct the groups for the `MPI_Win_start` and `MPI_Win_-post` calls. To determine the number of processes in the window object's group,

---

int **MPI_Win_get_group**(MPI_Win win, MPI_Group *group)

Table 4.22: C routine for accessing the group of a window object

---

MPI_WIN_GET_GROUP(win, group, ierror)
        integer win, group, ierror

Table 4.23: Fortran routine for accessing the group of a window object

and the rank of the calling process in this group, we can access the window object's group with `MPI_Win_get_group`. This call returns a group that is the same as the group of the communicator that was used in creating the window object. Once we have this group, we can find the size and rank of the calling process by using `MPI_Group_size` and `MPI_Group_rank`, respectively. We free the group with `MPI_Group_free`. This example does not include the code to create the window object or initialize the window memory. C and Fortran bindings for `MPI_Win_-get_group` are shown in Tables 4.22 and 4.23, respectively.

In the code in Figure 3.8, the targets (neighbors) for the `MPI_Put` operations are `top_nbr` and `bottom_nbr`. The code to create the group is simply

```
int nInGroup=0;
MPI_Win_get_group(win, &group);
if (bottom_nbr != MPI_PROC_NULL)
    ranks[nInGroup++] = bottom_nbr;
if (top_nbr != MPI_PROC_NULL)
    ranks[nInGroup++] = top_nbr;
MPI_Group_incl(group, nInGroup, ranks, &nbr_group);
MPI_Group_free(&group);
```

This code is careful to handle the possibility that either `bottom_nbr` or `top_nbr` is `MPI_PROC_NULL`. If both are `MPI_PROC_NULL`, `MPI_Group_incl` will return a valid empty group `MPI_GROUP_EMPTY`. Because the ghost points are exchanged, this group is also the group of processes that are the origin processes for `MPI_Put` calls that target this process. Thus, the `to_group` of `MPI_Win_start` and the `from_group` of `MPI_Win_post` are the same in this case.

Second, we replace the `MPI_Win_fence` that precedes the RMA operations in Figure 3.8 with

```
MPI_Win_post(nbr_group, 0, win);
MPI_Win_start(nbr_group, 0, win);
```

and we replace the `MPI_Win_fence` that follows the RMA operations with

```
MPI_Win_complete(win);
MPI_Win_wait(win);
```

4.11.3 Performance Optimizations for Scalable Synchronization

The two calls used to initiate scalable synchronization for RMA (`MPI_Win_start` and `MPI_Win_post`) take an `assert` argument. This assert value can be used by an MPI implementation to provide improved performance in the same way that the `assert` argument to `MPI_Win_fence` can be used (see Section 3.8.2).

Three `assert` values may be used with `MPI_Win_post`. Recall that `MPI_-Win_post` begins an exposure epoch for the local window; thus, assert values that tell the implementation about changes to the local window before or after the `MPI_Win_post` call may be helpful. The three assert values are the following:

MPI_MODE_NOSTORE. The local window was not updated by local stores (or local get or receive calls) since the last call to `MPI_Win_complete`.

MPI_MODE_NOPUT. The local window will not be updated by put or accumulate calls between this `MPI_Win_post` call and the matching `MPI_Win_wait` call.

MPI_MODE_NOCHECK. The matching `MPI_Win_start` calls have not been issued by any process that is an origin of RMA operations that have this process as the target. In addition, those `MPI_Win_start` calls *must* also specify `MPI_MODE_NOCHECK` as their `assert` value.

The only `assert` value defined for `MPI_Win_start` is `MPI_MODE_NOCHECK`. This can be used only when the matching `MPI_Win_post` calls on the target processes have already been called and have specified `MPI_MODE_NOCHECK` as part of their `assert` argument.

Unlike the `MPI_Win_fence` case, these assert values are less likely to be useful. For example, many programs will perform stores to the local window before beginning an exposure epoch with `MPI_Win_post` (eliminating `MPI_MODE_NOSTORE` as a valid assert value). Using RMA get operations instead of RMA put or accumulate operations by the origin processes would allow `MPI_MODE_NOPUT` to be used as an `assert` value, but that is not a good reason to prefer RMA get over put. The assert value `MPI_MODE_NOCHECK` requires some outside synchronization to ensure that the conditions for its use are met; these are similar to those needed for a ready send (such as `MPI_Rsend`).

The info key `no_locks` may be used with a `MPI_Win_create` call if `MPI_-Win_lock` and `MPI_Win_unlock` are never used with the created window object. Just as for programs that use `MPI_Win_fence` to complete RMA operations, this can be an important optimization.

4.12 Summary

This chapter has covered two major topics: passive target RMA and scalable synchronization. The majority of the chapter has focused on passive target RMA: remote access without active cooperation by the target process. This provides a true one-sided operation, compared with the active target RMA introduced in Chapter 3 that relies on all processes, both origin and target, calling `MPI_Win_fence`. The passive target synchronization, using `MPI_Win_lock` and `MPI_Win_unlock` to define an access epoch, is designed to allow the widest portability and performance by an MPI implementation.

However, the looseness of the synchronization (the nonblocking lock) requires more care with other operations. We showed how to use `MPI_Fetch_and_op` to construct an atomic counter, which can be used to implement a mutual exclusion or mutex operations. With this mutex, we showed how to implement a distributed array library whose RMA operations have different semantics than MPI's. We also used a distributed list example to compare a shared-memory implementation with MPI RMA; this example will help users who wish to port an application to a distributed-memory system using MPI.

The third form of RMA synchronization defined by the MPI standard is another form of active target synchronization, but one that identifies the target and origin processes for any RMA operation. This allows an MPI implementation to provide a synchronization mechanism that is as scalable as the application. We illustrated this by revisiting the ghost-point-exchange example introduced in Chapter 3, replacing calls to `MPI_Win_fence` with the scalable synchronization routines `MPI_Win_-post`, `MPI_Win_start`, `MPI_Win_complete`, and `MPI_Win_wait`.

5 Using Shared Memory with MPI

Combining all the MPI concepts, such as point-to-point messaging, collective communication, and remote memory access communication, is a highly complex task even though these concepts are designed to integrate and interoperate. The recent hardware trend toward large shared-memory multi- and many-core architectures often forces programmers to mix MPI with a different shared-memory model to achieve the highest performance or lowest memory consumption. Commonly used shared-memory models are POSIX threads and OpenMP. Some programmers even integrate POSIX shared-memory calls into their code in order to expose memory directly to other processes. While MPI-3's remote memory access aims to reduce the performance gap between messaging and direct access, it still requires an explicit copy before the data can be used, whereas data can be loaded directly into the CPU cache in shared-memory systems. The interaction between MPI and external programming models is complex and can cause deadlocks, data loss, and erroneous computations in rare cases. How to mix MPI and other programming models is discussed in Chapter 6.

Sharing memory between MPI processes can often achieve much of the desired speedup and reduction in memory consumption. It is also simpler to integrate into existing code bases and simpler to program. The main reason for the simplicity is *disciplined sharing*. As illustrated in Figure 5.1, POSIX threaded or OpenMP programs share the whole heap[1] across all threads, which allows one thread to tamper with the state of every other thread. This global shared-everything model can lead to complex and subtle bugs, however. In contrast, MPI traditionally employs a shared-nothing philosophy as shown in Figure 5.2. In this mode, a rogue thread is isolated and can corrupt only process-local memory and can thus easily be identified. Even though the thread could send MPI messages, corrupting remote state through random, buggy messages is much more unlikely because the remote side has to explicitly call a receive function to receive each message. As we will discuss, however, shared memory has several benefits when used with care. For example, if a limited amount of memory is shared in a disciplined way between processes, bugs can affect only the explicitly shared regions. This leads to simpler programming and debugging. In addition, since the method integrates with existing MPI programs and maintains the point-to-point and collective semantics between all processes (even if they share memory), it is easy to integrate in existing programs. While MPI programmers could use POSIX shared memory, POSIX shared memory

---

[1] The heap is the part of the process's memory that is used for dynamically allocated space, such as memory from `malloc`.

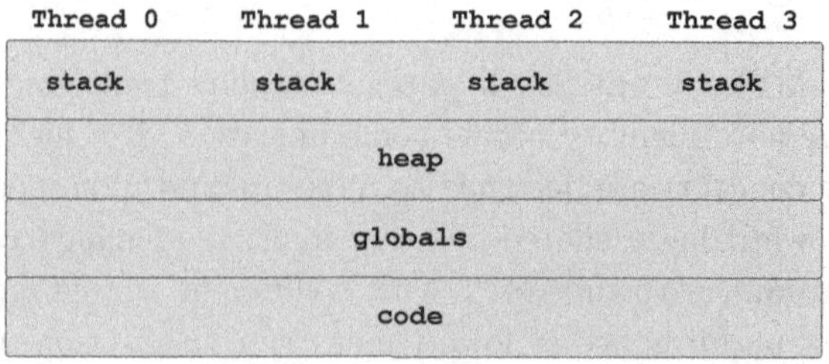

Figure 5.1: Full memory sharing in threaded environments

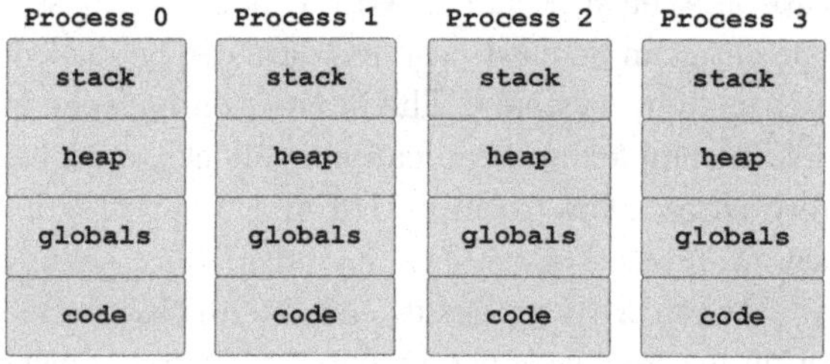

Figure 5.2: Standard MPI semantics—no sharing

is not portable across all architectures and may pose other challenges, for example, cleanup of stale shared memory regions.

MPI-3 standardizes *shared-memory windows*, a portable mechanism to expose a process's memory to other processes in a disciplined way, as conceptually shown in Figure 5.3. This shared memory can be accessed by CPU load/store instructions just as POSIX shared memory or memory shared among OpenMP threads. All shared memory is logically attached to an MPI window. Hence, all remote memory access functions described in Chapters 3 and 4 can also be used on shared-memory windows just as on other MPI windows. Yet, MPI provides no consistency or coherency guarantees for direct load/store accesses. Here, users need to consult the details of the target architecture and may need to issue additional calls such as memory fences.

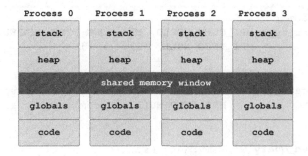

Figure 5.3: MPI-3 shared window semantics—disciplined sharing

5.1 Using MPI Shared Memory

MPI's shared memory can generally be used in the same way as any other shared-memory system. Thus use cases and possible algorithms are virtually unlimited. Here, we present three examples for common usage patterns. We then discuss the exact semantics of each function. The function names are intuitive, and further details about them can be found in Section 5.2.

5.1.1 Shared On-Node Data Structures

Many codes, for example from the quantum-chemistry domain, require large lookup tables that are global to the computation and often constant (unchanging). The most space-efficient design would be to have a single table distributed across all processes and accessed by remote calls (e.g., RMA). For performance efficiency, however, the data is often replicated at each process, causing the memory demands of the application to grow linearly with the number of processes. This memory requirement is especially dramatic in the quickly growing many-core designs when a process is run on each of the n cores and data is replicated n times, even though the hardware often supports direct memory loads and stores.

In MPI-3 shared memory, one simply allocates a shared memory window for the shared data and keeps one copy per many-core node instead of one copy per core. This approach largely alleviates the memory problem because the number of cores in supercomputers is growing much faster than the number of nodes.

In the simplest model, the data is only read after it has been initialized. Thus the data can be written collectively, followed by a memory fence and an MPI synchronization before it is accessed. The code in Figure 5.4 illustrates an example.

```
MPI_Comm shmcomm;
MPI_Comm_split_type(MPI_COMM_WORLD, MPI_COMM_TYPE_SHARED, 0,
                    MPI_INFO_NULL, &shmcomm);

MPI_Win win;
MPI_Win_allocate_shared(local_size*sizeof(double), sizeof(double),
                    MPI_INFO_NULL, shmcomm, &mem, &win);
MPI_Aint sz;
double *ptr;
MPI_Win_shared_query(win, myrank, &sz,
                    &dispunit, &ptr); // get my pointer
double *base_ptr;
MPI_Win_shared_query(win, MPI_PROC_NULL, &sz,
                    &dispunit, &base_ptr); // get win base

// initialize window data
for(i = 0; i < local_size; ++i) ptr[i] = ...;

__sync(); // intrinsic for memory barrier

MPI_Barrier(shmcomm);

// read shared data field (all ranks, relative to base_ptr)
... = base_ptr[...];

MPI_Win_free(&win);
```

Figure 5.4: Example showing the allocation of shared memory and load/store access to that memory

5.1.2 Communication through Shared Memory

A second use case of shared memory is for directly accessing remote memory in a computation without communicating data explicitly (the hardware/cache coherence protocol will communicate the data transparently). This method has the potential to accelerate communication between processes on the same shared-memory node and to reduce the pressure on the memory subsystem. However, because of complex interactions in the cache coherence protocols and false sharing that may lead to excessive cache line transfers, this approach is not always fastest in practice. Copying the data to memory that is accessed exclusively by one thread can improve performance.

```
MPI_Comm_split_type(comm, MPI_COMM_TYPE_SHARED, 0,
                    MPI_INFO_NULL, &shmcomm);
// ... compute neighbors north etc. in shmcomm
MPI_Win_allocate_shared(size*sizeof(double), sizeof(double),
                        info, shmcomm, &mem, &win);
MPI_Win_shared_query(win, north, &sz, &dispunit, &northptr);
MPI_Win_shared_query(win, south, &sz, &dispunit, &southptr);
MPI_Win_shared_query(win, east, &sz, &dispunit, &eastptr);
MPI_Win_shared_query(win, west, &sz, &dispunit, &westptr);

for(iter=0; iter<niters; ++iter) {
 MPI_Win_fence(0, win); // start new access and exposure epoch
 if(north != MPI_PROC_NULL) // the north "communication"
  for(int i=0; i<bx; ++i) a2[ind(i+1,0)]=northptr[ind(i+1,by)];
 if(south != MPI_PROC_NULL) // the south "communication"
  for(int i=0; i<bx; ++i) a2[ind(i+1,by+1)]=southptr[ind(i+1,1)];
 if(east != MPI_PROC_NULL) // the east "communication"
  for(int i=0; i<by; ++i) a2[ind(bx+1,i+1)]=eastptr[ind(1,i+1)];
 if(west != MPI_PROC_NULL) // the west "communication"
  for(int i=0; i<by; ++i) a2[ind(0,i+1)]=westptr[ind(bx,i+1)];

 update_grid(&a1, &a2); // apply operator and swap arrays
}
```

Figure 5.5: Example code for 2-D stencil communication through a shared memory window

Arguably, just copying the data directly into the destination buffer can provide substantial benefits in practice [55]. The example in Figure 5.5 shows our stencil code implemented with communication through a shared memory window. We assume that all neighbors are members of the shared memory window (an extension to the general case is straightforward but would clutter the example).

For more complex operations using lock/unlock epochs, additional synchronizations, e.g., MPI_Win_sync or platform-specific calls, may be necessary, depending on the memory consistency model of the underlying hardware. This issue is expected to be clarified further in future revisions of the MPI standard.

Many advanced schemes are already implemented in MPI libraries to transparently accelerate the performance of regular MPI on-node communication. These schemes often require fast shared-memory synchronization and synergistic copying [16] in order to provide highest performance. Thus, it may be hard to design a

```
OPI_Alloc(&send_buffer, max_particles);

pack_particle_buffer(send_buffer, particle_data);

//Pass ownership of our send buffer.
OPI_Igive(&send_buffer, count, datatype,
    neighbor_rank, TAG, MPI_COMM_WORLD, &reqs[0]);

//Take ownership of a new receive buffer.
OPI_Itake(&recv_buffer, count, datatype,
    neighbor_rank, TAG, MPI_COMM_WORLD, &reqs[1]);

MPI_Waitall(2, reqs, MPI_STATUSES_IGNORE);

unpack_particle_buffer(recv_buffer, particle_data);

//Always return the receive buffer.
OPI_Free(&recv_buffer);
```

Figure 5.6: Example code for ownership passing

faster, correct, and portable method for communication in shared memory. If the goal is to copy data from one process to another, we recommend using normal MPI operations instead of shared-memory windows.

Yet, one particularly simple and effective use of shared memory in communication is *ownership passing*. Here, data is not copied from the sender to the receiver; instead, the buffer that contains the data is passed between the two. This uses the shared-memory hardware directly but guarantees that only one process has access to the data buffer at any time. It thus avoids the complex interactions between multiple processes sharing the same data and elegantly integrates into existing message-passing codes. To demonstrate a possible interface, Figure 5.6 shows a brief example for the boundary communication in a particle code, originally proposed by Friedley et al. [17].

The OPI_ functions are library functions written on top of MPI. In the example, buffers are allocated from a shared-memory window by OPI_Alloc, and the message is prepared in the allocated buffer. Then, the ownership of the buffer is sent to the destination process (which must also have access to the shared memory window) by OPI_Igive. The destination process receives an incoming buffer with OPI_Itake. After transferring the ownership, the sender process cannot access the buffer that has been sent (in the example, the function `OPI_Igive` invalidates the pointer when it completes). Furthermore, after a buffer has been processed, it is given back to the pool for future communications with `OPI_Free`. In this example, arbitrary MPI buffers can be transferred but support for noncontiguous datatypes may be tricky and is thus not further discussed.

This simple example illustrates how shared memory can be used in a "message-passing style," which can be integrated easily into existing programs and potentially achieve significant speedups. The implementation of such a system is nontrivial, but it can be wrapped as a portable library atop MPI shared-memory windows. For details and further optimizations, see [17].

In general, performance programming in shared-memory systems can be tricky because of the interactions between the cache-coherence protocol and the algorithms. Even though this is not part of MPI, users of shared-memory windows are confronted with these complications. We advise users to carefully study the details of the hardware protocols in order to exploit highest performance. Some guidance for cache-coherent systems can be found in [55].

5.1.3   Reducing the Number of Subdomains

Another use case overlaps the two previous cases and demonstrates a higher-level use for shared memory windows. Some computational methods, such as the additive Schwarz method [57, 60], are sensitive to the domain decomposition of the problem. More precisely, such methods perform worse or require more iterations to converge with a finer-grained decomposition. If this is the case, then shared memory windows can be used to reduce the number of separate pieces and still allow parallel computations within each piece. Here, one could have one domain per many-core node and coordinate the computation through fast shared memory.

We now discuss each of the functions involved in MPI shared memory allocation in detail.

5.2   Allocating Shared Memory

The call `MPI_Win_allocate_shared` allocates memory that is accessible by all other processes in the communicator. This call relies on shared-memory features of the underlying hardware and can thus be called only with communicators of which all processes reside in a shared memory domain (e.g., a compute node). In this function, each process exposes local memory to all other processes in the window.

---

int **MPI_Win_allocate_shared**(MPI_Aint size, int disp_unit, MPI_Info info,
  MPI_Comm comm, void *baseptr, MPI_Win *win)

int **MPI_Win_shared_query**(MPI_Win win, int rank, MPI_Aint *size, int *disp_unit,
  void *baseptr)

Table 5.1: C bindings for shared memory window allocation and query calls

---

MPI_WIN_ALLOCATE_SHARED(size, disp_unit, info, comm, baseptr, win, ierror)
  integer disp_unit, info, comm, win, ierror
  integer(kind=MPI_ADDRESS_KIND) size, baseptr

MPI_WIN_SHARED_QUERY(win, rank, size, disp_unit, baseptr, ierror)
  integer win, rank, disp_unit, ierror
  integer(kind=MPI_ADDRESS_KIND) size, baseptr

Table 5.2: Fortran bindings for shared memory window allocation and query calls

A process can expose no memory by specifying zero as the size. The C and Fortran bindings for the function are given in Tables 5.1 and 5.2, respectively.

The call to MPI_Win_allocate_shared returns a process-local pointer to the shared memory region allocated by the calling process. This pointer can be used for normal memory operations, and this memory can also be accessed by remote processes. However, the addresses for the allocated memory segments are meaningful only at the calling process; they will not refer to the correct memory location at any other process (except by coincidence) and thus should never be communicated. The function MPI_Win_shared_query can be used to retrieve the local base addresses of other processes. The address returned by this function is the address valid on the calling process for the shared-memory segment of process rank. The retrieved address is valid only at the process that called MPI_Win_shared_query.

As mentioned above, the communicator passed to MPI_Win_allocate_shared must include only processes that reside on an architecture that supports direct load/store access through shared memory. A programmer may not always be able to easily determine the largest communicator for which all processes can share memory. Therefore, MPI provides the function MPI_Comm_split_type that can create such communicators. The C and Fortran bindings are shown in Tables 5.3 and 5.4, respectively. If MPI_COMM_TYPE_SHARED is passed as split_type,

---

int **MPI_Comm_split_type**(MPI_Comm comm, int split_type, int key, MPI_Info info,
　　　　MPI_Comm *newcomm)

Table 5.3: C interface for communicator creation for shared-memory windows

---

MPI_COMM_SPLIT_TYPE(comm, split_type, key, info, newcomm, ierror)
　　　　integer comm, split_type, key, info, newcomm, ierror

Table 5.4: Fortran interface for communicator creation for shared-memory windows

then the call produces subcommunicators that span shared-memory domains of the largest possible size. The MPI standard also allows implementations to define their own split types to help expose platform-specific capabilities to applications, such as for creating communicators that span single NUMA (non-uniform memory access) domains or single nodes. We recommend that users consult the documentation of the specific implementation for specific details. As for MPI_Comm_split, the key argument is used to determine the ranks of the processes in the new communicator. Ties are broken according to the ranks in the group of the input communicator; thus, using 0 for the key ensures that the ranks of the new communicator are ordered the same way as they were in the input communicator.

Figure 5.7 shows an example in which MPI_Comm_split_type is called on MPI_COMM_WORLD with six processes distributed unevenly on three shared-memory nodes. The collective call returns three different communicators (each calling process is part of exactly one communicator, and thus each process is returned only its own communicator). Programmers can use the normal MPI communicator, group, and collective functions to query which process is in the same split communicator and thus can share memory using shared-memory windows. For example, the routine MPI_Group_translate_ranks can be used to determine which process in one group corresponds to the same process in another group.

5.3 Address Calculation

We have not yet discussed address calculation across process boundaries. While each process can query the local addresses of all processes, one may sometimes wish to view the complete shared-memory segment (the combination of all processes' contribution) as a single consecutive memory location.

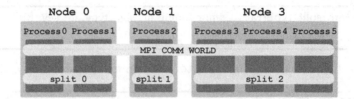

Figure 5.7: Illustration of using MPI_Comm_split_type to create shared-memory windows on three shared-memory nodes with different numbers of processes

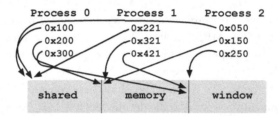

Figure 5.8: Default contiguous memory allocation scheme

By default, MPI-3 follows the "principle of least surprise," meaning that the memory allocated in the same shared-memory window is consecutively addressable. For example, if three processes allocate 0x100 bytes each, then the first byte of process 1 starts after the last byte of process 0. This feature enables convenient address calculation across process boundaries; for example, process 0 can easily compute the offset of the 10th element at process 1. While this enables address arithmetic, the MPI implementation is still allowed to assign each process a different (virtual) base address for the window. Figure 5.8 illustrates an example with three processes sharing a single window, with each process allocating 0x100 bytes.

Since any number of processes can specify size=0 to MPI_Win_allocate_-shared, it may not be trivial to determine the shared memory segment of the first process (the base address of the window). To enable users to easily determine the base address of contiguous shared memory windows, MPI provides a feature whereby if the function MPI_Win_shared_query is called with MPI_PROC_-NULL as the rank, it will return the address of the first byte in the shared memory window, regardless of which process allocated it.

Contiguous allocation may hinder performance because most systems do not al-

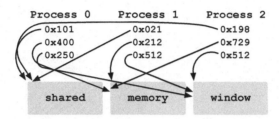

Figure 5.9: Noncontiguous memory allocation scheme using the info key
`alloc_shared_noncontig`

low address remapping at arbitrary sizes (cf. Section 3.8). Therefore, in order
to create contiguous addresses for all processes, the memory is usually allocated
by a single process contiguously and segmented virtually [31]. If the system has
multiple NUMA regions, the entire memory may be allocated in a single NUMA
region to guarantee consecutive addressing. Such allocation, however, may lead
to severe performance degradation for memory accesses on some NUMA architectures. To avoid incurring this performance penalty, the user can allow the MPI
implementation to allocate memory noncontiguously by passing an `MPI_Info` object to `MPI_Win_allocate_shared` with the key `alloc_shared_noncontig`
set to `true`. When this info key is passed, the implementation is not bound to consecutive addressing, as shown in Figure 5.9, and can allocate memory in a NUMA
domain close to each process. However, it also means that the programmer can no
longer compute the base address of the shared memory segment of another process
by simply using the base address at the calling process and the size of each segment
and must instead use the query function `MPI_Win_shared_query`. If `MPI_-
Win_shared_query` is called on a noncontiguous window with `MPI_PROC_NULL`
as the `rank`, it returns the base address of the first process that specified `size`
greater than `0`.

6 Hybrid Programming

What is hybrid programming? Many definitions exist. Here's the one we will use: the use of multiple programming models or systems in the same application. A programming model is an abstraction about a way to program; message passing is a programming model. A programming system is a specification (most likely with a realization) that implements parts or all of one or more programming models. MPI is a programming system; the specification is the standard document, and the realization is one of the implementations. For users of MPI, adding an additional programming system, such as threads or OpenMP, creates a hybrid programming environment. These are common choices because they are designed for a shared-memory environment and exploit hardware support for load and store access. Another option for shared memory within a node was discussed in Chapter 5. Hybrid programming has the benefit of combining several programming models or systems that can be optimized for different parts of the computing environment. Getting good performance from a hybrid model can be difficult, however, and requires understanding how the different systems may interact.

6.1 Background

MPI was designed when processors typically occupied more than one chip; it was common for floating point and even cache memory to be on separate chips. The model of a single process per compute element (processor in MPI terms) was a good fit to the hardware of the day. Shared-memory systems with multiple processors also existed, however, and threads were already of interest. As the original MPI was developed, an effort was made to make the specification thread safe. This meant, for example, avoiding the notion of a "current" message, which was used in some other message-passing programming models. And to a large extent, the design met that goal. However, one case was missed, having to do with the use of `MPI_Probe` or `MPI_Iprobe` to determine, for example, the size of a message and then use MPI to receive that message. Implicit in that is a notion of current message—the message that was probed. As developers began to use threads more aggressively, this oversight came to light. MPI-3 added a new way to probe and receive messages in a thread-safe manner, which we discuss in Section 6.7.

As developers and users gained experience with threads, performance tradeoffs became apparent. While threads, used either by users in their code or within the MPI implementation itself, offer many advantages, they come with a cost. Code must ensure that any access to data that *might* be shared is properly protected against conflicting accesses or updates by separate threads in the same process.

The cost of this guarantee is often high, requiring interaction with the memory system. This was apparent to the developers of MPI implementations shortly after MPI-1 was released and is the reason that MPI-2 introduced `MPI_Init_thread` as well as several support routines to learn about the thread environment. Section 6.2 discusses some of the issues of using threads.

6.2 Thread Basics and Issues

Throughout this book we have referred constantly to *processes* as the entities that communicate with one another. A process may be defined loosely as an address space together with a current state consisting of a program counter, register values, and a subroutine call stack. The fact that a process has only one program counter means that it is doing only one thing at a time; we call such a process *single threaded*. Multiple processes may be executed on a single processor through timesharing, so in some sense the processor is doing more than one thing at a time, but the process isn't.

An important generalization of the process is the situation in which processes have multiple program counters (with associated register values and stacks) sharing the process's address space. The (program counter, register set, stack) triple is called a *thread* and is much like a process in its own right except that it does not have an address space of its own.

The motivation for threads is to allow a concurrent programming model within a single process, with rapid switching of control of the CPU from one thread to another possible because little or no memory management is involved. It also provides a way to program multiple cores in a single processor chip, with each thread possibly running on a separate core simultaneously with the other threads.

Individual threads are not visible outside a process. Therefore, MPI communication among multithreaded processes does not address individual threads; the threads of a process can perform MPI operations on behalf of their process. Using threads in conjunction with message passing can be extremely convenient for several reasons:

- Threads provide a natural implementation of nonblocking communication operations. A thread can be created to do a blocking receive operation. As long as this blocks only the thread and not the process, it has the effect of a nonblocking receive. The same applies to sends.

- Threads are the parallel programming model of choice for "symmetric multiprocessing" shared-memory machines.

- Threads can improve performance by helping make highly latent systems more "latency tolerant."

6.2.1 Thread Safety

In order for threads to be used in conjunction with a message-passing library, the library must be designed to work well with threads. This property is called *thread safety*. Thread safety means that multiple threads can be executing message-passing library calls without interfering with one another. Thread *un*safety occurs when the message-passing system is expected to hold certain parts of the process state, and it is impossible to hold that process state for more than one thread at a time. For example, before threads were commonplace, some libraries used the concept of "the most recently received message" to avoid passing a status argument stored on the process's stack. That is, user code looked something like

```
recv(msg, type);
src = get_src();
len = get_len();
```

This approach works in the single-threaded case; but in the multithreaded case, several receives may be in progress simultaneously, and when get_src is called, it may not be clear for which message the source is supposed to be returned. MPI solves this problem by returning the source as part of the status object, which normally resides on the stack of a specific thread. This problem of a resource that is owned by the message-passing library instead of by the user thread can arise in the case of other data structures as well, such as message buffers, error fields, or "current" contexts. MPI has been carefully engineered to be thread safe in its semantics (with one exception described in Section 6.7), and implementors are encouraged to provide thread-safe implementations, so that MPI can work hand in hand with thread libraries.

For an application to use MPI with threads, it isn't enough that the implementation of MPI be thread safe. The thread library must be aware of the MPI implementation to the extent that execution of a blocking operation will cause the current thread to yield control to another thread in the process rather than cause the process to block. When a message arrives, a thread waiting for it should be made runnable again. Furthermore, when a system call is made, the operating system should block only the thread that made the call, not all threads, or much of the flexibility of user-level threads is lost.

Today, the POSIX standard [40], also known as *Pthreads*, is the most widely used definition for threads on Unix systems, although the limitations of threads defined as a library are well known [4]. Threads are also available in other programming models; for example, threads are a core part of Java, threads are part of C++11, and they are also part of OpenMP [52], which is essentially a thread-based extension for C and Fortran.

Threads are a widely used programming paradigm for shared-memory multicore processors. MPI can be used to program networks of such machines precisely because it is designed to be thread safe. Threads may also be used by a compiler to provide parallelism with little or no direct involvement by the programmer.

6.2.2   Performance Issues with Threads

While threads often provide a convenient programming model, the power and flexibility of threads does not come for free. Several sources of performance challenges arise with threaded programming. One of the most obvious and often the most significant in terms of performance cost is to ensure that threads that are accessing and updating the same data do so in a way that doesn't mangle the data. For example, if two threads are updating the same linked list, they need to be careful to ensure that both don't change the same "next" pointer to the element that they are inserting. The extra coordination needed to avoid this sort of problem introduces extra overhead. And since it is often impossible to tell in advance whether a conflict of this type will arise, that overhead is paid for all accesses. On most systems, the mechanisms for ensuring correctness in this case, such as thread locks or mutexes, are expensive and may take hundreds of processor clock cycles or more. Moreover, it is appallingly easy to make a mistake when writing programs that update shared state, leading to bugs that are hard to find because they depend on the exact timing of the accesses of the threads to the data.

Another performance hazard is more subtle. Even if two threads are accessing different data, if that data is on the same cache line, the system may cause a cache line flush or reload from memory every time the other thread accesses that cache line. So even if the program is written to keep the data that each thread accesses disjoint from other threads, this *false sharing* can cause a significant loss of performance.

The way that the system schedules threads and assigns threads to cores also can make a large difference in performance. For many applications that use threads to provide an event-driven execution model, the most efficient approach usually is to schedule all threads in the process on the same or on nearby cores (nearby in the sense of sharing cache). For computational science applications, however, this is usually the worst possible assignment of threads to cores—in most cases, the code has been designed so that all threads are working on different parts of the same problem, for example, different parts of a large array. In that case, not only do you want the threads assigned to different cores; you also want each thread to stay with the same core so as to make the best use of the cache memory. Note that there is no one right way to schedule threads to cores—the best choice depends on how those threads will run and what data they will access and update.

Now, what does this have to do with MPI? MPI, in the `MPI_THREAD_MULTIPLE` mode that allows the general use of threads, defines the interaction of threads with MPI in a simple way. Specifically, a multithreaded MPI program executes an arbitrary interleaving of the code from each of the threads, subject to any coordination between the threads, such as thread locks. There are no restrictions on how the threads may share MPI objects. MPI allows, for example, one thread to create a request and another to test or wait on it. All the issues in memory synchronization that we discussed in Chapters 3, 4, and 5 apply here as well. Thus, the MPI implementation must be careful to be thread safe, and this often means ensuring that data structures are safely updated when multiple threads may access them. Since memory synchronization is almost always expensive, being thread safe comes with a cost.

6.2.3 Threads and Processes

Thread systems where the operating system (the kernel) is not involved in managing the individual threads are called *user threads*. User threads tend to be faster than *kernel threads* (that is, the time that it takes to switch between threads within the same process is typically smaller with user threads), but often have the restriction that some system calls will block all threads in the process containing the thread that made the system call, not just the calling thread. Such system calls often include `read`, `write`, `recv`, and `send`. This tradeoff in performance versus generality can make it difficult to write truly portable multithreaded programs, since the application cannot assume that the entire process will not be blocked when a thread calls a library routine. The POSIX thread (Pthreads) specification does not specify whether the threads are user or kernel; it is up to the threads implementation.

6.3   MPI and Threads

The MPI-1 standard was designed to be thread safe: with the exception of `MPI_-Probe` and `MPI_Iprobe`, no global state (other than whether MPI was initialized) or notion of "current value" exists in the MPI-1 specification. In MPI-2, `MPI_-File_seek` has the same thread-safety issues as `MPI_Probe`; however, a thread-safe alternative is to use the explicit-offset versions of the I/O routines (e.g., `MPI_-File_read_at`).

The MPI-2 standard benefited from experiences in using threads and building thread-safe MPI implementations. For example, the portability problems experienced by multithreaded applications because of the differences between the capabilities of user and kernel threads led the MPI Forum to require that MPI calls block only the calling thread. This requirement still doesn't address the issue of user versus kernel threads; but if the application uses MPI for all interprocess communication and I/O and makes no explicit system calls, a multithreaded MPI application (assuming that the MPI implementation provides the necessary level of thread support as defined below) is portable, even if the thread system provides only user threads.

The MPI Forum also required that correct MPI programs not attempt to have multiple threads complete the same nonblocking MPI operation. For example, it is invalid to start a nonblocking MPI operation in one thread and then allow several threads to call `MPI_Wait` or `MPI_Test` on the same request object at the same time. It is permissible, of course, to have one thread start a nonblocking MPI operation and have a different thread complete it, as long as there is no possibility that two threads will try to complete (or test) the same operation. This restriction allows MPI implementations to provide high performance in operations involving request objects because the implementation can rely on the fact that only one (user-defined) thread will ever operate on the request.

Another issue has been the performance tradeoffs between multithreaded and single-threaded code. While having multiple threads enables an application to use multiple processors or to perform alternate work while a high-latency operation, such as I/O, proceeds, multithreaded code also requires operations to guard against inconsistent updates to the same memory location from different threads (see Section 6.2.2). These additional operations, particularly if they involve software locks or system calls, can be expensive. Some vendors have provided both single-threaded and multithreaded libraries, but then an application (and even more so, a library) is faced with the question of whether it has linked with the right library. If not, the application will still run but will suffer occasional and mysterious errors.

These experiences are most clearly shown in the function added in MPI-2 to initialize an MPI program: `MPI_Init_thread`. This function, in addition to the `argc` and `argv` arguments of `MPI_Init`, requests a level of thread support and

---

int **MPI_Init_thread**(int *argc, char ***argv, int required, int *provided)

Table 6.1: C binding for initializing MPI when threads may be used

returns the level of thread support that was granted. Here are the kinds of thread support, in order of increasing generality:

MPI_THREAD_SINGLE. Only one (user) thread.

MPI_THREAD_FUNNELED. Many user threads, but only the main thread (the one that initialized MPI) may make MPI calls.

MPI_THREAD_SERIALIZED. Many user threads, but only one thread may make MPI calls at a time (the user must guarantee this).

MPI_THREAD_MULTIPLE. Free for all. Any thread may make MPI calls at any time.

All values are integers and are ordered so that the more general value is greater than all the more restrictive levels of support.

The C and Fortran bindings for MPI_Init_thread are shown in Tables 6.1 and 6.2, respectively. An MPI implementation is permitted to return any of these values as the value of provided. For example, an MPI implementation that is not thread safe will always return MPI_THREAD_SINGLE. On the other hand, an MPI implementation could be provided in several different versions, using the value of required to determine which to choose (through dynamic linking of the libraries), and reporting the value provided. This approach allows the MPI implementor and the MPI user to choose whether to pay any performance penalty that might come with a fully multithreaded MPI implementation.

The function MPI_Init_thread can be used instead of MPI_Init. That is, while an MPI-1 program starts with MPI_Init and ends with MPI_Finalize, an MPI program can start with either MPI_Init or MPI_Init_thread. Regardless of whether MPI_Init or MPI_Init_thread is called, the MPI program must end with a call to MPI_Finalize (there is no "MPI_Finalize_thread"). In addition, the MPI standard requires that the thread in each process that called MPI_Init or MPI_Init_thread, which MPI calls the *main thread*, also be the (only) thread in that process that calls MPI_Finalize.

Note that the value of required does *not* need to be the same on each process that calls MPI_Init_thread. An MPI implementation may choose to give the

---

MPI_INIT_THREAD(required, provided, ierror)
      integer required, provided, ierror

Table 6.2: Fortran binding for initializing MPI when threads may be used

same value of `provided`, of course. We will see below an example where different levels of thread support may be chosen.

The most thread-friendly level of support is `MPI_THREAD_MULTIPLE`. When this level of support is provided, MPI routines may be used in any combination of threads. Such an MPI implementation is called *thread compliant*.

`MPI_Init` initializes MPI to the `MPI_THREAD_SINGLE` level of thread support. However, some MPI implementations may provide an extension to select the level of thread support provided by `MPI_Init` based on command-line arguments to `mpiexec` or environment variables.

No MPI routines exist to create a thread; that task is left to other tools, which may be compilers or libraries. In the next section, we show an example where the new thread is created by using a Pthreads library call. In an OpenMP program, the compiler may create the additional threads. By leaving the exact method of thread creation to other standards, MPI ensures that programs may use any thread approach that is available (as long as it is consistent with the MPI implementation).

6.4   Yet Another Version of **NXTVAL**

One example that we have used is that of a "next value" routine that increments a counter and returns the value. In *Using MPI* [26], we used this example in Section 7.1 to illustrate the use of `MPI_Comm_split`, ready sends, and multiple completions. In Section 4.4 of this book, we developed a version that used remote memory access. In this section we consider a solution to the same problem that uses threads.

Specifically, we will dedicate a thread to providing the counter. This thread will use a blocking receive to wait for requests for a new value and will simply return the data with a blocking send.

The code in Figure 6.1 is reasonably simple. Only a few items need mentioning. The process with rank zero creates the thread in `init_counter`. Any process, including the one with rank zero, may then call `counter_nxtval` to fetch the current value and increment it by the value of `incr`. The `stop_counter` routine uses an `MPI_Barrier` first to ensure that no process is still trying to use the

```
#define EXIT_TAG 1
void *counter_routine(MPI_Comm *counterCommP)
{
 int incr, ival = 0;
 MPI_Status status;
 while (1) {
  MPI_Recv(&incr, 1, MPI_INT, MPI_ANY_SOURCE, MPI_ANY_TAG,
           *counterCommP, &status);
  if (status.MPI_TAG == EXIT_TAG) return 0;
  MPI_Send(&ival, 1, MPI_INT, status.MPI_SOURCE, 0,
           *counterCommP);
  ival += incr;
 }
 return 0;
}
/* We discuss how to eliminate this global variable in the text */
static pthread_t thread_id;
void init_counter(MPI_Comm comm, MPI_Comm *counterCommP)
{
 int rank;
 MPI_Comm_dup_with_info(comm, MPI_INFO_NULL, counterCommP);
 MPI_Comm_rank(comm, &rank);
 if (rank == 0)
 pthread_create(&thread_id, NULL, counter_routine, counterCommP);
}
/* Any process can call this to fetch and increment by val */
void counter_nxtval(MPI_Comm counter_comm, int incr, int *val)
{
 MPI_Send(&incr, 1, MPI_INT, 0, 0, counter_comm);
 MPI_Recv(val, 1, MPI_INT, 0, 0, counter_comm, MPI_STATUS_IGNORE);
}
/* Every process in counter_comm (including rank 0!) must call
   this */
void stop_counter(MPI_Comm *counterCommP)
{
 int rank;
 MPI_Barrier(*counterCommP);
 MPI_Comm_rank(*counterCommP, &rank);
 if (rank == 0) {
  MPI_Send(MPI_BOTTOM, 0, MPI_INT, 0, EXIT_TAG, *counterCommP);
  pthread_join(thread_id, NULL);
 }
 MPI_Comm_free(counterCommP);
}
```

Figure 6.1: Version of nxtval using threads

counter. The process with rank zero then sends a message to itself, but this message is received in `counter_routine`, which is running in a separate thread. Receiving that message causes `counter_routine` to exit, thereby terminating that thread. The `pthread_join` call in `stop_counter` causes the process that created the thread to wait until the thread finishes.

This code depends on the MPI guarantee that a blocking MPI call blocks only the calling thread, not all the threads in the process. Without this requirement, a thread-safe implementation of MPI would have little value. This does require the `MPI_THREAD_MULTIPLE` mode. However, only one process needs this level of thread support. If no other processes are using threads, they could specify `MPI_THREAD_SINGLE` as the required level of thread support.

The variable `thread_id` is global in Figure 6.1. This prevents more than one counter from being active at any time in any single process. However, we all know that global variables are bad. Fortunately, MPI provides a convenient way to attach this variable to the output communicator, `counter_comm_p`, through the use of attributes. Attributes are covered in more detail in Section 12.3.

6.5   Nonblocking Version of `MPI_Comm_accept`

An example of a blocking collective operation whose nonblocking version we would like to have is `MPI_Comm_accept`. Because `MPI_Comm_accept` is not a nonblocking operation, it cannot be canceled. This means that an MPI program that calls `MPI_Comm_accept` cannot continue until the `MPI_Comm_accept` returns. To handle this situation, a program that uses `MPI_Comm_accept` to allow, but not require, another MPI program to attach to it should make a "dummy" connect request to satisfy the `MPI_Comm_accept`.

For example, in Section 10.3.2, we show a program that allows a visualization program to connect to it to allow the visualization program to draw data as it is being computed. But what if we do not want to require the visualization program to connect before proceeding with the computation? We can start by placing the `MPI_Comm_accept` in a separate thread. Doing so allows the program to continue even while the `MPI_Comm_accept` is waiting. However, the program cannot exit until the `MPI_Comm_accept` completes. The easiest way to handle this situation is to have the same program connect to itself to complete the connection, as shown in Figure 6.2.

To allow for this case, we also change the initial connect and accept code so that the first communication is an integer that indicates either a normal (e.g.,

```
integer exit_msg, server
parameter (exit_msg = -1)
...
call MPI_COMM_CONNECT(port_name, MPI_INFO_NULL, 0, &
                      MPI_COMM_SELF, server, ierr)
call MPI_BCAST(exit_msg, 1, MPI_INTEGER, MPI_ROOT, &
               server, ierr)
call MPI_COMM_DISCONNECT(server, ierr)
```

Figure 6.2: Code to connect and terminate a connection

visualization client) connection or an exit message. We use an intercommunicator broadcast to ensure that all the participating processes receive the message.

6.6 Hybrid Programming with MPI

Today, virtually all processors contain multiple cores that access shared memory. These *multicore* processors are an evolution of the symmetric multiprocessor. Many multicore processors, and virtually all multichip nodes, are examples of a NUMA shared-memory processor. On these processors, the approach of combining message passing with shared-memory techniques (such as threads) can provide an effective programming model. This approach is often called *hybrid* or *mixed-model* programming.

MPI was designed to encourage hybrid programming. The thread-safe design has made it relatively easy to use MPI with programs that use either implicit, compiler-based parallelism or explicit, user-programmed parallelism. In this model, the most common MPI thread mode is MPI_THREAD_FUNNELED: only one thread performs MPI calls. The other threads are used only for compute tasks. Using MPI with this model is simple: in fact, it often amounts to nothing more than using a compiler switch to enable the automatic generation by the compiler of multithreaded code for loops. In other cases (e.g., when using OpenMP [52]), a few changes or annotations to the code must be made to enable the thread-based parallelization of loops.

However, if library routines might be called by some of the compute threads, additional care must be exercised. In the MPI_THREAD_FUNNELED mode, a library routine that is called by a thread may wish to ensure that it be allowed to perform MPI calls. By calling MPI_Query_thread, the library can discover the level of thread support , which returns the level of thread support that has been provided. If the level is MPI_THREAD_FUNNELED, only the "main" thread may make MPI

---

int **MPI_Query_thread**(int *provided)

int **MPI_Is_thread_main**(int *flag)

Table 6.3: C routines to discover the level of thread support

---

MPI_QUERY_THREAD(provided, ierror)
        integer provided, ierror

MPI_IS_THREAD_MAIN(flag, ierror)
        logical flag
        integer ierror

Table 6.4: Fortran routines to discover the level of thread support

calls. A thread can determine whether it is the main thread by calling `MPI_Is_thread_main`, which returns a logical value indicating whether the calling thread is the same thread that called `MPI_Init` or `MPI_Init_thread`. The C and Fortran bindings for these calls are given in Tables 6.3 and 6.4, respectively.

Figure 6.3 shows how a library routine can determine that it has an adequate level of thread support. To simplify the `if` tests, this code takes advantage of the ordering of the values of the levels of thread support. Note that `MPI_Query_thread` and `MPI_Is_thread_main` may be used even when MPI is initialized with `MPI_Init` instead of `MPI_Init_thread`.

Using MPI programs with OpenMP. Some systems for thread-based parallelism, such as OpenMP [52], allow the user to control the number of threads with environment variables. Unfortunately, MPI does not require that the environment variables (or `argc` and `argv`) be propagated to every process by the MPI implementation. Therefore, instead of using the environment variables directly, you should specifically set the number of threads to use. Since many MPI implementations start the process with rank 0 in `MPI_COMM_WORLD` with the user's environment, the code in Figure 6.4 can be used. The routine `omp_get_num_threads` will return the number of threads, in case you wish to check that the requested number of threads was provided.

This section only touches on a few of the issues of using OpenMP with MPI. For more on using OpenMP, particularly performance issues and use in a hybrid model, see *Using OpenMP* [9].

```
int thread_level, thread_is_main;

MPI_Query_thread(&thread_level);
MPI_Is_thread_main(&thread_is_main);
if (thread_level > MPI_THREAD_FUNNELED ||
    (thread_level == MPI_THREAD_FUNNELED && thread_is_main)) {
    ... we may make MPI calls
}
else {
    printf("Error! Routine makes MPI calls\n\
This thread does not support them\n");
    return 1;
}
...
```

Figure 6.3: Code to test for the necessary level of thread support. Note that if the thread_level is MPI_THREAD_SERIALIZED, the user must ensure that no other thread makes MPI calls when this library may be making MPI calls.

```
    MPI_Comm_rank(MPI_COMM_WORLD, &rank);
    if (rank == 0) {
        nthreads_str = getenv("OMP_NUM_THREADS");
        if (nthreads_str)
            nthreads = atoi(nthreads_str);
        else
            nthreads = 1;
    }
    MPI_Bcast(&nthreads, 1, MPI_INT, 0, MPI_COMM_WORLD);
    omp_set_num_threads(nthreads);
```

Figure 6.4: Code to set the number of OpenMP threads from within an MPI program

6.7 MPI Message and Thread-Safe Probe

One place where MPI is not fully thread safe is in the use of `MPI_Probe` and
`MPI_Iprobe` to check for a message and then receive that message with a call to
`MPI_Recv`. For example, a common use of a probe call is to allocate space for a
message before receiving it, as follows:

```
MPI_Status status;
MPI_Probe(MPI_ANY_SOURCE, MPI_ANY_TAG, comm, &status);
MPI_Get_count(&status, MPI_INT, &msgsize);
buf = (int*) malloc(msgsize*sizeof(int));
MPI_Recv(buf, msgsize, MPI_INT, status.MPI_SOURCE,
         status.MPI_TAG, comm, MPI_STATUS_IGNORE);
```

In a single-threaded program, MPI guarantees that the message that the `MPI_-
Probe` call returned information about in the `status` argument is the one that
will be received by the subsequent call to `MPI_Recv`. In a multithreaded program, however, it is not possible to guarantee this behavior. Consider the following
sequence of events:

```
Thread 1                          Thread 2
MPI_Probe(...,&status)            MPI_Probe(...,&status)
buf=malloc(...)                   buf=malloc(...)
MPI_Recv(buf,...,
         status.MPI_SOURCE,
         status.MPI_TAG,comm,
         ...)
                                  ... thread 2 is delayed
                                  MPI_Recv(buf,...,
                                           status.MPI_SOURCE,
                                           status.MPI_TAG,comm,
                                           ...)
```

In this example, both threads probe the same message, whose details are returned in
`status`. Both threads then allocate space for this message. Thread 1 then receives
the message (because in this case thread 1 was the first to call `MPI_Recv`). But
when thread 2 attempts to receive the message, that message has already been
received by thread 1. The program will probably fail at this point—either receiving
a message of the wrong length or blocking while attempting to receive a message
that no longer exists.

Before MPI-3, in order to avoid this problem, a program needed to use some
separate thread-synchronization mechanism to ensure that only one thread at a
time executes the `MPI_Probe` to `MPI_Recv` section of code.

```
#define EXIT_TAG 65535
MPI_Message message;
MPI_Status  status;
...
while (1) {
 MPI_Mprobe(MPI_ANY_SOURCE, MPI_ANY_TAG, comm, &message,
            &status);
 /* Check for an all-done message */
 if (status.MPI_TAG == EXIT_TAG) break;
 /* Allocate space for data */
 MPI_Get_count(&status, MPI_BYTE, &msgsize);
 buf = (char *)malloc(msgsize);
 MPI_Mrecv(buf, msgsize, MPI_BYTE, &message, &status);
 ... operate on data in buf
 free(buf);
}
```

Figure 6.5: Code to receive messages of unknown size from other processes

MPI-3 fixed this problem by introducing a new MPI object, called MPI_-Message, and new routines to probe for and receive probed messages. The use of these routines is similar to the MPI_Probe/MPI_Recv sequence above, but with an additional parameter, MPI_Message, to indicate the specific message that has been probed and that is to be received. An example of the use of these new routines is shown in Figure 6.5, which describes code that receives and processes incoming messages. Multiple threads can safely execute this same code (though each thread will need to receive the exit message).

Just as for MPI_Probe, there is a nonblocking version of the routine to probe and return information on a message if present. The use of this routine is shown in Figure 6.6. The C and Fortran bindings for these routines are shown in Tables 6.5 and 6.6, respectively.

There are a few differences between the regular probe and the mprobe routines. First, once a message has been matched by MPI_Mprobe or MPI_Improbe, no other probe or receive operation can match that message. It must be received by calling MPI_Mrecv or MPI_Imrecv. This is necessary if multiple threads are to use the mprobe routines to look for messages. Second, there is a predefined MPI_-Message, MPI_MESSAGE_NO_PROC, which is the message returned by either of the mprobe routines to a message with source MPI_PROC_NULL. Note that this special message does not need to be received, but if it is, the status object will have

```
#define EXIT_TAG 65535
MPI_Message message;
MPI_Status   status;
MPI_Request req;
...
while (1) {
    MPI_Improbe(MPI_ANY_SOURCE, MPI_ANY_TAG, comm, &flag,
                &message, &status);
    if (!flag) {
        ... do some local work
    }
    else {
        /* Check for an all-done message */
        if (status.MPI_TAG == EXIT_TAG) break;
        /* Allocate space for data */
        MPI_Get_count(&status, MPI_BYTE, &msgsize);
        buf = (char *)malloc(msgsize);
        MPI_Imrecv(buf, msgsize, MPI_BYTE, &message, &req);
        /* ... do some local work while the message arrives */
        MPI_Wait(&req, &status);
        /* ... operate on data in buf */
        free(buf);
    }
}
```

Figure 6.6: Code to receive messages of unknown size from other processes in a nonblocking manner

a source of MPI_PROC_NULL, a tag of MPI_ANY_TAG, and a count of 0. These are the same values returned by a regular receive with a source of MPI_PROC_NULL.

Readers of the MPI 3.0 standard should note that there was an unfortunate inconsistency in the Fortran binding for MPI_Improbe, for both the Fortran 9x and the new Fortran 2008 bindings. The flag argument should have been declared LOGICAL but instead was declared as an INTEGER. This will be fixed in the MPI 3.0 errata and in MPI 3.1.

---

int **MPI_Mprobe**(int source, int tag, MPI_Comm comm, MPI_Message *message,
           MPI_Status *status)

int **MPI_Improbe**(int source, int tag, MPI_Comm comm, int *flag,
           MPI_Message *message, MPI_Status *status)

int **MPI_Mrecv**(void* buf, int count, MPI_Datatype datatype,
           MPI_Message *message, MPI_Status *status)

int **MPI_Imrecv**(void* buf, int count, MPI_Datatype datatype,
           MPI_Message *message, MPI_Request *request)

Table 6.5: C bindings for MPI message routines

MPI_MPROBE(source, tag, comm, message, status, ierror)
           integer source, tag, comm, message, status(MPI_STATUS_SIZE),
              ierror

MPI_IMPROBE(source, tag, comm, flag, message, status,ierror)
           integer source, tag, comm, message, status(MPI_STATUS_SIZE),
              ierror
           logical flag

MPI_MRECV(buf, count, datatype, message, status, ierror)
           <type> buf(*)
           integer count, datatype, message, status(MPI_STATUS_SIZE), ierror

MPI_IMRECV(buf, count, datatype, message, request, ierror)
           <type> buf(*)
           integer count, datatype, message, request, ierror

Table 6.6: Fortran bindings for MPI message routines

7 Parallel I/O

In this chapter we describe the parallel I/O capabilities of MPI, sometimes referred to as MPI-IO. We begin with simple example programs that demonstrate the basic use of MPI for I/O and then move on to programs that demonstrate various advanced I/O features of MPI. We also explain how the I/O features of MPI must be used in order to achieve high performance.

7.1 Introduction

In the past, many parallel applications performed I/O either by having each process write to a separate file or by having all processes send their data to one process that gathers all the data and writes it to a single file. Application developers chose these approaches because of historical limitations in the I/O capabilities of many parallel systems: either parallel I/O from multiple processes to a common file was not supported, or, if supported, the performance was poor. On modern parallel systems, however, these limitations no longer exist. With sufficient and appropriately configured I/O hardware and modern parallel and high-performance file systems, such as PVFS, GPFS, or Lustre, one can achieve both high performance and the convenience of a single file by having multiple processes directly access a common file. The I/O interface in MPI is specifically designed to support such accesses and to enable implementations to deliver high performance for such accesses. The interface supports various features—such as noncontiguous accesses, collective I/O, and hints—that are essential for high-performance parallel I/O.

We note that the I/O functions in MPI are for unformatted binary file I/O—similar to the POSIX I/O functions `read` and `write` or the C library functions `fread` and `fwrite`. MPI does not have any functions for formatted text I/O equivalent to `fprintf` and `fscanf` in C.

7.2 Using MPI for Simple I/O

Let us begin with another simple example: a parallel program in which processes need to read data from a common file. Let us assume that there are n processes, each needing to read $(1/n)$th of the file, as shown in Figure 7.1.

7.2.1 Using Individual File Pointers

Figure 7.2 shows one way of writing such a program with MPI. It has the usual functions one would expect for I/O: an open, a seek, a read, and a close. Let us

FILE

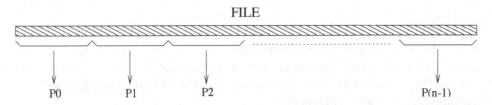

P0   P1   P2   P(n-1)

Figure 7.1: Example with n processes, each needing to read a chunk of data from a common file

look at each of the functions closely. MPI_File_open is the function for opening a file. The first argument to this function is a communicator that indicates the group of processes that need to access the file and that are calling this function. We use MPI_COMM_WORLD as the communicator because all processes in this example need to open and thereafter access a common file called /pfs/datafile. The file name is passed as the second argument to MPI_File_open.

The MPI standard does not specify the format of file names; instead, implementations have the freedom to define the format they support. One can expect that implementations will support familiar naming conventions. For example, implementations running in Unix environments can be expected to support the usual Unix file-naming conventions. In this example and many other examples in this chapter, we use the file name /pfs/datafile (for no particular reason). This name refers to a file called datafile stored in the directory /pfs. Readers can replace this file name with a file name of their choice. The directory name can be expected to be optional in most implementations—if the name is not specified, the implementation will use a default directory such as the directory from where the program is run.

The third argument to MPI_File_open specifies the mode of access; we use MPI_MODE_RDONLY because this program only reads from the file. The fourth argument, called the *info* argument, allows the user to pass hints to the implementation. In this simple example, we don't pass any hints; instead, we pass a null info argument, MPI_INFO_NULL. In Section 7.7 we will consider in detail the issue of passing hints to the implementation. MPI_File_open returns a *file handle* in the last argument. This file handle is to be used for future operations on the open file.

All I/O functions return an integer error code. For simplicity, we don't check error codes in any of the examples in this chapter; we assume that the functions return successfully. The usual MPI methods of error handling, error codes, and classes apply to the I/O functions as well. Note that, unlike the rest of MPI, the

```
/* read from a common file using individual file pointers */
#include "mpi.h"

#define FILESIZE (1024 * 1024)

int main(int argc, char **argv)
{
    int *buf, rank, nprocs, nints, bufsize;
    MPI_File fh;
    MPI_Status status;

    MPI_Init(&argc,&argv);
    MPI_Comm_rank(MPI_COMM_WORLD, &rank);
    MPI_Comm_size(MPI_COMM_WORLD, &nprocs);

    bufsize = FILESIZE/nprocs;
    buf = (int *) malloc(bufsize);
    nints = bufsize/sizeof(int);

    MPI_File_open(MPI_COMM_WORLD, "/pfs/datafile", MPI_MODE_RDONLY,
                  MPI_INFO_NULL, &fh);
    MPI_File_seek(fh, rank*bufsize, MPI_SEEK_SET);
    MPI_File_read(fh, buf, nints, MPI_INT, &status);
    MPI_File_close(&fh);

    free(buf);
    MPI_Finalize();
    return 0;
}
```

Figure 7.2: C program to perform the I/O needed in Figure 7.1 using individual file pointers

default error handler for the MPI I/O functions is `MPI_ERRORS_RETURN` instead of `MPI_ERRORS_ABORT`. Thus it is very important to check the error codes returned by the MPI I/O functions.

After opening the file, each process moves its local file pointer, called *individual file pointer* in MPI, to the location in the file from which the process needs to read data. We use the function `MPI_File_seek` for this purpose. The first argument to `MPI_File_seek` is the file handle returned by `MPI_File_open`. The second argument specifies the offset in the file to seek to, and the third argument `MPI_-SEEK_SET` specifies that the offset must be calculated from the head of the file. File offsets in C are of an implementation-defined type called `MPI_Offset`. The implementation will define `MPI_Offset` to be an integer type of size large enough to represent the largest file size supported by the implementation (for example, an 8-byte integer). We specify the offset to `MPI_File_seek` as a product of the rank of the process and the amount of data (in bytes) to be read by each process. (The offset to `MPI_File_seek` in this example must be specified as a number of bytes because we are using what is known as the default file view. We will consider the issue of file views in detail in Section 7.3.) The file size, which is used in the offset calculation, is specified as a constant in this program for simplicity. However, one can also determine the file size by using the function `MPI_File_get_size`.

We use the function `MPI_File_read` for reading data. On each process, this function reads data from the current location of the process's individual file pointer for the open file. The first argument to `MPI_File_read` is the file handle. The second argument is the address of the buffer in memory into which data must be read. The next two arguments specify the amount of data to be read. Since the data is of type integer, we specify it as a count of the number of integers to be read. The final argument is a status argument, which is the same as the status argument in MPI communication functions, such as `MPI_Recv`. One can determine the amount of data actually read by using the functions `MPI_Get_count` or `MPI_-Get_elements` on the status object returned by `MPI_File_read`, but we don't bother to do so in this example. In most cases, passing `MPI_STATUS_IGNORE` is preferable when the status object is not needed. `MPI_File_read` increments the individual file pointer on each process by the amount of data read by that process. We then close the file using the function `MPI_File_close`.

The five functions, `MPI_File_open`, `MPI_File_seek`, `MPI_File_read`, `MPI_File_write`, and `MPI_File_close`, are actually sufficient to write any I/O program. These functions are quite similar in functionality to their Unix counterparts. The other I/O functions in MPI are for performance, portability, and convenience. Although these five functions can be used as a quick start to using

int **MPI_File_open**(MPI_Comm comm, const char *filename, int amode,
            MPI_Info info, MPI_File *fh)

int **MPI_File_seek**(MPI_File fh, MPI_Offset offset, int whence)

int **MPI_File_read**(MPI_File fh, void *buf, int count, MPI_Datatype datatype,
            MPI_Status *status)

int **MPI_File_write**(MPI_File fh, const void *buf, int count, MPI_Datatype datatype,
            MPI_Status *status)

int **MPI_File_close**(MPI_File *fh)

Table 7.1: C bindings for the five basic I/O functions in MPI

MPI for I/O and for easily porting Unix I/O programs to MPI, we strongly recommend that users not stop here. For real benefits with using MPI for I/O, one must use its special features, such as support for noncontiguous accesses and collective I/O, described in the rest of this chapter.

The C and Fortran bindings for the five basic I/O functions in MPI are given in Tables 7.1 and 7.2.

7.2.2   Using Explicit Offsets

MPI_File_read and MPI_File_write are called *individual-file-pointer functions* because they use the current location of the individual file pointer of each process as the location from where to read/write data. MPI also provides another set of functions, called *explicit-offset functions* (MPI_File_read_at and MPI_-File_write_at), which don't use the individual file pointer. In these functions, the file offset is passed directly as an argument to the function. A separate seek is therefore not needed. If multiple threads of a process are accessing the same file, the explicit-offset functions, rather than the individual-file-pointer functions, must be used for thread safety.

Figure 7.3 shows how the same example of Figure 7.1 can be implemented by using MPI_File_read_at instead of MPI_File_read. We use Fortran this time in order to show how the I/O functions in MPI can be used from Fortran. Other than a difference in programming language, the only difference in this example is that MPI_File_seek is not called; instead, the offset is passed as an argument to MPI_File_read_at. We also check how much data was actually read by

---

MPI_FILE_OPEN(comm, filename, amode, info, fh, ierror)
        character*(*) filename
        integer comm, amode, info, fh, ierror

MPI_FILE_SEEK(fh, offset, whence, ierror)
        integer fh, whence, ierror
        integer(kind=MPI_OFFSET_KIND) offset

MPI_FILE_READ(fh, buf, count, datatype, status, ierror)
        <type> buf(*)
        integer fh, count, datatype, status(MPI_STATUS_SIZE), ierror

MPI_FILE_WRITE(fh, buf, count, datatype, status, ierror)
        <type> buf(*)
        integer fh, count, datatype, status(MPI_STATUS_SIZE), ierror

MPI_FILE_CLOSE(fh, ierror)
        integer fh, ierror

Table 7.2: Fortran bindings for the five basic I/O functions in MPI

using `MPI_Get_count` on the status object returned by `MPI_File_read_at`. The individual file pointer is neither used nor incremented by the explicit-offset functions.

File offsets are of type `integer (kind=MPI_OFFSET_KIND)` in Fortran. `MPI_OFFSET_KIND` is a constant defined by the MPI implementation in the include file `mpif.h` and in the Fortran modules `mpi` and `mpi_f08`. `MPI_OFFSET_KIND` defines an integer of size large enough to represent the maximum file size supported by the implementation.

Notice how we have passed the file offset to `MPI_File_read_at` in Fortran. We did not pass the expression `rank*nints*INTSIZE` directly to the function. Instead we defined a variable `offset` of type `integer (kind=MPI_OFFSET_-KIND)`, assigned the value of the expression to it, and then passed `offset` as a parameter to `MPI_File_read_at`. We did so because, in the absence of function prototypes, if we passed the expression directly to the function, the compiler would pass it as an argument of type `integer`. The MPI implementation expects an argument of type `integer (kind=MPI_OFFSET_KIND)`, which could be (and often is) of size larger than `integer`. For example, on many machines integers are of size four bytes, whereas file offsets may be defined to be of size eight bytes in order to support large files. In such cases, passing an integer expression as the

```fortran
! read from a common file using explicit offsets
PROGRAM main
    use mpi

    integer FILESIZE, MAX_BUFSIZE, INTSIZE
    parameter (FILESIZE=1048576, MAX_BUFSIZE=1048576, INTSIZE=4)
    integer buf(MAX_BUFSIZE), rank, ierr, fh, nprocs, nints
    integer status(MPI_STATUS_SIZE), count
    integer (kind=MPI_OFFSET_KIND) offset

    call MPI_INIT(ierr)
    call MPI_COMM_RANK(MPI_COMM_WORLD, rank, ierr)
    call MPI_COMM_SIZE(MPI_COMM_WORLD, nprocs, ierr)

    call MPI_FILE_OPEN(MPI_COMM_WORLD, '/pfs/datafile', &
                       MPI_MODE_RDONLY, MPI_INFO_NULL, fh, ierr)
    nints = FILESIZE/(nprocs*INTSIZE)
    offset = rank * nints * INTSIZE
    call MPI_FILE_READ_AT(fh, offset, buf, nints, MPI_INTEGER, &
                          status, ierr)
    call MPI_GET_COUNT(status, MPI_INTEGER, count, ierr)
    print *, 'process ', rank, 'read ', count, 'integers'

    call MPI_FILE_CLOSE(fh, ierr)
    call MPI_FINALIZE(ierr)
END PROGRAM main
```

Figure 7.3: Fortran program to perform the I/O needed in Figure 7.1 using explicit offsets

offset parameter in Fortran would result in a runtime error that is hard to debug. Many users make this mistake; for example, they directly pass 0 as the offset. The problem can be avoided by passing only variables of the correct type (`integer (kind=MPI_OFFSET_KIND)`) to functions that take file offsets or displacements as arguments. A high quality implementation of the `mpi_f08` module will detect these errors and is one reason why the MPI standard strongly encourages the use of the most recent Fortran module for MPI.

C and Fortran bindings for the explicit-offset functions are given in Tables 7.3 and 7.4.

---

int **MPI_File_read_at**(MPI_File fh, MPI_Offset offset, void *buf, int count,
            MPI_Datatype datatype, MPI_Status *status)

int **MPI_File_write_at**(MPI_File fh, MPI_Offset offset, const void *buf, int count,
            MPI_Datatype datatype, MPI_Status *status)

Table 7.3: C bindings for the explicit-offset functions

MPI_FILE_READ_AT(fh, offset, buf, count, datatype, status, ierror)
            <type> buf(*)
            integer fh, count, datatype, status(MPI_STATUS_SIZE), ierror
            integer(kind=MPI_OFFSET_KIND) offset

MPI_FILE_WRITE_AT(fh, offset, buf, count, datatype, status, ierror)
            <type> buf(*)
            integer fh, count, datatype, status(MPI_STATUS_SIZE), ierror
            integer(kind=MPI_OFFSET_KIND) offset

Table 7.4: Fortran bindings for the explicit-offset functions

7.2.3 Writing to a File

In the above example, if we wanted to write to the file instead of reading, we would simply replace MPI_File_read with MPI_File_write in Figure 7.2 and MPI_-File_read_at with MPI_File_write_at in Figure 7.3. In addition, in both programs, we would need replace the flag MPI_MODE_RDONLY that was passed to MPI_File_open with the two flags MPI_MODE_CREATE and MPI_MODE_-WRONLY. MPI_MODE_CREATE is necessary to create the file if it doesn't already exist. MPI_MODE_WRONLY indicates that the file is being opened for writing only. In C, we can pass two (or more) flags by using the bitwise-or operator as follows: MPI_MODE_CREATE | MPI_MODE_WRONLY. In Fortran, we can use the addition operation: MPI_MODE_CREATE + MPI_MODE_WRONLY. The flag MPI_MODE_-RDWR must be used if the file is being opened for both reading and writing.

We note that to create a file with MPI_File_open, most implementations would require that the directory containing the file (specified in the file name) exist before the call to MPI_File_open. (The Unix open function also requires this.) Users can create the directory, for example, with the Unix command mkdir before running the program.

A file can be deleted by using the function MPI_File_delete in an MPI program or by using a file-deletion command, such as rm, from the command prompt.

7.3   Noncontiguous Accesses and Collective I/O

In the preceding section we saw how to use MPI for a simple example where the I/O request of each process is contiguous. I/O of this kind could also be done with regular Unix I/O functions. In many parallel scientific applications, however, each process needs to access lots of small pieces of data located noncontiguously in the file. One way to access noncontiguous data is to use a separate function call to read/write each small contiguous piece, as in Unix I/O. Because of high I/O latency, however, accessing small amounts of data at a time is *very* expensive. A great advantage of MPI over Unix I/O is the ability in MPI to access noncontiguous data with a single function call. Combined with that is the ability to specify—with the help of a class of read/write functions called *collective I/O functions*—that a group of processes need to access a common file at about the same time. By using these two features, the user can provide the implementation with the entire (noncontiguous) access information of a process as well as information about which set of processes are accessing the file simultaneously. The implementation can use this information to perform certain optimizations that can improve performance significantly. These optimizations typically involve merging several small accesses and making few large requests to the file system [67].

7.3.1   Noncontiguous Accesses

Let us first see how MPI supports noncontiguous accesses in the file. MPI has a notion of a *file view*, which we did not explain in the two example programs so far, but it was implicitly used nonetheless. A file view in MPI defines which portion of a file is "visible" to a process. A read or write function can access data only from the visible portion of the file; all other data will be skipped. When a file is first opened, the entire file is visible to the process, and MPI treats the file as consisting of all bytes (not integers, floating-point numbers, etc.). The user can read any byte or write to any byte in the file. The individual file pointer of each process and also the shared file pointer (discussed in Section 7.6) are set to offset 0 when the file is opened.

It is possible and often desirable to change a process's file view by using the function MPI_File_set_view. This may be done for two reasons:

- To indicate the type of data that the process is going to access, for example, integers or floating-point numbers, rather than just bytes. This is particularly necessary for file portability, that is, if the user wants to access the file later on from a different machine with a different data representation. We will consider this issue further in Section 7.9.

- To indicate which parts of the file should be skipped, that is, to specify noncontiguous accesses in the file.

For accessing data using the individual file pointer or explicit offsets, each process can specify a different view if it needs to. For accessing data with the shared file pointer, however, all processes must specify the same view (see Section 7.6). The function for setting the file view is `MPI_File_set_view`; the view can be changed any number of times during the program.

MPI datatypes, both basic and derived, are used to specify file views. File views are specified by a triplet: *displacement*, *etype*, and *filetype*. The displacement indicates the number of bytes (always bytes!) to be skipped from the start of the file. It can be used, for example, to skip reading the header portion of a file if the file contains a header. The etype is the basic unit of data access. It can be any MPI basic or derived datatype. All file accesses are performed in units of etype (no less). All offsets in the file (for example, file-pointer locations, offsets passed to the explicit-offset functions) are specified in terms of the number of etypes. For example, if the etype is set to `MPI_INT`, the individual and shared file pointers can be moved by a number of integers, rather than bytes.

The filetype is an MPI basic or derived datatype that specifies which portion of the file is visible to the process and of what type is the data. The filetype either must be the same as the etype or must be a derived datatype constructed out of etypes.[1] The file view of a process begins from the displacement and consists of multiple contiguous copies of the filetype. This is similar to the use of the datatype argument in the `MPI_Send` function, with the additional displacement.

When a file is first opened, the displacement is 0, and the etype and filetype are both `MPI_BYTE`. This is known as the default file view. The two programs we considered in the preceding section (Figures 7.2 and 7.3) use the default file view.

Figure 7.4 shows an example of a file view consisting of a displacement of five integers, an etype of `MPI_INT`, and a filetype consisting of two integers followed by a gap of four integers. The figure shows how the file is "tiled" with this filetype.

---

[1] A restriction on filetypes is that a filetype must specify only monotonically nondecreasing offsets in the file. For example, a derived datatype that specifies offsets in the order {2, 6, 5, 7, 4} cannot be used as a valid filetype. We consider this issue further in Section 7.4.5.

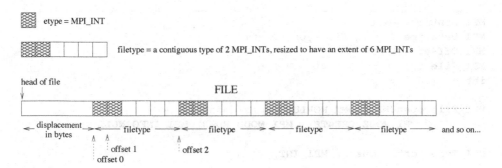

Figure 7.4: Example of file view

Once this view is set, only the shaded portions of the file will be read/written by any read/write function; the blank unshaded portions will be skipped. Figure 7.5 shows the corresponding C code for setting this view. We first create a contiguous derived datatype consisting of two integers. We then set a gap of four integers at the end of this datatype, by using the function `MPI_Type_create_resized` with a lower bound of zero and an extent of `6 * sizeof(int)`. We commit the resized datatype, and the committed datatype is used as the filetype. The etype is `MPI_INT`, and the displacement is `5 * sizeof(int)`.

The arguments passed to `MPI_File_set_view` are the file handle, displacement, etype, filetype, data representation, and info (hints). We consider data representation and hints in Sections 7.9 and 7.7, respectively. Here we set the data representation to the default value `native`, which means the data representation in the file is the same as in memory, and we pass `MPI_INFO_NULL` as the info argument.

When this program is run, the single `MPI_File_write` call will result in 1,000 integers written to the file in a noncontiguous fashion as defined by the file view: an initial gap of size equal to five integers, then two integers of data, then a gap of size four integers, followed again by two integers of data, then a gap of size four integers, and so forth. File views thus provide a powerful way of specifying noncontiguous accesses in the file. Any noncontiguous access pattern can be specified because any MPI derived datatype can be used to define the file view.

C and Fortran bindings for `MPI_File_set_view` and `MPI_Type_create_-resized` are given in Tables 7.5 and 7.6.

```
MPI_Aint lb, extent;
MPI_Datatype etype, filetype, contig;
MPI_Offset disp;
MPI_File fh;
int buf[1000];

MPI_File_open(MPI_COMM_WORLD, "/pfs/datafile",
          MPI_MODE_CREATE | MPI_MODE_RDWR, MPI_INFO_NULL, &fh);

MPI_Type_contiguous(2, MPI_INT, &contig);
lb = 0;
extent = 6 * sizeof(int);
MPI_Type_create_resized(contig, lb, extent, &filetype);
MPI_Type_commit(&filetype);

disp = 5 * sizeof(int); /* assume displacement in this file
                           view is of size equal to 5 integers */
etype = MPI_INT;

MPI_File_set_view(fh, disp, etype, filetype, "native",
            MPI_INFO_NULL);
MPI_File_write(fh, buf, 1000, MPI_INT, MPI_STATUS_IGNORE);
```

Figure 7.5: C code to set the view shown in Figure 7.4.

---

int **MPI_File_set_view**(MPI_File fh, MPI_Offset disp, MPI_Datatype etype,
          MPI_Datatype filetype, const char *datarep, MPI_Info info)

int **MPI_Type_create_resized**(MPI_Datatype oldtype, MPI_Aint lb, MPI_Aint extent,
          MPI_Datatype *newtype)

Table   7.5:   C   bindings   for   MPI_File_set_view   and
MPI_Type_create_resized

MPI_FILE_SET_VIEW(fh, disp, etype, filetype, datarep, info, ierror)
            integer fh, etype, filetype, info, ierror
            character*(*) datarep
            integer(kind=MPI_OFFSET_KIND) disp

MPI_TYPE_CREATE_RESIZED(oldtype, lb, extent, newtype, ierror)
            integer oldtype, newtype, ierror
            integer(kind=MPI_ADDRESS_KIND) lb, extent

Table 7.6: Fortran bindings for `MPI_File_set_view` and `MPI_Type_create_resized`

Figure 7.6: Example with n processes, each needing to read blocks of data from the file, the blocks being distributed in a round-robin (block-cyclic) manner among processes.

7.3.2 Collective I/O

Now let us consider the use of *collective* I/O functions together with noncontiguous accesses. We use a different example, shown in Figure 7.6. The difference between this example and the first example we considered in this chapter (Figure 7.1) is that each process in this case reads smaller blocks of data distributed in a round-robin (block-cyclic) manner in the file. With Unix I/O, the only way to read this data would be to read each block separately, because the Unix `read` function allows the user to access only a single contiguous piece of data at a time. One can also do the same with MPI (by using the default file view), but one can do better. Instead of making several read calls, one can define the noncontiguous file view of each process in order to read data with a single function, and one can use a collective read function to specify that all processes need to read data. The corresponding code is given in Figure 7.7. A good MPI implementation will be able to deliver much better performance if the user expresses the I/O in the program in this manner, rather than using Unix-style I/O. Let's go through this program in detail.

The constant `FILESIZE` specifies the size of the file in bytes. `INTS_PER_BLK`

```
/* noncontiguous access with a single collective I/O function */
#include "mpi.h"

#define FILESIZE      1048576
#define INTS_PER_BLK  16

int main(int argc, char **argv)
{
    int *buf, rank, nprocs, nints, bufsize;
    MPI_File fh;
    MPI_Datatype filetype;

    MPI_Init(&argc,&argv);
    MPI_Comm_rank(MPI_COMM_WORLD, &rank);
    MPI_Comm_size(MPI_COMM_WORLD, &nprocs);

    bufsize = FILESIZE/nprocs;
    buf = (int *) malloc(bufsize);
    nints = bufsize/sizeof(int);

    MPI_File_open(MPI_COMM_WORLD, "/pfs/datafile", MPI_MODE_RDONLY,
                  MPI_INFO_NULL, &fh);

    MPI_Type_vector(nints/INTS_PER_BLK, INTS_PER_BLK,
                    INTS_PER_BLK*nprocs, MPI_INT, &filetype);
    MPI_Type_commit(&filetype);
    MPI_File_set_view(fh, INTS_PER_BLK*sizeof(int)*rank, MPI_INT,
                  filetype, "native", MPI_INFO_NULL);

    MPI_File_read_all(fh, buf, nints, MPI_INT, MPI_STATUS_IGNORE);
    MPI_File_close(&fh);

    MPI_Type_free(&filetype);
    free(buf);
    MPI_Finalize();
    return 0;
}
```

Figure 7.7: C program to perform the I/O needed in Figure 7.6. Each process reads noncontiguous data with a single collective read function.

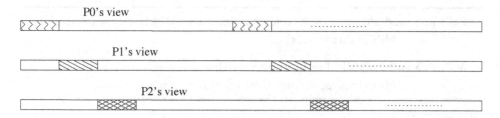

Figure 7.8: The file views created by the program in Figure 7.7

specifies the size of each of the blocks that a process needs to read; the size is specified as the number of integers in the block. Each process needs to read several of these blocks distributed in a cyclic fashion in the file. We open the file using MPI_File_open and specify MPI_COMM_WORLD as the communicator, because all processes access a common file /pfs/datafile. Next we construct the file view. For specifying the filetype, we create a derived datatype of type "vector" by using the function MPI_Type_vector. The first argument to this function is the number of blocks each process needs to read. The second argument is the number of integers in each block. The third argument is the number of integers between the starting elements of two consecutive blocks that a process needs to read. The fourth argument is the type of each data item—MPI_INT in this case. The newly created vector datatype is returned in the fifth argument. We commit this datatype and then use it as the filetype argument for MPI_File_set_view. The etype is MPI_INT. Note how we use the displacement argument of MPI_-File_set_view to specify the file offset from where the view of each process begins. The displacement is specified (in bytes, always) as the product of the size of the block and the rank of the process. As a result, the file view of each process is a vector datatype starting from the displacement, as illustrated in Figure 7.8.

I/O is performed by using the collective version of MPI_File_read, called MPI_File_read_all. Notice that there is no difference in the parameter list of MPI_File_read and MPI_File_read_all. The only difference is that MPI_-File_read_all is defined to be a *collective I/O function*, as suggested by the _-all in its name. Collective means that the function must be called by every process in the communicator that was passed to the MPI_File_open function with which the file was opened. This communicator information is implicitly contained in the file handle passed to MPI_File_read_all. MPI_File_read, on the other hand, may be called independently by any subset of processes and is therefore known as an *independent I/O function*.

---

int **MPI_File_read_all**(MPI_File fh, void *buf, int count, MPI_Datatype datatype,
              MPI_Status *status)

int **MPI_File_write_all**(MPI_File fh, const void *buf, int count,
              MPI_Datatype datatype, MPI_Status *status)

Table 7.7: C bindings for `MPI_File_read_all` and `MPI_File_write_all`

MPI_FILE_READ_ALL(fh, buf, count, datatype, status, ierror)
              <type> buf(*)
              integer fh, count, datatype, status(MPI_STATUS_SIZE), ierror

MPI_FILE_WRITE_ALL(fh, buf, count, datatype, status, ierror)
              <type> buf(*)
              integer fh, count, datatype, status(MPI_STATUS_SIZE), ierror

---

Table 7.8: Fortran bindings for `MPI_File_read_all` and `MPI_File_write_all`

When a process calls an independent I/O function, the implementation has no idea what other processes might do and must therefore satisfy the request of each process individually. When a process calls a collective I/O function, however, the implementation knows exactly which other processes will also call the same collective I/O function, each process providing its own access information. The implementation may, therefore, choose to wait for all those processes to reach the function, in order to analyze the access requests of different processes and service the combined request efficiently. Although the request of one process may consist of numerous small noncontiguous pieces the combined request of all processes may be large and contiguous, as in Figure 7.6. Optimization of this kind is broadly referred to as collective I/O [13, 12, 65], and it can improve performance significantly. Therefore, the user should, when possible, use the collective I/O functions instead of independent I/O functions. We consider this issue further in Section 7.10.

C and Fortran bindings for `MPI_File_read_all` and `MPI_File_write_all` are given in Tables 7.7 and 7.8. Collective versions also exist for the explicit-offset functions, `MPI_File_read_at` and `MPI_File_write_at`.

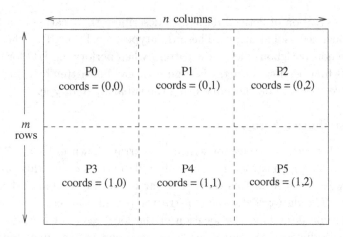

2D array distributed on a 2 x 3 process grid

Figure 7.9: A 2-D array of size m rows and n columns distributed among six processes arranged as a 2×3 logical grid. The array is to be written to a common file containing the global array in row-major order (as in C).

7.4 Accessing Arrays Stored in Files

In this section we demonstrate how MPI makes it easy to access subarrays and distributed arrays (both regularly and irregularly distributed) stored in files. I/O of this kind is very commonly needed in parallel programs.

Many parallel programs have one or more multidimensional arrays distributed among processes in some manner. Each array must be read from or written to a file in which the storage order corresponds to that of the global array in either row-major order (as in C programs) or column-major order (as in Fortran programs). Figure 7.9 shows such an example. A two-dimensional array of size m rows and n columns is distributed among six processes arranged as a 2×3 logical grid. The array must be written to a common file containing the global array in row-major (C) order. Clearly the local array of each process is not located contiguously in the file: each row of the local array of a process is separated by rows of the local arrays of other processes. MPI provides a convenient way of describing I/O of this kind and performing it with a single I/O function call. If the user uses the collective I/O functions, the MPI implementation may also be able to deliver high performance for this kind of access, even though the accesses are noncontiguous.

Two datatype constructors, called *darray* and *subarray*, are defined in MPI that facilitate the creation of derived datatypes describing the location of a local array within a linearized global array. These datatypes can be used as the filetype to describe the noncontiguous file-access pattern when performing I/O for distributed arrays. Let's first see how the array in Figure 7.9 can be written by using the darray datatype. We then will do the same using the subarray datatype.

7.4.1 Distributed Arrays

Figure 7.10 shows the program for writing the array shown in Figure 7.9 by using the darray datatype constructor. The only difference between this program and the others we have seen in this chapter so far is the way in which the filetype is constructed. The darray datatype constructor provides an easy way to create a derived datatype describing the location of the local array of a process within a linearized multidimensional global array for common regular distributions. The distributions supported are the array distributions defined in High Performance Fortran (HPF), namely, block, cyclic, and the general block-cyclic or cyclic(k) distribution [42]. The array can have any number of dimensions; and each dimension can be distributed in any of the above ways, or the dimension can be replicated (that is, not distributed). The input to the darray constructor consists of the array size and distribution information and the rank of the process whose local array is the one to be described. The output is a derived datatype describing the layout of the local array of that process within the linearized global array for the specified distribution. One can create such a derived datatype by using other MPI datatype constructors, but doing so is more difficult. Therefore, these array datatype constructors were added to MPI as convenience functions.

The first argument to `MPI_Type_create_darray` is the number of processes over which the array is distributed, six in this case. The second argument is the rank of the process whose local array is the one to be described, which in this case is the process calling the function. The third argument is the number of dimensions of the global array (and also the local array). The fourth argument is an array that specifies the size of the global array in each dimension. The fifth argument is an array specifying the way in which the global array is distributed in each dimension. In this example, we specify a block distribution using `MPI_DISTRIBUTE_BLOCK`. The sixth argument specifies the distribution parameter for each dimension, that is, the k in a cyclic(k) distribution. For block and cyclic distributions, which don't need this parameter, this argument is specified as `MPI_DISTRIBUTE_DFLT_-DARG`. The seventh argument is an array specifying the number of processes along each dimension of the logical process grid over which the array is distributed. The

```
gsizes[0] = m;      /* no. of rows in global array */
gsizes[1] = n;      /* no. of columns in global array*/

distribs[0] = MPI_DISTRIBUTE_BLOCK;   /* block distribution */
distribs[1] = MPI_DISTRIBUTE_BLOCK;   /* block distribution */

dargs[0] = MPI_DISTRIBUTE_DFLT_DARG; /* default block size */
dargs[1] = MPI_DISTRIBUTE_DFLT_DARG; /* default block size */

psizes[0] = 2;   /* no. of processes in vertical dimension
                     of process grid */
psizes[1] = 3;   /* no. of processes in horizontal dimension
                     of process grid */

MPI_Comm_rank(MPI_COMM_WORLD, &rank);
MPI_Type_create_darray(6, rank, 2, gsizes, distribs, dargs,
                    psizes, MPI_ORDER_C, MPI_FLOAT, &filetype);
MPI_Type_commit(&filetype);

MPI_File_open(MPI_COMM_WORLD, "/pfs/datafile",
            MPI_MODE_CREATE | MPI_MODE_WRONLY,
            MPI_INFO_NULL, &fh);

MPI_File_set_view(fh, 0, MPI_FLOAT, filetype, "native",
                MPI_INFO_NULL);

local_array_size = num_local_rows * num_local_cols;
MPI_File_write_all(fh, local_array, local_array_size,
                MPI_FLOAT, &status);

MPI_File_close(&fh);
```

Figure 7.10: C program for writing the distributed array of Figure 7.9 to a common file using a "darray" datatype as the filetype

process grid is always assumed to have the same number of dimensions as the global array. If the array is not distributed along a particular dimension, the number of processes for that dimension must be specified as 1. For example, a 100×100 array can be distributed over 4 processes arranged as a 2×2 grid, or 1×4 grid, or 4×1 grid. The ordering of processes in the grid is *always* assumed to be row-major, as in the case of virtual Cartesian process topologies in MPI. If a program assumes a different ordering of processes, one cannot use the darray constructor but instead must use subarray or other derived datatype constructors. We discuss this issue further in Section 7.4.2.

The eighth argument to `MPI_Type_create_darray` specifies the storage order of the local array in memory and also of the global array in the file. It can be specified as either `MPI_ORDER_C` or `MPI_ORDER_FORTRAN`, which corresponds, respectively, to row-major ordering as in C or column-major ordering as in Fortran. The ninth argument is the datatype describing the type of each array element, which in this example is `MPI_FLOAT`. The function returns in the last argument a derived datatype that describes the layout of the local array of the specified process within the linearized global array for the specified distribution. We commit this datatype and set the file view using this datatype as the filetype. For maximum performance, we call the collective write function `MPI_File_write_all` and not an independent write function. Note that the count and datatype passed to `MPI_-File_write_all` describe the memory layout of the local array. In this example we assume that the local array is contiguously allocated in memory. We therefore specify the datatype as `MPI_FLOAT` and the count as the number of elements in the local array. In Section 7.4.4, we will consider an example in which the local array is noncontiguous in memory, and we will see how to construct a derived datatype that describes the memory layout.

7.4.2   A Word of Warning about Darray

Although the darray datatype is convenient to use, one must be careful about using it because it assumes a very specific definition of data distribution—the exact definition of the distributions in HPF [42]. This assumption matters particularly when in a block distribution the size of the array in any dimension is not evenly divisible by the number of processes in that dimension. In such a case, HPF defines the block size to be obtained by a ceiling division of the array size and the number of processes.[2] If one assumes a different definition in a program, such as floor division

---

[2]The ceiling division of two integers i and j is defined as $\lceil i/j \rceil = (i+j-1)/j$. For example, $\lceil 5/4 \rceil = 2$. Therefore, a block distribution of an array of size 5 on 4 processes is defined as 2

(which is regular integer division, for example, $\lfloor 5/4 \rfloor = 1$), one cannot use the darray constructor because the resulting datatype will not match the distribution. Furthermore, darray assumes that the ordering of processes in the logical grid is always row-major, as in the virtual Cartesian process topologies of MPI (see Figure 7.9). If a program follows a different ordering, such as column-major, the datatype returned by darray will be incorrect for that program.

If one follows a different definition of distribution or a different process-grid ordering, one can use the subarray datatype instead. For this datatype, the location (starting coordinates) of the local array in the global array must be specified explicitly. The subarray datatype, however, will work only for block distributions, not cyclic or cyclic(k) distributions (because one cannot specify a stride in any dimension). In cases where subarray is also not applicable, one can create the derived datatype explicitly by using some of the general constructors defined in MPI, such as indexed or struct. *Any* data layout can be specified by (recursively) using the other datatype constructors; it's just easier to use darray or subarray wherever it works.

7.4.3 Subarray Datatype Constructor

The subarray datatype constructor can be used to create a derived datatype that describes the layout of a subarray within a linearized array. One describes the subarray by its starting coordinates and size in each dimension. The example of Figure 7.9 can also be written by using subarray instead of darray, because the local array of each process is effectively a subarray of the global array. Figure 7.11 shows the "subarray version" of the program in Figure 7.10. This program is a bit more complicated than the darray version because we have to specify the subarray explicitly. In darray, the subarray is implicitly specified by specifying the data distribution.

We use the process-topology function `MPI_Cart_create` to create a virtual Cartesian process grid. We do this purely for convenience: it allows us to find the coordinates of each process within the two-dimensional grid (with the function `MPI_Cart_coords`) and use these coordinates to calculate the global indices of the first element of the local array of each process.

The first argument to `MPI_Type_create_subarray` is the number of dimensions of the array. The second argument is the size of the array in each dimension. The third argument is the size of the subarray in each dimension. The fourth argument specifies the starting coordinates of the subarray in each dimension of

---

elements on processes 0 and 1, 1 element on process 2, and 0 elements on process 3.

```
gsizes[0] = m;   /* no. of rows in global array */
gsizes[1] = n;   /* no. of columns in global array*/

psizes[0] = 2;   /* no. of processes in vertical dimension
                        of process grid */
psizes[1] = 3;   /* no. of processes in horizontal dimension
                        of process grid */

lsizes[0] = m/psizes[0];   /* no. of rows in local array */
lsizes[1] = n/psizes[1];   /* no. of columns in local array */

dims[0] = 2;
dims[1] = 3;
periods[0] = periods[1] = 1;
MPI_Cart_create(MPI_COMM_WORLD, 2, dims, periods, 0, &comm);
MPI_Comm_rank(comm, &rank);
MPI_Cart_coords(comm, rank, 2, coords);

/* global indices of the first element of the local array */
start_indices[0] = coords[0] * lsizes[0];
start_indices[1] = coords[1] * lsizes[1];

MPI_Type_create_subarray(2, gsizes, lsizes, start_indices,
                         MPI_ORDER_C, MPI_FLOAT, &filetype);
MPI_Type_commit(&filetype);

MPI_File_open(comm, "/pfs/datafile",
              MPI_MODE_CREATE | MPI_MODE_WRONLY,
              MPI_INFO_NULL, &fh);
MPI_File_set_view(fh, 0, MPI_FLOAT, filetype, "native",
              MPI_INFO_NULL);

local_array_size = lsizes[0] * lsizes[1];
MPI_File_write_all(fh, local_array, local_array_size,
                   MPI_FLOAT, &status);

MPI_File_close(&fh);
```

Figure 7.11: C program for writing the distributed array of Figure 7.9 to a common file using a "subarray" datatype as the filetype

---

int **MPI_Type_create_darray**(int size, int rank, int ndims, const int array_of_gsizes[],
                const int array_of_distribs[], const int array_of_dargs[],
                const int array_of_psizes[], int order, MPI_Datatype oldtype,
                MPI_Datatype *newtype)

int **MPI_Type_create_subarray**(int ndims, const int array_of_sizes[],
                const int array_of_subsizes[], const int array_of_starts[], int order,
                MPI_Datatype oldtype, MPI_Datatype *newtype)

Table 7.9: C bindings for darray and subarray datatype constructors

the array. The starting coordinates are always specified assuming that the array is indexed beginning from zero (even for Fortran arrays). For example, if a Fortran program contains an array A(1:100,1:100) and one wants to specify the subarray B(4:50,10:60), then the starting coordinates of B must be specified as (3,9). In other words, the C convention is always used. (Some convention is needed because Fortran allows arrays to be defined starting from any number, for example, X(50:100, 60:120).)

In the program in Figure 7.11, we calculate the starting index of the local array of a process in the global array as a function of the coordinates of the process in the process grid. For this we use the functions MPI_Cart_create and MPI_-Cart_coord. MPI_Cart_create creates the specified 2 × 3 logical process grid and returns a new communicator. MPI_Cart_coord returns the coordinates of a process in the process grid. The coordinates are as shown in Figure 7.9. We multiply the coordinates of the process by the size of the local array in each dimension to obtain the starting location of the process's local array in the global array.

The fifth argument to MPI_Type_create_subarray is the same as the order argument in MPI_Type_create_darray: it specifies the array storage order in memory and file. The sixth argument is the type of each element in the array, which could be any MPI basic or derived datatype. The function returns in the last argument a derived datatype corresponding to the layout of the subarray in the global array. We use this datatype as the filetype in MPI_File_set_view. In this example, the array is contiguously allocated in memory. Therefore, in the MPI_File_write_all call, we specify the memory datatype as MPI_FLOAT and the count as the number of floats in the local array.

C and Fortran bindings for the darray and subarray datatype constructors are given in Tables 7.9 and 7.10.

MPI_TYPE_CREATE_DARRAY(size, rank, ndims, array_of_gsizes, array_of_distribs,
        array_of_dargs, array_of_psizes, order, oldtype, newtype, ierror)
           integer size, rank, ndims, array_of_gsizes(*), array_of_distribs(*),
               array_of_dargs(*), array_of_psizes(*), order, oldtype, newtype,
               ierror

MPI_TYPE_CREATE_SUBARRAY(ndims, array_of_sizes, array_of_subsizes,
        array_of_starts, order, oldtype, newtype, ierror)
           integer ndims, array_of_sizes(*), array_of_subsizes(*),
             array_of_starts(*), order, oldtype, newtype, ierror

---

Table 7.10: Fortran bindings for darray and subarray datatype constructors

7.4.4 Local Array with Ghost Area

In many applications with distributed arrays, the local array is allocated with a few extra rows and columns in each dimension. This extra area, which is not really part of the local array, is often referred to as a *halo* or *ghost* area. The ghost area is used to store rows or columns belonging to neighboring processes that have been communicated via interprocess communication. These rows and columns are stored in the ghost area, and not in a separate buffer, in order to make the computational part of the code compact, convenient, and cache friendly and to avoid splitting any "do loops" that loop across the rows or columns of the local array. Figure 7.12 illustrates the idea of a ghost area.

If a local array has a ghost area around it, the local data is not located contiguously in memory. In the case of C arrays, for example, the rows of the local array in memory are separated by a few elements of ghost area. When such an array is written to a file, one usually does not want the ghost area to be written to the file since the data corresponding to that area will be written by another process. Instead of writing each row of the local array with a separate function, resulting in many I/O function calls, we can describe this noncontiguous memory layout in terms of an MPI derived datatype and specify this derived datatype as the datatype argument to a single `MPI_File_write_all` function. The entire data transfer, which is noncontiguous in both memory and file, can therefore be performed with a single function.

As Figure 7.12 illustrates, the local array is effectively a subarray of a larger array that includes the ghost area. Therefore, we can use a subarray datatype to describe the layout of the local array in the allocated memory space. The code for

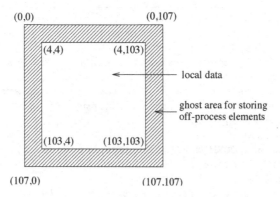

Figure 7.12: A local array of size (100,100) is actually allocated as a (108,108) array to provide a "ghost" area along the boundaries for storing off-process elements. The real data is stored starting from index (4,4). The local array is therefore noncontiguous in memory.

doing this is given in Figure 7.13.

Assume that the ghost area is of size four elements on each side in each dimension; in other words, there are four extra rows and columns on each side of the local array. We first create the filetype using a subarray datatype, open the file, and set the view to this type. This portion of the code is identical to the previous program in Figure 7.11. Then we create another subarray datatype to describe the memory layout of the local array. For this, we specify the size of the allocated array as the local array size plus eight in each dimension (four on each side). The starting location of the local array in the allocated array is (4,4), assuming zero-based indexing as required. We commit the resulting datatype returned by MPI_Type_create_subarray and use it as the datatype argument in MPI_File_write_all. (Recall that this argument describes memory layout, not file layout; the file layout is specified by the file view.) Since the entire local array is described by this datatype, we specify the count argument of MPI_File_write_all as 1.

7.4.5 Irregularly Distributed Arrays

MPI can also be used for accessing irregularly distributed arrays—by specifying the filetype appropriately. If combined with the use of collective I/O functions, an MPI implementation may even be able to deliver high performance for such accesses, which are normally considered difficult to optimize. An irregular distribution is one that cannot be expressed mathematically by a compact formula, unlike a block or

```
gsizes[0] = m;     gsizes[1] = n;
/* no. of rows and columns in global array*/
psizes[0] = 2;     psizes[1] = 3;
/* no. of processes in vertical and horizontal dimensions
   of process grid */
lsizes[0] = m/psizes[0];   /* no. of rows in local array */
lsizes[1] = n/psizes[1];   /* no. of columns in local array */
dims[0] = 2;    dims[1] = 3;
periods[0] = periods[1] = 1;
MPI_Cart_create(MPI_COMM_WORLD, 2, dims, periods, 0, &comm);
MPI_Comm_rank(comm, &rank);
MPI_Cart_coords(comm, rank, 2, coords);
/* global indices of the first element of the local array */
start_indices[0] = coords[0] * lsizes[0];
start_indices[1] = coords[1] * lsizes[1];
MPI_Type_create_subarray(2, gsizes, lsizes, start_indices,
                         MPI_ORDER_C, MPI_FLOAT, &filetype);
MPI_Type_commit(&filetype);
MPI_File_open(comm, "/pfs/datafile",
              MPI_MODE_CREATE | MPI_MODE_WRONLY,
              MPI_INFO_NULL, &fh);
MPI_File_set_view(fh, 0, MPI_FLOAT, filetype, "native",
                  MPI_INFO_NULL);
/* create a derived datatype that describes the layout of the
   local array in the memory buffer that includes the ghost
   area. This is another subarray datatype! */
memsizes[0] = lsizes[0] + 8; /* no. of rows in allocated array */
memsizes[1] = lsizes[1] + 8; /* no. of cols in allocated array */
start_indices[0] = start_indices[1] = 4;
/* indices of the first element of the local array in the
   allocated array */
MPI_Type_create_subarray(2, memsizes, lsizes, start_indices,
                         MPI_ORDER_C, MPI_FLOAT, &memtype);
MPI_Type_commit(&memtype);
MPI_File_write_all(fh, local_array, 1, memtype, &status);
MPI_File_close(&fh);
```

Figure 7.13: C program for writing a distributed array that is also noncontiguous in memory because of a ghost area

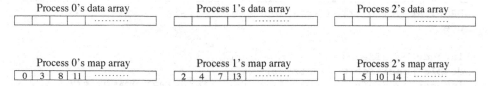

map array describes the location of each element of data array in the (common) file

Figure 7.14: Example of irregular file access. Each process has a local data array and a local map array. Each element of the map array indicates the location in the file of the corresponding element in the data array.

cyclic distribution. Therefore, we need another array—called a *map array*—that specifies the mapping of each element of the local array to the global array. An example of a map array is the output of a graph partitioner that partitions an unstructured mesh among processes based on some load-balancing criteria.

Let's consider an example in which an irregularly distributed array is to be written to a common file containing the global array in canonical order, as shown in Figure 7.14. Figure 7.15 shows the Fortran subroutine for performing this I/O. The main difference between this program and the ones we considered above for regularly distributed arrays is the construction of the datatype to be used as the filetype.

We note that the MPI standard specifies that the filetype used by any process must specify only monotonically nondecreasing offsets in the file (see Section 13.1.1 in [46]). For example, a derived datatype that specifies offsets in the order {2, 6, 5, 7, 4} cannot be used as a valid filetype. No such restriction exists on the datatype used to describe data layout in memory; it can specify memory offsets in any order. Therefore, the filetype created for an irregular distribution must always specify monotonically nondecreasing offsets. If the entries in the map array are not in nondecreasing order, the map array must first be reordered into nondecreasing order before it is used to create the filetype. The datatype describing the memory layout must be correspondingly permuted so that the desired distribution is still specified correctly.

Let us assume for simplicity that, in the program in Figure 7.15, the map array is already in monotonically nondecreasing order. We can therefore directly use the map array as an index into the file and use an indexed datatype as the filetype. Let us assume further that the map array specifies the location in units of local-array elements—double-precision numbers in this case—and not in bytes. We use the

```fortran
SUBROUTINE write_irreg_array(buf, map, bufsize)
  use mpi

  integer bufsize
  double precision buf(bufsize)
  integer map(bufsize), fh, filetype, status(MPI_STATUS_SIZE)
  integer (kind=MPI_OFFSET_KIND) disp
  integer i, ierr

  call MPI_FILE_OPEN(MPI_COMM_WORLD, '/pfs/datafile', &
                     MPI_MODE_CREATE + MPI_MODE_RDWR, &
                     MPI_INFO_NULL, fh, ierr)

  call MPI_TYPE_CREATE_INDEXED_BLOCK(bufsize, 1, map, &
                     MPI_DOUBLE_PRECISION, filetype, ierr)
  call MPI_TYPE_COMMIT(filetype, ierr)
  disp = 0
  call MPI_FILE_SET_VIEW(fh, disp, MPI_DOUBLE_PRECISION, &
                     filetype, 'native', MPI_INFO_NULL, ierr)

  call MPI_FILE_WRITE_ALL(fh, buf, bufsize, &
                     MPI_DOUBLE_PRECISION, status, ierr)

  call MPI_FILE_CLOSE(fh, ierr)

  return
END SUBROUTINE write_irreg_array
```

Figure 7.15: Fortran program for writing an irregularly distributed array

datatype constructor MPI_Type_create_indexed_block to create the indexed datatype. We pass as the first argument to MPI_Type_create_indexed_block the number of elements in the local data array. The second argument is the number of elements in each block, which we set to 1. The third argument is an array specifying the displacement of each block in the datatype; we pass the map array as this argument. The fourth argument is the type of each element, MPI_DOUBLE_-PRECISION in this case. The function returns the resulting derived datatype in the fifth argument. We commit this datatype and use it as the filetype in MPI_File_-set_view. We use a single collective write function, MPI_File_write_all, to write the entire array.

---

int **MPI_Type_create_indexed_block**(int count, int blocklength,
         const int array_of_displacements[], MPI_Datatype oldtype,
         MPI_Datatype *newtype)

Table 7.11: C binding for `MPI_Type_create_indexed_block`

MPI_TYPE_CREATE_INDEXED_BLOCK(count, blocklength,
         array_of_displacements, oldtype, newtype, ierror)
         integer count, blocklength, array_of_displacements(*), oldtype,
         newtype, ierror

Table 7.12: Fortran binding for `MPI_Type_create_indexed_block`

C and Fortran bindings for `MPI_Type_create_indexed_block` are given in Tables 7.11 and 7.12.

7.5 Nonblocking I/O and Split Collective I/O

MPI supports nonblocking versions of all independent read/write functions. The mechanism MPI provides for nonblocking I/O is similar to that for nonblocking communication. The nonblocking I/O functions are all named `MPI_File_ixxx`, for example, `MPI_File_iread` and `MPI_File_iwrite_at`, similar to the names `MPI_Isend` and `MPI_Irecv`. The nonblocking I/O functions return an `MPI_-Request` object, as do the nonblocking communication functions. One can use the usual MPI test/wait functions (`MPI_Test`, `MPI_Wait`, `MPI_Testany`, etc.) on the returned request object to test or wait for the completion of nonblocking I/O operations. By using nonblocking I/O functions, one can potentially overlap I/O with other computation/communication in the program, for example as shown below.

```
MPI_Request request;

MPI_File_iwrite_at(fh, offset, buf, count, datatype, &request);
for (i=0; i<1000; i++) {
    /* perform computation */
}
MPI_Wait(&request, &status);
```

How well I/O can be overlapped depends of course on the quality of the implementation.

---

int **MPI_File_iwrite_at**(MPI_File fh, MPI_Offset offset, const void *buf, int count,
             MPI_Datatype datatype, MPI_Request *request)

int **MPI_File_write_all_begin**(MPI_File fh, const void *buf, int count,
             MPI_Datatype datatype)

int **MPI_File_write_all_end**(MPI_File fh, const void *buf, MPI_Status *status)

Table   7.13:   C   bindings   for   `MPI_File_iwrite_at`,
`MPI_File_write_all_begin`, and `MPI_File_write_all_end`

For collective I/O, MPI supports only a restricted form of nonblocking I/O, called *split collective I/O*. To use split collective I/O, the user must call a "begin" function (for example, `MPI_File_read_all_begin`) to start the collective I/O operation and an "end" function (for example, `MPI_File_read_all_end`) to complete the operation. The restriction is that the user can have only one split collective I/O operation active at a time on any given file handle. In other words, the user cannot issue two begin functions on the same file handle without calling an end function to complete the first begin. Since this restriction exists, a split collective begin does not return an `MPI_Request` object or any other object. A split collective end, by definition, matches the previously called split collective begin on that file handle. The MPI standard allows an implementation to perform the collective I/O operation entirely during the begin function, or entirely during the end function, or in the "background," between the begin and end functions.

An example of using split collective I/O is as follows:

```
MPI_File_write_all_begin(fh, buf, count, datatype);
for (i=0; i<1000; i++) {
    /* perform computation */
}
MPI_File_write_all_end(fh, buf, &status);
```

C and Fortran bindings for `MPI_File_iwrite_at`, `MPI_File_write_all_-begin`, and `MPI_File_write_all_end` are given in Tables 7.13 and 7.14.

7.6   Shared File Pointers

Thus far, we have seen two ways of specifying to MPI the location in the file from where data must be read/written: individual file pointers and explicit offsets. MPI also supports a third way of specifying the location: via the shared file pointer.

MPI_FILE_IWRITE_AT(fh, offset, buf, count, datatype, request, ierror)

                `<type>  buf(*)`

                integer fh, count, datatype, request, ierror

                integer(kind=MPI_OFFSET_KIND) offset

MPI_FILE_WRITE_ALL_BEGIN(fh, buf, count, datatype, ierror)

                `<type> buf(*)`

                integer fh, count, datatype, ierror

MPI_FILE_WRITE_ALL_END(fh, buf, status, ierror)

                `<type> buf(*)`

                integer fh, status(MPI_STATUS_SIZE), ierror

Table 7.14: Fortran bindings for `MPI_File_iwrite_at`, `MPI_File_write_all_begin`, and `MPI_File_write_all_end`

This is a file pointer whose value is shared among the processes belonging to the communicator passed to `MPI_File_open`. MPI provides two functions, `MPI_-File_read_shared` and `MPI_File_write_shared`, that read or write data starting from the current location of the shared file pointer. After a call to one of these functions, the shared file pointer is updated by the amount of data read or written. The next call to one of these functions from *any* process in the group will result in data being read or written from the new location of the shared file pointer. Contrast this with individual file pointers: a read or write operation on one process using the individual file pointer has no effect on the individual file pointer on any other process.

A process can explicitly move the shared file pointer (in units of etypes) by using the function `MPI_File_seek_shared`. MPI requires that all processes specify the same file view when using the shared file pointer. This restriction does not exist for individual file pointers and explicit offsets. Examples of applications where shared file pointers are useful are work sharing and writing log files.

Figure 7.16 shows a C example in which all processes need to write to a common log file and the order in which the writes appear in the file does not matter. We simply use the shared-file-pointer function `MPI_File_write_shared`. Therefore, we do not need to calculate file offsets. C and Fortran bindings for `MPI_File_write_shared` are given in Tables 7.15 and 7.16.

Nonblocking versions of the shared-file-pointer functions also exist, called `MPI_-File_iread_shared` and `MPI_File_iwrite_shared`. The collective I/O

```
/* writing to a common file using the shared file pointer */
#include "mpi.h"

int main(int argc, char *argv[])
{
  int buf[1000];
  MPI_File fh;

  MPI_Init(&argc, &argv);

  MPI_File_open(MPI_COMM_WORLD, "/pfs/datafile",
                MPI_MODE_RDONLY, MPI_INFO_NULL, &fh);
  MPI_File_write_shared(fh, buf, 1000, MPI_INT,
                        MPI_STATUS_IGNORE);
  MPI_File_close(&fh);

  MPI_Finalize();
  return 0;
}
```

Figure 7.16: A C example that uses the shared file pointer

---

int **MPI_File_write_shared**(MPI_File fh, const void *buf, int count,
                    MPI_Datatype datatype, MPI_Status *status)

Table 7.15: C binding for `MPI_File_write_shared`

MPI_FILE_WRITE_SHARED(fh, buf, count, datatype, status, ierror)
                <type> buf(*)
                integer fh, count, datatype, status(MPI_STATUS_SIZE), ierror

---

Table 7.16: Fortran binding for `MPI_File_write_shared`

functions that use shared file pointers are called `MPI_File_read_ordered` and `MPI_File_write_ordered`. With these functions, data will be read or written in the file as if the shared file pointer was accessed in order of process rank, hence the name "ordered." For example, in the case of `MPI_File_write_ordered`, process 0's data will appear first in the file, followed by process 1's data, and so on. Note that the implementation can still perform this I/O in parallel: since the function is collective, the implementation can determine the sizes of the requests of all processes, calculate the offsets in the file corresponding to a rank ordering of the writes, and then perform all the writes concurrently. As in the case of individual file pointers and explicit offsets, split collective versions are available, for example, `MPI_File_read_ordered_begin` and `MPI_File_read_ordered_end`.

7.7   Passing Hints to the Implementation

MPI provides users the option to pass "hints" to the implementation. For I/O, this can be done via the `info` argument to the functions `MPI_File_open`, `MPI_-File_set_view`, and `MPI_File_set_info`. In all programs so far, we have passed `MPI_INFO_NULL` as the info argument because we did not want to pass any hints. In many instances, however, one might want to pass hints. Examples of hints include the number of disks to stripe a file across, the striping unit, access pattern information, and file permissions. We briefly introduced the info argument in Chapter 1. Here we will see how info is used for I/O.

Recall that info is an opaque MPI object of type `MPI_Info` in C and `integer` in Fortran. Any number of (key, value) pairs can be added to an info object. When the info object is passed to an I/O function, such as `MPI_File_open`, `MPI_-File_set_view`, or `MPI_File_set_info`, each (key, value) pair serves as a hint associated with the file handle passed to the function. For example, if a key is `striping_unit` and the value is `1048576`, the user is requesting a striping unit of 1048576 (1 MB). Keys and values are both specified as character strings. MPI has reserved a set of keys whose meanings are defined in the standard; an implementation is free to define additional keys whose meanings are implementation specific. All hints are optional; a user need not provide any hints, and even if hints are provided, an implementation is free to ignore them. Hints do not change the semantics of a program, but they may help an implementation improve performance.

Figure 7.17 shows a simple program in which various hints are set, both predefined hints and hints specific to our implementation of the I/O functions in MPI, called ROMIO [63, 65, 66, 69]. The function `MPI_Info_create` creates an info object. `MPI_Info_set` adds (key, value) pairs to the info object. `MPI_Info_set` is

```
MPI_File fh;  MPI_Info info;

MPI_Info_create(&info);

/* FOLLOWING HINTS ARE PREDEFINED IN MPI */

/* no. of I/O devices across which the file should be striped */
MPI_Info_set(info, "striping_factor", "16");

/* the striping unit in bytes */
MPI_Info_set(info, "striping_unit", "1048576");

/* buffer size for collective I/O */
MPI_Info_set(info, "cb_buffer_size", "8388608");

/* no. of processes that should perform disk accesses
   during collective I/O */
MPI_Info_set(info, "cb_nodes", "16");

/* FOLLOWING ARE ADDITIONAL HINTS SUPPORTED BY ROMIO */

/* buffer size for data sieving in independent reads */
MPI_Info_set(info, "ind_rd_buffer_size", "2097152");

/* buffer size for data sieving in independent writes */
MPI_Info_set(info, "ind_wr_buffer_size", "1048576");

/* NOW OPEN THE FILE WITH THIS INFO OBJECT */
MPI_File_open(MPI_COMM_WORLD, "/pfs/datafile",
              MPI_MODE_CREATE | MPI_MODE_RDWR, info, &fh);

MPI_Info_free(&info);  /* free the info object */
```

Figure 7.17: Example of passing hints to the implementation

called several times in the program, each time to add a different (key, value) pair to the info object. The first four hints are predefined hints in MPI; the next two are ROMIO specific. Note that this program can be run with any MPI implementation: if an implementation does not understand a particular hint, it will be ignored.

The key striping_factor specifies the number of I/O devices (for example, disks) across which the file should be striped. striping_unit specifies the number of consecutive bytes of a file that are stored on a particular I/O device when a file is striped across I/O devices. The `striping_factor` and `striping_unit` hints are useful only if specified at the time the file is created in an `MPI_File_open` call with the mode `MPI_MODE_CREATE`. The key `cb_buffer_size` specifies the size of the temporary buffer that the implementation can use on each process when performing collective I/O. The key `cb_nodes` specifies the number of processes that should actually perform disk accesses during collective I/O. The keys `ind_-rd_buffer_size` and `ind_wr_buffer_size` are ROMIO-specific hints that specify the size of the temporary buffer ROMIO uses for data sieving, which is an optimization ROMIO performs in the case of noncontiguous, independent accesses.

Hints can be specified when the file is opened with `MPI_File_open`, or when setting the file view with `MPI_File_set_view`, or explicitly with the function `MPI_File_set_info`.

Querying the values of hints.   One can also query the values of hints being used by the implementation, if any, as shown in the code in Figure 7.18. `MPI_File_-get_info` returns a new info object containing the hints currently being used for the specified file. In this example, it contains the default values of hints being used. `MPI_Info_get_nkeys` returns the number of keys associated with the info object. We loop over the number of keys and, for each iteration of the loop, retrieve one key with the function `MPI_Info_get_nthkey` and its associated value with `MPI_Info_get`. Since `MPI_File_get_info` returns a new info object, we must free it using `MPI_Info_free`.

Note that we have defined `key` and `value` as character strings of length `MPI_-MAX_INFO_KEY` and `MPI_MAX_INFO_VAL`, respectively. These two MPI constants specify the maximum lengths of info key and value strings supported by the implementation. In C, the length specified by these constants includes the null terminating character. Therefore, there is no need to allocate a character buffer of size (`MPI_MAX_INFO_KEY+1`) or (`MPI_MAX_INFO_VAL+1`). In Fortran, there is no null terminating character; therefore, the values of the constants `MPI_MAX_-INFO_KEY` and `MPI_MAX_INFO_VAL` in Fortran are one less than in C.

Tables 7.17 and 7.18 give the C and Fortran bindings for the info functions used in Figures 7.17 and 7.18. We refer readers to the MPI standard for a complete list of the info keys predefined in MPI [46].

7.8   Consistency Semantics

MPI's consistency semantics for I/O specify the results when multiple processes perform I/O. Several scenarios are possible. We consider the common ones and

```
/* query the default values of hints being used */
#include "mpi.h"
#include <stdio.h>

int main(int argc, char **argv)
{
    int i, nkeys, flag, rank;
    MPI_File fh;
    MPI_Info info_used;
    char key[MPI_MAX_INFO_KEY], value[MPI_MAX_INFO_VAL];

    MPI_Init(&argc,&argv);
    MPI_Comm_rank(MPI_COMM_WORLD, &rank);

    MPI_File_open(MPI_COMM_WORLD, "/pfs/datafile",
                  MPI_MODE_CREATE | MPI_MODE_RDWR,
                  MPI_INFO_NULL, &fh);

    MPI_File_get_info(fh, &info_used);
    MPI_Info_get_nkeys(info_used, &nkeys);

    for (i=0; i<nkeys; i++) {
        MPI_Info_get_nthkey(info_used, i, key);
        MPI_Info_get(info_used, key, MPI_MAX_INFO_VAL,
                     value, &flag);
        printf("Process %d, Default: key = %s, value = %s\n",
               rank, key, value);
    }

    MPI_File_close(&fh);
    MPI_Info_free(&info_used);

    MPI_Finalize();
    return 0;
}
```

Figure 7.18: Querying the values of hints being used by the implementation

```
int MPI_Info_create(MPI_Info *info)

int MPI_Info_set(MPI_Info info, const char *key, const char *value)

int MPI_Info_get(MPI_Info info, const char *key, int valuelen, char *value, int *flag)

int MPI_Info_get_nkeys(MPI_Info info, int *nkeys)

int MPI_Info_get_nthkey(MPI_Info info, int n, char *key)

int MPI_Info_free(MPI_Info *info)

int MPI_File_get_info(MPI_File fh, MPI_Info *info_used)
```

Table 7.17: C bindings for the info functions used in Figures 7.17 and 7.18

```
MPI_INFO_CREATE(info, ierror)
        integer info, ierror

MPI_INFO_SET(info, key, value, ierror)
        integer info, ierror
        character*(*) key, value

MPI_INFO_GET(info, key, valuelen, value, flag, ierror)
        integer info, valuelen, ierror
        character*(*) key, value
        logical flag

MPI_INFO_GET_NKEYS(info, nkeys, ierror)
        integer info, nkeys, ierror

MPI_INFO_GET_NTHKEY(info, n, key, ierror)
        integer info, n, ierror
        character*(*) key

MPI_INFO_FREE(info, ierror)
        integer info, ierror

MPI_FILE_GET_INFO(fh, info_used, ierror)
        integer fh, info_used, ierror
```

Table 7.18: Fortran bindings for the info functions used in Figures 7.17 and 7.18

explain them with the help of examples. We refer readers to the MPI standard for a complete specification of the consistency semantics [46].

7.8.1 Simple Cases

In two scenarios consistency is not an issue:

1. *Read-only access*: If all processes are only reading from files and not performing any writes, each process will see exactly the data that is present in the file. This is true regardless of which communicator was used to open the file (MPI_COMM_SELF, MPI_COMM_WORLD, or some other).

2. *Separate files*: If each process accesses a *separate* file (that is, no file is shared among processes), MPI guarantees that the data written by a process can be read back by the same process at any time after the write.

More interesting is the situation when multiple processes access a *common* file and at least one process *writes* to the file. From the perspective of consistency semantics, a lot depends on which communicator was used to open the file. In general, MPI guarantees stronger consistency semantics if the communicator correctly specifies every process that is accessing the file (for example, MPI_COMM_WORLD) and weaker consistency semantics if the communicator specifies only a subset of the processes accessing the common file (for example, MPI_COMM_SELF). In either case, the user can take steps to guarantee consistency when MPI does not automatically guarantee consistency, as we will see below.

7.8.2 Accessing a Common File Opened with MPI_COMM_WORLD

Let us first consider the case where all processes access a common file and specify the communicator as MPI_COMM_WORLD when they open the file, and at least one process needs to write to the file. The simplest case of such access is when each process accesses a *separate portion* of the file, that is, there are no overlapping regions (bytes) in the file between the accesses of any two processes. In this case, MPI automatically guarantees that a process can read back the data it wrote without any extra synchronization. An example is shown below:

Process 0	Process 1
MPI_File_open(MPI_COMM_WORLD, "file", ... , &fh1)	MPI_File_open(MPI_COMM_WORLD, "file", ... , &fh2
MPI_File_write_at(fh1, 0, buf, 100, MPI_BYTE, ...)	MPI_File_write_at(fh2, 100, buf, 100, MPI_BYTE, ...)
MPI_File_read_at(fh1, 0, buf, 100, MPI_BYTE, ...)	MPI_File_read_at(fh2, 100, buf, 100, MPI_BYTE, ...)

Here, two processes open a common file with `MPI_COMM_WORLD`. Each process writes 100 bytes to different locations in the file and reads back only the data it just wrote. MPI guarantees that the data will be read correctly.

Now let's consider the same example but with a difference: let's assume that each process needs to read the data just written by the other process. In other words, the accesses of the two processes overlap in the file. With respect to consistency semantics, the situation now is dramatically different. When the accesses (or portions of the accesses) of any two processes overlap in the file, MPI does *not* guarantee that the data will automatically be read correctly. The user must take some extra steps to ensure correctness. There are three choices:

1. *Set atomicity to true*: Before the write on each process, change the file-access mode to *atomic* by using the function `MPI_File_set_atomicity` as follows.

Process 0	Process 1
MPI_File_open(MPI_COMM_WORLD, "file", ... , &fh1)	MPI_File_open(MPI_COMM_WORLD, "file", ... , &fh2
MPI_File_set_atomicity(fh1, 1)	MPI_File_set_atomicity(fh2, 1)
MPI_File_write_at(fh1, 0, buf, 100, MPI_BYTE, ...)	MPI_File_write_at(fh2, 100, buf, 100, MPI_BYTE, ...)
MPI_Barrier(MPI_COMM_WORLD)	MPI_Barrier(MPI_COMM_WORLD)
MPI_File_read_at(fh1, 100, buf, 100, MPI_BYTE, ...)	MPI_File_read_at(fh2, 0, buf, 100, MPI_BYTE, ...)

In the atomic mode, MPI guarantees that the data written by one process can be read immediately by another process. This is not guaranteed in the nonatomic mode, which is the default mode when the file is opened. In the above program, a barrier is used after the writes to ensure that each process has completed its write before the read is issued from the other process.

2. *Close the file and reopen it*: Another way to read the data correctly is to close the file after the write, reopen it, and then read the data written by the other process, as shown below.

Process 0	Process 1
MPI_File_open(MPI_COMM_WORLD, "file", ... , &fh1)	MPI_File_open(MPI_COMM_WORLD, "file", ... , &fh2
MPI_File_write_at(fh1, 0, buf, 100, MPI_BYTE, ...)	MPI_File_write_at(fh2, 100, buf, 100, MPI_BYTE, ...)
MPI_File_close(&fh1)	MPI_File_close(&fh2)
MPI_Barrier(MPI_COMM_WORLD)	MPI_Barrier(MPI_COMM_WORLD)
MPI_File_open(MPI_COMM_WORLD, "file", ... , &fh1)	MPI_File_open(MPI_COMM_WORLD, "file", ... , &fh2
MPI_File_read_at(fh1, 100, buf, 100, MPI_BYTE, ...)	MPI_File_read_at(fh2, 0, buf, 100, MPI_BYTE, ...)

By doing so, we ensure that there are no overlapping operations on the file handles returned from one collective open. The reads are performed with a different set of file handles that did not exist when the writes were performed. A barrier is used in this program for a similar reason as above: to ensure that each process has completed its close before the other process reopens the file.

3. *Ensure that no "write sequence" on any process is concurrent with any sequence (read or write) on another process*: This is a more complicated way of ensuring correctness. The words *sequence* and *write sequence* have a specific meaning in this context. A *sequence* is defined as a set of file operations bracketed by any pair of the functions `MPI_File_sync`,[3] `MPI_File_open`, and `MPI_File_close`. A sequence is called a *write sequence* if any of the data-access operations in the sequence are write operations. For example, the following three sets of operations are all sequences, and the first two are write sequences: sync–write–read–sync, open–write–write–close, and sync–read–read–close. We note that the first and last operations must be a sync, open, or close for the set of operations to be called a sequence. MPI guarantees that the data written by a process can be read by another process if the user arranges the program such that a *write* sequence on one process is not concurrent (in time) with *any* sequence (read or write) on any other process.

Figure 7.19 shows how to apply this rule to the above example where each process needs to read the data just written by the other process. To ensure that no write sequence on a process is concurrent with any sequence on the other process, we have to add sync functions to create a write sequence and use a barrier to separate them (in time) from the write sequence on the other process. We choose to let the write on process 0 occur first; we could have chosen the other way around. We add a sync after the write on process 0 in order to create the sequence open–write‗at–sync. Since `MPI_File_sync` is collective over the communicator with which the file was opened, namely, `MPI_COMM_WORLD`, the function must also be called on process 1. Then we call a barrier to separate this write sequence from the write sequence on process 1. Since the write sequence on process 1 must begin after this barrier, we first have to create a sequence by calling a sync on process 1 immediately after the barrier. Then we do the write, followed by another sync to complete the sequence. Because of the collective nature of `MPI_‑File_sync`, the function must be called on process 0 as well. Next we call a barrier to separate the write sequence on process 1 from the read sequence on process 0. Since the read sequence on process 0 must start after the barrier, we add a sync after the barrier, followed by the read. If we did not add this sync, the read sequence would start from the sync that is just before the barrier and, therefore, would not be time-separated from the write sequence

---

[3] The function `MPI_File_sync` explicitly synchronizes any cached file data with that on the storage device; `MPI_File_open` and `MPI_File_close` also have the same effect.

Process 0	Process 1
MPI_File_open(MPI_COMM_WORLD, "file", ... , &fh1) MPI_File_write_at(fh1, 0, buf, 100, MPI_BYTE, ...) MPI_File_sync(fh1)	MPI_File_open(MPI_COMM_WORLD, "file", ... , &fh2) MPI_File_sync(fh2) *(needed for collective operation)*
MPI_Barrier(MPI_COMM_WORLD)	MPI_Barrier(MPI_COMM_WORLD)
MPI_File_sync(fh1) *(needed for collective operation)*	MPI_File_sync(fh2) MPI_File_write_at(fh2, 100, buf, 100, MPI_BYTE, ...)
MPI_File_sync(fh1) *(needed for collective operation)*	MPI_File_sync(fh2)
MPI_Barrier(MPI_COMM_WORLD)	MPI_Barrier(MPI_COMM_WORLD)
MPI_File_sync(fh1) MPI_File_read_at(fh1, 100, buf, 100, MPI_BYTE, ...) MPI_File_close(&fh1)	MPI_File_sync(fh2) *(needed for collective operation)* MPI_File_read_at(fh2, 0, buf, 100, MPI_BYTE, ...) MPI_File_close(&fh2)

Figure 7.19: Two processes open a common file with MPI_COMM_WORLD and use the default nonatomic mode of access. Each process writes to the file and then needs to read the data just written by the other process. The syncs and barriers are needed for the data to be correctly written and read.

on process 1. The sync after the barrier on process 1 is needed because it is collective with the corresponding sync on process 0. It is not needed for consistency semantics because the read sequence on process 1 that starts from just before the barrier is already nonconcurrent with the previous write sequence on process 0.

We note that if the program had used the collective versions of the read/write functions, namely, MPI_File_write_at_all and MPI_File_read_at_all, we could not have used this method for achieving consistency. The reason is that since it is erroneous to separate collective operations among processes by inserting barriers in between, there is no way to make the write sequence on one process nonconcurrent with any other sequence on the other process. Therefore, in cases where multiple collective operations overlap, only the first two options for achieving consistency are available, namely, setting atomicity or closing and then reopening the file.

7.8.3   Accessing a Common File Opened with MPI_COMM_SELF

Now let's consider the case where all processes access a common file but specify MPI_COMM_SELF as the communicator when they open it. (Doing so is allowed, but we don't recommend it in general.) In this case, there is only one way to achieve consistency: the user must take steps to ensure that no write sequence on

Process 0	Process 1
MPI_File_open(MPI_COMM_SELF, "file", ... , &fh1)	MPI_File_open(MPI_COMM_SELF, "file", ... , &fh2)
MPI_File_write_at(fh1, 0, buf, 100, MPI_BYTE, ...)	
MPI_File_sync(fh1)	
MPI_Barrier(MPI_COMM_WORLD)	MPI_Barrier(MPI_COMM_WORLD)
	MPI_File_sync(fh2)
	MPI_File_write_at(fh2, 100, buf, 100, MPI_BYTE, ...)
	MPI_File_sync(fh2)
MPI_Barrier(MPI_COMM_WORLD)	MPI_Barrier(MPI_COMM_WORLD)
MPI_File_sync(fh1)	
MPI_File_read_at(fh1, 100, buf, 100, MPI_BYTE, ...)	MPI_File_read_at(fh2, 0, buf, 100, MPI_BYTE, ...)
MPI_File_close(&fh1)	MPI_File_close(&fh2)

Figure 7.20: The example in Figure 7.19 when the file is opened with
MPI_COMM_SELF

any process is concurrent with any sequence (read or write) on any other process. This is needed even if there are no overlapping accesses among processes, that is, even if each process accesses separate parts of the file. Changing the file-access mode to atomic does not help in this case.

Therefore, for our example where one process needs to read the data written by the other process, the only way to do it correctly when the file is opened with MPI_COMM_SELF is as shown in Figure 7.20. This is similar to Figure 7.19, the only difference being the communicator passed to MPI_File_open. Because of MPI_COMM_SELF, all collective operations, such as MPI_File_sync, effectively become local operations. Therefore, the syncs that were needed in Figure 7.19 for matching the corresponding collective sync on the other process are not needed here. Only those syncs needed for consistency semantics, that is, for creating sequences, are needed.

7.8.4 General Recommendation

Although multiple processes can access a common file by opening it with MPI_-COMM_SELF as the communicator, it is not advisable to do so. Users should strive to specify the right communicator to MPI_File_open—one that specifies all the processes that need to access the open file. Doing so not only provides the benefit of the stronger consistency semantics that MPI guarantees in such cases, but it can also result in higher performance. For example, one can then use the collective I/O functions, which allow the implementation to perform collective optimizations.

---

int **MPI_File_set_atomicity**(MPI_File fh, int flag)

int **MPI_File_sync**(MPI_File fh)

Table 7.19: C bindings for `MPI_File_set_atomicity` and `MPI_File_sync`

MPI_FILE_SET_ATOMICITY(fh, flag, ierror)
>   integer fh, ierror
>   logical flag

MPI_FILE_SYNC(fh, ierror)
>   integer fh, ierror

Table 7.20: Fortran bindings for `MPI_File_set_atomicity` and `MPI_File_sync`

Tables 7.19 and 7.20 give the C and Fortran bindings for the two functions introduced in this section, `MPI_File_set_atomicity` and `MPI_File_sync`.

7.9 File Interoperability

Unlike messages, files are persistent entities; they remain after the program ends. Therefore, some questions must be answered about MPI files:

- Are MPI files any different from the files normally created by the file system? In other words, can an MPI file be read by a non-MPI program?

- How can MPI files created on one machine be moved to another machine?

- How can MPI files written on one machine be read on another machine with a different data representation?

We answer these questions in this section.

7.9.1 File Structure

MPI files contain no more information about the application than what the application explicitly stores in the files. In other words, MPI files are not self-describing in any way; they are just like ordinary files in content.

For performance reasons, MPI does not specify how an implementation should physically create files, although logically an MPI program will always see the file as a linear sequence of bytes. For example, an implementation is free to store a file physically in a compressed format or divide the file into smaller files stored on the local disks of different machines or in some other way, as long as the user is able to access the file as a linear sequence of bytes from an MPI program.

If files created by an MPI implementation are different from regular files in the underlying file system, the MPI standard requires that the implementation provide a utility for users to convert an MPI file into a linear sequence of bytes. It must also provide utilities to perform familiar file operations, such as copying, deleting, and moving. Therefore, one can always access the data written by an MPI program from a non-MPI program—by converting the MPI file into a linear sequence of bytes if necessary. In most implementations, the files created are no different from the files created by the underlying file system, so one can directly use the regular file-system commands, such as `cp`, `rm`, `mv`, `ls`, and one also can directly access the files from a non-MPI program.

7.9.2 File Data Representation

Since different machines have different binary data representations—byte ordering, sizes of datatypes, etc.—files created on one machine may not be directly portable to other machines, unless these differences are accounted for. MPI provides users the option of creating portable files that can be read on other machines. This is done via the `datarep` parameter to `MPI_File_set_view`.

In all the examples we have considered so far in this chapter, we have used `native` as the value for the `datarep` parameter to `MPI_File_set_view`. This parameter specifies the data representation used to store various datatypes (integers, floating-point numbers) in the file. MPI supports multiple data representations. Three types of data representations are predefined in MPI: `native`, `internal`, and `external32`. Implementations are free to support additional representations. MPI also allows users to define new data representations and add them to an MPI implementation at run time by providing the necessary conversion functions.

In the `native` representation, data is stored in the file as it is in memory; no data conversion is performed. This is the default data representation. Since there is no data conversion, there is no loss in I/O performance or data precision. This representation cannot be used in heterogeneous environments where the processes accessing a file have different data representations in memory. Similarly, a file created with this representation cannot be read on a machine with a different data representation. In other words, files created with the `native` representation are not portable.

The `internal` representation is an implementation-defined representation that may provide some (implementation-defined) degree of file portability. For example, an MPI implementation can define an `internal` representation that is portable to any machine where that MPI implementation is supported. A different MPI implementation may or may not be able to read the file.

The `external32` representation is a specific data representation defined in MPI. It is basically a 32-bit big-endian IEEE format, with the sizes of all basic datatypes specified by MPI. For a complete specification of `external32`, see the MPI standard [46]. A file written with `external32` can be read with any MPI implementation on any machine. Since using `external32` may require the implementation to perform data conversion, however, it may result in lower I/O performance and some loss in data precision. Therefore, this representation should be used only if file portability is needed.

Note that an implementation may choose to use `external32` as the `internal` representation.

7.9.3   Use of Datatypes for Portability

Although `internal` and `external32` data representations enable file portability, portability is possible only if the user specifies the correct datatypes, and not `MPI_BYTE`, to the read/write functions and to `MPI_File_set_view`. Doing so allows the implementation to know what kind of datatype is being accessed and therefore perform the necessary type conversions. For example, to write an array of 100 integers, you should specify `count=100` and `datatype=MPI_INT` to the write function. You should not specify it as `count=400` and `datatype=MPI_BYTE` as you would with the Unix I/O interface.

Care must also be taken in constructing file views with derived datatypes because some derived-datatype constructors, such as `MPI_Type_create_struct`, take displacements in bytes. For constructing derived datatypes to be used in file views, these byte displacements must be specified in terms of their values for the file data representation, not for the data representation in memory. The function `MPI_File_get_type_extent` is provided for this purpose. It returns the extent of a datatype in the file data representation selected. Similarly, the initial displacement in the file view (the `disp` argument to `MPI_File_set_view`), which is also specified in bytes, must be specified in terms of its value for the file data representation.

```
MPI_Aint lb, extent, extent_in_file;
MPI_Datatype etype, filetype, contig;
MPI_Offset disp;
MPI_File fh;
int buf[1000];

MPI_File_open(MPI_COMM_WORLD, "/pfs/datafile",
              MPI_MODE_CREATE | MPI_MODE_RDWR,
              MPI_INFO_NULL, &fh);

MPI_File_set_view(fh, 0, MPI_BYTE, MPI_BYTE, "external32",
                  MPI_INFO_NULL);
MPI_File_get_type_extent(fh, MPI_INT, &extent_in_file);

MPI_Type_contiguous(2, MPI_INT, &contig);
lb = 0;
extent = 6 * extent_in_file;
MPI_Type_create_resized(contig, lb, extent, &filetype);
MPI_Type_commit(&filetype);

disp = 5 * extent_in_file;
etype = MPI_INT;

MPI_File_set_view(fh, disp, etype, filetype, "external32",
                  MPI_INFO_NULL);
MPI_File_write(fh, buf, 1000, MPI_INT, MPI_STATUS_IGNORE);
```

Figure 7.21: Writing portable files

We note that the datatypes passed as arguments to read/write functions specify the data layout in memory. They must always be constructed by using displacements corresponding to displacements in the memory data representation.

Let us now revisit the example of Figure 7.4 in which a process needs to access noncontiguous data located in a file as follows: an initial displacement of five integers, followed by groups of two contiguous integers separated by gaps of four integers. We saw in Figure 7.5 how to set the view for this example for a nonportable file using the native data representation. Now let's do the same for a portable file using external32. The code is shown in Figure 7.21.

When a file is first opened, the default data representation is native. To change the data representation to external32, we have to call the function MPI_File_-set_view. But in this example, we run into a small problem. To create the derived

---

int **MPI_File_get_type_extent**(MPI_File fh, MPI_Datatype datatype,
        MPI_Aint *extent)

Table 7.21: C binding for `MPI_File_get_type_extent`

MPI_FILE_GET_TYPE_EXTENT(fh, datatype, extent, ierror)
        integer fh, datatype, ierror
        integer(kind=MPI_ADDRESS_KIND) extent

Table 7.22: Fortran binding for `MPI_File_get_type_extent`

datatype to be used as the filetype, we need to know the extent of an integer in the
`external32` data representation. We can, of course, look up the value in the MPI
standard, but we would like to find it at run time using the function specifically
provided for the purpose, namely, `MPI_File_get_type_extent`. The problem
is that this function takes a file handle (and not a data representation) as argument,
which means that the data representation for the file must be set before calling this
function. Hence, we need to call `MPI_File_set_view` twice: once just to set the
data representation to `external32` (with dummy values for displacement, etype,
and filetype) and once again with the real displacement, etype, and filetype after
the extent of an integer in the file has been determined by using `MPI_File_-`
`get_type_extent`.[4] Instead of using `sizeof(int)` as in Figure 7.4, we use
`extent_in_file` to calculate `disp` and to create the filetype. The file created
by this program can be read with any MPI implementation on any machine.

   C and Fortran bindings for `MPI_File_get_type_extent` are given in Tables 7.21 and 7.22.

7.9.4   User-Defined Data Representations

MPI also allows the user to define new data representations and register them with
the MPI implementation. The user must provide the necessary conversion functions,
which the implementation will use to convert from memory to file format and vice
versa. This provides a powerful method for users to write data in a representation

---

[4]This could have been avoided if MPI had a function that took a data-representation string
and a communicator as arguments (instead of a file handle) and returned the extent of a datatype
in that representation. Alas, since MPI has no such function, we have to do it in this roundabout
fashion.

that an MPI implementation may not support by default. We refer the reader to the MPI standard [46] for details of this feature.

7.10   Achieving High I/O Performance with MPI

In this section we describe how MPI must be used in order to achieve high I/O performance.We examine the different ways of writing an I/O application with MPI and see how these choices affect performance.

7.10.1   The Four "Levels" of Access

Any application has a particular "I/O access pattern" based on its I/O needs. The same I/O access pattern, however, can be presented to the I/O system in different ways, depending on which I/O functions the application uses and how. We classify the different ways of expressing I/O access patterns in MPI into four "levels," level 0 through level 3 [64]. We explain this classification with the help of a simple example, accessing a distributed array from a file, which is a common access pattern in parallel applications such as the mesh-based examples discussed in Chapter 1. The principle applies to other access patterns as well.

Consider a two-dimensional array distributed among 16 processes in a (block, block) fashion as shown in Figure 7.22. The array is stored in a file corresponding to the global array in row-major order, and each process needs to read its local array from the file. The data distribution among processes and the array storage order in the file are such that the file contains the first row of the local array of process 0, followed by the first row of the local array of process 1, the first row of the local array of process 2, the first row of the local array of process 3, then the second row of the local array of process 0, the second row of the local array of process 1, and so on. In other words, the local array of each process is located noncontiguously in the file.

Figure 7.23 shows four ways in which a user can express this access pattern in MPI. In level 0, each process does Unix-style accesses—one independent read request for each row in the local array. Level 1 is similar to level 0 except that it uses collective I/O functions, which indicate to the implementation that all processes that together opened the file will call this function, each with its own access information. Independent I/O functions, on the other hand, convey no information about what other processes will do. In level 2, each process creates a derived datatype to describe the noncontiguous access pattern, defines a file view, and calls

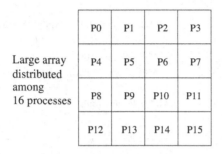

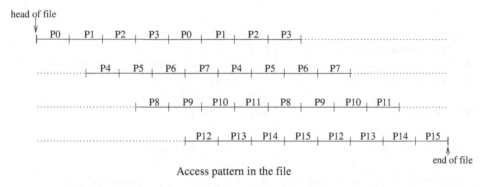

Access pattern in the file

Figure 7.22: Distributed-array access

independent I/O functions. Level 3 is similar to level 2 except that it uses collective I/O functions.

The four levels represent increasing amounts of data per request, as illustrated in Figure 7.24.[5] The more the amount of data per request, the greater the opportunity for the implementation to deliver higher performance. Users must therefore strive to express their I/O requests as level 3 rather than level 0. How good the performance is at each level depends, of course, on how well the implementation takes advantage of the extra access information at each level.

If an application needs to access only large, contiguous pieces of data, level 0 is equivalent to level 2, and level 1 is equivalent to level 3. Users need not create derived datatypes in such cases, since level-0 requests themselves will likely perform well. Most real parallel applications, however, do not fall into this category. Instead,

---

[5]In this figure, levels 1 and 2 represent the same amount of data per request; but, in general, when the number of noncontiguous accesses per process is greater than the number of processes, level 2 represents more data than level 1.

```
MPI_File_open(..., "filename", ..., &fh)        MPI_File_open(MPI_COMM_WORLD, "filename", ..., &fh
for (i=0; i<n_local_rows; i++) {                for (i=0; i<n_local_rows; i++) {
   MPI_File_seek(fh, ...)                          MPI_File_seek(fh, ...)
   MPI_File_read(fh, row[i], ...)                  MPI_File_read_all(fh, row[i], ...)
}                                               }
MPI_File_close(&fh)                             MPI_File_close(&fh)
```

Level 0
(many independent, contiguous requests)

Level 1
(many collective, contiguous requests)

```
MPI_Type_create_subarray(..., &subarray, ...)   MPI_Type_create_subarray(.., &subarray, ...)
MPI_Type_commit(&subarray)                      MPI_Type_commit(&subarray)
MPI_File_open(..., "filename", ..., &fh)        MPI_File_open(MPI_COMM_WORLD, "filename", ..., &fh
MPI_File_set_view(fh, ..., subarray, ...)       MPI_File_set_view(fh, ..., subarray, ...)
MPI_File_read(fh, local_array, ...)             MPI_File_read_all(fh, local_array, ...)
MPI_File_close(&fh)                             MPI_File_close(&fh)
```

Level 2
(single independent, noncontiguous request)

Level 3
(single collective, noncontiguous request)

Figure 7.23: Pseudo-code that shows four ways of accessing the data in Figure 7.22 with MPI

each process in a parallel application may need to access a number of relatively small, noncontiguous portions of a file. From a performance perspective, it is critical that this access pattern be expressed in the I/O interface, because it enables the implementation to optimize the I/O request. The optimizations typically allow the physical I/O to take place in large, contiguous chunks, with higher performance, even though the user's request may be noncontiguous.

For example, our implementation, ROMIO, performs an optimization called *data sieving* for level-2 requests. The basic idea is as follows: instead of reading noncontiguous data with lots of separate read calls to the file system, ROMIO reads large chunks from the file and extracts, in memory, the data that is really needed. For level-3 requests, ROMIO performs collective I/O: it analyzes the requests of different processes, merges the requests as much as possible, and makes large parallel reads/writes for the combined request. Details of both these optimizations can be found in [67].

Users, therefore, must ensure that they describe noncontiguous access patterns in terms of a file view and then call a single I/O function; they must not try to

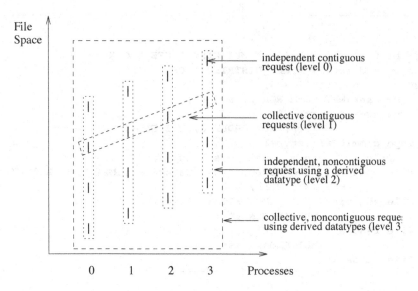

File Space

independent contiguous request (level 0)

collective contiguous requests (level 1)

independent, noncontiguous request using a derived datatype (level 2)

collective, noncontiguous reque: using derived datatypes (level 3

0   1   2   3   Processes

Figure 7.24: The four levels representing increasing amounts of data per request

access each contiguous portion separately as in Unix I/O. Figure 7.25 shows the detailed code for creating a derived datatype, defining a file view, and making a level-3 I/O request for the distributed-array example of Figure 7.22. It is similar to the example in Figure 7.10.

We note that the MPI standard does not *require* an implementation to perform any of these optimizations. Nevertheless, even if an implementation does not perform any optimization and instead translates level-3 requests into several level-0 requests to the file system, the performance would be no worse than if the user directly made level-0 requests. Therefore, there is no reason not to use level-3 requests (or level-2 requests where level-3 requests are not possible).

7.10.2   Performance Results

Table 7.23 shows the performance for writing a 3-D distributed array of size 1024^3 on the IBM Blue Gene/Q (Mira) at Argonne National Laboratory and the Blue Waters system (Cray XE6/XK7) at NCSA. On both systems the test was run with 256 MPI processes (32 nodes with 8 ranks per node on BG/Q and 16 nodes with 16 ranks per node on Blue Waters), and we measured the performance for level-0, level-2, and level-3 requests. The systems have different amounts of I/O hardware and different file systems (GPFS on BG/Q and Lustre on Blue Waters),

```
gsizes[0] = num_global_rows;
gsizes[1] = num_global_cols;
distribs[0] = distribs[1] = MPI_DISTRIBUTE_BLOCK;
dargs[0] = dargs[1] = MPI_DISTRIBUTE_DFLT_DARG;
psizes[0] = psizes[1] = 4;
MPI_Comm_rank(MPI_COMM_WORLD, &rank);
MPI_Type_create_darray(16, rank, 2, gsizes, distribs, dargs,
                psizes, MPI_ORDER_C, MPI_FLOAT, &filetype);
MPI_Type_commit(&filetype);
local_array_size = num_local_rows * num_local_cols;
MPI_File_open(MPI_COMM_WORLD, "/pfs/datafile", MPI_MODE_RDONLY,
                MPI_INFO_NULL, &fh);
MPI_File_set_view(fh, 0, MPI_FLOAT, filetype, "native",
                MPI_INFO_NULL);
MPI_File_read_all(fh, local_array, local_array_size,
                MPI_FLOAT, &status);
MPI_File_close(&fh);
```

Figure 7.25: Detailed code for the distributed-array example of Figure 7.22 using a level-3 request

	Level 0	Level 2	Level 3
Blue Gene/Q	–	39	2,685
Blue Waters	142	137	2,839

Table 7.23: I/O bandwidth in MB/s for writing a 3-D distributed array of size 1024^3 with 256 processes on BG/Q and Blue Waters

so we don't intend to compare performance among the two systems but rather to compare the performance of the different levels of access on a particular system. The results make evident the substantial advantage of writing the program in a way that makes level-3 requests rather than level 0 or 1. (On the BG/Q, for this array size, the level-0 test took too long to complete, so we don't show the result with level 0.)

7.11   An Example Application

To illustrate the use MPI-IO functionality, let us consider an example from a real application in astrophysics. The application uses several three-dimensional arrays that are distributed among processes using a block distribution in all three dimensions. The arrays fit entirely in memory. Every few iterations, some of the arrays must be written to files for three purposes: data analysis, checkpointing (for later restart), and visualization. The storage order of data in all files is required to be the same as it would be if the program were run with a single process. In other words, the arrays must be stored in column-major order of the global array. There are two reasons for this requirement: to be able to restart the program with a different number of processes from the program that created the restart file, and to analyze and visualize the data with conventional tools on desktops. The easiest way to achieve these goals is to write the data to a single file in some canonical order. The alternative way of writing to separate files and postprocessing them is clumsy and inconvenient.

The data in the data-analysis and restart files is organized as follows. Each file begins with a small "header" consisting of six floating-point variables that have the same values on all processes. Following this header are six arrays appended one after another in the same file. The visualization data is stored in four separate files, each of which has a six-variable header followed by a single array. Every few iterations, the application writes out new data-analysis and visualization files and overwrites the previously written restart file.

Implementing the I/O with MPI. We describe how to write the restart file using MPI; the data-analysis file is identical, and the visualization file is similar—actually simpler, since it has only one array.

Figure 7.26 shows the code for writing the restart file. We first write the six-variable header (assume that the six variables have already been collected into a single buffer called `header`). Since all processes have the same values for the header, any one process can write it. We choose to let process 0 write the header. Now we need to define the file view in a way that the header is automatically skipped and the arrays can be written with a single function call each. We create a darray datatype for use as the filetype, similar to the one in the program in Figure 7.10. We fill in various one-dimensional arrays, which are used as parameters to the darray datatype constructor. Here, `gsizes` contains the size of the global array in each dimension; `distribs` specifies that the distribution is a block distribution in each dimension; and `dargs` specifies the default distribution argument. We set all entries in `psizes` to zero for use in the function `MPI_Dims_create`. `MPI_-Dims_create` creates a logical process grid of the specified number of dimensions. If `psizes` specifies a nonzero value in any dimension, `MPI_Dims_create` will use that value as the number of processes in that dimension. We want `MPI_Dims_-`

`create` to calculate the number of processes in each dimension; therefore, we pass a zero-filled `psizes`.

MPI_Type_create_darray returns a datatype, which we first commit and then use as the filetype to MPI_File_set_view. The displacement is specified as the size of the header in bytes, namely, six times the size of a floating-point number. This will cause the header portion of the file to be skipped in subsequent writes. The etype is specified as MPI_FLOAT. Recall that the file view is defined as a *tiling* of the file, starting at the displacement, followed by multiple copies of the filetype appended contiguously one after another. Therefore, with this view, we can simply write all six arrays with six calls to MPI_File_write_all. local_array_size is the size of the local array in terms of the number of floating-point numbers. After each write, the individual file pointer on each process is automatically incremented by the number of etypes written, skipping all holes. The file pointer will therefore point to the offset in the file where the write of the next array from this process should begin. Consequently, no explicit file-pointer manipulation is needed.

We note that we have used the darray datatype and MPI_Dims_create for simplicity. All the warnings about darray mentioned in Section 7.4.2 apply here. If an application does not follow the same definition of data distribution or logical-process ordering as the darray datatype, one must not use darray but must use subarray instead.

Reading the header.   When the header needs to be read from a file, for example during a restart, the read can be implemented in one of the following ways:

- Process 0 can read the header and broadcast it to all other processes.

- All processes can read the header directly by using a collective read function, such as MPI_File_read_all.

- All processes can read the header directly by using an independent read function, such as MPI_File_read.

Since headers are usually small, the read-broadcast method is usually the best method to use. In the case of collective reads, the implementation may analyze the request and then choose to implement it using a read-broadcast. Analyzing the request involves interprocess communication, and hence overhead, which can be avoided if the user does the read-broadcast directly. The third option, independent reads from each process, will result in too many small I/O requests.

```
MPI_File_open(MPI_COMM_WORLD, "/pfs/restartfile",
             MPI_MODE_CREATE | MPI_MODE_WRONLY,
             MPI_INFO_NULL, &fh);

MPI_Comm_size(MPI_COMM_WORLD, &nprocs);
MPI_Comm_rank(MPI_COMM_WORLD, &rank);
if (rank == 0)
    MPI_File_write(fh, header, 6, MPI_FLOAT, &status);

for (i=0; i<3; i++) {
    gsizes[i] = global_size_in_each_dim;
    distribs[i] = MPI_DISTRIBUTE_BLOCK;
    dargs[i] = MPI_DISTRIBUTE_DFLT_DARG;
    psizes[i] = 0;
}
MPI_Dims_create(nprocs, 3, psizes);
MPI_Type_create_darray(nprocs, rank, 3, gsizes, distribs, dargs,
                       psizes, MPI_ORDER_FORTRAN, MPI_FLOAT,
                       &filetype);
MPI_Type_commit(&filetype);

MPI_File_set_view(fh, 6*sizeof(float), MPI_FLOAT, filetype,
                  "native", MPI_INFO_NULL);

MPI_File_write_all(fh, array1, local_array_size, MPI_FLOAT,
                   MPI_STATUS_IGNORE);
MPI_File_write_all(fh, array2, local_array_size, MPI_FLOAT,
                   MPI_STATUS_IGNORE);
MPI_File_write_all(fh, array3, local_array_size, MPI_FLOAT,
                   MPI_STATUS_IGNORE);
MPI_File_write_all(fh, array4, local_array_size, MPI_FLOAT,
                   MPI_STATUS_IGNORE);
MPI_File_write_all(fh, array5, local_array_size, MPI_FLOAT,
                   MPI_STATUS_IGNORE);
MPI_File_write_all(fh, array6, local_array_size, MPI_FLOAT,
                   MPI_STATUS_IGNORE);
MPI_File_close(&fh);
```

Figure 7.26: Writing the restart file

7.12   Summary

The I/O interface in MPI provides many features that can help users achieve high
I/O performance in parallel applications. The most important of these features
are the ability for users to specify noncontiguous data layouts in memory and file
using MPI datatypes, the ability to specify the group of processes participating in
collective I/O operations, and the ability to pass hints to the implementation. In
particular, in applications with noncontiguous access patterns, users must strive to
express the I/O in terms of level-3 requests (noncontiguous, collective), rather than
level-0 requests (Unix-style).

8 Coping with Large Data

Over the past several years, systems with large amounts of memory per node have become commonly available. For example, even laptops have 8 gigabytes (GB) of memory, a Blue Gene/Q node has 16 GB of memory, each node on Blue Waters (Cray XE6/XK7) has 32–64 GB of memory, and cluster nodes also routinely have 32–64 GB of memory. As a result, users with memory-intensive applications are allocating data structures larger than 2 GB in size, which is larger than what can be represented with a signed 32-bit integer. In this chapter, we refer to data of such size as *large data*.

8.1 MPI Support for Large Data

A common misunderstanding is that MPI cannot handle large data. This misunderstanding arises from the fact that the "count" parameter in all MPI communication and I/O functions is defined as an `int` in C, which is typically a 32-bit quantity on most systems[1]. Therefore, if you allocate an array of 4 GB characters, for example, you will not be able to send it with a single `MPI_Send` with `count=4GB` and `datatype=MPI_CHAR` because, as a signed 32-bit integer, you cannot set `count` to a value greater than or equal to 2 GB.

One solution to this problem would be for the MPI Forum to define a second set of all communication and I/O functions with a different count parameter that an implementation can define to be of the right size. However, the forum decided not to pursue this approach since it would result in too many additional functions. Instead, the forum adopted an approach that takes advantage of existing support for derived datatypes in MPI, which needed the addition of only a small number of new support or query functions.

8.2 Using Derived Datatypes

As described in *Using MPI* [26], all MPI data movement functions move data in "count" units of a datatype. The datatype can be a basic datatype corresponding to a language type or a derived datatype created out of multiple instances of a basic datatype by using the datatype construction functions in MPI.

The way to send and receive large data, therefore, is to define a large enough datatype so that the count parameter can be made correspondingly smaller so as

---

[1]An `int` in C could have other lengths, such as 16 or 64 bits, but 32 bits is now nearly universal, and for simplicity of the discussion in this chapter, we will assume that an `int` is 32 bits.

---

int **MPI_Type_get_extent_x**(MPI_Datatype datatype, MPI_Count *lb,
          MPI_Count *extent)

int **MPI_Type_get_true_extent_x**(MPI_Datatype datatype, MPI_Count *lb,
          MPI_Count *extent)

int **MPI_Type_size_x**(MPI_Datatype datatype, MPI_Count *size)

Table 8.1: C routines for accessing the size of large datatypes

to fit within 2 GB. For example, in the case of a 4 GB character array, one could define a contiguous datatype of four `MPI_CHAR`s and call `MPI_Send` with a count of 1 GB, as shown in the following code snippet.

```
/* to send a 4 GB array of characters */
MPI_Type_contiguous(4, MPI_CHAR, &newtype);
MPI_Type_commit(&newtype);
count = 1024*1024*1024;
MPI_Send(buf, count, newtype, dest, tag, MPI_COMM_WORLD);
```

The new functions that needed to be added were new versions of some existing support functions, such as functions to query the size or extent of a datatype, in order to ensure that the output parameters of these functions were of the right size. For this purpose, a new type was defined in the MPI standard, called `MPI_Count` in C and `INTEGER (KIND=MPI_COUNT_KIND)` in Fortran.

The size of the `MPI_Count` type is determined by the MPI implementation, with the restriction that it must be large enough to represent an address in memory and an offset in a file. In other words, it must be at least as large as the larger of the `MPI_Aint` and `MPI_Offset` types. The new functions to query the size and extent of large datatypes are shown in Tables 8.1 and 8.2 for C and Fortran, respectively. Note that, compared with the already existing corresponding functions, the new functions have a suffix of `_x` and that the `size`, `lb`, and `extent` parameters are of type `MPI_Count`.

8.3   Example

In Chapter 7 we showed results of using parallel I/O to write out a 3-D mesh that was distributed across all processes into a single file. This example is drawn from the code that was used for those results. It has the following features:

MPI_TYPE_GET_EXTENT_X(datatype, lb, extent, ierror)
        integer datatype, ierror
        integer(kind = MPI_COUNT_KIND) lb, extent

MPI_TYPE_GET_TRUE_EXTENT_X(datatype, true_lb, true_extent, ierror)
        integer datatype, ierror
        integer(kind=MPI_COUNT_KIND) true_lb, true_extent

MPI_TYPE_SIZE_X(datatype, size, ierror)
        integer datatype, ierror
        integer(kind=MPI_COUNT_KIND) size

Table 8.2: Fortran routines for accessing the size of large datatypes

1. It uses a darray datatype to create the distributed array that will be used in the file view.

2. It prints the range of bytes used in the file (when `verbose` flag is true).

3. The amount of memory needed is `meshLsize`, which could be more than 2 GB (limit of signed 32-bit integer).

The code is shown in Figure 8.1.

8.4 Limitations of This Approach

Although this method of handling large data can be used in most cases, it has a few limitations.[2]

8.4.1 Collective Reduction Functions

One limitation is in the use of collective reduction functions, such as `MPI_Reduce` or `MPI_Allreduce`, for large data. Users commonly call these functions with one of the predefined reduction operations in MPI, such as `MPI_SUM`, `MPI_MIN`, or `MPI_MAX`. However, MPI specifies that these predefined operations can be used only if the datatype passed to the collective function is a basic datatype. If the datatype is a derived datatype, none of the predefined reduction operations can be used. Instead, you must use the so-called user-defined reduction operations; that

---

[2]http://lists.mpi-forum.org/mpi-forum/2014/05/2772.php,
   https://svn.mpi-forum.org/trac/mpi-forum-web/ticket/430

```
MPI_Type_create_darray(wsize, wrank, ndims, array_of_gsizes,
                        array_of_distribs, array_of_dargs,
                        array_of_psizes, order, MPI_INT,
                        &darrayType);
MPI_Type_commit(&darrayType);

if (verbose) {
    MPI_Count lb, extent;
    MPI_Type_get_extent_x(darrayType, &lb, &extent);
    printf("Datatype: lb = %lld, extent = %lld\n",
           (long long)lb, (long long)extent);
    MPI_Type_get_true_extent_x(darrayType, &lb, &extent);
    printf("Datatype: true lb = %lld, true extent = %lld\n",
           (long long)lb, (long long)extent);
}
MPI_Type_size_x(darrayType, &meshLsize);

...
err = MPI_File_set_view(fh, 0, MPI_INT, darrayType,
                        "native", MPI_INFO_NULL);
```

Figure 8.1: Example use of MPI_Count routines to work with darray types

is, you must define the reduction operation yourself by using MPI_Op_create and pass the newly created operation to the collective function.

For example, if you want to perform a sum reduction on an array of size 4G integers, you cannot simply create a contiguous datatype of four integers and call MPI_Reduce with a count of 1G and MPI_SUM as the reduction operation. Instead, you must either call MPI_Reduce multiple times using a count less than 2G and MPI_INT as the datatype, or you must define your own reduction operation that works on a derived datatype and call MPI_Reduce with this operation and the derived datatype.

8.4.2   Irregular Collectives

Another limitation is in the case of the irregular collectives, such as MPI_Gatherv, MPI_Alltoallv, or MPI_Alltoallw, for large data. The problem with the "v" collectives is that each process can send unequal amounts of data, but there is only one datatype parameter to the function. Depending on how different are the amounts of data sent from each process, it may not be possible to define the same "large" datatype to describe the data from all processes.

MPI_Alltoallw supports multiple datatypes but has a different problem in that the displacements are defined as int and are used as an absolute displacement into the buffer, not scaled by the extent of the datatype as in the "v" collectives. The limitation of an int-defined explicit displacement is that you can never offset into a buffer beyond 2 GB.

For these irregular collectives, one solution is to simply implement them as a series of point-to-point operations, although it may not result in the best performance. Another solution is to use the neighborhood collective function, MPI_Neighbor_-alltoallw, which we discussed in Chapter 2. This function performs an irregular alltoall operation among nearest neighbors as defined by a virtual process topology. (You would have to first define such a virtual topology, which is also explained in Chapter 2.) The advantage of using MPI_Neighbor_alltoallw is that, unlike in MPI_Alltoallw, the displacement parameters are defined as MPI_Aint and hence can be used to index into a buffer beyond 2 GB.

9 Support for Performance and Correctness Debugging

Building parallel codes that are both correct and fast is difficult. This chapter describes some of the features of MPI that can help with identifying and fixing both performance and correctness problems.

From the beginning, MPI provided support for building tools to help debug MPI programs. The profiling interface, introduced in MPI-1 and described in *Using MPI*, Section 7.6, is a powerful way to build tools that can work on top of an MPI program, in most cases without requiring any change in the application code. However, this interface is limited to intercepting calls to MPI routines. When diagnosing a performance problem, more information is often needed. For example, how long did an MPI_Recv wait before the message arrived? How many messages were in the message queue waiting to be received? Answering these questions accurately requires help from the MPI implementation, which *may* maintain this sort of data. In fact, many MPI implementations have some internal performance instrumentation that the developers may use in their own performance tuning. With the new tools interface introduced in MPI-3, MPI provides a standard way for users and for other tools to access whatever performance data the MPI implementation can provide. This interface provides access to *performance variables* and is described in Section 9.1.2.

Of course, identifying a performance problem is only the first step. An MPI implementation may provide parameters that can change the performance, for example, by selecting a different algorithm for an MPI collective operation or changing how point-to-point messages are sent. The MPI tools interface also provides access to variables defined by the implementation that control the behavior of the implementation; these *control variables* are described in Section 9.1.1. We describe these before covering the performance variables because the interface is similar to but simpler than that for the performance variables.

MPI also provides users with other ways to help the implementation perform better. These include the use of MPI Info for *hints* and the use of *assertions*. These usually represent information about the application that is independent of a particular MPI implementation. Some of these are described in Section 9.2.

In Section 9.3 we briefly describe an interface that allows debuggers and other tools to access information about a running MPI program. While not part of the MPI standard, this interface is widely implemented, and a specification document has been created by the MPI Forum. Together, these interfaces allow applications and tools to provide comprehensive information for the analysis and control of an MPI application.

---

int **MPI_T_init_thread**(int required, int *provided)

int **MPI_T_finalize**(void)

Table 9.1: Bindings for initializing and finalizing the MPI_T interface

9.1 The Tools Interface

Large codes commonly have internal instrumentation to help the developers understand the performance and behavior of the code, as well as variables that control
the behavior of the code. Most, if not all, implementations of MPI have such data
and variables. However, the exact choice of variables and data are specific to each
implementation. The MPI tools, or MPI_T, interface is intended to give users and
tool developers a way to discover what variables are available, to learn what sort
of data they provide or features they control, and to access and update them.

For both performance and control variables, there are several common concepts.
Because no predefined variables are required of all MPI implementations, the available variables are identified by an integer index starting at zero. The number of
available variables may increase (but not decrease) during the execution of an MPI
program. For example, the first time a routine is used, code may be dynamically
loaded into the executable, making additional variables available.

To access a particular variable, you must first create a *handle*. With this handle,
the MPI implementation can provide low-overhead access to the internal variable;
for example, the handle could be a pointer to the variable itself or to a small structure containing a pointer to the variable. By using a handle, the implementation
details are hidden from the user while providing opportunities for a high-efficiency
implementation.

The MPI_T interface, unlike the rest of MPI, is not language independent and is
defined only for standard C. The reason has to do with the complexity of returning
data of different types (e.g., integer or floating point) with the same routine in
standard Fortran. Although such a definition can be done, the MPI Forum decided
to specify only a C interface. Fortran users will need to write C routines that they
can call from Fortran.

Figure 9.1 shows sample code for initializing and finalizing the MPI_T interface.
The function bindings are shown in Table 9.1.

Error returns. Because the MPI_T routines may be used before MPI is initialized
or after MPI is finalized, the MPI_T routines do not use the MPI error class and

```
...
MPI_Init_thread(0, 0, required, &provided);
MPI_T_init_thread(required, &provided);

... Mix MPI and MPI_T calls

MPI_T_finalize();
MPI_Finalize();
...
```

Figure 9.1: All use of MPI_T routines must be between the MPI_T initialize and finalize routines

code system. Instead, the MPI_T routines return an error code. The value MPI_-SUCCESS is returned on success. The MPI standard specifies all the error values that each of the MPI_T routines may return. In this book, we mention only a few of the error values. Unlike MPI, however, the default behavior on error is not to cause the program to fail, hence; you must be vigilant in checking error returns from the MPI_T routines. In our examples, we perform a simple check; you may wish to provide more detail when an error occurs.

9.1.1 Control Variables

Control variables allow the user to influence how the MPI implementation works. For example, many MPI implementations send short messages immediately (often called *eager protocol*), whereas longer messages are sent only when the matching receive is posted (often called *rendezvous protocol*). The definition of "short" is a parameter in the code and, if the MPI implementation chooses, can be exposed to the programmer as a control variable.

First, we need to discover the available control variables. Rather than rely on documentation, MPI provides a way to determine from within an MPI program what control variables are defined. This approach is called *introspection*. We need two routines for this: one to tell us how many control variables are defined and the other to return information on each of the control variables. These routines are shown Table 9.2 and their use in the program in Figure 9.2.

The key routine is MPI_T_cvar_get_info, which has many parameters. Let's first look at the ones that we use in this program.

cvar_index. This is the index, from 0 to num_cvar-1, of the control variable.

```
#include <stdio.h>
#include "mpi.h"

/* Lengths for statically allocated character arrays */
#define MAX_NAME_LEN 128
#define MAX_DESC_LEN 1024
int main(int argc, char *argv[])
{
  int        i, num_cvar, nameLen, verbosity, descLen, binding;
  int        required = MPI_THREAD_SINGLE, provided, err, scope;
  char       name[MAX_NAME_LEN], desc[MAX_DESC_LEN];
  MPI_T_enum enumtype;
  MPI_Datatype datatype;

  MPI_Init_thread(0, 0, required, &provided);
  MPI_T_init_thread(required, &provided);

  MPI_T_cvar_get_num(&num_cvar);
  printf("%d MPI Control Variables\n", num_cvar);
  for (i=0; i<num_cvar; i++) {
   nameLen = sizeof(name);
   descLen = sizeof(desc);
   err = MPI_T_cvar_get_info(i, name, &nameLen, &verbosity,
                             &datatype, &enumtype, desc,
                             &descLen, &binding, &scope);

   printf("\t%-32s\t%s\n", name, desc);
  }

  MPI_T_finalize(); /* No test on return because we're
                       about to exit */
  MPI_Finalize();
  return 0;
}
```

Figure 9.2: Program to print the available control variables and their descriptions

---

int **MPI_T_cvar_get_num**(int *num)

int **MPI_T_cvar_get_info**(int cvar_index, char *name, int *name_len, int *verbosity,
            MPI_Datatype *datatype, MPI_T_enum *enumtype, char *desc,
            int *desc_len, int *binding, int *scope)

int **MPI_T_cvar_get_index**(const char *name, int *cvar_index)

Table 9.2: Routines to query number and properties of control variables and to find a control variable by name

name. The name of the control variable is returned here. This must have length `name_len`.

name_len. On input, the length of `name`; on output, the number of characters used, including the null terminator.

desc. A text description of the control variable. It must have length `desc_len`. A null pointer is permitted for `desc`, in which case no description is returned.

desc_len. On input, the length of `desc`; on output, the number of characters used, including the null terminator.

An example of some of the output of this program is shown below. This output is from the MPICH implementation of MPI and shows only the first two of the control variables defined by MPICH.

```
57 MPI Control Variables
        MPIR_CVAR_ALLTOALL_SHORT_MSG_SIZE        the short message
algorithm will be used if the per-destination message size (sendcount
*size(sendtype)) is <= this value
        MPIR_CVAR_ALLTOALL_MEDIUM_MSG_SIZE        the medium message
algorithm will be used if the per-destination message size (sendcount
*size(sendtype)) is <= this value and larger than ALLTOALL_SHORT_MSG_SIZE
...
```

What are the other parameters for? They provide information about the use of the control variable. These output parameters are as follows:

verbosity describes the intended audience for the control variable. The values have names of the form `MPI_T_VERBOSITY_<user>_<detail>`. For example, the values include `MPI_T_VERBOSITY_USER_BASIC`, `MPI_T_-VERBOSITY_TUNER_DETAIL`, and `MPI_T_VERBOSITY_MPIDEV_ALL`, which are respectively basic controls for an MPI program user, detailed controls for someone tuning an MPI program for performance, and all controls for the developer of the MPI implementation itself. All nine combinations of user and detail are defined by MPI.

binding indicates whether the control variable is specific to a particular MPI object. A common value for this is `MPI_T_BIND_NO_OBJECT`. In contrast, a control variable whose binding was `MPI_T_BIND_T_COMM` would apply to a specific MPI communicator.

scope describes whether the control variable may be modified and, if so, whether it can be modified on a single process or must be modified consistently on a group of processes. Typical values include `MPI_T_SCOPE_CONSTANT` for a value that cannot be changed, `MPI_T_SCOPE_LOCAL` for a value that can be changed and can be a different value on each process, and `MPI_T_SCOPE_-ALL_EQ` for a value that can be changed but must be the same on every process. An example of a local control variable is one that turns debugging output on or off. An example of a `MPI_T_SCOPE_ALL_EQ` control variable is one that controls the choice of algorithm or algorithm parameter in collective communication. The variables in the example above, which control the parameters in the implementation of the `MPI_Alltoall` routine, are examples of this kind of scope.

datatype indicates the kind of data stored in the control variable—for example, is it an `int` or a `double`? Because this needs to be a value that can be used in a test, the corresponding MPI datatype is returned. So, if the control variable is an `int`, the value `MPI_INT` will be returned.

enumtype is used only if `MPI_INT` is returned for the `datatype`. If the value is `MPI_T_ENUM_NULL`, then this value is not an `enum`. Otherwise, the value returned is really a C enum type, and a separate set of `MPI_T` routines is used to determine how to convert the value of the control variable into the `enum` value name. Those routines are not described in this book; see the MPI-3 standard for details on their use.

When accessing or modifying a control variable, you should be sure to check the `datatype`, `binding`, and `scope`. In the examples below, we will ensure that we have the values that we expect. Chapter 14 in the MPI-3 standard [46] provides a complete list of the valid values for these parameters.

---

int **MPI_T_cvar_handle_alloc**(int cvar_index, void *obj_handle,
            MPI_T_cvar_handle *handle, int *count)

int **MPI_T_cvar_handle_free**(MPI_T_cvar_handle *handle)

int **MPI_T_cvar_read**(MPI_T_cvar_handle handle, void* buf)

int **MPI_T_cvar_write**(MPI_T_cvar_handle handle, const void* buf)

Table 9.3: C bindings for routines to access and modify control variables

Changing a control variable. How do you access or modify a control variable? MPI provides a wo-step process. First, you must associate a *handle* with the control variable. This handle is used to read or write the control variable. You can then free the handle (and any resources that the MPI implementation needed for the handle). This process is best described by example; Figure 9.3 shows how one control variable is read and modified. Table 9.3 shows the C bindings for the routines needed for this example.

Figure 9.3 has several steps. First, both MPI and MPI_T are initialized. Second, we must find the index that corresponds to the control variable that we want to access. In MPI 3.0, this was a fairly awkward step—the only way to do this was to search through all the available control variables by using the MPI_T_cvar_get_info routine that we used in Figure 9.2 to access the name of each control variable. Fortunately, the MPI Forum has introduced a new routine, MPI_T_cvar_get_index, that, given a control variable name, returns the index. This routine should appear in MPI 3.1, which is expected to be released at the end of 2014.

In the example we also check that we found the control variable; if not, this simple code just aborts.

The call to MPI_T_cvar_handle_alloc creates the handle to be used in accessing the control variable. The first argument is the index of the control variable, which we determined in the for loop. The next argument is needed only if the *binding* of the control variable is *not* MPI_T_BIND_NO_OBJECT. If an object is required, this should be a pointer to that object. The last two values are returned. The first is the handle; this is of type MPI_T_cvar_handle and will be used in the routines to read and write the control variable. The second is the number of values in the control variable. Typically, this will be one; but if the control variable was, for example, an array of three ints, then this value would be 3. Note that the

```c
#include <stdio.h>
#include "mpi.h"
#define MAX_NAME_LEN 128
#define MAX_DESC_LEN 1024
int main(int argc, char *argv[] )
{
  int          cidx, eagersize, nvals, err;
  int          required = MPI_THREAD_SINGLE, provided;
  MPI_T_cvar_handle chandle;
  MPI_T_enum   enumtype;
  MPI_Datatype datatype;

  MPI_Init_thread(0, 0, required, &provided);
  MPI_T_init_thread(required, &provided);

  /* Lookup the index for the desired variable */
  err = MPI_T_cvar_get_index("MPIR_CVAR_CH3_EAGER_MAX_MSG_SIZE",
                             &cidx);
  if (err != MPI_SUCCESS) MPI_Abort(0, MPI_COMM_WORLD);

  /* Create a handle for it */
  err = MPI_T_cvar_handle_alloc(cidx, NULL, &chandle,
                                &nvals);
  if (nvals != 1)
    printf("Unexpected number of values = %d\n", nvals);

  err = MPI_T_cvar_read(chandle, &eagersize);
  printf("Eager size = %d\n", eagersize);

  eagersize = 1024;
  err = MPI_T_cvar_write(chandle, &eagersize);
  err = MPI_T_cvar_read(chandle, &eagersize);
  if (eagersize != 1024) printf("Failed to reset eagersize!\n");

  MPI_T_cvar_handle_free(&chandle);
  MPI_T_finalize();    /* No test on return because we're about
                          to exit */
  MPI_Finalize();
}
```

Figure 9.3: Code to change the eager limit in MPICH

code calls `MPI_T_cvar_handle_free` to free this handle when it is no longer needed.

With this preparation, accessing and modifying the control variable is easy. The routine `MPI_T_cvar_read` takes as input argument the handle and stores the value of the control variable in the location pointed at by the `buf` argument—in this case, `eagersize`. Similarly, `MPI_T_cvar_write` stores the given value (pointed at by the `buf` argument) in the control variable.

Note that this code reads the value after writing it. This approach is not necessary but is often a good consistency check. For clarity of the example, error returns from the `MPI_T` routines were not checked but should be checked in real code.

9.1.2 Performance Variables

Performance problems arise in parallel programs from many sources. Some of the most common ones are load imbalance, late receives, receive queue congestion, and network contention. An MPI implementation may provide a way to detect these problems or at least to suggest what may be the problem.

For example, load imbalance—which is the uneven distribution of work among processes, leading to inefficiencies when a process runs out of work and must wait for others to catch up—is often indicated by MPI communication routines that block, waiting for the source process to send them data. In fact, users often confuse load imbalance for slow MPI communication. Some MPI implementations may record the amount of time spent waiting for data to arrive; by accessing this value, the user (or the performance expert attempting to tune the code) can discover that a load imbalance is likely.

Another example is late receives. If data is sent before a matching receive has been posted at the destination, the MPI implementation must either store the message and data, requiring an extra copy, or must wait to send the data until the receive has been posted. If the implementation maintains a queue of unexpected messages, checking the length of this queue can indicate whether late-posted receives may be the problem.

A related example is receive-queue congestion, where many receives are posted, and posted early enough to match the sends, but they are posted in the "wrong" order, causing the MPI implementation to spend time searching through the queue. If the implementation keeps track of how many queue elements are examined, then examining the value of this variable can suggest that the send and/or the receives are issued in the wrong order.

Our final example is network contention. In the simplest case, it occurs when multiple messages are routed over the same physical network link, causing the total bandwidth to be shared—and thus for each communication to see reduced performance. Some network hardware keeps track of such events; and if the MPI implementation provides access to that data, one can discover that contention is reducing the performance of the application.

The `MPI_T` performance interface provides a way for a user or a tool to examine whatever performance variables are provided by the implementation. By combining that data with an understanding of how the implementation works, even abstractly, you may be able to determine the source of the performance problem. You'll note that this is a vague statement—determining what the provided information means often requires someone experienced in tuning MPI programs. The goal of the `MPI_T` interface is twofold: to encourage MPI implementations to provide this data, and to provide a portable way to access the data, in the hope that more user-friendly tools will take advantage of it.

You may be wondering why the MPI Forum didn't specify an easy way to get to the performance variables common to every MPI implementation, for example, the number of unexpected messages received. The reason is that even something as apparently obvious as the number of unexpected messages is not an MPI concept—it is a common but not necessary part of an implementation. An implementation might use a different approach to processing messages for which no receive has yet been posted (for example, in one implementation such messages were rejected at the receiver, and the sender had to resend them later). Since the `MPI_T` interface is intended to enable an MPI implementation to expose implementation-specific features, it is neither possible nor desirable to define variables that all MPI implementations must provide.

Since no performance variables are required by the MPI standard, our first example shows how to print out the names and description for all the performance variables that are available when the MPI program starts. The code in Figure 9.4 will print all available performance variables as well as a description of the variables and some basic properties, such as whether the variables may only be read. Note both the similarities and differences with the code to print all control variables shown in Figure 9.2. Among the differences from the control variables are several return values. These include the following:

var_class. The *class* of the performance variable. The class indicates, for example, whether the variable is a counter or a timer. This is discussed more below. In addition, a performance variable is uniquely determined by the pair of values

```c
#include <stdio.h>
#include <string.h>
#include "mpi.h"

int main(int argc, char *argv[])
{
  int          provided, err;
  int          numPvar, nameLen, descLen, verbosity, varClass;
  int          binding, isReadonly, isContinuous, isAtomic, i;
  char         name[128], desc[1024];
  MPI_T_enum   enumtype;
  MPI_Datatype datatype;

  MPI_Init_thread(0, 0, MPI_THREAD_SINGLE, &provided);
  err = MPI_T_init_thread(MPI_THREAD_SINGLE, &provided);
  if (err) MPI_Abort(MPI_COMM_WORLD, 0);

  err = MPI_T_pvar_get_num(&numPvar);
  if (err) MPI_Abort(MPI_COMM_WORLD, 0);
  printf("%d MPI Performance Variables\n", numPvar);

  for (i=0; i<numPvar; i++) {
   nameLen = sizeof(name);
   descLen = sizeof(desc);
   err = MPI_T_pvar_get_info(i, name, &nameLen, &verbosity,
                    &varClass, &datatype, &enumtype, desc,
                    &descLen, &binding, &isReadonly,
                    &isContinuous, &isAtomic);
   if (err) MPI_Abort(MPI_COMM_WORLD, 0);
   printf("\t%s\tClass=%d\tReadonly=%s\tContinuous=%s\tAtomic=%s\t%s\n",
     name, varClass, isReadonly ? "T" : "F",
     isContinuous ? "T" : "F", isAtomic ? "T" : "F", desc);
  }
  MPI_T_finalize();   /* No test on return because we're about
                         to exit */
  MPI_Finalize();
  return 0;
}
```

Figure 9.4: Simple program to list the performance variables that are available when an MPI program starts

---

int **MPI_T_pvar_get_num**(int *num)

int **MPI_T_pvar_get_info**(int pvar_index, char *name, int *name_len, int *verbosity,
                int *var_class, MPI_Datatype *datatype, MPI_T_enum *enumtype,
                char *desc, int *desc_len, int *binding, int *isreadonly,
                int *iscontinuous, int *isatomic)

int **MPI_T_pvar_get_index**(const char *name, int var_class, int *pvar_index)

Table 9.4: Routines to query number and properties of performance variables and to find a performance variable from its name and class

name and var_class. This is in contrast to control variables, which are uniquely specified by just their name.

readonly. Indication of whether the variable can be written or reset by the user.

continuous. Indication of whether the variable can be stopped by the user, preventing further changes.

atomic. Indication of whether the variable can be read and reset atomically, avoiding race conditions.

The variable class is the most important part of these. MPI defines a number of different classes. The following are the most common classes:

MPI_T_PVAR_CLASS_LEVEL. The amount of use of a resource. For example, this might provide the number of currently posted receives.

MPI_T_PVAR_CLASS_COUNTER. The number of occurrences of an event, such as the number of times a message has arrived but no receive was posted for the message.

MPI_T_PVAR_CLASS_HIGHWATERMARK. A class similar to MPI_T_PVAR_CLASS_LEVEL, but reports the maximum value of the resource.

MPI_T_PVAR_CLASS_LOWWATERMARK. A class similar to MPI_T_PVAR_CLASS_LEVEL, but reports the minimum value of the resource.

MPI_T_PVAR_CLASS_TIMER. The amount of time spent executing some part of the MPI library. If the datatype for this performance variable is MPI_DOUBLE, then the value is in seconds; otherwise, it is implementation defined (but must be explained in the desc field).

In addition, the following variable classes are defined:

MPI_T_PVAR_CLASS_SIZE. The *fixed* size of a resource, for example, the available memory for buffering, assuming that value is indeed fixed.

MPI_T_PVAR_CLASS_STATE. The *state* of the system. This class of variable should be represented by an enum type. Such variables are likely to be *readonly*.

MPI_T_PVAR_CLASS_PERCENTAGE. The percentage utilization of a resource, expressed as a double value between 0.0 and 1.0.

MPI_T_PVAR_CLASS_AGGREGATE. A sum of values from an event, rather than a count of the number of occurrences. For example, a variable of class MPI_T_PVAR_CLASS_COUNTER might be used to count the number of messages sent; a variable of this type is used to count the number of bytes sent in those messages.

MPI_T_PVAR_CLASS_GENERIC. An implementation-specific performance variable, used for anything that doesn't fit into one of the predefined classes.

For each of these variable classes, there exist restrictions on the type of data that can be returned (except for MPI_T_PVAR_CLASS_GENERIC). Most values must be of C type unsigned, unsigned long, unsigned long long, or double, with the corresponding MPI datatypes of MPI_UNSIGNED, MPI_UNSIGNED_LONG, MPI_-UNSIGNED_LONG_LONG, or MPI_DOUBLE.

Once you have found the performance variable that you are interested in, you need to access it. The process is similar to that for control variables but with an additional step, namely, the creation of a *session*. The session enables different parts of the code to access and modify a performance variable in a way that is specific to that part of the code. In some sense, a session serves the same role as a communicator—it provides a way to isolate the use of a performance variable to a specific module, library, or part of the code. A session is created with MPI_T_-pvar_session_create; this is a local (not a collective) call.

Once a session is created, you can create a *handle*. Like control variables, the handle will be used to access and modify the performance variable. A handle is created with MPI_T_pvar_handle_alloc.

---

int **MPI_T_pvar_session_create**(MPI_T_pvar_session *session)

int **MPI_T_pvar_handle_alloc**(MPI_T_pvar_session session, int pvar_index,
        void *obj_handle, MPI_T_pvar_handle *handle, int *flag)

int **MPI_T_pvar_handle_free**(MPI_T_pvar_session session,
        MPI_T_pvar_handle *handle)

int **MPI_T_pvar_session_free**(MPI_T_pvar_session *session)

int **MPI_T_pvar_start**(MPI_T_pvar_session session, MPI_T_pvar_handle handle)

int **MPI_T_pvar_stop**(MPI_T_pvar_session session, MPI_T_pvar_handle handle)

int **MPI_T_pvar_read**(MPI_T_pvar_session session, MPI_T_pvar_handle handle,
        void* buf)

int **MPI_T_pvar_write**(MPI_T_pvar_session session, MPI_T_pvar_handle handle,
        const void* buf)

Table 9.5: C bindings for routines to access and modify performance variables

We are almost ready to read the value of the variable. Some variables are updated continuously by the implementation; these return true (1) for the iscontinuous parameter. These are the most common type. Other variables, however, can be stopped and started by the user, and begin in the stopped state. These variables must be started before they will begin to gather data. The routine MPI_T_pvar_-start starts a performance variable, and MPI_T_pvar_stop stops one. You do not need to stop a performance variable in order to read it, but stopping a variable does guarantee that the variable is not updated once stopped.

Like control variables, performance variables may be read and (if the isreadonly flag was false) written. The corresponding routines, MPI_T_pvar_-read and MPI_T_pvar_write, take both the performance variable session and handle.

The code in Figures 9.5 and 9.6 illustrates the use of performance variables. The code in Figure 9.5 sets up the performance variable session and handle, calls a test program, and then reads and prints the value read. The test program in Figure 9.6 sends many messages, then receives them in the reverse of the order from which they were sent. For most MPI implementations, this message pattern will cause the implementation to search the entire unexpected queue, finding the message after examining every message. While this may seem a perverse way to order the searches, applications can produce similar orderings when receiving from multiple processes and then specifying a particular order for executing the receives. Try this test, changing the number of messages and the order of receives.

9.2   Info, Assertions, and MPI Objects

MPI allows users to provide two types of information about the behavior of their application. *Hints* are suggestions from the application about choices that may improve performance; hints may be ignored by the implementation. *Assertions* are statements about behavior that are guarantees from the programmer to the MPI implementation—if the program makes an assertion that is not true, the implementation may produce erroneous results. In MPI, most hints are communicated through the use of an `MPI_Info` value; assertions are usually integer values passed to an MPI routine. In both cases, the user does not have to provide either hints or assertions—the program will be correct without them. They can, however, improve the performance of an application.

Hints and assertions in MPI differ from control variables in that they express features of the application or are suggestions, rather than a way to directly control the implementation. Thus, unlike control variables described in Section 9.1.1, they are portable.

Why are these important? The MPI implementation must base its implementation decisions on what information it has. Typcially, all a routine knows is that it has been called; a sophisticated implementation may also have kept track of recent uses of the routine. However, knowing more about the specific state of the application or about the properties of use can permit the implementation to perform optimizations that would either be incorrect for other situations or less efficient.

A good example is the assertions for the synchronization in one-sided communication. `MPI_Win_fence` provides a number of assertion values that describe what MPI one-sided calls or local changes to the memory window have occurred before or will occur after the call. This provides information unavailable to the MPI implementation. Note that if the user makes an assertion that is incorrect, the program is erroneous.

A good example of the use of hints is for parallel I/O. A number of values exist for optimizing the performance of collective I/O, such as `cb_block_size`, described in Section 7.7. Users can set these values based on their experience with their parallel file system and the sequence of I/O operations performed by their application. A hint is different from a control variable because the implementation

```c
#include <stdio.h>
#include <string.h>
#include "mpi.h"

int main(int argc, char *argv[])
{
  int          provided, lcount, err, pidx, isContinuous;
  double       qtimestart, qtime;
  MPI_T_enum   enumtype;        MPI_Datatype datatype;
  MPI_T_pvar_session session;   MPI_T_pvar_handle handle;

  MPI_Init_thread(0, 0, MPI_THREAD_SINGLE, &provided);
  err = MPI_T_init_thread(MPI_THREAD_SINGLE, &provided);
  if (err) MPI_Abort(MPI_COMM_WORLD, 0);

  err = MPI_T_pvar_get_index("time_matching_unexpectedq",
                    MPI_T_PVAR_CLASS_TIMER, &pidx);

  if (err != MPI_SUCCESS) MPI_Abort(MPI_COMM_WORLD, 0);
  /* Determine whether we need to start the variable. MPI 3.1
     allows us to pass NULL for any return parameter that
     we ignore. */
  err = MPI_T_pvar_get_info(pidx, NULL, NULL, NULL, NULL,
                        NULL, NULL, NULL, NULL, NULL,
                        NULL, &isContinuous, NULL);

  err = MPI_T_pvar_session_create(&session);
  err = MPI_T_pvar_handle_alloc(session, pidx, NULL, &handle,
                        &lcount);
  err = MPI_T_pvar_read(session, handle, &qtimestart);
  if (!isContinuous) err = MPI_T_pvar_start(session, handle);
  TestProgram();
  if (!isContinuous) err = MPI_T_pvar_stop(session, handle);
  err = MPI_T_pvar_read(session, handle, &qtime);
  printf("Time searching unexpected queue = %e\n",
        qtime-qtimestart);
  /* No test on return from here on because we're about to
     exit */
  MPI_T_pvar_handle_free(session, &handle);
  MPI_T_pvar_session_free(&session);
  MPI_T_finalize();
  MPI_Finalize();
  return 0;
}
```

Figure 9.5: Example program to read the time spent searching the unexpected receive queue in MPICH (performance variable names are specific to an MPI implementation)

```
#include "mpi.h"
/* A simple program to send and receive in an inefficient order */
#define MAX_REQ 128
void TestProgram(void)
{
    MPI_Request sr[MAX_REQ], rr[MAX_REQ];
    int wrank, wsize, i, from, to, err;

    MPI_Comm_rank(MPI_COMM_WORLD, &wrank);
    MPI_Comm_size(MPI_COMM_WORLD, &wsize);

    from = 0;
    to   = wsize-1;

    if (wrank == from) {
        for (i=0; i<MAX_REQ; i++) {
            MPI_Isend((void*)0, 0, MPI_BYTE, to,
                        i, MPI_COMM_WORLD, &sr[i]);
        }
    }
    MPI_Barrier(MPI_COMM_WORLD); /* To ensure that the sends are
                                    posted before the receives */
    if (wrank == to) {
        for (i=0; i<MAX_REQ; i++) {
            MPI_Irecv((void*)0, 0, MPI_BYTE, from,
                        MAX_REQ-i-1, MPI_COMM_WORLD, &rr[i]);
        }
    }
    if (wrank == to) {
        MPI_Waitall(MAX_REQ, rr, MPI_STATUSES_IGNORE);
    }
    if (wrank == from) {
        MPI_Waitall(MAX_REQ, sr, MPI_STATUSES_IGNORE);
    }
}
```

Figure 9.6: Test program to post many sends before receives

---

int **MPI_Comm_set_info**(MPI_Comm comm, MPI_Info info)

int **MPI_Comm_get_info**(MPI_Comm comm, MPI_Info *info_used)

int **MPI_Win_set_info**(MPI_Win win, MPI_Info info)

int **MPI_Win_get_info**(MPI_Win win, MPI_Info *info_used)

Table 9.6: C routines to set and get the MPI info value on communicators and windows

need not pay any attention to the hint. Like control variables, hints may be defined by the implementation. Many implementations have provided their own I/O hints; you must check the documentation to discover their names, meanings, and valid values.

Because MPI_Info was a new feature added in MPI-2, communicators (defined in MPI-1) did not have hints. At the time MPI-1 was defined, it was thought that attributes could be used for implementation-specific hints. That approach was impractical, however, since there is no portable way to write code that uses implementation-defined attributes (these are the attributes that would be set with MPI_Comm_set_attr). Moreover, even though MPI-2 allowed info hints to be provided when an MPI window was created, one could not change the hints on a window after it was created. Because of the potential benefit of hints in helping an MPI implementation provide better performance, MPI-3 added routines to allow info hints to be set on communicators and windows; these are shown in Tables 9.6 and 9.7 for C and Fortran, respectively. While there are no predefined hints for communicators, and only a few for windows, implementations may provide additional hints. For example, several MPI implementors have said that they could provide better performance if they knew that MPI_ANY_SOURCE and MPI_ANY_-TAG would not be used for any receive on a particular communicator. An info value could be used to provide that information to the implementation.

In addition, MPI-3 has a new version of MPI_Comm_dup that takes an info object as an input argument; MPI_Comm_dup_with_info behaves exactly like MPI_-Comm_dup except that the info values in the new communicator are taken from the info argument instead of being copied from the input communicator. The C and Fortran bindings for this routine are shown in Tables 9.8 and 9.9, respectively.

Associating a new info object while duplicating a communicator subtly changes the behavior of communicator duplication. When MPI_Comm_dup duplicates a communicator, the new communicator gets copies of the attributes from the old

---

MPI_COMM_SET_INFO(comm, info, ierror)
    integer comm, info, ierror

MPI_COMM_GET_INFO(comm, info_used, ierror)
    integer comm, info_used, ierror

MPI_WIN_SET_INFO(win, info, ierror)
    integer win, info, ierror

MPI_WIN_GET_INFO(win, info_used, ierror)
    integer win, info_used, ierror

Table 9.7: Fortran routines to set and get the MPI info value on communicators and windows

---

int **MPI_Comm_dup_with_info**(MPI_Comm comm, MPI_Info info,
        MPI_Comm *newcomm)

Table 9.8: C routine to duplicate a communicator with a specified info

communicator, the topology information, and the info values. If one of those info values was a promise by the user to, for example, never use MPI_ANY_SOURCE, that promise would be propagated to the new, duplicated communicator. However, since MPI_Comm_dup is typically used by a library to create a private communicator for its own communication, it shouldn't be bound by any promises made by the user for the use of the original communicator. Figure 9.7 shows a way that a library routine can perform a communicator duplication and ensure that the new communicator, here newcomm, has only the hints that are valid for the library routines. If no hints are desired, the null info value, MPI_INFO_NULL, may be passed to MPI_Comm_-dup_with_info.

9.3   Debugging and the MPIR Debugger Interface

While MPI does not specify a debugger (or a compiler and linker), most parallel debuggers are able to work well with MPI programs, displaying all the processes in the MPI program and showing the state of the message queues. How did this situation come to be?

A little history is in order here. As MPI became successful, the question of how to debug MPI programs (as opposed to the general question of how to debug paral-

---

MPI_COMM_DUP_WITH_INFO(comm, info, newcomm, ierror)
     integer comm, info, newcomm, ierror

Table 9.9: Fortran routine to duplicate a communicator with a specified info

---

```
int MPE_Safe_comm_dup(MPI_Comm comm, MPI_Comm *newcomm)
{
    MPI_Info oldinfo, myinfo;
    char value[MPI_MAX_INFO_VAL];
    int   flag, err;

    MPI_Info_create(&myinfo);
    MPI_Comm_get_info(comm, &oldinfo);
    /* Look for the one info key we want to propagate to
       the new communicator */
    MPI_Info_get(oldinfo, "commfast", sizeof(value),
                 value, &flag);
    if (flag)
        MPI_Info_set(myinfo, "commfast", value);
    err = MPI_Comm_dup_with_info(comm, myinfo, newcomm);
    MPI_Info_free(&myinfo);
    MPI_Info_free(&oldinfo);
    return err;
}
```

Figure 9.7: Routine to safely duplicate a communicator, copying only the desired info values to the new communicator

lel programs) became important. Several debuggers for parallel programs already existed; what was needed was a way to (a) determine the processes known by the operating system that are part of the same MPI program (called *process acquisition*) and (b) access MPI-specific information about the state of message passing, since this is where many bugs in the parallel part of the application reside.

Because MPICH was already in wide use and open source, Jim Cownie, the lead developer of TotalView, working together with the MPICH developers, defined an interface to allow TotalView to discover all of the processes in an MPICH program and to access the internal message queues. This design was careful to define abstractions for the list of processes and for the message queues, so that any MPI implementation could provide this information to the debugger. The interface was described in a paper [11], and an open-source implementation was included in MPICH. This interface was defined for MPI-1 only. Subsequent work looked at extensions to dynamic processes (which changed the assumptions behind the process-acquisition design) and were described in [21]. But none of these provided a formal description; in addition, changes in both the typical environment and programming languages made the interfaces obsolescent—for example, when defined, four-byte addresses were common, and C ints were appropriate for sizes of objects.

To address these issues, the MPI Forum has produced two "companion" documents to the MPI standard that define an interface that an MPI implementation may provide in order to allow a parallel debugger to provide a more MPI-friendly environment to the programmer. The first document, "MPIR Process Acquisition Interface," describes how a parallel debugger can determine all the processes in a running MPI application. The name "MPIR" comes from the original definition in the MPICH implementation, in which the names of internal utility routines began with MPIR. The second document, "MPI Message Queue Dumping Interface," provides an abstract view of message queues and a way for a parallel debugger to access them. While these interfaces are intended primarily for the implementors of MPI and of parallel debuggers, other tool developers can use them as well.

Note that neither performance nor control variables provide access to the kind of data provided by these interfaces.

9.4   Summary

This chapter has touched on some of the features that are available in MPI to control and gather information about the performance of an application. Many of these features are intended to enable the development of tools that will provide user-oriented information and guidance; you should investigate those before using these features directly. But the fact that you *can* access this information is one of the reasons that MPI is the often the right tool for high-performance parallel computing.

10 Dynamic Process Management

In this chapter we describe the MPI approach for creating new MPI processes *by* MPI processes. We also describe how separately started MPI applications can establish contact and exchange MPI messages with one another.

The MPI-1 standard did not say anything about how processes are started. Process startup took place outside an MPI program, and an MPI process called `MPI_Comm_size` to find out how many processes were started and `MPI_Comm_rank` to find out which process it was. The number of processes was thus fixed no later than when `MPI_Init` returned.

The MPI-2 standard added the capability for an MPI program to create new processes and communicate with them, and also for two separately started MPI programs to connect and communicate with each other (similar to a client-server environment). This functionality is referred to in MPI as dynamic process management.

10.1 Intercommunicators

Before we plunge into this chapter, let us review the concept of MPI *intercommunicators*. These are a relatively obscure part of MPI, but play a more prominent role in the area of dynamic process management, where they turn out to be just what is needed to express the communication pattern. A "normal" MPI communicator is, strictly speaking, an *intracommunicator*. It consists of a context and a group of processes. The distinguishing feature of an intercommunicator is that associated with it are *two* groups of processes, referred to (from the point of view of a specific process) as the *local* group (the group containing the process) and the remote group. Processes are identified by rank in group, as usual, but a message sent to a process with a particular rank using an intercommunicator always goes to the process with that rank in the remote group. Figure 10.1 shows a message sent from process 0 (in its local group) to process 1. Since it is sent in an intercommunicator, it goes to the process with rank 1 in the remote group. Intercommunicators can be used in both point-to-point and collective operations, and communication is always from one group to another.

10.2 Creating New MPI Processes

In MPI, the basic function for creating new processes is `MPI_Comm_spawn`. The key features of `MPI_Comm_spawn` are the following:

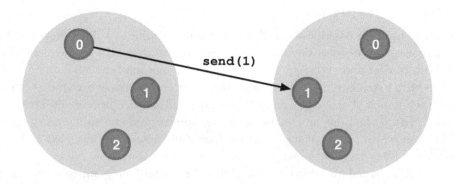

Figure 10.1: Message passing with an intercommunicator

- It is a collective operation over the spawning processes (called the *parents*) and also collective with the calls to MPI_Init in the processes that are spawned (called the *children*).

- It returns an intercommunicator in which, from the point of view of the parents, the local group contains the parents and the remote group contains the children.

- The new processes have their own MPI_COMM_WORLD.

- The function MPI_Comm_get_parent, called from the children, returns an intercommunicator containing the children as the local group and the parents as the remote group.

These features are illustrated in Figure 10.2.

10.2.1 Parallel cp: A Simple System Utility

Let us consider an example in which processes are created dynamically: a simple utility program that does a parallel copy, that is, copies a file from the local disk of a machine to the local disks of other machines in a cluster without a shared file system. Let us suppose that our login- and compile-server is called dion and the "compute" nodes are called belmont0, belmont1, and so on. We expect to frequently have to copy a file from dion to the local file systems of some subset of the belmonts. We would like it to look like the ordinary Unix cp command but function as a parallel copy. That is, if we say

```
pcp 0-63 mandelworker /tmp/mandelworker
```

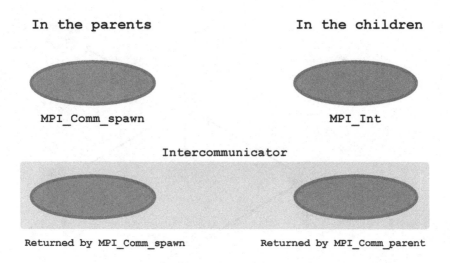

Figure 10.2: Spawning processes. Ovals are intracommunicators containing several processes.

we want the file `mandelworker` to be copied from its local place on `dion` to the `/tmp` directory on the first 64 `belmonts`.

Figure 10.3 shows our `pcp` program in action. Process 0 is reading the input file and broadcasting it, one block at a time, to all the other processes, who are writing it to local disk. This program has three forms of parallelism.

- All the processes are doing file I/O in parallel.

- Much of the message passing takes place in parallel. For example, the message from process 1 to process 3 is being transmitted concurrently with the message from process 2 to process 5.

- By breaking the file into blocks, we also achieve *pipeline* parallelism. This type of parallelism arises, for example, from the concurrency of the message from process 0 to process 1 with the message from process 1 to process 3.

In this example, even process 0, which is reading the file, makes a copy of it. An alternative semantics for `pcp` would be to assume that the file is already in place on process 0 and, therefore, process 0 does not write the output file.

The code for the beginning of the master part of the `pcp` program is shown in Figure 10.4. The first step is to parse the expression for the machines to copy the file to and create a file containing those machine names. Let us assume that the function

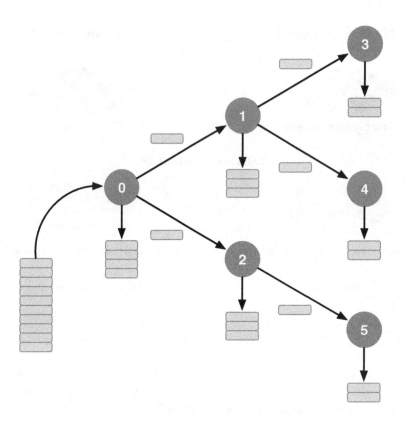

Figure 10.3: Multiple levels of parallelism in pcp

makehostlist parses the first argument and writes out a hostfile (whose name is given by the second argument) that can be understood by our implementation of MPI_Comm_spawn. The number of workers specified is returned as the third argument of makehostlist. We then pass the name of this file to MPI_Comm_-spawn via info, in order to create pcp workers on each of the target machines. Therefore the call

```
makehostlist(argv[1], "targets", &num_hosts);
```

writes out a file called targets containing the appropriate host names. We need to pass this information to the system that starts up new processes. Since job scheduling and process startup systems have not been standardized, no standard MPI format exists for this information. Instead, this information is passed to

```c
#include "mpi.h"
#include <unistd.h>
#include <string.h>
#include <stdio.h>
#include <sys/types.h>
#include <sys/stat.h>
#include <fcntl.h>
#define BUFSIZE    256*1024
#define CMDSIZE    80
int main(int argc, char *argv[])
{
    int      num_hosts, mystatus, allstatus, done, numread;
    int      infd, outfd;
    char     outfilename[MAXPATHLEN], controlmsg[CMDSIZE];
    char     buf[BUFSIZE];
    char     soft_limit[20];
    MPI_Info hostinfo;
    MPI_Comm pcpworkers, all_processes;

    MPI_Init(&argc, &argv);

    makehostlist(argv[1], "targets", &num_hosts);
    MPI_Info_create(&hostinfo);
    MPI_Info_set(hostinfo, "file", "targets");
    sprintf(soft_limit, "0:%d", num_hosts);
    MPI_Info_set(hostinfo, "soft", soft_limit);
    MPI_Comm_spawn("pcp_worker", MPI_ARGV_NULL, num_hosts,
                   hostinfo, 0, MPI_COMM_SELF, &pcpworkers,
                   MPI_ERRCODES_IGNORE);
    MPI_Info_free(&hostinfo);
    MPI_Intercomm_merge(pcpworkers, 0, &all_processes);
```

Figure 10.4: Beginning of master part of parallel copy program

MPI_Comm_spawn via an info object. We create an MPI_Info object containing "targets" as the value of the reserved key (for use with MPI_Comm_spawn) file. This info key simply tells MPI_Comm_spawn to look in the file targets for information, in a format specific to the MPI implementation, about how to perform the operation. We assume here that the file may contain the names of the processors to spawn processes on. The info key soft is also used to allow MPI_-Comm_spawn to return successfully even if it was unable to start all the requested processes. Next, the call

```
MPI_Comm_spawn("pcp_worker", MPI_ARGV_NULL, num_hosts, hostinfo,
          0, MPI_COMM_SELF, &pcpworkers,
          MPI_ERRCODES_IGNORE);
```

creates the workers. For simplicity we leave out error checking at this point, passing MPI_ERRCODES_IGNORE instead of an array for returning the error codes.

We immediately convert the intercommunicator pcpworkers that contains both the calling process and the processes created by MPI_Comm_spawn into an intracommunicator with MPI_Intercomm_merge. The output intracommunicator, all_processes, will be used for all subsequent communication between the workers and the master.

The code for the middle of the master part of the pcp program is shown in Figure 10.5. We attempt to open the input file. If we fail, we broadcast a message to the workers telling them to exit immediately. If we succeed, we broadcast a "ready" message instead.

Next we broadcast the name of the output file, and all processes attempt to open it. To test whether the file opened successfully, we use an MPI_Allreduce with MPI_MIN as the operation. Thus, if any process fails to open the output file, all processes will know (since allstatus will be set to −1). In this case all processes call MPI_Finalize and exit. If all processes receive a 0 in allstatus (MPI_Allreduce ensures that all processes get the same result), then all files have been successfully opened. (If we replaced MPI_MIN as the operation in the MPI_Allreduce of the mystatus variable with MPI_MINLOC, we could indicate the rank of the failed process as well.)

The first part of the worker code is shown in Figure 10.6. This code is similar to the code for the master except that the workers need to call MPI_Comm_get_-parent to establish contact with process 0, and workers do no argument processing and print no messages.

At the end of the sections of code for both master and worker that we have looked at so far, all processes have successfully opened the necessary files. The second part

```
strcpy(outfilename, argv[3]);
if ((infd = open(argv[2], O_RDONLY)) == -1) {
  fprintf(stderr, "input %s does not exist\n", argv[2]);
  sprintf(controlmsg, "exit");
  MPI_Bcast(controlmsg, CMDSIZE, MPI_CHAR, 0, all_processes);
  MPI_Finalize();
  return -1 ;
} else {
  sprintf(controlmsg, "ready");
  MPI_Bcast(controlmsg, CMDSIZE, MPI_CHAR, 0, all_processes);
}
MPI_Bcast(outfilename, MAXPATHLEN, MPI_CHAR, 0,
          all_processes);
if ((outfd = open(outfilename, O_CREAT|O_WRONLY|O_TRUNC,
      S_IRWXU)) == -1)
  mystatus = -1;
else
  mystatus = 0;
MPI_Allreduce(&mystatus, &allstatus, 1, MPI_INT, MPI_MIN,
              all_processes);
if (allstatus == -1) {
  fprintf(stderr, "Output file %s could not be opened\n",
          outfilename);
  MPI_Finalize();
  return 1 ;
}
```

Figure 10.5: Middle of master part of parallel copy program

of the master code is shown in Figure 10.7. It simply reads the file a block at a time and broadcasts the blocks to the workers. Note that before sending each block it sends the length as well. This approach handles the (possibly) short block at the end and the end-of-file condition, since all processes in an MPI_Bcast (the root that is sending and the other processes that are receiving) must specify the *same* buffer length.[1] An alternative approach would be to use a structure containing an int field for the length of the data and a fixed-sized array of char for the buffer; a single MPI_Bcast would send both the numread value and the data read. Only in the last MPI_Bcast call would more data be sent (and ignored) than

[1]This is unlike the send/receive case, where the sender specifies the length of data but the receiver specifies the *maximum* buffer length, providing the MPI_Status argument to determine the actual size received.

```
#include "mpi.h"
#include <unistd.h>
#include <stdio.h>
#include <sys/types.h>
#include <sys/stat.h>
#include <fcntl.h>
#define BUFSIZE    256*1024
#define CMDSIZE    80
int main(int argc, char *argv[])
{
    int       mystatus, allstatus, done, numread;
    char      outfilename[MAXPATHLEN], controlmsg[CMDSIZE];
    int       outfd;
    char      buf[BUFSIZE];
    MPI_Comm workercomm, all_processes;

    MPI_Init(&argc, &argv);

    MPI_Comm_get_parent(&workercomm);
    MPI_Intercomm_merge(workercomm, 1, &all_processes);
    MPI_Bcast(controlmsg, CMDSIZE, MPI_CHAR, 0,
              all_processes);
    if (strcmp(controlmsg, "exit") == 0) {
        MPI_Finalize();
        return 1;
    }
    MPI_Bcast(outfilename, MAXPATHLEN, MPI_CHAR, 0,
              all_processes);
    if ((outfd = open(outfilename, O_CREAT|O_WRONLY|O_TRUNC,
                      S_IRWXU)) == -1)
        mystatus = -1;
    else
        mystatus = 0;
    MPI_Allreduce(&mystatus, &allstatus, 1, MPI_INT, MPI_MIN,
                  all_processes);
    if (allstatus == -1) {
        MPI_Finalize();
        return -1;
    }
```

Figure 10.6: First part of worker for parallel copy program

```
    /* at this point all files have been successfully opened */
    done = 0;
    while (!done) {
        numread = read(infd, buf, BUFSIZE);
        MPI_Bcast(&numread, 1, MPI_INT, 0, all_processes);
        if (numread > 0) {
            MPI_Bcast(buf, numread, MPI_BYTE, 0, all_processes);
            write(outfd, buf, numread);
        }
        else {
            close(outfd);
            done = 1;
        }
    }
    MPI_Comm_free(&pcpworkers);
    MPI_Comm_free(&all_processes);
    MPI_Finalize();
    return 0;
}
```

Figure 10.7: End of master part of parallel copy program

was needed. The second part of the worker code, which matches this structure, is shown in Figure 10.8. At the end, all processes free the intercommunicator created by MPI_Comm_spawn and the merged intracommunicator before exiting.

The primary difference between spawn in MPI and that of earlier message-passing systems is the collective nature of the operation. In MPI, a group of processes collectively creates another group of processes, and all of them synchronize (via MPI_Comm_spawn in the parents and MPI_Init in the children), thus preventing race conditions and allowing the necessary communication infrastructure to be set up before any of the calls return.

C and Fortran bindings for the dynamic process management functions used in the parallel copy example are given in Tables 10.1 and 10.2, respectively.

10.2.2   Matrix-Vector Multiplication Example

Our matrix-vector multiplication example uses the same algorithm employed in Chapter 3 of *Using MPI* [26]. Instead of having all processes started outside the program, however, we will start only the master process and have it start the workers with MPI_Comm_spawn. The most obvious difference between this version

```
/* at this point all files have been successfully opened */

done = 0;
while (!done) {
    MPI_Bcast(&numread, 1, MPI_INT, 0, all_processes);
    if (numread > 0) {
        MPI_Bcast(buf, numread, MPI_BYTE, 0, all_processes);
        write(outfd, buf, numread);
    }
    else {
        close( outfd );
        done = 1;
    }
}
MPI_Comm_free(&workercomm);
MPI_Comm_free(&all_processes);
MPI_Finalize();
return 0;
}
```

Figure 10.8: End of worker part of parallel copy program

int **MPI_Comm_spawn**(const char *command, char *argv[], int maxprocs,
        MPI_Info info, int root, MPI_Comm comm, MPI_Comm *intercomm,
        int array_of_errcodes[])

int **MPI_Comm_get_parent**(MPI_Comm *parent)

int **MPI_Intercomm_merge**(MPI_Comm intercomm, int high,
        MPI_Comm *newintracomm)

Table 10.1: C bindings for the functions used in the parallel copy example

---

MPI_COMM_SPAWN(command, argv, maxprocs, info, root, comm, intercomm,
          array_of_errcodes, ierror)
          character*(*) command, argv(*)
          integer info, maxprocs, root, comm, intercomm, array_of_errcodes(*),
          ierror

MPI_COMM_GET_PARENT(parent, ierror)
          integer parent, ierror

MPI_INTERCOMM_MERGE(intercomm, high, newintracomm, ierror)
          integer intercomm, newintracomm, ierror
          logical high

Table 10.2: Fortran bindings for the functions used in the parallel copy example

and the other version is that the master and the workers are each separate main programs. First let us consider the beginning of the code for the master process, shown in Figure 10.9.

We expect to start this program with

```
mpiexec -n 1 master
```

The program multiplies the matrix a by the vector b and stores the result in c. The parallelism comes from performing the dot products of the rows of a with b in parallel. We assume that there are more rows of a than there are processes, so that each process will do many dot products. For this example, we do *not* assume that all processes execute at the same speed; hence we adopt a *self-scheduling* algorithm for load-balancing purposes. The master process sends rows, one by one, to the worker processes; and when a worker finishes with a row, it sends the result (the dot product) back to the master. If more rows remain to be done, the master sends a row to the worker that just completed a row. From the master's point of view, work is handed out to whichever worker has become idle. From the worker's point of view, it receives a job, works on that job, and sends the result back to the master, simultaneously requesting a new task. The master itself does not compute any dot products. In this way all the workers are kept busy, even if they work at different speeds.

This algorithm is not a particularly good way to parallelize matrix-vector multiplication, but it demonstrates self-scheduling algorithms well. The algorithm is the same one used in *Using MPI* [26], but here we do not determine the number of workers until after the master has started, in order to illustrate both MPI_Comm_spawn

```fortran
! Matrix-vector multiply, with spawning of workers
PROGRAM main
  use mpi
  integer MAX_ROWS, MAX_COLS
  parameter (MAX_ROWS = 1000, MAX_COLS = 1000)
  double precision a(MAX_ROWS,MAX_COLS), b(MAX_COLS), c(MAX_ROWS)
  double precision buffer(MAX_COLS), ans
  integer workercomm

  integer ierr, status(MPI_STATUS_SIZE)
  integer i, j, numsent, sender, numworkers
  integer anstype, rows, cols

  call MPI_INIT(ierr)
! master decides how many workers to spawn, say 10
  numworkers = 10
  call MPI_COMM_SPAWN('worker', MPI_ARGV_NULL, numworkers, &
                 MPI_INFO_NULL, 0, MPI_COMM_WORLD, &
                 workercomm, MPI_ERRCODES_IGNORE, ierr)
! master initializes and then dispatches
  rows   = 100
  cols   = 100
! initialize a and b
  do j = 1,cols
     b(j) = 1
     do i = 1,rows
        a(i,j) = i
     enddo
  enddo
  numsent = 0
! send b to each worker
  call MPI_BCAST(b, cols, MPI_DOUBLE_PRECISION, MPI_ROOT, &
                 workercomm, ierr)
```

Figure 10.9: First part of master for matrix-vector multiplication

and the use of `MPI_Bcast` on an intercommunicator. The first part of the master program is shown in Figure 10.9. The only variables new for this version are the intercommunicator `workercomm`, which will be constructed by `MPI_Comm_spawn`, and the variable `numworkers`, which holds the number of workers.

In general, a program of this type would do some sort of calculation to determine how many workers to spawn. As we will see in Section 10.2.5, it can also obtain advice from the system on how many workers it can spawn. To simplify this example, we assume that the master somehow decides to create ten workers, and so we simply set `numworkers` equal to `10`. The call that creates the workers and the corresponding intercommunicator is

```
call MPI_COMM_SPAWN('worker', MPI_ARGV_NULL, numworkers, &
                    MPI_INFO_NULL, 0, MPI_COMM_WORLD, &
                    workercomm, MPI_ERRCODES_IGNORE, ierr)
```

(The Fortran version of) `MPI_Comm_spawn` has nine arguments. The first is the executable file to be run by the new processes. The second argument is an array of strings to represent the "command line" arguments to the executable. Here, since we are not passing the workers any command-line arguments, we use the predefined constant `MPI_ARGV_NULL`. The third argument is the number of workers to start. Extra information (such as what machines to start the worker processes on), and perhaps even site-specific hints to the job scheduler, can be given in the fourth argument, the `info` argument. Here, we just pass the predefined constant `MPI_-INFO_NULL` and defer to Section 10.2.5 a fuller discussion of its use with `MPI_-Comm_spawn`. The call to `MPI_Comm_spawn` is collective (over the communicator specified in the sixth argument), and the first four arguments need not be presented at all of the processes (although they must, of course, be syntactically correct) but will be interpreted only at the "root" process, specified in the fifth argument. Here we specify `0`, since there is only one master process. The sixth argument is the communicator over which this call is collective, here `MPI_COMM_WORLD`.[2]

Next come the output arguments. The seventh argument, here `workercomm`, will be set to be the intercommunicator containing both the master (in the local group) and the workers (in the remote group). The next argument is an array of error codes, one for each new process to be created, but we can (and here do) pass the special constant `MPI_ERRCODES_IGNORE` instead, to indicate that we are not going to check the individual error codes. The overall error code (the last argument in Fortran or the function value returned in C) can be checked to see

---

[2]Since there is only one process, we could also have used `MPI_COMM_SELF`.

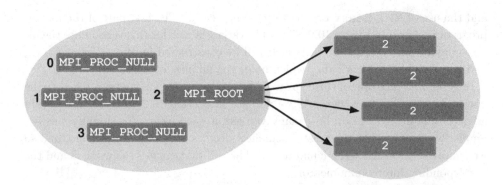

Figure 10.10: Intercommunicator broadcast. The argument used as the `root` field is given inside the box representing each process. In this example, process 2 in the group on the left is broadcasting to every process in the group on the right.

whether `MPI_Comm_spawn` was successful as a whole. If it is `MPI_SUCCESS`, then all processes were successfully created, and all potential communication, both with and among the new processes, is enabled.

10.2.3   Intercommunicator Collective Operations

Next the master initializes the matrix a and the vector b and uses the collective operation `MPI_Bcast` to send b to the workers. For intercommunicators, the broadcast occurs from the root in the *local* group to all the processes in the *remote* group, which in this case are the workers. Because there are two groups, the root process indicates itself by using the special value `MPI_ROOT`. The processes receiving the broadcast specify the rank of the root in the other group, just as they would if there were a single group. (Here, where the local group has only one member, the effect is not different from the case in which all processes are in the same (intra)communicator, but in general an intercommunicator `MPI_Bcast` is quite different from an intracommunicator `MPI_Bcast`.) If more than one process is in the group that contains the root, those processes specify `MPI_PROC_NULL` as the root value. Figure 10.10 illustrates an intercommunicator broadcast.

Note that (at this point) we don't have an intracommunicator containing the master and the workers; we could create one with the MPI function `MPI_Intercomm_-merge` as we did in Section 10.2.1, but it will not be necessary in this example.

10.2.4   Intercommunicator Point-to-Point Communication

The rest of the master code is shown in Figure 10.11. It is similar to the nonspawn version of the code (Figure 3.6 in *Using MPI* [26]). The major difference is that the ranks of the workers go from 0 to numworkers-1, since the master is addressing them, not in MPI_COMM_WORLD, but in the remote group of the intercommunicator workercomm. The master sends all the workers a row to work with, receives answers from the workers, and then sends out new rows until all rows are done. Then it sends a message with tag 0 to each worker to tell it that the computation is over. The master then prints the vector c, which is the product of a and b.

The code for the workers is shown in Figure 10.12. It is similar to the worker part of the original version (Figure 3.7 in *Using MPI* [26]). The new feature here is that after MPI_Init, the workers can communicate with one another, through their MPI_COMM_WORLD, which contains all processes spawned with the same MPI_-Comm_spawn call, but not with the master. In this example, the worker processes do not communicate with each other; they need communicate only with the master. To obtain a communicator containing the master, the workers do

```
call MPI_COMM_GET_PARENT(parentcomm, ierr)
```

This returns in parentcomm the intercommunicator created by the collective call to MPI_Comm_spawn in the master and MPI_Init in the workers. The local group of this communicator (from the workers' point of view) is the same as the group of their MPI_COMM_WORLD. The remote group is the set of processes that collectively called MPI_Comm_spawn, which in this case consists of just the master. The workers address the master as rank 0 in parentcomm during the exchange of rows and dot products. When the workers get the "all done" message (tag=0), they call MPI_Finalize and exit.

10.2.5   Finding the Number of Available Processes

The MPI Forum spent some time and effort debating whether one could incorporate into the MPI standard an interface to a job scheduler. It turned out that the variety of schedulers and their interfaces, coupled with the great variety in the types of requests that users wanted to make of their resource managers, made this too difficult. Therefore, MPI's dynamic process management defers to some other possible library any interaction with the scheduler. The one feature remaining from this discussion that did enter the standard (although only as an optional feature) is MPI_UNIVERSE_SIZE, an attribute of MPI_COMM_WORLD. The term "optional" here means that an MPI implementation need not provide a value for the attribute;

```fortran
!  send a row to each worker; tag with row number
   do i = 1,min(numworkers,rows)
     do j = 1,cols
        buffer(j) = a(i,j)
     enddo
     call MPI_SEND(buffer, cols, MPI_DOUBLE_PRECISION, i-1, &
                   i, workercomm, ierr)
     numsent = numsent+1
   enddo
   do i = 1,rows
     call MPI_RECV(ans, 1, MPI_DOUBLE_PRECISION, &
                   MPI_ANY_SOURCE, MPI_ANY_TAG, &
                   workercomm, status, ierr)
     sender      = status(MPI_SOURCE)
     anstype     = status(MPI_TAG)               ! row is tag value
     c(anstype) = ans
     if (numsent .lt. rows) then                 ! send another row
       do j = 1,cols
          buffer(j) = a(numsent+1,j)
       enddo
       call MPI_SEND(buffer, cols, MPI_DOUBLE_PRECISION, &
                     sender, numsent+1, workercomm, ierr)
       numsent = numsent+1
     else
       call MPI_SEND(buffer, 0, MPI_DOUBLE_PRECISION, sender, &
                     0, workercomm, ierr)
     endif
   enddo

!  print the answer
   do i = 1,rows
     print *, "c(", i, ") = ", c(i)
   enddo
   call MPI_COMM_FREE(workercomm, ierr)
   call MPI_FINALIZE(ierr)
END PROGRAM main
```

Figure 10.11: Second part of master for matrix-vector multiply

```fortran
! worker program for matrix-vector multiplication
PROGRAM main
      use mpi
      integer MAX_COLS
      parameter (MAX_COLS = 1000)
      double precision b(MAX_COLS)
      double precision buffer(MAX_COLS), ans

      integer i, ierr, status(MPI_STATUS_SIZE)
      integer row, cols, rows, rank
      integer parentcomm

      call MPI_INIT(ierr)
      call MPI_COMM_GET_PARENT(parentcomm, ierr)
!     the master is now rank 0 in the remote group of the
!     parent intercommunicator.
!     workers receive b, then compute dot products until
!     done message received
      rows = 100
      cols = 100
      call MPI_BCAST(b, cols, MPI_DOUBLE_PRECISION, 0, &
                     parentcomm, ierr)
      call MPI_COMM_RANK(MPI_COMM_WORLD, rank, ierr)
      if (rank .lt. rows) then
         ! skip if more processes than work
         do
            call MPI_RECV(buffer, cols, MPI_DOUBLE_PRECISION, 0, &
                          MPI_ANY_TAG, parentcomm, status, ierr)
            if (status(MPI_TAG) .eq. 0) exit
            row = status(MPI_TAG)
            ans = 0.0
            do i = 1,cols
               ans = ans+buffer(i)*b(i)
            enddo
            call MPI_SEND(ans, 1, MPI_DOUBLE_PRECISION, 0, row, &
                          parentcomm, ierr)
         enddo
      endif
      call MPI_COMM_FREE(parentcomm, ierr)
      call MPI_FINALIZE(ierr)
END PROGRAM main
```

Figure 10.12: Worker part of matrix-vector multiply

but if such a value is provided, it works as follows. MPI_UNIVERSE_SIZE provides
to the MPI application information on how many processes can usefully be run.
The application can then use this information to determine how many "additional"
processes can usefully be spawned. The value of MPI_UNIVERSE_SIZE, even if
provided, is not a hard limit; rather, it is a "best guess" by the implementation of
how many processes could exist.

The value of the attribute MPI_UNIVERSE_SIZE may be determined by the
implementation in many ways. It could come from an environment variable set
either by the user or by the system. It could come from runtime interaction with
a job scheduler, or it could be set by the process manager. One logical approach is
to have MPI_UNIVERSE_SIZE set by mpiexec. That is, in an environment with
both a scheduler and a process manager,[3]

```
mpiexec -n 1 -universe_size 10 matvec-master
```

could perform three functions:

- request 10 "slots" from the job scheduler,

- request from the process manager that 1 process running matvec_master
  be started, and

- arrange for the value of MPI_UNIVERSE_SIZE to be set to 10.

Then the matvec_master program would know that 9 more processes could be
started without requiring additional interaction with the scheduler.

Now let us consider the use of MPI_UNIVERSE_SIZE with MPI_Comm_spawn.
The beginning of matvec_master modified to use MPI_UNIVERSE_SIZE is
shown in Figure 10.13. Features of the program not in our earlier MPI_Comm_-
spawn examples are the following:

- It uses MPI_UNIVERSE_SIZE to decide how many processes to spawn.

- It checks the error codes from the attempts to spawn processes.

Let us step through this program. We call MPI_Comm_get_attr to see whether
the attribute MPI_UNIVERSE_SIZE has been set. If it has, we spawn as many
processes as the value of MPI_UNIVERSE_SIZE tells us are available. Since the

_____

[3]The argument -universe_size is not a standard argument for mpiexec; it is shown here as
an example that some implementations may provide. Other possibilities for specifying the value
of MPI_UNIVERSE_SIZE include an environment variable or configuration parameter.

```fortran
integer softinfo
integer (kind=MPI_ADDRESS_KIND) universe_size
logical universe_size_flag
integer numworkers, usize, i, errcodes(10)

call MPI_COMM_GET_ATTR(MPI_COMM_WORLD, MPI_UNIVERSE_SIZE, &
            universe_size, universe_size_flag, ierr)
if (universe_size_flag) then
    usize = universe_size - 1
    call MPI_COMM_SPAWN('worker', MPI_ARGV_NULL, usize,&
                    MPI_INFO_NULL, 0, MPI_COMM_WORLD, &
                    workercomm, errcodes, ierr)
else
    call MPI_INFO_CREATE(softinfo, ierr)
    call MPI_INFO_SET(softinfo, 'soft', '1:10', ierr)
    call MPI_COMM_SPAWN('worker', MPI_ARGV_NULL, 10, &
                    softinfo, 0, MPI_COMM_WORLD, &
                    workercomm, errcodes, ierr)
    call MPI_INFO_FREE(softinfo, ierr)
endif
call MPI_COMM_REMOTE_SIZE(workercomm, numworkers, ierr)
do i=1, 10
    if (errcodes(i) .ne. MPI_SUCCESS) then
        print *, 'worker ', i, ' did not start'
    endif
enddo
print *, 'number of workers = ', numworkers
```

Figure 10.13: Modification of the master part of the matrix-vector program to use MPI_UNIVERSE_SIZE to specify the number of available processes

master process counts as one process, we spawn one less than the value of the attribute itself. On the other hand, if there is no such attribute (universe_-size_flag = 0), then we take a more conservative approach. We create an MPI_Info object and use it to describe a "soft" request for any number of processes between one and ten. Here we use the predefined info key soft and specify a range of numbers of processes using the same form as for the -soft argument to mpiexec. We also pass an array of error codes to be filled in, and we check for success.

Recall that MPI_Comm_spawn returns an intercommunicator (workercomm in this case) in which the remote group consists of the newly spawned processes. We

```
char            *worker_argv[2];
...
worker_argv[0] = argv[3];
worker_argv[1] = NULL;
MPI_Comm_spawn("pcp_worker", worker_argv, num_hosts, hostinfo,
               0, MPI_COMM_SELF, &pcpworkers,
               MPI_ERRCODES_IGNORE);
```

Figure 10.14: Passing command-line arguments to spawned processes

use MPI_Comm_remote_size to find out the size of this group, which is the number of workers.

In C, the value returned by MPI_Comm_get_attr is a pointer to an integer containing the value, rather than the value itself. This is the same as for the other predefined attributes such as MPI_TAB_UB. The code for accessing the value of MPI_UNIVERSE_SIZE from C follows:

```
int *universe_size_ptr, universe_size_flag;
...
MPI_Comm_get_attr(MPI_COMM_WORLD, MPI_UNIVERSE_SIZE,
                  &universe_size_ptr, &universe_size_flag);
if (universe_size_flag) {
    printf("Number of processes available is %d\n",
           *universe_size_ptr);
}
```

10.2.6 Passing Command-Line Arguments to Spawned Programs

In our examples so far, we have used MPI_ARGV_NULL to indicated that the spawned programs are called with no command-line arguments. It is often helpful to pass command-line parameters to the spawned programs. For example, in the parallel copy example in Section 10.2.1, instead of using MPI_Bcast to send the name of the output file to each worker, we could have started the processes with a single command-line argument containing the name of the output file. The change to the master program (Figure 10.4) is shown in Figure 10.14.

The argv argument to MPI_Comm_spawn is different from the argv parameter in a C main in two ways: it does not contain the name of the program (the value of argv[0] in main), and it is null terminated (rather than using an argc parameter containing the argument count, as main does). In Fortran, the code is similar. An array of character is used; an entirely blank string indicates the end of the list.

---

int **MPI_Comm_spawn_multiple**(int count, char *array_of_commands[],
        char **array_of_argv[], const int array_of_maxprocs[],
        const MPI_Info array_of_info[], int root, MPI_Comm comm,
        MPI_Comm *intercomm, int array_of_errcodes[])

Table 10.3: Spawning multiple executables in C

MPI_COMM_SPAWN_MULTIPLE(count, array_of_commands, array_of_argv,
        array_of_maxprocs, array_of_info, root, comm, intercomm,
        array_of_errcodes, ierror)
          integer count, array_of_info(*), array_of_maxprocs(*), root, comm,
            intercomm, array_of_errcodes(*), ierror
          character*(*) array_of_commands(*), array_of_argv(count, *)

Table 10.4: Spawning multiple executables in Fortran

What if we would like to pass separate command-line arguments to each of the new processes? MPI offers a separate function, `MPI_Comm_spawn_multiple`, for this purpose as well as for starting processes that use different executable files. The C and Fortran bindings are shown in Tables 10.3 and 10.4, respectively. Basically, the first four arguments specifying the command name, argument vector, number of processes, and info have become arrays of size `count`, which is the first argument.

10.3 Connecting MPI Processes

Some applications are naturally constructed from several separate programs. One example used in *Using MPI* [26] and in the MPI standard is that of a climate simulation constructed from two programs: a simulation of the ocean and a simulation of the atmosphere. In fact, this example was used in *Using MPI* to discuss intercommunicators. Another popular example is one that connects a visualization program to a simulation program. We will consider this example below.

One advantage of the approach in this section is that the choice of visualization program can be made at run time; this is different from having the simulation program spawn the visualization program. The approach also can work when complexities of the runtime environment make it difficult to start the visualization process either with `mpiexec` or with `MPI_Comm_spawn`.

Much of discussion in the MPI standard on connecting MPI processes talks about *clients* and *servers*. While many of the concepts and issues are shared with traditional client/server models, a number of differences do exist. We prefer to think of the MPI model as a *peer-to-peer* model where one process accepts connections and the other process requests the connection. Because the MPI model for connecting processes does not address traditional client/server issues such as fault tolerance, we prefer to avoid the terms "client" and "server."

10.3.1   Visualizing the Computation in an MPI Program

Often when running a simulation, one wishes to visualize the progress of the simulation, perhaps by using three-dimensional graphics to draw the current state of the solution on the mesh being used to approximate the problem. As our example of interconnecting two MPI programs we enhance the Poisson solver described in Section 3.6 to connect with a visualization program.

We modify the program as follows:

1. The program creates a port and accepts a connection on that port. A *port* is nothing but a name that another program can use to connect to the program that created the port. As expected, the result of connecting to another MPI program is an intercommunicator connecting the two programs.

2. At each iteration, the solver sends the current solution to the visualization program using intercommunicator communication operations.

Our first version assumes that the visualization program is actually a single process. In fact, the visualization program is simple, as is shown in Figure 10.15. At each iteration, the program receives the iteration number, using a point-to-point intercommunicator operation, and the mesh itself, using `MPI_Gatherv` in an intercommunicator collective operation. The code to initialize the arguments needed by `MPI_Gatherv` uses `MPI_Gather` (also in intercommunicator form) to receive the amount of data that each process in the server will send to this program. The actual graphics drawing is done by the routine `DrawMesh`.

The routine `MPI_Comm_connect` establishes the connection to the other program. Because we choose to have the visualization program connect to the computation program, the visualization program is the *client* of the computation program (the processes that call `MPI_Comm_connect` are always the clients). The input arguments to `MPI_Comm_connect` are the port name, an `info` value, the rank of a "lead" or root process, and an intracommunicator. We will discuss the port name below; it is simply a character string, although its value is determined by the

```
#include "mpi.h"
#define MAX_PROCS 128
#define MAX_MESH 512*512
int main(int argc, char *argv[])
{
  MPI_Comm server;
  int      it, i, nprocs, rcounts[MAX_PROCS], rdispls[MAX_PROCS];
  double   mesh[MAX_MESH];
  char     port_name[MPI_MAX_PORT_NAME];

  MPI_Init(0, 0);

  gets(port_name);   /* we assume only one process
                        in MPI_COMM_WORLD */
  MPI_Comm_connect(port_name, MPI_INFO_NULL, 0, MPI_COMM_WORLD,
                   &server);
  MPI_Comm_remote_size(server, &nprocs);

  /* Get the number of data values from each process */
  MPI_Gather(MPI_BOTTOM, 0, MPI_DATATYPE_NULL,
             rcounts, 1, MPI_INT, MPI_ROOT, server);
  /* Compute the mesh displacements */
  rdispls[0] = 0;
  for (i=0; i<nprocs-1; i++)
      rdispls[i+1] = rdispls[i] + rcounts[i];

  while (1) {
      MPI_Recv(&it, 1, MPI_INT, 0, 0, server, MPI_STATUS_IGNORE);
      if (it < 0) break;
      MPI_Gatherv(MPI_BOTTOM, 0, MPI_DATATYPE_NULL,
                  mesh, rcounts, rdispls, MPI_DOUBLE,
                  MPI_ROOT, server);
      DrawMesh(mesh);
      }
  MPI_Comm_disconnect(&server);
  MPI_Finalize();
  return 0;
}
```

Figure 10.15: Visualization program

MPI implementation. In this version of the example, we read the port name from standard input.

Enhancements to this program could run the visualization routine in a separate thread, allowing the user to rotate, scale, and otherwise interact with the data visually, while the code shown here updates the data each time a new iteration becomes available. Of course, the code uses the appropriate facilities (such as a thread mutex) to ensure that the drawing routine always has a consistent data set and not a mixture of several iterations.

10.3.2   Accepting Connections from Other Programs

We must modify the solver to accept the connection from the visualization program and send to it the data to be visualized. The changes are shown in Figure 10.16. The first item to note is that these changes are all additions; the original program is unchanged. For example, if the program was using MPI_COMM_WORLD before, it continues to use the same communicator for the computational part of the code. The second item to note is that this program is in Fortran, while our visualization client program is in C. MPI provides for language interoperability, including the ability of programs in different languages to send messages to each other.

The changes to the program come in three places. The first place creates a port that the client program to connect to. To do so, we call MPI_Open_port, which returns a port name. As usual, an info value may be used to request implementation-specific behavior when requesting a port; in this case, we use MPI_-INFO_NULL to get the default behavior. A port name is simply a character string, and we print it out. The client program must provide to MPI_Comm_connect this printed value; it is read with the gets statement in Figure 10.15.

Once the port is open, the program allows another MPI program to connect to it by calling MPI_Comm_accept. This is a collective call over all processes in the input communicator (the fourth argument), with the input arguments (such as the port name) valid at the specified root, which is process 0 in this case. An info argument is provided here as well to allow for implementation-specific customization. This is a blocking collective call that returns an intercommunicator.

The middle part of the code sends data to the client process, starting with information on the decomposition of the data in the computational process and continuing with the iteration count and current result within the iteration loop. These communication operations match the communication calls in the visualization client.

```fortran
character*(MPI_MAX_PORT_NAME) port_name
integer    client
...
if (myid .eq. 0) then
    call MPI_OPEN_PORT(MPI_INFO_NULL, port_name, ierr)
    print *, port_name
endif
call MPI_COMM_ACCEPT(port_name, MPI_INFO_NULL, 0, &
                     MPI_COMM_WORLD, client, ierr);
! Send the information needed to send the mesh
call MPI_GATHER(mesh_size, 1, MPI_INTEGER, &
               MPI_BOTTOM, 0, MPI_DATATYPE_NULL, &
               0, client, ierr)
....
! For each iteration, send the local part of the mesh
if (myid .eq. 0) then
    call MPI_SEND(it, 1, MPI_INTEGER, 0, 0, client, ierr)
endif
call MPI_GATHERV(mesh, mesh_size, MPI_DOUBLE_PRECISION, &
               MPI_BOTTOM, 0, 0, &
               MPI_DATATYPE_NULL, 0, client, ierr)
...
! Disconnect from client before exiting
if (myid .eq. 0) then
    call MPI_CLOSE_PORT(port_name, ierr)
endif
call MPI_COMM_DISCONNECT(client, ierr)
call MPI_FINALIZE(ierr)
```

Figure 10.16: Modifications to Poisson example to accept connections from the visualization program and to send data to it

---

int **MPI_Open_port**(MPI_Info info, char *port_name)

int **MPI_Close_port**(const char *port_name)

int **MPI_Comm_accept**(const char *port_name, MPI_Info info, int root,
                MPI_Comm comm, MPI_Comm *newcomm)

int **MPI_Comm_connect**(const char *port_name, MPI_Info info, int root,
                MPI_Comm comm, MPI_Comm *newcomm)

int **MPI_Comm_disconnect**(MPI_Comm *comm)

Table 10.5: C bindings for client/server functions

The final part of the program closes the port and disconnects from the client by calling `MPI_Close_port` and `MPI_Comm_disconnect`. The `MPI_Close_-port` call frees up port; after the `MPI_Close_port` call, the port name returned by `MPI_Open_port` is no longer valid.

The call to `MPI_Comm_disconnect` ensures that all communication on the communicator has completed before returning; this is the difference between this function and `MPI_Comm_free`.

The C and Fortran bindings for the routines used in these examples are in Tables 10.5 and 10.6, respectively.

If the server needs to manage multiple connections at once, it must use a separate thread (see Chapter 6) for each `MPI_Comm_accept` call. The client need not be changed. Using a thread also allows the server to handle the case of no connections, as we will see in the next chapter.

10.3.3 Comparison with Sockets

The MPI routines for connecting two groups of processes follow a simple model that is similar to the Unix sockets model (see [62] for a description of sockets). A comparison with that model illustrates some of the differences as well as the motivation for the design. The correspondences are shown below:

MPI_Open_port. The socket routines `socket`, `bind`, and `listen` provide a similar function. At the end of `bind`, a port specified by an IP address and a port number is defined. The `listen` call prepares the port to receive connection requests. One major difference is that the port number is an

---

MPI_OPEN_PORT(info, port_name, ierror)
        character*(*) port_name
        integer info, ierror

MPI_CLOSE_PORT(port_name, ierror)
        character*(*) port_name
        integer ierror

MPI_COMM_ACCEPT(port_name, info, root, comm, newcomm, ierror)
        character*(*) port_name
        integer info, root, comm, newcomm, ierror

MPI_COMM_CONNECT(port_name, info, root, comm, newcomm, ierror)
        character*(*) port_name
        integer info, root, comm, newcomm, ierror

MPI_COMM_DISCONNECT(comm, ierror)
        integer comm, ierror

Table 10.6: Fortran bindings for client/server

input value for `bind`, whereas it is part of the output value (as part of the `port_name`) for `MPI_Open_port`.

MPI_Comm_accept. The socket routine `accept` establishes the connection and returns a new socket.

MPI_Comm_connect. The socket routines `socket` and `connect` are used to connect to a port.

The differences between these approaches are also important. The most important is that the socket interface establishes a connection between two processes (or threads), whereas the MPI interface connects two groups of processes. In addition, the socket interface provides very fine control on the connection mechanism. For example, the socket operations can be placed into a nonblocking mode (with an `fcntl` call on the socket file descriptor). Because Unix file descriptors are used, an application can use `select` or `poll` to manage multiple `listen` (that is, `MPI_Comm_accept`) operations within a single process (or thread).

Other features of the socket interface, such as control over timeouts, can be accomplished through implementation-specific `info` options. For example, an implementation could provide the info key `timeout` with value in milliseconds; passing

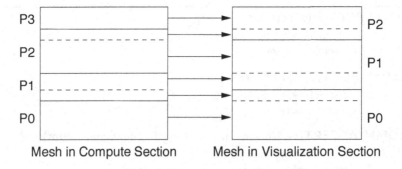

Figure 10.17: Data transfers between the simulation program (4 processes) and the visualization program (3 processes). Solid lines indicate the decomposition of the mesh among processes. Arrows indicate the transfers that take place. Dashed lines show the division of the mesh in terms of the other group of processes.

an info object containing this key to MPI_Comm_accept would allow the implementation to time out the connection attempt.

10.3.4 Moving Data between Groups of Processes

If the data is large, the visualization program itself may need to be parallel. In this case, we need to send a data structure that is distributed in one way on one group of processes to a different distribution on another group of processes.

For simplicity, we will consider the case of two different one-dimensional decompositions as illustrated in Figure 10.17. Each process on the left must send data to one or more processes on the right. One approach would be to use a collection of intercommunicator point-to-point operations (using nonblocking sends and receives to ensure that the operations don't cause deadlock or sequentialization), but we will illustrate an alternative approach using the intercommunicator collective routine MPI_Alltoallv.

The routine MPI_Alltoallv is a more flexible version of the routine MPI_-Alltoall. In the intracommunicator form, each process sends different data to every other process. In the intercommunicator version, each process in one group sends different data to every other process in the other group. In our case, every process is not sending to every other process. For those processes to which no data is being sent, we simply set the sendcount for those destinations to zero. The code in Figure 10.18 computes the sendcounts and sdispls arguments for MPI_Alltoallv, where the calling process has rows s to e of the mesh, and the

```
r_s   = 1
displ = 0
do i=0, viz_numprocs-1
    if (s .ge. r_s + m(i)) then
        sendcounts(i) = 0
        sdispls(i)  = 0
    elseif (e .lt. r_s) then
        sendcounts(i) = 0
        sdispls(i)  = 0
    else
        sendcounts(i) = min(e - s + 1, r_s + m(i) - s) * nx
        sdispls(i)    = displ
        displ         = displ + sendcounts(i)
    endif
    r_s = r_s + m(i)
enddo
```

Figure 10.18: Code to compute arguments for MPI_Alltoallv

decomposition on the visualization server is given by the array m, where m(i) is the number of rows on process i.

MPI_Alltoallv may be preferable to individual send and receive operations when MPI is being used over a wide-area network. For example, the visualization program may be running on a local graphics workstation while the computational program may be running on a remote supercomputer. Using MPI_Alltoallv allows an MPI implementation to better optimize the movement of data between the two systems, because the entire data motion is concisely described by the arguments to MPI_Alltoallv.

10.3.5   Name Publishing

In the example above, the port name is moved between the server and the client by using print to print the name onto standard output and gets to read the name from standard input. This is completely general but more than a little awkward. Fortunately, MPI provides a partial solution. We can think of the

```
print *, port_name
```

step as *publishing* the port name to the outside world. Similarly, the

```
gets(port_name);
```

Visualization Program:

```
MPI_Lookup_name("Poisson", MPI_INFO_NULL, port_name);
MPI_Comm_connect(port_name, MPI_INFO_NULL, 0, MPI_COMM_WORLD,
                 &server);
```

Simulation Program:

```
character*(MPI_MAX_PORT_NAME) port_name
integer    client
...
if (myid .eq. 0) then
    call MPI_OPEN_PORT(MPI_INFO_NULL, port_name, ierr)
    call MPI_PUBLISH_NAME('Poisson', MPI_INFO_NULL, &
                          port_name, ierr)
endif
call MPI_COMM_ACCEPT(port_name, MPI_INFO_NULL, 0, &
                     MPI_COMM_WORLD, client, ierr);
...
if (myid .eq. 0) then
    call MPI_UNPUBLISH_NAME('Poisson', MPI_INFO_NULL, &
                            port_name, ierr)
    call MPI_CLOSE_PORT(port_name, ierr)
endif
```

Figure 10.19: Code changes to the example in Figures 10.15 and 10.16 to use name publishing

call in the client is asking the user to look up the port name. MPI provides an alternative to printing and reading that is called a *name service*. In the MPI approach, a program may associate a port name with a private name chosen by the programmer. This private name is called the *service name*. A port name is associated with a service name by calling the routine MPI_Publish_name; the association may be removed by calling MPI_Unpublish_name.

A process that needs a particular port name may look it up by passing the service name to MPI_Lookup_name. Since the service name is defined by the programmer rather than the MPI implementation (or runtime system), the service name may be hard-coded into the application.

Figure 10.19 shows the changes that must be made to the visualization and simulation programs to allow them to use the MPI name publishing routines rather than print and gets. The C and Fortran bindings for the name service routines

int **MPI_Publish_name**(const char *service_name, MPI_Info info,
             const char *port_name)

int **MPI_Unpublish_name**(const char *service_name, MPI_Info info,
             const char *port_name)

int **MPI_Lookup_name**(const char *service_name, MPI_Info info, char *port_name)

Table 10.7: C bindings for name publishing

MPI_PUBLISH_NAME(service_name, info, port_name, ierror)
             integer info, ierror
             character*(*) service_name, port_name

MPI_UNPUBLISH_NAME(service_name, info, port_name, ierror)
             integer info, ierror
             character*(*) service_name, port_name

MPI_LOOKUP_NAME(service_name, info, port_name, ierror)
             character*(*) service_name, port_name
             integer info, ierror

Table 10.8: Fortran bindings for name publishing

are given in Tables 10.7 and 10.8, respectively.

Name publishing has a number of limitations. The most important limitation is that since the service names are chosen by the programmer, two programmers can choose the same service name for two different applications. No perfect solution to this problem exists, but a number of approaches can be used to reduce the chance for trouble. For example, commercial distributed-computing systems provide a central clearing house for service names. The programmer requests a service name and is given a name that is guaranteed to be unique (at least within the domain that the distributed-computing system is running over, which is all that is required). The downsides to this approach are that the names are often long strings of seemingly random characters and that a central registry of names must be maintained, even as the domain of available computers changes. Furthermore, each user of the client and server must acquire its own service names.

A simpler but slightly less robust approach is for the service name to include the user's login name (this allows multiple users to use the same program without having their service names collide). For example, instead of using `"Poisson"` as the service name for the visualization client, we might use the code

```
sprintf(service_name, "Poisson-%s", cuserid(NULL));
```

The routine `cuserid` returns the name of user associated with the calling process. There is no direct Fortran equivalent, but one usually can access this information through an implementation-specific way (if necessary, calling a C routine to perform the operation).

Another limitation of the name-service routines is that an MPI implementation is not required to provide a usable name service. That is, the routines `MPI_Publish_name`, `MPI_Unpublish_name`, and `MPI_Lookup_name` must be provided, but they can return failure for all operations.[4]

10.4   Design of the MPI Dynamic Process Routines

Programmers who are used to the simple Unix command `ssh` or Unix function `fork` can find the MPI approach to dynamic process management complex. This section explains some of the reasons for the MPI approach.

10.4.1   Goals for MPI Dynamic Process Management

The design of the MPI dynamic process routines maintains the properties that have made MPI successful: portability, determinism, scalability, and performance. In addition, it exploits the power of MPI communicators (particularly intercommunicators) to accomplish this with basically two new functions: `MPI_Comm_spawn` and `MPI_Comm_get_parent`.

Portability.   The most basic requirement is that users be able to write portable applications that can run in a variety of job-scheduling/process-management environments. This seemingly simple requirement is in fact one of the most demanding. Job scheduling and process management environments are very different in different systems. For example, commodity clusters offer a wide variety of flexible and powerful options. But many supercomputing systems provide fewer features, trading flexibility for performance. Furthermore, to optimize communication, some systems take advantage of the fact that the collection of processes is unchanging. Changes to the communication layout are expensive and may require collective operations.

---

[4]By default, errors are fatal; therefore, checking the return value from these routines requires changing the error handler for `MPI_COMM_WORLD`.

Moreover, the division of labor between a job scheduler and a process starter, while natural, is not universal. The MPI model assumes only that a new collection of processes can be started and connected together and to the parent processes. This capability is close to what most environments require to start a regular MPI job, and the MPI Forum felt that this would be portable.

Determinism.   The semantics of dynamic process creation must be carefully designed to avoid race conditions. In MPI, every process is a member of at least one communicator. The collection of processes in a communicator must be unchanging. If it isn't, collective operations (such as `MPI_Allreduce`) no longer have well-defined meanings. Adding processes to an MPI "job" requires the creation of a new communicator. Removing processes requires freeing the communicators, window objects, and MPI file objects that contain the exiting processes. The requirement of determinism dictated the use of communicators and collective operations in creating processes. Note that the "two-party" approach used in some systems that create one process at a time can be implemented in MPI by simply using `MPI_COMM_SELF` as the communicator for the spawning process and using a soft spawn of one process in `MPI_Comm_spawn`. The MPI approach permits this use but also allows for scalably spawning large numbers of processes that are provided with efficient interprocess communications.

Scalability and performance.   One of the ways in which MPI achieves scalability and performance is through the use of collective operations that concisely describe an operation that involves large numbers of processes. Rather than create new processes through individual requests to a job manager and process creator, MPI allows the programmer to make a single request for a large number of processes that will belong to a single group (one of the two groups in the intercommunicator returned by `MPI_Comm_spawn`).

In summary, when trying to understand the design choices for the MPI dynamic process routines, one should think not of what can be done on a cluster of machines running some variety of Unix but of what would be required for a supercomputer that provides only a batch-scheduling interface. The MPI design allows a program to run on either kind of system without change.

10.4.2   What MPI Did Not Standardize

We have noted that several features are dependent on the MPI implementation. The MPI Forum spent a great deal of time discussing these, but in the end concluded no approach was both general enough to maintain the portability of MPI and powerful enough to provide a useful facility for users of MPI. This situation was particularly true for the interface to the job scheduler and process manager.

Many job schedulers provide a rich command language for specifying the resources to be used for a job. These may include specific software releases, hardware (cache size or CPU speed), and even priorities (for example, a processor with set A of capabilities or, if that is not available, then one with set B). Some research systems have provided limited subsets of these capabilities, and the MPI Forum considered following their lead. In the end, however, the forum felt that any specific choice was worse than no choice at all. Instead, the forum invented the `MPI_Info` argument as a general hook for providing implementation-specific information to `MPI_Comm_-spawn`. This general "hints" mechanism for providing a portable way to specify implementation-specific information was so useful that it was applied to the I/O and RMA routines as well.

Although unfortunately the MPI Forum could not standardize the job-manager and process-startup interface, users face exactly the same situation for file names. While users of Unix systems may feel that file names are standard, important differences with other operating systems remain. For example, with Windows, valid characters are different, the directory-separator character is different, and Unix has no "drive" letter. Even within Unix, different file-system implementations offer different performance and correctness properties; specifying the file name can select completely different file system environments.

11 Working with Modern Fortran

Fortran was designed from the beginning to support aggressive optimization, including code transformations by the compiler to optimize memory motion and code placement. With Fortran 90, the Fortran language added features that permit the checking of the types of arguments passed to a routine, the use of arrays and subsets of an array (called *array sections*), the creation of user-defined datatypes (similar to `structs` in C), and ways to use a variable to point at another object (called *pointers* in Fortran, but these are not identical to pointers in C or C++). The evolution of Fortran has provided both opportunities and challenges for using MPI with Fortran.

With Fortran 2008 [47], more features were added to Fortran to precisely define the interoperation of Fortran programs with C, rather than relying on the characteristics of implementations. These *almost* make it possible to define a Fortran module that would permit Fortran programs to call the C binding of MPI directly, with no intervening routine call to translate between the Fortran and C implementations.

The Fortran interface defined in MPI-3 has the following goals:

1. Provide comprehensive checking of arguments, ensuring that the correct number and types of arguments are provided.

2. Enable the use of optional arguments, particularly for the common case of ignoring the `ierror` argument.

3. Support array sections as parameters to communication routines.

4. Avoid correctness problems caused by the use of nonblocking routines.

Unfortunately, Fortran 2008 alone is insufficient to meet these goals, particularly for items 1 and 3. As explained in this chapter, it requires an extension to the Fortran 2008 standard, known as TS 29113 (which is expected to become part of the Fortran standard).

11.1 The `mpi_f08` Module

With MPI-3, the recommended interface for Fortran programs is the `mpi_f08` module. This module takes advantage of new features in Fortran to provide enhanced usability for Fortran users. It is a major change from the older `mpif.h` include file and `mpi` module. The major differences for users are these:

- MPI handles have unique handle types instead of `INTEGER`. Thus, instead of declaring a communicator handle with `INTEGER comm`, you now use

Type(MPI_Comm) :: comm. The name of the type in Fortran is the same as the name used in the C Binding.

- The ierror argument used for returning an error code is now optional.

- Memory allocation (e.g., MPI_Alloc_mem) now uses a standard way to return a pointer to memory by using the ISO_C_BINDING type C_PTR. See Section 4.3.2.

- Most arguments are declared with a Fortran INTENT.

- New constants, described below, indicate whether Fortran subarrays may be used in calls to MPI routines or whether the Fortran attribute ASYNCHRONOUS may be used to avoid subtle but serious problems with communication buffers in nonblocking MPI routines.

Figure 11.1 shows a simple code that exploits some of the features of the mpi_f08 module.

Many of the benefits of this interface are most apparent when developing code, because the compiler can detect more user errors than with the previous interfaces. For example, if the tag value (an INTEGER) and the communicator are interchanged in the call to MPI_ISEND, the compiler can now detect that and report an error at compile time, because the type of a communicator is no longer INTEGER.

Some issues remain, however, particularly because Fortran 2008 alone lacks some features that are needed to define a useful module for MPI. For this reason, the MPI Forum defined an interface based on Fortran 2008 plus an extension, TS 29113, which is expected to become part of the Fortran standard. The words "expected to become" combined with the fact that few, if any, Fortran compilers fully implemented Fortran 2008 and TS 29113 when the MPI-3 standard was approved, led the MPI Forum to define a number of versions of the mpi_f08 module, depending on the capabilities of the Fortran compiler. We cover some of the issues below.

11.2 Problems with the Fortran Interface

MPI has struggled to define an interface to Fortran that is both correct and useful. The major issues were "choice" arguments, nonblocking routines, and array sections. This section provides some background on these issues and what issues remain.

```fortran
program main
use mpi_f08
type(MPI_Comm)       :: comm
type(MPI_Datatype) :: rtype
type(MPI_Request)   :: req
integer              :: myrank
real, asynchronous :: a(100)     ! see text on asynchronous
!
call mpi_init()
call mpi_comm_dup(MPI_COMM_WORLD, comm)
call mpi_type_contiguous(100, MPI_REAL, rtype)
call mpi_comm_rank(comm, myrank)
if (myrank .eq. 0) then
  call mpi_isend(a, 1, rtype, 1, 0, comm, req)
  call mpi_wait(req, MPI_STATUS_IGNORE)
elseif (myrank .eq. 1) then
  call mpi_recv(a, 1, rtype, 0, 0, comm, MPI_STATUS_IGNORE)
endif
call mpi_comm_free(comm)
call mpi_type_free(rtype)
call mpi_finalize()
!
end
```

Figure 11.1: Simple program using the mpi_f08 module. Note that all ierror arguments were left off; this code relies on the default abort-on-error behavior of MPI.

11.2.1 Choice Parameters in Fortran

The MPI standard has many places where a communication buffer of any type may be used; these are sometimes called "choice" parameters. An example is the send buffer in MPI_SEND. Unfortunately, Fortran has no anonymous pointer (equivalent to void* in C) and requires, even for Fortran 77, that each parameter to a routine have a single type. Thus, calling MPI_SEND with an INTEGER array as the send buffer at one place in a program and with a REAL array at another place was incorrect in MPI-1, although few Fortran compilers of the time enforced this rule.

MPI-2 introduced an mpi module (for non-Fortran programmers, a Fortran module is a sort of compiled header file). By using features of Fortran 90, one can define several interfaces for the same routine name (also called overloading); thus, it became possible to create an mpi module file that would allow a correct program to be

written that called, for example, MPI_SEND with both INTEGER and REAL buffers.
However, the module file had to explicitly enumerate every possibility—including
each possible array dimension. For example, a REAL array with one dimension
is different from an array with two dimensions. To correctly implement the mpi
module in standard Fortran 90 was impractical, so many implementations provided
interfaces only for the routines that did not take "choice" arguments—parameters
that had type void* in the corresponding C binding. This issue is still the case
through Fortran 2008, but an extension to Fortran 2008, TS 29113, adds a way to
specify an anonymous parameter with TYPE(*), DIMENSION(..). Note, however, that the MPI 3.0 standard is a bit misleading in its discussion of different
Fortran interfaces prior to those that include TS 29113—it isn't possible to create
a valid mpi or mpi_f08 module using only standard Fortran. Without TS 29113,
the interface must rely on an implementation-specific directive or compiler option
to turn off some of the argument checking. On the plus side, most Fortran compilers
have provided such an option since at least 2010.

What does this mean for the user? As Fortran compilers implement TS 29113, the
mpi_f08 module will become a complete interface specification for every MPI routine, providing enhanced compile-time argument checking. Until then, you should
be aware that since an MPI implementation must rely on the abilities of the Fortran
compiler when compiling Fortran code, the interface specification may be incom-
plete or rely on features of a particular Fortran compiler that may disable some of
the argument checking, even for the rest of your program.

11.2.2   Nonblocking Routines in Fortran

Fortran was carefully designed to permit aggressive optimization. For example,
most forms of pointer aliasing, one of the banes of optimizers for C or C++ code,
aren't allowed in Fortran. This design makes it easier for compilers to move code
even across subroutine or function calls, and, since the original definition of MPI,
compilers have become more willing to perform such transformations.

For example, consider this Fortran code (note that we take advantage of the fact
that the ierror argument is optional in the Fortran 2008 binding for MPI):

```
INTEGER :: rbuf(1000000), rval
TYPE(MPI_Request) :: req
call MPI_IRECV(rbuf, 1000000, MPI_INTEGER, &
               0, 0, MPI_COMM_WORLD, req)
call MPI_WAIT(req, MPI_STATUS_IGNORE)
rval = rbuf(1)
```

This code seems straightforward, and the C version of the code would do exactly what it looks like this code is doing. But because Fortran has no pointer aliasing and no notion of a nonblocking routine (outside of its own I/O support), the compiler knows that, in a valid Fortran program, the `MPI_WAIT` call can have no effect on `rbuf`. Thus, the compiler could execute the code in this way,

```
INTEGER :: rbuf(1000000), rval
TYPE(MPI_Request) :: req
call MPI_IRECV(rbuf, 1000000, MPI_INTEGER, &
               0, 0, MPI_COMM_WORLD, req)
rval = rbuf(1)
call MPI_WAIT(req, MPI_STATUS_IGNORE)
```

since as far as the compiler knows, after `MPI_IRECV` returns, `rbuf` won't change. And because `rbuf` is defined as a large array, the compiler might want to deallocate it as soon as possible—in this case, as soon as the value `rbuf(1)` is read and stored into `rval`.

The MPI-3 standard includes a discussion of this issue in Section 17.1.17. In Fortran 2003 and Fortran 2008, it may be possible to use the `ASYNCHRONOUS` attribute to indicate that the contents of a variable may be changed asynchronously by some other agent; in the Fortran standard, this refers to nonblocking I/O in Fortran but prevents the compiler moving the code. Using `ASYNCHRONOUS`, our example code now looks like the following:

```
INTEGER, ASYNCHRONOUS :: rbuf(1000000)
INTEGER :: rval
TYPE(MPI_Request) :: req
call MPI_IRECV(rbuf, 1000000, MPI_INTEGER, &
               0, 0, MPI_COMM_WORLD, req)
call MPI_WAIT(req, MPI_STATUS_IGNORE)
rval = rbuf(1)
```

A Fortran compiler, however, is permitted to ignore `ASYNCHRONOUS` if it doesn't implement true nonblocking I/O. The user can detect this case by checking the variable `MPI_ASYNC_PROTECTS_NONBLOCKING` defined by the `mpi_f08` module. If the variable is set to `.TRUE.`, the user can use `ASYNCHRONOUS` to indicate to the compiler that a variable may be changed after an MPI nonblocking routine returns. If set to `.FALSE.`, it means the `ASYNCHRONOUS` attribute is ignored by the compiler. MPI, however, provides a solution for this case. A special routine is provided that does nothing, but the Fortran compiler doesn't know that. By calling this routine, `MPI_F_SYNC_REG`, and passing it the variable (`rbuf` in our example),

the Fortran compiler is prevented from moving code involving rbuf across the call
to MPI_F_SYNC_REG. A more portable version of our example is the following:

```
INTEGER, ASYNCHRONOUS :: rbuf(1000000)
INTEGER :: rval
TYPE(MPI_Request) :: req
call MPI_IRECV(rbuf, 1000000, MPI_INTEGER, &
               0, 0, MPI_COMM_WORLD, req)
call MPI_WAIT(req, MPI_STATUS_IGNORE)
if (.not. MPI_ASYNC_PROTECTS_NONBLOCKING) then
    call MPI_F_SYNC_REG(rbuf)
endif
rval = rbuf(1)
```

Because the value of MPI_ASYNC_PROTECTS_NONBLOCKING is constant, a good
compiler should eliminate the test and, if the value is .TRUE., the call to MPI_-
F_SYNC_REG.

In other cases involving nonblocking routines (whether it is point-to-point, one-
sided, I/O, or collective) a Fortran compiler is permitted to move code in a way
that might not be expected by the programmer; the MPI-3 standard details these
in Section 17.1.17.

11.2.3 Array Sections

Starting with Fortran 90, Fortran introduced a number of array operations and
functions. In particular, one can describe a regular subarray of a larger array
using subscript *triplets*. For example, the statement A(3:17,2:8:3) describes
a variable containing the third through seventeenth rows (the 3:17) and columns
two, five, and eight (2:8:3; the third value is the *stride*). A colon in an array
reference indicates that all values for the given dimension are to be used. This
feature can be convenient; for example, to send the seventeenth row of a matrix
(stored in Fortran's column major order), the code is just

```
real :: A(50,50)
...
call MPI_Isend(A(17,:), 50, MPI_REAL, 0, 0, MPI_COMM_WORLD)
```

However, this requires that the MPI implementation understands how the Fortran
compiler passes such subarrays to routines. The mpi_f08 module provides the
value MPI_SUBARRAYS_SUPPORTED to indicate whether the MPI implementation
understands the Fortran subarray syntax. This value is best used either in a sep-

arate program that prints out the value, or as a test to see whether the code will work properly. An example is the following:

```fortran
real :: A(50,50)
...
if (.not. MPI_SUBARRAYS_SUPPORTED) then
    print *, 'This code requires subarray support from MPI'
    call MPI_ABORT(MPI_COMM_WORLD, 1)
endif
call MPI_Isend(A(17,:), 50, MPI_REAL, 0, 0, MPI_COMM_WORLD)
```

Because MPI datatypes provide an alternative solution (in this case, a simple vector datatype, constructed with `MPI_TYPE_VECTOR`), rather than have code for the case `MPI_SUBARRAYS_SUPPORTED = .FALSE.`, it is usually better to use MPI datatypes when portability is required.

11.2.4 Trouble with `LOGICAL`

Fortran defines a `LOGICAL` type with values `.TRUE.` and `.FALSE.`. While a Fortran compiler may implement these as integers with the values 1 and 0, respectively (the values used in C), doing so is not required by the standard. Thus, unlike the numeric types and the address or pointer types, no direct correspondence exists between a Fortran `LOGICAL` and any native C type. This issue was overlooked in the preparation of the original Fortran 2008 binding in the MPI-3.0 standard, which defines the Fortran subroutines, functions, and abstract interfaces with `BIND(C)`, so that compilers could generate code from Fortran directly to a C implementation of the MPI library with no intervening "wrapper" routine (a routine to translate between the C and Fortran types). As a result of this oversight, all the Fortran 2008 bindings presented in the MPI-3.0 standard had to be changed, as you will find in the MPI-3.0 errata. Other changes have also been made to the Fortran interface, for both Fortran 9x (`mpi` module) and Fortran 2008 (`mpi_f08` module); make sure that you check both the errata to the MPI-3.0 standard as well as the standard itself for any questions about the Fortran interface.

12 Features for Libraries

In this chapter we consider some advanced features of MPI that are particularly useful to library writers. We also summarize the MPI functions that we did not discuss in either this book or in *Using MPI*.

12.1 External Interface Functions

MPI defines a set of functions, called *external interface functions*, that enable users to do certain things that would otherwise require access to the source code of an MPI implementation. These functions include functions for decoding datatypes, creating request objects for new nonblocking operations (called *generalized requests*), filling in the `status` object, and adding new error codes and classes. The external interface functions are useful to library writers. They can be used, for example, to layer the MPI I/O functions on top of any MPI implementation that supports the MPI external interface functions. Our implementation of the MPI I/O functions (ROMIO) uses this feature and therefore works with multiple MPI implementations [66].

12.1.1 Decoding Datatypes

An MPI datatype is an opaque object that describes data layout. In many cases, such as for layering the MPI I/O functions, it is necessary to know what a datatype represents. Without functions for decoding datatypes, it is not possible to do so unless one has access to the internal representation of datatypes in the MPI implementation. Such an approach is clearly nonportable. MPI, therefore, has defined a mechanism by which users can portably decode a datatype. Two functions are provided for this purpose: `MPI_Type_get_envelope` and `MPI_Type_get_-contents`. To see how these functions can be used, let's write a simple program to determine whether a given datatype is a derived datatype of type hvector and, if so, print the count, blocklength, and stride that was used to create this hvector type. This program is shown in Figure 12.1.

We first call the function `MPI_Type_get_envelope` to determine whether the given datatype is of type hvector. The first argument to this function is the datatype itself. The function returns in the last argument a constant, called `combiner`, that indicates the kind of datatype. For example, it returns `MPI_COMBINER_NAMED` if the datatype is a predefined (basic) datatype, `MPI_COMBINER_INDEXED` if it is an indexed datatype, and so on. For derived datatypes, however, it is not sufficient just to know the kind of datatype; we also need to know how that derived datatype

```c
#include "mpi.h"
#include <stdio.h>
#include <stdlib.h>

void is_type_hvector(MPI_Datatype datatype)
{
 int nints, nadds, ntypes, combiner, *ints;
 MPI_Aint *adds;
 MPI_Datatype *types;

 MPI_Type_get_envelope(datatype, &nints, &nadds, &ntypes,
            &combiner);

 if (combiner != MPI_COMBINER_HVECTOR)
  printf("not type_hvector\n");
 else {
  printf("is type_hvector\n");
  ints = (int *) malloc(nints*sizeof(int));
  adds = (MPI_Aint *) malloc(nadds*sizeof(MPI_Aint));
  types = (MPI_Datatype *) malloc(ntypes*sizeof(MPI_Datatype));

  MPI_Type_get_contents(datatype, nints, nadds, ntypes,
              ints, adds, types);
  printf("count = %d, blocklength = %d, stride = %ld\n",
         ints[0], ints[1], adds[0]);
  free(ints);
  free(adds);
  free(types);
 }
}
```

Figure 12.1: Code that checks if a given datatype is of type hvector and, if so, prints the count, blocklength, and stride

was constructed. The three arguments, `nints`, `nadds`, and `ntypes`, are output parameters that help us in this regard. `nints` tells us how many integer parameters were used in the constructor function that created `datatype`, `nadds` tells us how many address-sized parameters were used, and `ntypes` tells us how many datatypes were used. We use these values to allocate buffers of the right size and pass them to the function `MPI_Type_get_contents` in order to retrieve all the parameters that were used to create `datatype`.

For an hvector datatype in our example program, `MPI_Type_get_-envelope` returns `combiner=MPI_COMBINER_HVECTOR`, `nints=2`, `nadds=1`, and `ntypes=1`. We allocate three arrays, called `ints`, `adds`, and `types`, of sizes `nints`, `nadds`, and `ntypes`, respectively. We next call `MPI_Type_get_-contents` with `datatype` as the first parameter; then the three values `nints`, `nadds`, and `ntypes`; and finally the three arrays `ints`, `adds`, and `types`. The implementation will fill these arrays with the parameters that were used in the construction of `datatype`. For each kind of derived datatype (contiguous, vector, indexed, etc.), the MPI standard specifies exactly how these arrays are filled. For an hvector datatype, `ints[0]` and `ints[1]` contain the count and blocklength that were passed to the hvector constructor function, `adds[0]` contains the stride, and `types[0]` contains a datatype equivalent to the datatype passed to the hvector constructor.

We can recursively call `MPI_Type_get_envelope` and `MPI_Type_get_-contents` on the returned datatype until we reach a basic datatype. In this way, recursively constructed datatypes can be recursively decoded.

We note that `MPI_Type_get_contents` must be called only for derived datatypes. It is erroneous to call this function for a basic datatype, and, in fact, there is no reason to do so. One can determine the type of a basic datatype by simply doing a comparison check, such as "`if (datatype == MPI_INT)`." One cannot use a C `switch` statement, however, because `MPI_INT`, `MPI_DOUBLE`, and so forth are not necessarily compile-time constants.

C and Fortran bindings for the datatype decoding functions are given in Tables 12.1 and 12.2.

12.1.2 Generalized Requests

MPI enables users to define new nonblocking operations, create `MPI_Request` objects for them, and use any of the usual MPI functions, such as `MPI_Test`, `MPI_Wait`, or their variants, to test or wait for the completion of these operations. Such requests are called *generalized requests*.

---

int **MPI_Type_get_envelope**(MPI_Datatype datatype, int *num_integers,
        int *num_addresses, int *num_datatypes, int *combiner)

int **MPI_Type_get_contents**(MPI_Datatype datatype, int max_integers,
        int max_addresses, int max_datatypes, int array_of_integers[],
        MPI_Aint array_of_addresses[], MPI_Datatype array_of_datatypes[])

Table 12.1: C bindings for `MPI_Type_get_envelope` and `MPI_Type_get_contents`

MPI_TYPE_GET_ENVELOPE(datatype, num_integers, num_addresses,
        num_datatypes, combiner, ierror)
        integer datatype, num_integers, num_addresses, num_datatypes,
        combiner, ierror

MPI_TYPE_GET_CONTENTS(datatype, max_integers, max_addresses,
        max_datatypes, array_of_integers, array_of_addresses,
        array_of_datatypes, ierror)
        integer datatype, max_integers, max_addresses, max_datatypes,
        array_of_integers(*), array_of_datatypes(*), ierror
        integer(kind=MPI_ADDRESS_KIND) array_of_addresses(*)

Table 12.2: Fortran bindings for `MPI_Type_get_envelope` and `MPI_Type_get_contents`

To understand how generalized requests can be used, let's consider the example of implementing the nonblocking write function `MPI_File_iwrite` on top of its blocking version, `MPI_File_write`, using a thread. We have split the code into two figures: Figure 12.2 contains the function `MPI_File_iwrite`, and Figure 12.3 contains other functions used in Figure 12.2.

Implementing `MPI_File_iwrite`. In the implementation of `MPI_File_-iwrite`, we first allocate a structure called `params` and fill it with various parameters that we want to pass to the thread function `write_thread` and to the callback functions associated with the generalized request (explained below). We directly fill into this structure the parameters `fh`, `buf`, and `count` that were passed to `MPI_File_iwrite`. We do not store the original datatype directly because the

```
#include "mpi.h"
#include <pthread.h>

typedef struct {
    MPI_File fh;
    const void *buf;
    int count;
    MPI_Datatype *datatype;
    MPI_Request *request;
    MPI_Status *status;
} params_struct;

void *write_thread(void *ptr);

int MPI_File_iwrite(MPI_File fh, const void *buf, int count,
                    MPI_Datatype datatype, MPI_Request *request)
{
    pthread_t thread;
    params_struct *params;
    MPI_Status *status;

    status = (MPI_Status *) malloc(sizeof(MPI_Status));
    params = (params_struct *) malloc(sizeof(params_struct));
    params->fh = fh;
    params->buf = buf;
    params->count = count;
    params->status = status;
    MPI_Type_dup(datatype, params->datatype);

    MPI_Grequest_start(query_fn, free_fn, cancel_fn,
                       (void *) params, request);
    params->request = request;
    pthread_create(&thread, NULL, write_thread, (void *) params);
    /* A more sophisticated implementation should remember thread
       to enable cancel */
    pthread_detach( thread );
    return MPI_SUCCESS;
}
```

Figure 12.2: Implementing `MPI_File_iwrite` on top of `MPI_File_write` using generalized requests and threads. The functions `write_thread`, `query_fn`, `free_fn`, and `cancel_fn` are defined in Figure 12.3.

```c
void *write_thread(void *ptr)
{
  params_struct *params;

  params = (params_struct *) ptr;
  MPI_File_write(params->fh, params->buf, params->count,
                 *(params->datatype), params->status);
  MPI_Grequest_complete(*(params->request));
  return 0;
}

int query_fn(void *extra_state, MPI_Status *status)
{
  params_struct *params;
  MPI_Count count;

  params = (params_struct *) extra_state;
  MPI_Get_elements_x(params->status, *(params->datatype), &count);
  MPI_Status_set_elements_x(status, *(params->datatype), count);
  MPI_Status_set_cancelled(status, 0);
  return MPI_SUCCESS;
}

int free_fn(void *extra_state)
{
  free(((params_struct *) extra_state)->status);
  MPI_Type_free(((params_struct *) extra_state)->datatype);
  free(extra_state);
  return MPI_SUCCESS;
}

int cancel_fn(void *extra_state, int complete)
{
  return MPI_SUCCESS;
}
```

Figure 12.3: Definitions of functions used in the code in Figure 12.2

user may free the datatype immediately after `MPI_File_iwrite` returns.[1] We instead create a duplicate of the datatype using `MPI_Type_dup` and store this duplicate. We also dynamically allocate a `status` object and store a pointer to it in the `params` structure. We do so because we need to pass this `status` object around the various callback functions: we will use it as the status argument to `MPI_File_write`, and we will query its contents in order to fill the corresponding status object for the generalized request. The `status` object, therefore, must remain allocated until the generalized request is freed.

The function to create a generalized request is `MPI_Grequest_start`. The name is somewhat misleading: this function does not actually start any operation; it just creates a new request object that can be associated with the new nonblocking operation being defined. We must start the nonblocking operation separately, and we do so by using the POSIX [40] function `pthread_create`, which creates a new thread.[2]

The first three arguments to `MPI_Grequest_start` are callback functions that we must provide. The MPI implementation will use these callback functions when `MPI_Test`, `MPI_Wait`, `MPI_Cancel`, and other such MPI functions are called on the generalized request. We explain below how we have implemented these callback functions. The fourth argument to `MPI_Grequest_start` is an extra-state argument, which the implementation does not use itself but simply passes to the callback functions each time they are called. We pass the `params` structure as this argument. The implementation returns a `request` object, called *generalized request*, as the fifth argument. To the user, this generalized request is like any other request object returned by a nonblocking MPI function. Any of the usual functions, such as `MPI_Test` or `MPI_Wait`, can be called on this object. The implementation will invoke the callback functions to implement test, wait, and other operations on the generalized request.

We start the nonblocking write with a call to `pthread_create`, which creates a new thread within the process. The ID of the newly created thread is returned in the first argument. The second argument specifies the attributes for the new thread; we just pass a null argument, which means that the default thread attributes will be used. The third argument specifies the function that the thread will execute. In this

---

[1]MPI allows the user to free an MPI object after the routine that begins a nonblocking operation; the MPI implementation internally retains all necessary information about the object until the nonblocking operation completes.

[2]Note that if we used the thread to call a blocking system routine, such as `write`, we would need to ensure that the thread was a kernel thread, as discussed in Chapter 6. Since we will use an MPI call for the I/O, MPI guarantees that calling the MPI blocking routine will block only the thread, not the process.

example, the function is `write_thread`. The final argument is the parameter that the thread will pass to the function `write_thread`; we pass the `params` structure as this argument. Since `write_thread` is run as a separate thread, `pthread_-create` returns without waiting for `write_thread` to complete. As a result, the function `MPI_File_iwrite` returns with the write operation initiated but not completed, that is, as a nonblocking write operation.

The `write_thread` routine. In the function `write_thread`, we simply call the blocking version (`MPI_File_write`) of the nonblocking function being implemented. The parameters passed to this function are extracted from the `params` structure. Since this is a blocking function, it returns only after the write has completed. After it returns, we call the function `MPI_Grequest_complete` to inform the implementation that the operation associated with the generalized request has completed. Only after `MPI_Grequest_complete` has been called will the implementation return `flag=true` when the user calls `MPI_Test` on the request. Similarly, `MPI_Wait` will return only after `MPI_Grequest_complete` has been called.

Let's now see how we have implemented the three callback functions passed to `MPI_Grequest_start`.

The `query_fn` routine. The MPI implementation will call `query_fn` to fill the status object for the request. This will occur, for example, when `MPI_Test` or `MPI_Wait` are called on the request. The implementation will pass to `query_fn` the `params` structure that we passed as the `extra_state` argument to `MPI_-Grequest_start`. The second argument passed to `query_fn` is a status object that we must fill. To fill the status object, we use the functions `MPI_Status_-set_elements_x` and `MPI_Status_set_cancelled`, which also are external interface functions defined in MPI. The function `MPI_Get_elements_x` is the version of `MPI_Get_elements` that provides the result as an `MPI_Count` rather than an `int`.

Recall that the `params` structure contains a status object that was filled by `MPI_File_write` in the function `write_thread`. We use the routine `MPI_-Get_elements_x` to retrieve the number of basic elements that were written by `MPI_File_write`. We then use `MPI_Status_set_elements_x` to enter the same value in the status object passed by the MPI implementation to `query_fn`. Note that there is no function like `MPI_Status_set_count` in MPI for setting the value to be returned when `MPI_Get_count` is called on the status object. This is because the implementation can calculate the count from the number of basic elements that we have specified using `MPI_Status_set_elements_x`.

We also need to specify in the status object if the request had been successfully canceled in response to an `MPI_Cancel` called by the user. The user can check whether the cancellation was successful by using the function `MPI_-Test_cancelled`. In this simple example, we do not support cancellation of requests; therefore, we simply pass 0 as the second argument to `MPI_Status_-set_cancelled`.

The `free_fn` routine. The MPI implementation will invoke the callback function `free_fn` to free all resources allocated by the user for implementing the generalized request. `free_fn` will be invoked when the generalized request is freed, for example, with `MPI_Test`, `MPI_Wait`, or `MPI_Request_free`. The implementation also passes to `free_fn` the `extra_state` argument (`params` structure) that we passed to `MPI_Grequest_start`. In the `free_fn`, we free the data structures that we allocated in the implementation of `MPI_File_iwrite`, namely, the status object and the duplicated datatype stored in the `params` structure and then the `params` structure itself.

The `cancel_fn` routine. The MPI implementation will invoke the callback function `cancel_fn` when the user attempts to cancel the nonblocking operation using `MPI_Cancel`. The implementation will pass `complete=true` to `cancel_-fn` if `MPI_Grequest_complete` has already been called on the request (by the separate thread executing the function `write_thread`); otherwise, it will pass `complete=false`. This lets us know whether the nonblocking operation has already completed and therefore cannot be canceled. In this simple example, however, we do not support cancellation anyway. Therefore, we simply return `MPI_-SUCCESS`.

Note that in order to know whether the request was successfully canceled, the user must call `MPI_Test_cancelled`. Calling `MPI_Test_cancelled` will cause the implementation to invoke the `query_fn` in which we set the canceled field of the status object to 0, indicating that the request was not canceled.

We stress the fact that the mechanism for generalized requests in MPI does *not* start nonblocking operations, nor does it cause them to progress or complete. The user must use some other mechanism (for example, threads) to take care of initiation, progress, and completion of the operation. MPI needs to be informed

int **MPI_Grequest_start**(MPI_Grequest_query_function *query_fn,
            MPI_Grequest_free_function *free_fn,
            MPI_Grequest_cancel_function *cancel_fn, void *extra_state,
            MPI_Request *request)

typedef int **MPI_Grequest_query_function**(void *extra_state, MPI_Status *status)

typedef int **MPI_Grequest_free_function**(void *extra_state)

typedef int **MPI_Grequest_cancel_function**(void *extra_state, int complete)

int **MPI_Grequest_complete**(MPI_Request request)

int **MPI_Get_elements_x**(const MPI_Status *status, MPI_Datatype datatype,
            MPI_Count *count)

int **MPI_Status_set_elements_x**(MPI_Status *status, MPI_Datatype datatype,
            MPI_Count count)

int **MPI_Status_set_cancelled**(MPI_Status *status, int flag)

Table 12.3: C bindings for the MPI functions for generalized requests and for filling the status object. `MPI_Grequest_query_function`, `MPI_Grequest_free_function`, and `MPI_Grequest_cancel_function` are not MPI functions; they show the calling sequences for the callback functions passed to `MPI_Grequest_start`.

only of the completion of the generalized request (by calling `MPI_Grequest_-complete`).

C and Fortran bindings for the MPI functions for generalized requests and for filling the status object are given in Tables 12.3 and 12.4.

12.1.3   Adding New Error Codes and Classes

A layered library, such as an implementation of the MPI I/O functions on top of an MPI implementation, may need to add new error codes and classes to the ones already defined by the MPI implementation. These would allow the user to call the usual MPI functions on error code and classes, namely, `MPI_Error_class` to determine the error class to which an error code belongs and `MPI_Error_string` to retrieve a text string associated with the error code. MPI provides three functions for adding new error codes and classes: `MPI_Add_error_class`, `MPI_Add_-`

MPI_GREQUEST_START(query_fn, free_fn, cancel_fn, extra_state, request, ierror)
          integer request, ierror
          external query_fn, free_fn, cancel_fn
          integer(kind=MPI_ADDRESS_KIND) extra_state

subroutine QUERY_FN(extra_state, status, ierror)
          integer status(MPI_STATUS_SIZE), ierror
          integer(kind=MPI_ADDRESS_KIND) extra_state

subroutine FREE_FN(extra_state,ierror)
          integer ierror
          integer(kind=MPI_ADDRESS_KIND) extra_state

subroutine CANCEL_FN(extra_state, complete, ierror)
          integer ierror
          integer(kind=MPI_ADDRESS_KIND) extra_state
          logical complete

MPI_GREQUEST_COMPLETE(request, ierror)
          integer request, ierror

MPI_GET_ELEMENTS_X(status, datatype, count, ierror)
          integer status(MPI_STATUS_SIZE), datatype, ierror
          integer(kind=MPI_COUNT_KIND) count

MPI_STATUS_SET_ELEMENTS_X(status, datatype, count, ierror)
          integer status(MPI_STATUS_SIZE), datatype, ierror
          integer(kind=MPI_COUNT_KIND) count

MPI_STATUS_SET_CANCELLED(status, flag, ierror)
          integer status(MPI_STATUS_SIZE), ierror
          logical flag

Table 12.4: Fortran bindings for `MPI_Grequest_start` and `MPI_Grequest_complete`. `query_fn`, `free_fn`, and `cancel_fn` are not MPI functions; they show the calling sequences for the callback functions passed to `MPI_Grequest_start`.

---

int **MPI_Add_error_class**(int *errorclass)

int **MPI_Add_error_code**(int errorclass, int *errorcode)

int **MPI_Add_error_string**(int errorcode, const char *string)

Table 12.5: C bindings for the functions for adding new error codes and classes

`error_code`, and `MPI_Add_error_string`. As an example, let's see how a layered library of the MPI I/O functionality can add the I/O error class `MPI_-ERR_AMODE`, an error code associated with this class, and the corresponding error strings to the MPI implementation. The program fragment is shown in Figure 12.4.

Note that an error class indicates a particular kind of error in general. Multiple error codes, corresponding to more specific errors, can be associated with an error class. In this example, we define a new error class, `MPI_ERR_AMODE`, and a specific error code, `MPIO_ERR_AMODE_COMB`, associated with this class. We use `MPIO_`, and not `MPI_`, for the error code because error codes are not predefined in MPI; only error classes are. We have defined the error code and class as external variables because they need to be used in other parts of the layered I/O library.

We use the function `MPI_Add_error_class` to create a new error class called `MPI_ERR_AMODE`. The MPI implementation assigns a value to the new error class; we cannot directly assign a value to it ourselves. We use the function `MPI_Add_-error_code` to create a new error code, `MPIO_ERR_AMODE_COMB`, associated with the error class `MPI_ERR_AMODE`. The implementation assigns a value to this error code. Next we use the function `MPI_Add_error_string` to associate a text string with the new error class and error code. Note that the string associated with the error class indicates a general error about amode, whereas the string associated with the error code indicates a very specific error. After the new error code and class have been added in this fashion, users can use the functions `MPI_Error_class` and `MPI_Error_string` on the new error code and class.

C and Fortran bindings for `MPI_Add_error_class`, `MPI_Add_error_code`, and `MPI_Add_error_string` are given in Tables 12.5 and 12.6.

12.2 Mixed-Language Programming

Library writers often write a library in one language (for example, C) and provide interfaces to it (called wrappers) from other languages (for example, Fortran and C++). MPI provides features that make it possible for a program written in one

```
extern int MPI_ERR_AMODE;          /* error class */
extern int MPIO_ERR_AMODE_COMB;    /* error code */

MPI_Add_error_class(&MPI_ERR_AMODE);
MPI_Add_error_code(MPI_ERR_AMODE, &MPIO_ERR_AMODE_COMB);
MPI_Add_error_string(MPI_ERR_AMODE,
"Error related to the amode passed to MPI_File_open");
MPI_Add_error_string(MPIO_ERR_AMODE_COMB,
"MPI_MODE_RDWR and MPI_MODE_RDONLY cannot be specified together");
```

Figure 12.4: Adding new error codes and classes to an MPI implementation. In this example, a layered library of the MPI I/O functionality adds the error class MPI_ERR_AMODE, an error code associated with this class, and the corresponding error strings to the MPI implementation.

MPI_ADD_ERROR_CLASS(errorclass, ierror)
       integer errorclass, ierror

MPI_ADD_ERROR_CODE(errorclass, errorcode, ierror)
       integer errorclass, errorcode, ierror

MPI_ADD_ERROR_STRING(errorcode, string, ierror)
       integer errorcode, ierror
       character*(*) string

Table 12.6: Fortran bindings for the functions for adding new error codes and classes

language to call MPI functions implemented in another language. The two languages that MPI supports are C and Fortran. MPI also allows programs written in different languages to send messages to one another; we considered such an example in Chapter 10.

Let us consider the example of implementing the Fortran interface for the MPI function MPI_File_write on top of its C implementation. The code is shown in Figure 12.5. When a user compiles a Fortran program containing a call to the "external" function MPI_File_write, the compiler creates an object file in which this function is named according to some convention followed by the compiler. For example, some compilers convert the function name to all lower-case letters and append an underscore at the end, some compilers add a double underscore at the end, some don't add an underscore, and some convert the function name to all

```
#include "mpi.h"

void mpi_file_write_(MPI_Fint *fh, void *buf, int *count,
                     MPI_Fint *datatype, MPI_Fint *status,
                     MPI_Fint *err)
{
  MPI_File fh_c;
  MPI_Datatype datatype_c;
  MPI_Status status_c;

  fh_c = MPI_File_f2c(*fh);
  datatype_c = MPI_Type_f2c(*datatype);
  *err = (MPI_Fint) MPI_File_write(fh_c, buf, *count, datatype_c,
                                   &status_c);
  MPI_Status_c2f(&status_c, status);
}
```

Figure 12.5: Implementing the Fortran interface for MPI_File_write

capital letters. For the Fortran program to link correctly, we must define the name of the C wrapper function according to the convention followed by the Fortran compiler. Let's assume that the Fortran compiler converts the function name to lower case and adds an underscore. Therefore, we name the wrapper function mpi_file_write_.

The argument list to this function takes into account the fact that parameters to functions in Fortran are passed by reference (as addresses) and that handles to MPI objects in Fortran are defined to be of type integer. Since an integer in Fortran may not be of the same size as an integer in C, MPI provides a datatype called MPI_Fint in C, which represents an integer of the same size as a Fortran integer. Therefore, all arguments to mpi_file_write_ other than the user's buffer are of type MPI_Fint*.

Before we can call the C function MPI_File_write, the Fortran handles to MPI objects must be converted to C handles. MPI provides handle conversion functions to convert from C handles to Fortran handles and vice versa. We use MPI_File_f2c to convert the Fortran file handle to a C file handle and MPI_Type_f2c to convert the Fortran datatype handle to a C datatype handle. Then we call the C function MPI_File_write and pass it the C file handle and the C datatype. Since status is an output parameter, we define a new C status object and pass it to the function. After the function returns, we call MPI_Status_c2f,

---

MPI_File **MPI_File_f2c**(MPI_Fint file)

MPI_Datatype **MPI_Type_f2c**(MPI_Fint datatype)

int **MPI_Status_c2f**(const MPI_Status *c_status, MPI_Fint *f_status)

Table 12.7: Bindings for the conversion functions used in Figure 12.5

which copies all the information contained in the C status object into the Fortran status object passed by the user. Note that `MPI_Status_c2f` is slightly different from handle conversion functions such as `MPI_File_c2f`, because `status` objects are explicitly allocated by the user and are not system objects. Handle conversion functions merely convert handles between languages, whereas `MPI_Status_c2f` actually copies all the information contained in a C status object (a structure of type `MPI_Status`) into a user-supplied Fortran status object (an integer array of size `MPI_STATUS_SIZE`).

The MPI standard specifies that datatypes defined in any language can be used in any other language after the handles have been converted appropriately using `MPI_Type_f2c` or `MPI_Type_c2f` (see Section 2.2.6 of [22]). For example, if the Fortran call to `MPI_File_write` specifies the datatype `MPI_COMPLEX`, the Fortran wrapper function can pass this datatype to the C function `MPI_File_-write` after handle conversion with `MPI_Type_f2c`.

Similar conversion functions are provided for all other MPI objects, namely, groups, communicators, requests, window objects, info, and op. All handle conversion functions are defined in C only; they do not have Fortran bindings.

The bindings for the conversion functions used in Figure 12.5 are given in Table 12.7.

12.3   Attribute Caching

MPI allows users to cache user-defined information on certain MPI objects, such as communicators, datatypes, and windows. This feature of MPI is particularly useful to library writers. MPI-1 supports this feature on communicators only. MPI extended attribute caching to datatypes and windows. Let us consider an example in which a library needs to decode a derived datatype and create a "flattened" version of the datatype consisting of a list of offsets and lengths for use later in the program. Flattening of datatypes is needed, for example, in a layered library that implements the MPI I/O functionality. Storing this flattened information on the datatype itself by using attribute caching is very handy here because of the following reasons:

- The flattened information can be easily accessed whenever the datatype is passed to the library.

- When the user frees the datatype using `MPI_Type_free`, the MPI implementation also frees the flattened information using the delete function that was provided when the flattened information was cached as an attribute on the datatype. If the flattened information is instead stored in some other way, such as in a table or list indexed by the datatype handle, one cannot ensure that the flattened information will be freed when the user frees the datatype. If the flattened information is not freed when the user frees the datatype and if the MPI implementation reuses the same datatype handle for a newly created derived datatype, there is a danger of the library using the old flattened information for the new datatype. Attribute caching eliminates this problem.

Figures 12.6 and 12.7 show the code for caching a flattened version of a datatype as an attribute on the datatype. To store the flattened information, we use a structure of type `flat_struct`, which contains an array of offsets, an array of lengths, the number of entries (n) in these two arrays, and a reference count to avoid creating multiple copies of this structure when the datatype is duplicated using `MPI_Type_dup`. We do not show the actual code for flattening a datatype; it can be written along the lines of Figure 12.1 by using the functions `MPI_Type_get_envelope` and `MPI_Type_get_contents` recursively.

We use the function `MPI_Type_create_keyval` to create a new attribute key that, together with an associated value, can be cached on a datatype. The first two parameters to `MPI_Type_create_keyval` are callback functions—a copy function and a delete function—that we must provide. They are described below. MPI returns in the third argument a key that we can use to cache an attribute value on the datatype. The fourth argument is an extra-state argument, which MPI will simply pass on to the callback functions. We use the function `MPI_Type_set_attr` to store this key on the datatype and associate the flattened datatype as the value of this key. Attribute values are address-sized integers; therefore, we store a pointer to the flattened datatype as the attribute value.

The copy and delete callback functions for the attribute key are defined in Figure 12.7. MPI will call the copy function when the datatype is duplicated using `MPI_Type_dup`. In the copy function, we merely increment the reference count by

```
#include "mpi.h"

typedef struct {
  MPI_Aint *offsets;
  int *lengths;
  int n;  /*no. of entries in the offsets and lengths arrays*/
  int ref_count; /* reference count */
} flat_struct;

void Flatten_datatype(MPI_Datatype datatype)
{
  flat_struct *flat_dtype;
  int key;

  flat_dtype = (flat_struct *) malloc(sizeof(flat_struct));
  flat_dtype->ref_count = 1;

  /* code for allocating memory for the arrays "offsets" and
     "lengths" and for flattening the datatype and filling in the
     offsets and lengths arrays goes here */

  MPI_Type_create_keyval(Copy_fn, Delete_fn, &key, (void *) 0);
  MPI_Type_set_attr(datatype, key, flat_dtype);
}
```

Figure 12.6: Using attribute caching on datatypes to cache a flattened version of a datatype on the datatype itself. The copy and delete functions for the attribute key are defined in Figure 12.7.

one. We also set the flag parameter to 1 to indicate that we want this attribute to be cached on the duplicated datatype. If flag is set to 0, the attribute will be deleted from the duplicated datatype. In the attr_val_out parameter, we must return the attribute value associated with this key on the duplicated datatype. In this case, the value is the same as the value on the original datatype, namely, a pointer to the flattened datatype structure, which MPI passes in the attr_val_in parameter.

Although both attr_val_in and attr_val_out are of type void*, they are defined differently. attr_val_in is the value itself, which is an address-sized variable and therefore of type void*. attr_val_out, however, is an output parameter; MPI will pass the address of the new attribute value as this parameter. attr_val_out is therefore an address of an address-sized variable, which is also

```
int Copy_fn(MPI_Datatype datatype, int key, void *extra_state,
            void *attr_val_in, void *attr_val_out, int *flag)
{
  ((flat_struct *) attr_val_in)->ref_count += 1;
  *((flat_struct **) attr_val_out) = (flat_struct *) attr_val_in;
  *flag = 1;
  return MPI_SUCCESS;
}

int Delete_fn(MPI_Datatype datatype, int key, void *attr_val,
              void *extra_state)
{
  flat_struct *flat_dtype;

  flat_dtype = (flat_struct *) attr_val;
  flat_dtype->ref_count -= 1;
  if (flat_dtype->ref_count == 0) {
    free(flat_dtype->offsets);
    free(flat_dtype->lengths);
    free(flat_dtype);
  }
  return MPI_SUCCESS;
}
```

Figure 12.7: Definitions of the copy and delete functions used in Figure 12.6

defined as void*. Since attr_val_out is the address of the new attribute value
and attr_val_in is the input value itself, we *cannot* simply do

```
attr_val_out = attr_val_in;
```

Instead we do

```
*((flat_struct **) attr_val_out) = (flat_struct *) attr_val_in;
```

MPI will call the delete function when the datatype is freed using MPI_Type_-
free. In the delete function, we decrement the reference count. If the count is
zero after decrementing, we free the memory allocated for the flattened datatype.

C and Fortran bindings for the attribute caching functions used in this example
are given in Tables 12.8 and 12.9.

For cases where no special copy or delete functions are needed, MPI provides
"do-nothing" functions. These are MPI_COMM_NULL_COPY_FN and MPI_COMM_-

---

int **MPI_Type_create_keyval**(MPI_Type_copy_attr_function *type_copy_attr_fn,
              MPI_Type_delete_attr_function *type_delete_attr_fn, int *type_keyval,
              void *extra_state)

typedef int **MPI_Type_copy_attr_function**(MPI_Datatype oldtype,int type_keyval,
              void *extra_state, void *attribute_val_in,void *attribute_val_out,
              int *flag)

typedef int **MPI_Type_delete_attr_function**(MPI_Datatype type, int type_keyval,
              void *attribute_val, void *extra_state)

int **MPI_Type_set_attr**(MPI_Datatype type, int type_keyval, void *attribute_val)

Table 12.8: C bindings for the attribute caching functions used in Section 12.3.
`MPI_Type_copy_attr_function` and `MPI_Type_delete_attr_function`
are not MPI functions; they show the calling sequences for the callback functions
passed to `MPI_Type_create_keyval`.

`NULL_DELETE_FN` for communicator attributes, `MPI_TYPE_NULL_COPY_FN` and
`MPI_TYPE_NULL_DELETE_FN` for datatype attributes, and `MPI_WIN_NULL_-`
`COPY_FN` and `MPI_WIN_NULL_DELETE_FN` for window object attributes.

12.4 Using Reduction Operations Locally

Sometimes library writers implement complex operations that need to work with
multiple datatypes and user-defined MPI operations. Let us consider the nonblocking specialized prefix sum routine from Section 2.4.1. The prefix sum uses different
binary operations depending on the process rank, multiplication for even and division for odd ranks. This is currently hard-coded into the example. To make it
generic, one could change the type of the op field in the structure `MY_Request`
to `MPI_Op` and extend the function invocation interface to accept the two operations, e.g., `void MY_Ioperation(double *sbuf, double *rbuf, int
count, MPI_Op mulop, MPI_Op divop, MPI_Comm comm, MY_Request
*req)`. The invocation would then save the `mulop` or `divop` to the op field.

In MPI-2, it would be impossible to implement the function `MY_Progress`
because one could not apply MPI operations locally. MPI-2.2 added the function `MPI_Reduce_local` to enable this functionality. This function accepts two
buffers, a datatype, and a count. Both buffers must contain `count` elements of
type `datatype`. The first one is a data input buffer and the second one is an input

---

MPI_TYPE_CREATE_KEYVAL(type_copy_attr_fn, type_delete_attr_fn, type_keyval,
          extra_state, ierror)
    external type_copy_attr_fn, type_delete_attr_fn
    integer type_keyval, ierror
    integer(kind=MPI_ADDRESS_KIND) extra_state

subroutine TYPE_COPY_ATTR_FN(oldtype, type_keyval, extra_state,
          attribute_val_in, attribute_val_out, flag, ierror)
    integer oldtype, type_keyval, ierror
    integer(kind=MPI_ADDRESS_KIND) extra_state, attribute_val_in,
          attribute_val_out
    logical flag

subroutine TYPE_DELETE_ATTR_FN(type, type_keyval, attribute_val, extra_state,
          ierror)
    integer type, type_keyval, ierror
    integer(kind=MPI_ADDRESS_KIND) attribute_val, extra_state

MPI_TYPE_SET_ATTR(type, type_keyval, attribute_val, ierror)
    integer type, type_keyval, ierror
    integer(kind=MPI_ADDRESS_KIND) attribute_val

Table 12.9: Fortran bindings for the attribute caching functions used in Section 12.3. `type_copy_attr_fn` and `type_delete_attr_fn` are not MPI functions; they show the calling sequences for the callback functions passed to `MPI_Type_create_keyval`.

---

int **MPI_Reduce_local**(const void* inbuf, void* inoutbuf, int count,
          MPI_Datatype datatype, MPI_Op op)

Table 12.10: C binding for local reduction

MPI_REDUCE_LOCAL(inbuf, inoutbuf, count, datatype, op, ierror)
    <type> inbuf(*), inoutbuf(*)
    integer count, datatype, op, ierror

Table 12.11: Fortran binding for local reduction

and output buffer. `MPI_Reduce_local` applies the binary operation `op` to each
of the `count` elements in each buffer and returns the result in `inoutbuf`. The
operation `op` can be any MPI predefined or user-defined operation. Tables 12.10
and 12.11 show the C and Fortran bindings for `MPI_Reduce_local`, respectively.

A possible implementation of the function `My_Progress` is shown in Figure 12.8.
A similar mechanism can be used to enable different datatypes. The code is left as
an exercise for the reader.

12.5 Error Handling

In this section we describe MPI's support for handling errors in programs.

12.5.1 Error Handlers

MPI associates an error handler function with each communicator, window object,
and file handle. If an error occurs in an MPI function, the implementation will
invoke the associated error handler. The default error handler for communicators
and window objects is `MPI_ERRORS_ARE_FATAL`, whereas for file handles it is
`MPI_ERRORS_RETURN`. In other words, if the default error handlers are set and
an error occurs in a non-I/O function, the program will abort, whereas if an error
occurs in an I/O function, the implementation will *try to* continue execution by
returning an appropriate error code.

MPI provides functions to create a new error handler, to associate it with a communicator, window object, or file handle, and to explicitly invoke an error handler.
Let's consider the case of file handles. The function for creating a new error handler
that can be associated with a file handle is `MPI_File_create_errhandler`; the
function for associating an error handler with a file handle is `MPI_File_set_-`
`errhandler`; and the function for explicitly invoking the error handler associated
with a file handle is `MPI_File_call_errhandler`. The routine `MPI_File_-`
`get_errhandler` returns the error handler associated with a file handle. Similar
functions exist for communicators and window objects.

The default error handler for all files can be changed by calling `MPI_File_-`
`set_errhandler` with a null file handle, `MPI_FILE_NULL`, before any file is
opened in the program. This method (of passing a null handle), however, cannot be used for communicators and window objects. The default error handler for
all communicators can be changed by changing the error handler associated with
`MPI_COMM_WORLD` immediately after MPI is initialized. Newly created communicators will inherit the new error handler from the "parent" communicator. There

```
int MY_Progress(MY_Request *req) {

  _opcomm *oc = ... /* query opcomm attribute from req->comm */

  /* start duplicating communicator */
  if (oc == NULL) {
    MPI_Comm_idup(req->comm, &req->comm, &oc->dupreq);
    oc = (_opcomm*)malloc(sizeof(_opcomm));
    oc->duped = 0;
    ... = oc; /* attach op as opcomm attribute to comm */
  } else if (oc->duped == 0) {
    int flag = 0;
    MPI_Test(&oc->dupreq, &flag, MPI_STATUS_IGNORE);
    if (flag) oc->duped = 1;
    else return 0;
  }

  if (!req->recvstarted && req->r > 0) {
    MPI_Irecv(req->rbuf, req->count, MPI_DOUBLE, req->r-1, 99,
              req->comm, &req->rreq);
    req->recvstarted = 1;
  }

  int flag, i;
  MPI_Test(&req->rreq, &flag, MPI_STATUS_IGNORE);
  if (flag == 1) {
    MPI_Reduce_local(req->sbuf, req->rbuf, req->count, MPI_DOUBLE,
                     req->op);
    if (req->r < req->s)
      MPI_Isend(req->rbuf, req->count, MPI_DOUBLE, req->r+1,
                99, req->comm, &req->sreq);
  }

  flag = 0;
  MPI_Test(&req->sreq, &flag, MPI_STATUS_IGNORE);
  if (flag == 1) return 1;
  else return 0;
}
```

Figure 12.8: Example implementation of My_Progress

is no way to change the default error handler for all window objects; it must be changed explicitly for each window object by using `MPI_Win_set_errhandler`.

12.5.2   Error Codes and Classes

Almost all MPI functions in C and Fortran return an error code. In C, the error code is the return value of the MPI function; in Fortran, it is the `ierror` argument to the function. If the function returns successfully, the error code is set to `MPI_-SUCCESS`; if not, an implementation-defined error code is returned. Error codes can be mapped onto standard MPI error classes by using the function `MPI_Error_-class`. The function `MPI_Error_string` can be used to obtain a text string corresponding to the error code. The error classes defined in MPI for I/O and remote memory operations are listed in Tables 12.12 and 12.13, respectively. Other error classes defined in MPI—for dynamic process management, info functions, and some miscellaneous functions—are listed in Table 12.14. The error classes defined in MPI-1 are given in Chapter 7 of *Using MPI* [25].

For example, consider the following program fragment. For demonstration purposes, we use both methods of printing an error message: via error classes and via error strings.

```
errcode = MPI_File_open(MPI_COMM_WORLD, "/pfs/datafile",
                        MPI_MODE_RDONLY, MPI_INFO_NULL, &fh);
if (errcode != MPI_SUCCESS) {
    MPI_Error_class(errcode, &errclass);
    if (errclass == MPI_ERR_NO_SUCH_FILE)
        printf("File does not exist\n");
    else {
        MPI_Error_string(errcode, str, &len);
        printf("%s\n", str);
    }
}
```

12.6   Topics Not Covered in This Book

MPI has additional routines that we have not covered in this book. They include the following.

- Routines to add and retrieve printable names to MPI objects:
  `MPI_Comm_set_name`, `MPI_Comm_get_name`, `MPI_Win_set_name`,
  `MPI_Win_get_name`, `MPI_Type_set_name`, and `MPI_Type_get_name`

`MPI_ERR_FILE`	Invalid file handle
`MPI_ERR_NOT_SAME`	Collective argument not identical on all processes or collective routines called in a different order by different processes
`MPI_ERR_AMODE`	Error related to the amode passed to `MPI_File_open`
`MPI_ERR_UNSUPPORTED_DATAREP`	Unsupported datarep passed to `MPI_File_set_view`
`MPI_ERR_UNSUPPORTED_OPERATION`	Unsupported operation, such as seeking on a file that supports sequential access only
`MPI_ERR_NO_SUCH_FILE`	File does not exist
`MPI_ERR_FILE_EXISTS`	File exists
`MPI_ERR_BAD_FILE`	Invalid file name (e.g., path name too long)
`MPI_ERR_ACCESS`	Permission denied
`MPI_ERR_NO_SPACE`	Not enough space
`MPI_ERR_QUOTA`	Quota exceeded. Note that both "quota" and "space" are not MPI concepts and are provided as error classes because they are common error conditions in using files
`MPI_ERR_READ_ONLY`	Read-only file or file system
`MPI_ERR_FILE_IN_USE`	File operation could not be completed because the file is currently open by some process
`MPI_ERR_DUP_DATAREP`	Conversion functions could not be registered because a data representation identifier that was already defined was passed to `MPI_Register_datarep`
`MPI_ERR_CONVERSION`	An error occurred in a user-supplied data conversion function
`MPI_ERR_IO`	Other I/O error

Table 12.12: Error classes for I/O

MPI_ERR_WIN	Invalid win argument
MPI_ERR_BASE	Invalid base argument
MPI_ERR_SIZE	Invalid size argument
MPI_ERR_DISP	Invalid disp argument
MPI_ERR_LOCKTYPE	Invalid locktype argument
MPI_ERR_ASSERT	Invalid assert argument
MPI_ERR_RMA_CONFLICT	Conflicting accesses to window
MPI_ERR_RMA_SYNC	Wrong synchronization of RMA calls
MPI_ERR_RMA_RANGE	Target memory is not part of the window (in the case of a window created with MPI_WIN_CREATE_DYNAMIC, target memory is not attached)
MPI_ERR_RMA_ATTACH	Memory cannot be attached (e.g., because of resource exhaustion)
MPI_ERR_RMA_SHARED	Memory cannot be shared (e.g., some process in the group of the specified communicator cannot expose shared memory)
MPI_ERR_RMA_FLAVOR	Passed window has the wrong flavor for the called function

Table 12.13: Error classes for RMA operations

- A routine to create an MPI connection out of an existing non-MPI connection: MPI_Comm_join

- Additional routines for I/O, including: MPI_File_get_amode, MPI_File_get_atomicity, MPI_File_get_byte_offset, MPI_File_get_group, MPI_File_get_position, MPI_File_get_position_shared, MPI_File_get_view, MPI_File_iread_at, MPI_File_preallocate, MPI_File_read_all_begin, MPI_File_read_all_end, MPI_File_read_at_all_begin, MPI_File_read_at_all_end, MPI_File_set_size, MPI_File_write_at_all_begin, MPI_File_write_at_all_end, MPI_File_write_ordered_begin, and MPI_File_write_ordered_end.

- Additional non-blocking versions of all collective communication and computation routines; these perform the same operation and have the same binding as their blocking versions, with the addition of an MPI_Request *

Dynamic Process Management

MPI_ERR_SPAWN	Unable to spawn specified number of processes
MPI_ERR_PORT	Named port does not exist or has been closed
MPI_ERR_SERVICE	An attempt to unpublish a name that has not been published or has already been unpublished
MPI_ERR_NAME	Service name has not been published

Info Functions

MPI_ERR_INFO	Invalid info value
MPI_ERR_INFO_KEY	Size of info key exceeds MPI_MAX_INFO_KEY
MPI_ERR_INFO_VALUE	Size of info value exceeds MPI_MAX_INFO_-VAL
MPI_ERR_INFO_NOKEY	Key not defined in info object

Miscellaneous

MPI_ERR_KEYVAL	Invalid attribute key
MPI_ERR_NO_MEM	Out of memory in MPI_Alloc_mem
MPI_ERR_BASE	Invalid base argument to MPI_Free_mem

Table 12.14: Other error classes defined in MPI

argument: MPI_Iallgather, MPI_Iallgatherv, MPI_Ialltoallv, MPI_Ialltoallw, MPI_Iexscan, MPI_Igather, MPI_Igatherv, MPI_Ineighbor_allgather, MPI_Ineighbor_allgatherv, MPI_Ineighbor_alltoall, MPI_Ineighbor_alltoallv, MPI_Ineighbor_alltoallw, MPI_Ireduce, MPI_Ireduce_scatter, MPI_Ireduce_scatter_block, MPI_Iscan, MPI_Iscatter, and MPI_Iscatterv.

- Additional routines for manipulating info objects: MPI_Info_delete, MPI_Info_dup, and MPI_Info_get_valuelen.

- Routines to provide information on the categories of control and performance variables: MPI_T_Category_changed, MPI_T_Category_get_categories, MPI_T_Category_get_cvars, MPI_T_Category_get_info, MPI_T_Category_get_num, and MPI_T_Category_get_pvars.

- Routines to provide the names of on integer-valued performance and control variables that are enumerations: `MPI_T_Enum_get_info` and `MPI_T_Enum_get_item`.

- Routines to reset or to read and reset a performance variable: `MPI_T_pvar_readreset` and `MPI_T_pvar_reset`.

- Routines to pack and unpack from a specified external data representation: `MPI_Pack_external` and `MPI_Unpack_external`, and to get the packed size in this external data representation: `MPI_Pack_external_size`.

- Routines to return a datatype for basic Fortran datatypes based on the range and precision of the Fortran datatype: `MPI_Type_create_f90_integer`, `MPI_Type_create_f90_real`, and `MPI_Type_create_f90_complex`. `MPI_Type_match_size` returns a datatype of the correct type (e.g., `real`) with a specific size.

- Routines that don't fit anywhere else: `MPI_Comm_compare`, which compares two communicators and returns their degree of similarity; `MPI_Comm_delete_attr`, `MPI_Type_delete_attr`, `MPI_Type_free_keyval`, and `MPI_Type_get_attr` that work with attributes; `MPI_Get_elements` and `MPI_Status_set_elements` that support `int` lengths rather than `MPI_Count` lengths; `MPI_Graph_get` for information about a communicator with a graph topology; `MPI_Request_get_status`, which provides access to the `MPI_Status` values associated with an `MPI_Request`; `MPI_Register_datarep`, which allows users to define their own data representation function to be used with file I/O; `MPI_Win_get_errhandler`, which provides access to the error handler associated with an `MPI_Win`; and `MPI_Win_flush_all` and `MPI_Win_flush_local_all`, which are the all-process versions of `MPI_Win_flush` and `MPI_Win_flush_local`, respectively.

Although these routines did not find a natural place in our book, they may be just what you need. For example, the routines for naming MPI objects can allow an MPI-aware debugger to print more detailed information about an MPI object. We encourage you to consider these routines when developing an application.

13 Conclusions

From reading this book you should understand that MPI is not just an interface for simple message-passing-style communication in parallel programs. The advanced features of MPI added in the MPI-2 and MPI-3 standards enable you to do much more. For example, MPI provides a rich interface for performing efficient parallel file I/O, dynamic process management functionality that enables you to write client-server or master-worker-style programs, an interface for one-sided programming that allows you to directly access the memory of another process, a well-defined threading model that allows you to program in a hybrid shared-memory and message-passing model, and various other features that enable scalability to the largest systems. In other words, MPI provides a sophisticated, portable, and scalable parallel programming environment.

We conclude with a discussion of the current status of MPI implementations, current efforts of the MPI Forum in defining future versions of the MPI standard, and MPI on future exascale systems.

13.1 MPI Implementation Status

Implementations of MPI are widely available both from vendors and from open-source projects. You can use MPI on almost any platform. Most implementations support all the MPI-2 features. A notable exception is that dynamic process management functions are not supported on IBM and Cray supercomputers, mostly because of complications with the resource managers on those systems and a lack of demand for that functionality from users of those systems. Implementations of MPI-3 features are increasingly becoming available. The open-source MPICH implementation of MPI has supported all of MPI-3 since November 2012. Vendor implementations derived from MPICH (e.g., Intel, IBM, Cray) either already do or will soon support these new features. A recent release of the Open MPI implementation also supports MPI-3. In other words, you should be able to use in practice what you have learned from this book.

13.2 Future Versions of the MPI Standard

Since the official release of the MPI-3 standard in September 2012, the MPI Forum has continued to meet every three months to discuss extensions to be included in future versions of the MPI standard. The next version of the MPI standard, MPI 3.1, is expected to be released by the end of 2014. It will have minor additions, clarifications, and bug fixes to MPI-3. The next major release of the standard,

MPI 4.0, will be released a year or two after that and is likely to include major new features such as support for fault tolerance. Fault tolerance has been discussed in the MPI Forum for several years, but the fault tolerance working group did not converge on a single proposal in time for inclusion in MPI-3. The group has made significant progress since then, and it is expected that MPI-4 will include support for fault tolerance. Another extension being discussed is to enable multiple threads of a process to communicate by using their own rank in a communicator, in order to enable implementations to support hybrid programming more efficiently.

13.3 MPI at Exascale

Today's fastest system (Tianhe-2) has a peak performance of 54.9 petaflops/sec. Over the next 8–10 years, exascale systems are expected to be available. These systems will be at least 20 times faster than the fastest system of today. The main difference between these systems and today's systems will likely not be in the total number of nodes but in the number of cores per node, which is expected to be 20–200 times higher than today. All indications are that MPI will continue to have a major role to play on exascale systems, in a hybrid programming style in conjunction with other programming models. MPI's support for hybrid programming as well as extensions being discussed for MPI-4 (most notably, fault tolerance, as described above) will help ensure that MPI can be used effectively on these systems. The sheer number of components in an exascale system will require resilience and fault tolerance from all components of the software stack, including MPI and the application. MPI's support for error handlers as well as the additional support for fault tolerance being considered for MPI-4 should help provide this needed feature for exascale.

A MPI Resources on the World Wide Web

Here we describe how to get access to MPI-related material on the Internet.

Examples of MPI programs. All the examples used in this book are available on the web at `http://www.mcs.anl.gov/mpi/using-advanced-mpi`, `http://www.unixer.de/using-advanced-mpi`, or by searching the web for "Using Advanced MPI: Modern Features of the Message-Passing Interface Examples." In addition, any errata items for this book will be made available at these web sites.

MPI implementations. The MPICH implementation, written by authors of this book and others, is freely available and may be downloaded from the web at `www.mpich.org`. The MPICH distribution includes examples and test programs. Most of the test programs may be used with any MPI implementation.

The MPI standard. The MPI standard is available in PDF on the web at `http://www.mpi-forum.org`. Errata for MPI-1, MPI-2, and MPI-3 are also available there.

A great deal of information on parallel-programming projects and tools is available on the web. We encourage you to investigate other sites on the web for other resources on MPI and parallel computing.

References

[1] R. Alverson, D. Roweth, and L. Kaplan. The Gemini system interconnect. In *2010 IEEE 18th Annual Symposium on High Performance Interconnects (HOTI)*, pages 83–87, Aug 2010.

[2] F. Andre, D. Herman, and J.-P. Verjus. *Synchronization of Parallel Programs.* Scientific Computing Series. MIT Press, Cambridge, MA, 1985.

[3] Satish Balay, Mark F. Adams, Jed Brown, Peter Brune, Kris Buschelman, Victor Eijkhout, William D. Gropp, Dinesh Kaushik, Matthew G. Knepley, Lois Curfman McInnes, Karl Rupp, Barry F. Smith, and Hong Zhang. PETSc users manual. Technical Report ANL-95/11 - Revision 3.4, Argonne National Laboratory, 2013.

[4] Hans-J. Boehm. Threads cannot be implemented as a library. In *Proceedings of the 2005 ACM SIGPLAN Conference on Programming Language Design and Implementation*, PLDI '05, pages 261–268, New York, NY, USA, 2005. ACM.

[5] Hans-J. Boehm and Sarita V. Adve. You don't know jack about shared variables or memory models. *Commun. ACM*, 55(2):48–54, February 2012.

[6] Dan Bonachea and Jason Duell. Problems with using MPI 1.1 and 2.0 as compilation targets for parallel language implementations. *IJHPCN*, 1(1/2/3):91–99, 2004.

[7] Franck Cappello, Al Geist, Bill Gropp, Laxmikant Kale, Bill Kramer, and Marc Snir. Toward exascale resilience. *International Journal of High Performance Computing Applications*, 23(4):374–388, 2009.

[8] Franck Cappello, Al Geist, William Gropp, Sanjay Kale, Bill Kramer, and Marc Snir. Toward exascale resilience: 2014 update. *Supercomputing frontiers and innovations*, 1(1), 2014. Open Access, http://superfri.org/superfri/article/view/14.

[9] Barbara Chapman, Gabriele Jost, and Ruud van der Paas. *Using OpenMP: Portable Shared Memory Parallel Programming.* MIT Press, Cambridge, MA, 2008.

[10] Dong Chen, Noel A. Eisley, Philip Heidelberger, Robert M. Senger, Yutaka Sugawara, Sameer Kumar, Valentina Salapura, David L. Satterfield, Burkhard

Steinmacher-Burow, and Jeffrey J. Parker. The IBM Blue Gene/Q interconnection network and message unit. In *Proceedings of 2011 International Conference for High Performance Computing, Networking, Storage and Analysis*, SC '11, pages 26:1–26:10, New York, NY, USA, 2011. ACM.

[11] James Cownie and William Gropp. A standard interface for debugger access to message queue information in MPI. In Jack Dongarra, Emilio Luque, and Tomàs Margalef, editors, *Recent Advances in Parallel Virtual Machine and Message Passing Interface*, volume 1697 of *Lecture Notes in Computer Science*, pages 51–58. Springer Verlag, 1999.

[12] Juan Miguel del Rosario, Rajesh Bordawekar, and Alok Choudhary. Improved parallel I/O via a two-phase run-time access strategy. In *Proceedings of the Workshop on I/O in Parallel Computer Systems at IPPS '93*, pages 56–70, April 1993. Also published in *Computer Architecture News*, 21(5):31–38, December 1993.

[13] Phillip Dickens and Rajeev Thakur. Evaluation of collective I/O implementations on parallel architectures. *Journal of Parallel and Distributed Computing*, 61(8):1052–1076, August 1, 2001.

[14] James Dinan, Sriram Krishnamoorthy, Pavan Balaji, Jeff R. Hammond, Manojkumar Krishnan, Vinod Tipparaju, and Abhinav Vishnu. Noncollective communicator creation in MPI. In *Proceedings of the 18th European MPI Users' Group Conference on Recent Advances in the Message Passing Interface*, EuroMPI'11, pages 282–291, Berlin, Heidelberg, 2011. Springer-Verlag.

[15] Tarek El-Ghazawi, William Carlson, Thomas Sterling, and Katherine Yelick. *UPC: Distributed Shared Memory Programming*. John Wiley & Sons, NJ, June 2005. $89.95 0-471-22048-5.

[16] A. Friedley, G. Bronevetsky, A. Lumsdaine, and T. Hoefler. Hybrid MPI: Efficient message passing for multi-core systems. In *IEEE/ACM International Conference on High Performance Computing, Networking, Storage and Analysis (SC13)*, November 2013.

[17] A. Friedley, T. Hoefler, G. Bronevetsky, and A. Lumsdaine. Ownership passing: Efficient distributed memory programming on multi-core systems. In *Proceedings of the 18th ACM SIGPLAN Symposium on Principles and Practice of Parallel Programming*, pages 177–186. ACM, February 2013.

[18] M. Gardner. The fantastic combinations of John Conway's new solitaire game "life". *Scientific American*, 223:120–123, October 1970.

[19] P. Ghysels and W. Vanroose. Hiding global synchronization latency in the preconditioned conjugate gradient algorithm. *Parallel Computing*, 40(7):224–238, 2014. 7th Workshop on Parallel Matrix Algorithms and Applications.

[20] Sergei Gorlatch. Send-receive considered harmful: Myths and realities of message passing. *ACM Trans. Program. Lang. Syst.*, 26(1):47–56, January 2004.

[21] Christopher Gottbrath, Brian Barrett, William D. Gropp, Ewing "Rusty" Lusk, and Jeff Squyres. An interface to support the identification of dynamic MPI 2 processes for scalable parallel debugging. In Bernd Mohr, Jesper Larsson Träff, Joachim Worringen, and Jack Dongarra, editors, *Recent Advances in Parallel Virtual Machine and Message Passing Interface*, number LNCS 4192 in Lecture Notes in Computer Science, pages 115–122. Springer, September 2006.

[22] William Gropp, Steven Huss-Lederman, Andrew Lumsdaine, Ewing Lusk, Bill Nitzberg, William Saphir, and Marc Snir. *MPI—The Complete Reference: Volume 2, The MPI-2 Extensions*. MIT Press, Cambridge, MA, 1998.

[23] William Gropp, Ewing Lusk, Nathan Doss, and Anthony Skjellum. A high-performance, portable implementation of the MPI Message-Passing Interface standard. *Parallel Computing*, 22(6):789–828, 1996.

[24] William Gropp, Ewing Lusk, and Anthony Skjellum. *Using MPI: Portable Parallel Programming with the Message Passing Interface*. MIT Press, Cambridge, MA, 1994.

[25] William Gropp, Ewing Lusk, and Anthony Skjellum. *Using MPI: Portable Parallel Programming with the Message Passing Interface*, 2nd edition. MIT Press, Cambridge, MA, 1999.

[26] William Gropp, Ewing Lusk, and Anthony Skjellum. *Using MPI: Portable Parallel Programming with the Message Passing Interface*, 3rd edition. MIT Press, Cambridge, MA, 2014.

[27] William Gropp, Ewing Lusk, and Rajeev Thakur. *Using MPI-2: Advanced Features of the Message-Passing Interface*. MIT Press, Cambridge, MA, 1999.

[28] William D. Gropp. *Users Manual for bfort: Producing Fortran Interfaces to C Source Code*. Mathematics and Computer Science Division, Argonne National Laboratory, March 1995. Technical report ANL/MCS-TM 208.

[29] William D. Gropp and Ewing Lusk. Fault tolerance in MPI programs. *International Journal of High Performance Computer Applications*, 18(3):363–372, 2004.

[30] J. M. D. Hill, B. McColl, D. C. Stefanescu, M. W. Goudreau, K. Lang, S. B. Rao, T. Suel, T. Tsantilas, and R. H. Bisseling. BSPlib: The BSP programming library. *Parallel Computing*, 24(14):1947–1980, December 1998.

[31] T. Hoefler, J. Dinan, D. Buntinas, P. Balaji, B. Barrett, R. Brightwell, W. Gropp, V. Kale, and R. Thakur. MPI + MPI: A new hybrid approach to parallel programming with MPI plus shared memory. *Journal of Computing*, May 2013. doi: 10.1007/s00607-013-0324-2.

[32] T. Hoefler and S. Gottlieb. Parallel zero-copy algorithms for Fast Fourier Transform and Conjugate Gradient using MPI datatypes. In *Recent Advances in the Message Passing Interface (EuroMPI'10)*, number LNCS 6305 in Lecture Notes in Computer Science, pages 132–141. Springer, September 2010.

[33] T. Hoefler, W. Gropp, M. Snir, and W. Kramer. Performance modeling for systematic performance tuning. In *International Conference for High Performance Computing, Networking, Storage and Analysis (SC'11), SotP Session*, November 2011.

[34] T. Hoefler and A. Lumsdaine. Message progression in parallel computing — to thread or not to thread? In *Proceedings of the 2008 IEEE International Conference on Cluster Computing*. IEEE Computer Society, October 2008.

[35] T. Hoefler, R. Rabenseifner, H. Ritzdorf, B. R. de Supinski, R. Thakur, and J. L. Traeff. The scalable process topology interface of MPI 2.2. *Concurrency and Computation: Practice and Experience*, 23(4):293–310, August 2010.

[36] T. Hoefler, T. Schneider, and A. Lumsdaine. Characterizing the influence of system noise on large-scale applications by simulation. In *International Conference for High Performance Computing, Networking, Storage and Analysis (SC'10)*, November 2010.

[37] T. Hoefler, C. Siebert, and A. Lumsdaine. Scalable communication protocols for dynamic sparse data exchange. In *Proceedings of the 2010 ACM SIGPLAN*

Symposium on Principles and Practice of Parallel Programming (PPoPP'10), pages 159–168. ACM, January 2010.

[38] T. Hoefler and M. Snir. Generic topology mapping strategies for large-scale parallel architectures. In *Proceedings of the 2011 ACM International Conference on Supercomputing (ICS'11)*, pages 75–85. ACM, June 2011.

[39] T. Hoefler and M. Snir. Writing parallel libraries with MPI — common practice, issues, and extensions. In *Recent Advances in the Message Passing Interface - 18th European MPI Users' Group Meeting, EuroMPI 2011, Santorini, Greece, September 18-21, 2011. Proceedings*, volume 6960, pages 345–355. Springer, September 2011.

[40] IEEE/ANSI Std. 1003.1. Portable Operating System Interface (POSIX)–Part 1: System Application Program Interface (API) [C Language], 1996 edition.

[41] John Kim, Wiliam J. Dally, Steve Scott, and Dennis Abts. Technology-driven, highly-scalable dragonfly topology. *SIGARCH Comput. Archit. News*, 36(3):77–88, June 2008.

[42] Charles H. Koelbel, David B. Loveman, Robert S. Schreiber, Guy L. Steele Jr., and Mary E. Zosel. *The High Performance Fortran Handbook*. MIT Press, Cambridge, MA, 1993.

[43] Manojkumar Krishnan, Bruce Palmer, Abhinav Vishnu, Sriram Krishnamoorthy, Jeff Daily, and Daniel Chavarria. The global arrays user's manual. Technical report, Pacific Northwest National Laboratory, 2012.

[44] John M. Mellor-Crummey and Michael L. Scott. Algorithms for scalable synchronization on shared-memory multiprocessors. *ACM Trans. Comput. Syst.*, 9(1):21–65, February 1991.

[45] Message Passing Interface Forum. MPI-2: Extensions to the Message-Passing Interface, July 1997. `http://www.mpi-forum.org/docs/mpi2-report.pdf`.

[46] Message Passing Interface Forum. MPI: A Message-Passing Interface Standard, Version 3.0, September 2012. `http://mpi-forum.org/docs/mpi-3.0/mpi30-report.pdf`.

[47] M. Metcalf, J. Reid, and M. Cohen. *Modern Fortran Explained*. Numerical Mathematics and Scientific Computation. Oxford University Press, 2011.

[48] Maged M. Michael and Michael L. Scott. Simple, fast, and practical non-blocking and blocking concurrent queue algorithms. In *Proceedings of the 15th Annual ACM Symposium on Principles of Distributed Computing (PODC '96)*, pages 267–275. ACM, May 1996.

[49] J. Nieplocha, R. J. Harrison, and R. J. Littlefield. Global Arrays: A portable "shared-memory" programming model for distributed memory computers. In *Proceedings, Supercomputing '94: Washington, DC, November 14–18, 1994*, Supercomputing, pages 340–349. IEEE Computer Society Press, 1994.

[50] Jarek Nieplocha, Bruce Palmer, Vinod Tipparaju, Manojkumar Krishnan, Harold Trease, and Edoardo Aprà. Advances, applications and performance of the global arrays shared memory programming toolkit. *International Journal of High Performance Computing Applications*, 20(2):203–231, 2006.

[51] Robert W. Numrich. F--: A parallel extension to Cray Fortran. *Scientific Programming*, 6(3):275–284, 1997.

[52] OpenMP Application Program Interface, Version 4.0. www.openmp.org, 2013.

[53] OpenSHMEM web site. http://openshmem.org/.

[54] Fabrizio Petrini, Darren J. Kerbyson, and Scott Pakin. The case of the missing supercomputer performance: Achieving optimal performance on the 8,192 processors of ASCI Q. In *Proceedings of the 2003 ACM/IEEE Conference on Supercomputing*, SC '03, New York, NY, USA, 2003. ACM.

[55] S. Ramos and T. Hoefler. Modeling communication in cache-coherent SMP systems — A case-study with Xeon Phi. In *Proceedings of the 22nd International Symposium on High-Performance Parallel and Distributed Computing*, pages 97–108. ACM, June 2013.

[56] Timo Schneider, Robert Gerstenberger, and Torsten Hoefler. Micro-applications for communication data access patterns and MPI datatypes. In Jesper Larsson Träff, Siegfried Benkner, and Jack J. Dongarra, editors, *Recent Advances in the Message Passing Interface - 19th European MPI Users'*

Group Meeting, EuroMPI 2012, Vienna, Austria, September 23-26, 2012. Proceedings, volume 7490 of Lecture Notes in Computer Science, pages 121–131. Springer, 2012.

[57] H. A. Schwarz. Gesammelte Mathematische Abhandlungen, volume 2, pages 133–143. Springer, Berlin, 1890. First published in Vierteljahrsschrift der Naturforschenden Gesellschaft in Zürich, volume 15, 1870, pp. 272–286.

[58] Gautam Shah, Jarek Nieplocha, Jamshed Mirza, Chulho Kim, Robert Harrison, Rama K. Govindaraju, Kevin Gildea, Paul DiNicola, and Carl Bender. Performance and experience with LAPI—a new high-performance communication library for the IBM RS/6000 SP. In Proceedings of the 1st Merged International Parallel Processing Symposium and Symposium on Parallel and Distributed Processing (IPPS/SPDP-98), pages 260–266. IEEE Computer Society, March 30–April 3 1998.

[59] D. B. Skillicorn, Jonathan M. D. Hill, and W. F. McColl. Questions and answers about BSP. Technical Report PRG-TR-15-96, Oxford University Computing Laboratory, 1996.

[60] Barry F. Smith, Petter E. Bjørstad, and William Gropp. Domain Decomposition: Parallel Multilevel Methods for Elliptic Partial Differential Equations. Cambridge University Press, 1996.

[61] Marc Snir, Steve W. Otto, Steven Huss-Lederman, David W. Walker, and Jack Dongarra. MPI—The Complete Reference: Volume 1, The MPI Core, 2nd edition. MIT Press, Cambridge, MA, 1998.

[62] W. Richard Stevens. Unix Network Programming: Networking APIs: Sockets and XTI, volume 1. Prentice Hall, Englewood Cliffs, NJ, 2nd edition, 1998.

[63] Rajeev Thakur, William Gropp, and Ewing Lusk. An abstract-device interface for implementing portable parallel-I/O interfaces. In Proceedings of the 6th Symposium on the Frontiers of Massively Parallel Computation, pages 180–187. IEEE Computer Society Press, October 1996.

[64] Rajeev Thakur, William Gropp, and Ewing Lusk. A case for using MPI's derived datatypes to improve I/O performance. In Proceedings of SC98: High Performance Networking and Computing, November 1998.

[65] Rajeev Thakur, William Gropp, and Ewing Lusk. Data sieving and collective I/O in ROMIO. In *Proceedings of the 7th Symposium on the Frontiers of Massively Parallel Computation*, pages 182–189. IEEE Computer Society Press, February 1999.

[66] Rajeev Thakur, William Gropp, and Ewing Lusk. On implementing MPI-IO portably and with high performance. In *Proceedings of the 6th Workshop on I/O in Parallel and Distributed Systems*, pages 23–32. ACM Press, May 1999.

[67] Rajeev Thakur, William Gropp, and Ewing Lusk. Optimizing noncontiguous accesses in MPI-IO. *Parallel Computing*, 28(1):83–105, January 2002.

[68] Rajeev Thakur, William Gropp, and Brian Toonen. Optimizing the synchronization operations in MPI one-sided communication. *High Performance Computing Applications*, 19(2):119–128, 2005.

[69] Rajeev Thakur, Ewing Lusk, and William Gropp. Users guide for ROMIO: A high-performance, portable MPI-IO implementation. Technical Report ANL/MCS-TM-234, Mathematics and Computer Science Division, Argonne National Laboratory, revised July 1998.

[70] Jesper Larsson Träff. Implementing the MPI process topology mechanism. In *Proceedings of the 2002 ACM/IEEE Conference on Supercomputing*, SC '02, pages 1–14, Los Alamitos, CA, USA, 2002. IEEE Computer Society Press.

[71] L. G. Valiant. A bridging model for parallel computations. *Communications of the ACM*, 33(8):103–111, August 1990.

[72] John D. Valois. Lock-free linked lists using compare-and-swap. In *Proceedings of the Fourteenth Annual ACM Symposium on Principles of Distributed Computing*, pages 214–222, Ottawa, Ontario, Canada, August 1995.

[73] Thorsten von Eicken, Anindya Basu, Vineet Buch, and Werner Vogels and. U-Net: A user-level network interface for parallel and distributed computing. In *Proceedings of the 15th ACM Symposium on Operating Systems Principles (SOSP)*, pages 40–53. ACM Press, December 1995.

Subject Index

Function and Term Index

Scientific and Engineering Computation

William Gropp and Ewing Lusk, editors; Janusz Kowalik, founding editor

Using MPI: Portable Parallel Programming with the Message-Passing Interface, third edition, William Gropp, Ewing Lusk, and Anthony Skjellum, 2014

Using Advanced MPI: Modern Features of the Message-Passing Interface, William Gropp, Torsten Hoefler, Rajeev Thakur, and Ewing Lusk, 2014

Printed in the United States
by Baker & Taylor Publisher Services